BILINGUALISM
in the
SOUTHWEST

BILINGUALISM
in the
SOUTHWEST

Paul R. Turner, editor

COLLABORATING AUTHORS

Carroll G. Barber   Rolf Kjolseth
Russell N. Campbell   William L. Leap
Chester C. Christian, Jr.   Madeleine Mathiot
Lurline H. Coltharp   Charles Olstad
Mary Jane Cook   Jacob Ornstein
Ricardo J. Cornejo   Cecil Robinson
Kenneth Hale   Bernard Spolsky
Agnes Holm   Elizabeth W. Willink
Wayne Holm   Robert D. Wilson
Rodney W. Young

LC
3732
S59
B54

THE UNIVERSITY OF ARIZONA PRESS
Tucson, Arizona

About the Editor

PAUL R. TURNER's interest in bilingualism dates back to his field-work as a missionary-linguist among the Highland Chontals of Oaxaca, Mexico, from 1959 to 1963. The years of research, and association with a bilingual Indian community, led not only to the present volume but to a bilingual dictionary compiled by the editor and his wife, *Dictionary: Chontal to Spanish-English, Spanish to Chontal* (University of Arizona Press, 1971). Turner in 1967 joined the faculty of the University of Arizona Department of Anthropology, later becoming chairman of the linguistics committee. He earned his Ph.D. in anthropology at the University of Chicago in 1966, focusing his doctoral studies on the grammar of the Highland Chontal language.

THE UNIVERSITY OF ARIZONA PRESS

I. S. B. N.-0-8165-0379-6
L. C. No. 72-85440

in memory of
EDWARD P. DOZIER
who
exemplified the best in bilingualism

CONTENTS

PART II   AMERICAN INDIANS

Assumptions and Methods

Language Resources and Development

Cultural and Linguistic Interactions

PART III   SUGGESTIONS FOR FURTHER RESEARCH

About the Authors

CARROLL G. BARBER, a doctoral candidate in anthropology at the University of Arizona, also has been a research associate at Fisk University and has co-authored *The Negro American: A Selected and Annotated Bibliography for High Schools and Junior Colleges* (Amistad Research Center, Nashville, Tennessee, 1968). Here he updates his study in "Trilingualism in an Arizona Yaqui Village."

RUSSELL N. CAMPBELL, associate professor of English at the University of California at Los Angeles, completed his doctoral work in the department of linguistics at the University of Michigan in 1964. He has been president of the National Association of Teachers of English to Speakers of Other Languages (TESOL). Dr. Campbell has written textbooks for Thai and Vietnamese speakers to use in learning English and he is the co-author of *Insights into English Structure: A Programmed Text* (Prentice-Hall, 1969). His articles on bilingual teacher training have appeared in *Language Learning, TESOL Quarterly,* and other journals. He shares "Some Thoughts on Bilingual Education for Mexican-American Children in California."

CHESTER CHRISTIAN, writer of "Criteria for Cultural-Linguistic Subdivision in the Southwest," has been director of the Inter-American Institute and associate professor in the department of modern languages at the University of Texas at El Paso. He received his PhD degree in 1967 from the University of Texas at Austin in the Institute of Latin American Studies. The title of his dissertation was *Literary Representation and Sociological Analysis: Social Class in Latin America.* He has written articles on acculturation, bilingual education, and Latin American literature that have appeared in the *Modern Language Journal, Revista de Ciencias Sociales,* and the Georgetown University *Monograph Series on Language and Linguistics.*

LURLINE H. COLTHARP, writer of "Bilingual Onomastics: A Case Study," and professor of English and linguistics at the University of Texas at El Paso, has done extensive research on the Pachuco sub-dialect of Spanish and wrote her PhD dissertation on this topic: *The Influence of English on the "Language" of the Tirilones* (University of Texas at Austin), as well as a book, *The Tongue of the Tirilones: A Linguistic Study of a Criminal Argot* (The University of Alabama Press, 1965). Dr. Coltharp has authored articles on language laboratories, phonetics, and Indian names that have appeared in the *TESOL Quarterly* and *Password.* Her main interests lie in teaching English as a second language, dialect study, and onomastics.

MARY JANE COOK, associate professor of English at the University of Arizona, has also been director of the English as a Second Language Program at that school. She has authored a book on *English as a Second Language for Navajo*

[ix]

Beginners (Bureau of Indian Affairs, 1969) and a second one for Navajo first graders. Her articles have dealt with the present-day English language and TESOL for Navajo and other Southwestern Indian speakers and have been published in *Language Learning* and the *TESOL Quarterly*. Her article presents "Problems of Southwestern Indian Speakers in Learning English."

RICARDO J. CORNEJO has been curriculum coordinator for bilingual education in the Southwest Educational Development Laboratory of Austin, Texas. He received his PhD degree from the University of Texas at Austin in 1969 and the title of his dissertation was *Bilingualism: Study of the Lexicon of the Five-Year-Old Spanish-Speaking Children of Texas*. Dr. Cornejo has authored a book, *English Pronunciation for Spanish Speakers* (Southwest Educational Development Laboratory, 1970) and written articles on the audiovisual aspects of education and the teaching of Spanish to Spanish-speaking children that have appeared in *Pedagogía, Revista de* (Chile) and *Program Description: Bilingual Education*, SEDL. His article is "A Description of the Acquisition of Lexicon in the Speech of Bilingual Children."

KENNETH L. HALE who wrote "Some Comments on the Role of American Indian Linguistics in Bilingual Education," has been professor of linguistics at the Massachusetts Institute of Technology. He has done linguistic fieldwork in Australia, Mexico, and the American Southwest. His PhD dissertation, *A Papago Grammar* (University of Indiana, 1959), was a result of his continuing interest in the languages of the Southwest. He has written articles on diachronic and synchronic linguistic topics that have appeared in the *International Journal of American Linguistics, Oceanic Linguistics, Linguistics*, and other journals.

AGNES HOLM has been a teacher at the Rock Point School on the Navajo Reservation. She was an M.A. candidate at the University of New Mexico and was previously a research assistant with the Navajo Reading Study at the same school. She is co-editor of *An Analytical Bibliography of Navajo Reading Materials* (US Bureau of Indian Affairs Curriculum Bulletin No. 10, 1970).

WAYNE HOLM, principal of the Rock Point School on the Navajo Reservation, was the co-director of the Navajo Reading Study at the University of New Mexico and a PhD candidate at the same school. Mr. Holm has written articles on ESL for Navajos and community control of Navajo education that have been published in *Indian Education* and the *Journal of American Education*. He discusses language use in the classroom in "Bilagáana Bizaad: ESL/EFL in a Navajo Bilingual Setting."

ROLF KJOLSETH, an associate professor of sociology at the University of Colorado, has been president of the Research Committee on Sociolinguistics of the International Sociological Association and an editorial board member of the journal, *Language in Society*. He received his doctorate from the sociology department of the University of Colorado in 1968, writing his dissertation on the topic: *Structure and Process in Creative Conversation: An Exploratory Study of Gesture Dialogue*. Dr. Kjolseth is interested mainly in multilingualism and education in its relation to ethnic language maintenance and shift. He evaluates education programs in his article, "Bilingual Programs in the United States: For Assimilation or Pluralism?"

WILLIAM L. LEAP, assistant professor of anthropology at the American University, has done fieldwork among the Pueblo Indian villages of New Mexico which resulted in a PhD dissertation, *The Language of Isleta, New Mexico* (Southern Methodist University, 1970). He has written articles on Tiwa noun class semology, Tiwa historical and comparative constructions, and linguistic identity of the Piro language of the American Southwest that have appeared in *Anthropological Linguistics* and *Studies in Linguistics*. He makes further observations on Isleta in "Language Pluralism in a Southwestern Pueblo: Some Comments on Isletan English."

MADELEINE MATHIOT, writer of "English and Papago Compared," and associate professor of linguistics at the State University of New York at Buffalo, has been the principal investigator on two research projects sponsored by the Office of Education dealing with method in language and culture research. Her continuing interest in language and culture relations resulted in a PhD dissertation that was published as the book, *An Approach to the Cognitive Study of Language* (Indiana University, 1968). She has written articles on the cognitive significance of grammatical categories and folk narratives, lexicography, and theory and method in sociolinguistics that have appeared in the *American Anthropologist, Language,* and *Semiotica.*

CHARLES OLSTAD discusses the role of dialect Spanish in education in "The Local Colloquial in the Classroom." As associate professor of Spanish and assistant to the Head of the Department of Romance Languages at the University of Arizona, he has co-authored *Creative Spanish* (Harper and Row, 1965) and *Aspectos de la Literatura Española* (Xerox College Publishing, 1972). He has written articles on Spanish literature, the Spanish language, and bilingual education that have appeared in *Hispania, Romance Notes,* and *Arizona and the West.*

JACOB ORNSTEIN, professor of modern languages and linguistics at the University of Texas at El Paso, also has been co-director of that school's newly established Cross-Cultural Southwest Ethnic Group Study Center. He has taught at a number of universities and authored articles and books dealing with Spanish language and literature, Slavic linguistics, applied linguistics, sociolinguistics, and bilingualism. His articles have appeared in *Modern Language Journal, Language, Hispania,* and numerous other journals. His article, "Toward an Inventory of Interdisciplinary Tasks in Research on U.S. Southwest Bilingualism," offers many ideas for further research in this area.

CECIL ROBINSON, professor of English at the University of Arizona, has been director of bicultural programs in Chile and Brazil and director of NDEA institutes for teachers of Spanish-speaking bilinguals and Navajos in the American Southwest. He is author of the book, *With the Ears of Strangers: the Mexican in American Literature* (The University of Arizona Press, 1963) and has written articles on the literary and cultural relations between North and Hispanic America that have appeared in *The Yale Review, The American West, Southwestern American Literature,* and other journals. He continues this interest in "A Kaleidoscope of Images: Mexicans and Chicanos as Reflected in American Literature."

BERNARD SPOLSKY, associate professor in the departments of anthropology and elementary education at the University of New Mexico, has been chairman of the program in linguistics at that school. He is the principal investigator of the Navajo Reading Study and has co-authored *Computation in Linguistics: A Case Book* (Indiana University Press, 1966). He has written articles on translation, language testing, second language pedagogy, and Navajo language maintenance that have appeared in *Behavioral Science, International Review of Applied Linguistics, Language Learning,* and other journals. He joins Agnes and Wayne Holm in the writing of "English Loan Words in the Speech of Young Navajo Children."

ELIZABETH W. WILLINK presents her ideas on "Bilingual Education for Navajo Children." An education specialist for the Bureau of Indian Affairs at the Rock Point Boarding School, Chinle, Arizona, she received her PhD degree in education at the University of Arizona in 1968. The title of her dissertation was *A Comparison of Two Methods of Teaching English to Navajo Children* which was a result of her teaching experience among the Navajo that dates back to 1957. Dr. Willink has written articles in both Dutch and English on a variety of subjects and has been a news correspondent and radio reporter for the Netherland's Information Bureaus in the United States, Canada, Austria, and France.

ROBERT D. WILSON, associate professor of English at the University of California, Los Angeles, received his doctoral degree in the department of linguistics at the same university in 1965, writing his dissertation on the topic, *An Algorithm of Derived Constituent Structure.* Dr. Wilson is director of projects of CITE, INC. (Consultants in Total Education) and has been in charge of developing bilingual materials for the Navajos under a contract with the Bureau of Indian Affairs. He has also written English grammar textbooks for use in high schools in the Philippines and has co-produced a filmstrip and record series entitled, *Beginning Fluency in English as a New Language.* He presents his theories in "Assumptions for Bilingual Instruction in the Primary Grades of Navaho Schools."

RODNEY W. YOUNG, author of "The Development of Semantic Categories in Spanish-English and Navajo-English Bilingual Children," and assistant professor in the department of education at the University of Utah, has conducted research among bilingual Navajo and Spanish speakers for his PhD dissertation *Semantics as a Determiner of Linguistic Comprehension Across Language and Cultural Boundaries* (University of New Mexico, 1971). His interest in bilingualism centers on the meaning systems of the languages that are used by a single speaker.

Preface

The contributors to this volume belong to a number of different disciplines: anthropology, education, english, linguistics, sociology, and spanish. These disciplines, as well as others, have important contributions to make in the study of bilingualism, but bilingualism as a social reality is so complex that no one discipline with its limited perspective is adequate to the task. The publication of these articles is intended to encourage the kind of interdisciplinary exchange of ideas and cooperation that has been lacking in the past. In fact, future progress would seem to be dependent upon the type of problem-oriented research that is multidisciplinary in scope rather than restricted to the specific interest and approach of a single discipline.

The articles that have been included in this volume demonstrate the diversity of academic interest in the phenomena of bilingualism. This diversity is by editorial design as well as a result of the nature of the subject matter. Since relatively little is known about bilingualism, neither a fixed theoretical viewpoint nor a highly structured problem-solving approach would seem to be appropriate at this time. The variety of theoretical and empirical issues that are dealt with in this volume is intended to be a contribution to what has been traditionally an eclectic study.

Some of the articles are not only controversial but also present contradictory claims. This is to be expected in a subject area that until quite recently has been only of peripheral interest to the traditional disciplines. The study of bilingualism has political overtones which make it difficult for a scholar to be objective since his research can affect the lives of a number of people. On the other hand, there can be no question about the social relevancy of this research for the Southwest. Here live the largest concentrations of Mexican-Americans and Indians in the United States. Whatever bilingual problems exist elsewhere in our country also exist here, only to a greater degree.

The title of this volume more accurately would describe the situation in the Southwest if the term "multilingualism" were used rather than "bilingualism," since many people in the Southwest speak more than two languages and are not truly bilingual in any precise usage of the term. The term "bilingualism" though is not meant to be interpreted literally but instead applies to the habitual usage of two or more languages when speaking. Actually, research has not yet demonstrated whether a two-language situation differs significantly from a three- or four-language situation and it is not necessary to make a distinction in terminology until more is known about these various language situations.

The choice of the term "multilingualism" also might be preferred since "bilingualism" has been used in the Southwest in a pejorative way to refer to someone who is linguistically and socially disadvantaged. There is a certain amount of truth in this viewpoint because the dominant Anglo culture has made it a handicap for Mexican-American and Indian children to continue to possess their own distinctive language and culture. Had the American public, however, been more interested in the past in educating these children in terms of their special language and cultural abilities rather than subjecting them to the trauma of a melting pot experience, bilingualism could have been an asset instead of a liability.

The Southwest always has been characterized by culturally diverse groups which have resisted losing their uniqueness. The national melting pot process, for various historical, geographical, and cultural reasons, has not been as effective here as elsewhere in destroying a people's identity. Distinctive Indian languages are still the first languages learned by significant numbers of people and Spanish is spoken throughout the Southwest with Los Angeles reported to have the third largest concentration of Spanish speakers in the New World only exceeded by Mexico City and Guadalajara.

There seems to be a new respect on the part of educators and lawmakers for the kind of language diversity found in the Southwest as indicated by the passage of the 1968 Bilingual Education Act. A number of bilingual education projects in the Southwest with quite diverse aims and means are now being funded by the Office of Education. It remains to be seen how many of these bilingual projects will seek to use the native tongue and culture only as a vehicle to gain proficiency in English as contrasted with how many will consider both languages and cultures seriously in an attempt to educate balanced bilinguals. The collaborating authors of this volume appreciate the contribution which bilingualism can make to personal and community self-respect. A unifying theme in their articles is that anyone who speaks more than one language and participates in more than one culture is a privileged individual. He has been liberated from the intellectual provincialism of a single culture and should be more tolerant of those from other cultures.

The symposium, "Bilingualism in the Southwest," that was held during the joint annual meeting of the Southwestern Anthropological

Association and American Ethnological Society in Tucson, Arizona, April 29–May 1, 1971, generated so much interest that a decision was made to publish a book on this topic. Knowledgeable persons who have worked in the Southwest were encouraged to submit articles dealing with their interests in bilingualism, and this volume is the result.

I wish to express my appreciation to those individuals who made this volume possible: James Officer, who originally suggested having a symposium on bilingualism at the AES-SWAA meetings; the participants in that symposium; the collaborating authors; and Marshall Townsend and Douglas Peck of the University of Arizona Press for their assistance.

MEXICAN-AMERICANS

1. Bilingual Education Programs in the United States: For Assimilation or Pluralism?

ROLF KJOLSETH

This article describes two types of bilingual education programs: assimilation and pluralistic. The assimilation type promotes ethnic language shift while the pluralistic type promotes ethnic language maintenance. Kjolseth's analysis reveals that most bilingual programs in the United States—contrary to their usual statements of program goals—are of the assimilation type and encourage the loss of the ethnic mother tongue.

This is a revised version of a paper originally presented in the section on "Sociological Perspectives on Bilingual Education" of the Sociolinguistics Program at the Seventh World Congress of Sociology held in Varna, Bulgaria, September 14–19, 1970 and which appeared in the *Acts* of the Congress. The revised version was published in R. Kjolseth und F. Sack (hrsgs.) *Zur Soziologie der Sprache: Ausgewaehlte Schriften vom VII. Weltkongress der Soziologie*, appeared as a special issue of the *Koelner Zeitschrift fuer Soziologie und Sozialpsychologie*, November-December 1971, and in Bernard Spolsky (ed.), *The Language Education of Minority Children: Selected Readings* (Newbury House Publishers, 1972).

[3]

RECENT LEGISLATION[1] and financial support[2] for bilingual education programs in the United States are held by many to indicate a basic liberal break from an earlier "language policy" and social context which successfully assimilated several waves of the most diverse immigrant groups into mainstream monolingual American society.

One often hears, especially from those who are promoting these new programs, that they will favor cultural bilingualism and pluralism, that is, the democratic coexistence of ethnic and non-ethnic groups.

This paper seeks to examine critically this thesis within a sociolinguistic perspective. This perspective necessarily considers the relevance and effects of bilingual programs upon language use beyond the school and within the wider community.

However, an analysis of specific programs first must be prefaced by a few introductory remarks. These will touch upon the role of the school in community social change, sketch the concepts and method by which the analysis will proceed, and very briefly describe the social context of the communities in which these bilingual programs are embedded.

It would be a mistake to overestimate what any school can accomplish or to overvalue the significance of a student's performance if it is restricted only to the domain of the school itself. The school is only one domain in the life space of individuals and communities. Language cannot "live" there although it may receive important impulses. The life of a language depends first and foremost upon its *use*[3] in other domains. When a person has skills in two languages, this individual bilingualism, if it is to be stable, must be sustained by diglossic[4] norms of

---

[1] Federal legislation was enacted January 2, 1968 as Title VII of the Elementary and Secondary Education Act of 1965. The text of this law is reproduced by Andersson (1970, Vol. 2, 1–6).

[2] Although 45 million dollars was authorized for the first three fiscal years, actual appropriations, which are granted on a one-year basis, have been only half of that authorized. Fishman (1970) discusses the politics involved.

[3] Sociolinguistic research has clearly shown that there is no necessary, invariable, or universal correlation between *attitudes* towards a language (ethnolinguistics) and actual patterns of language *use* (dominance configuration) within a speech community. For an early treatment of language use patterns see Schmidt-Rohr (1933:178–192). Landmann (1968) offers a fascinating historical account of a case (Yiddish) where negative attitudes co-occurred with increasing use of the ethnic language and vice versa. Nevertheless, there is presently an inordinate research emphasis upon attitudes which tacitly assumes them to be adequate indicators of language behavior.

[4] "Diglossia," coined by Ferguson (1959) and expanded by Gumperz (1964) and Fishman (1965, 1967, 1971) describes or characterizes a society wherein two or more language varieties are normatively employed, each for separate, complimentary functions or domains. Diglossia is therefore a multilingual "opportunity structure" which sustains bilingualism in individuals who, as they move from a social context dominated by one language to another dominated by norms of appropriateness for a second language, will be constrained to switch idioms and so, in the normal round of everyday life will use both languages and thereby naturally maintain their bilingualism through the only means possible—use.

community language use (Fishman 1967). Hence a bilingual program which fosters bilingual use outside the school and norms of stable and balanced diglossia is one which can be said to promote linguistic pluralism whereas a program which restricts or inhibits bilingual use in other than school domains and erodes diglossic community norms is one which must be characterized as promoting linguistic assimilation.

In other words, a bilingual program's social effectiveness is seen in the school domain's qualitative and quantitative effect upon the *use* of each language in other community domains.

Hard evidence on varying programs' differential effects upon community language-use patterns must come from comparative empirical community research of diachronic shifts in the dominance configurations of specific groups. However, prior to this, a provisional and substitute route via secondary research can be used to cast some light on the question of the likely effects of bilingual programs as currently structured.

We can consider any bilingual program as being composed of a set of structural options resulting from basic policy decisions. I have considered a large set and selected a non-exclusive sub-set of some fifteen which appear most relevant[5] in terms of having a potential effect upon language use outside the school. Thus each of these options is held to be potentially relevant in affecting language use within the community either in the direction of ethnic language maintenance or shift depending upon whether the option is taken and/or how it is filled or operationalized.

To simplify this presentation, all the options judged likely to produce ethnic language shift can be collected into an ideal-typical and extreme "Assimilation Model" and all those options which tend to foster ethnic language maintenance into a polar "Pluralistic Model." These two models therefore represent two extremes on a continuum of possible structures of bilingual education programs.

However, before presenting the two models, a number of contextual restrictions are in order because it must be clear that no feature of a bilingual education program can be considered shift-, or maintenance-fostering in and of itself. It is only within specific sociocultural contexts of great complexity that any program feature takes on relevance in one direction or the other.

Although these contextual features themselves merit an entire essay, I can only index a few here in order to suggest the frame of reference to which this analysis is restricted.

[5] Gaarder (1967) discusses some of these program options, as does Mackey (1970).

To speak of bilingual programs in the United States, the site of one of the most massive language shifts in world history, while half the world's population is characterized by stable intra-group bilingualism (Macnamara 1967), is to speak of quite a special case. Furthermore, I will restrict the context of my remarks to bilingual programs for Spanish-speaking Americans—the nation's largest foreign language minority and second largest ethnic minority[6]—with particular reference to Mexican Americans, or, as many more recently prefer to designate themselves, Chicanos.

This groups's ancestors came as colonial conquerors in the 16th century and were in turn conquered in the 19th century.[7] Since then Mexican-Americans have continued to grow in numbers through natural increase[8] and continuing immigration.[9] They are concentrated primarily in urban centers in five Southwestern states[10] and possess a rich folk culture.[11] The overwhelming majority are poor[12] ("lower" class), politically

[6] Estimates vary because the government has not included language items in its census questionnaires and has grouped Mexican-Americans together with "whites." The Mexican-American Population Commission of California places the number of "Americans of Hispanic origin" at 9.2 million as of 1971. "Hispanic origin" includes, in order of relative magnitude, Mexicans, Puerto Ricans Cubans, and other Latin Americans. By conservative estimate (John and Horner 1971:2) there were more than 4 million Mexican-Americans in the United States by 1971. Fishman (1966:42) estimates 3.4 million claimants of Spanish as their mother tongue in 1960.

[7] Don Juan de Oñate arrived on the banks of the Rio Grande river on Ascension Day, 1598, claiming all the eye beheld for Spain (Steiner 1969:3-2). Mexican hegemony was broken by the war between Mexico and the United States in 1846, which U. S. General Ulysses S. Grant characterized as the "most unjust (war) ever waged by a stronger against a weaker nation." (Steiner 1969:362). As a consequence, Mexico lost what has since become Texas, New Mexico, Arizona, and much of California, Nevada, Utah, and Colorado—an area comprising one-third of the United States (Steiner 1969:57).

[8] According to the 1960 U.S. census, the median age of Mexican-Americans was 17 years and their high birth rate is reflected in 709 children under 5 years of age per 1,000 women age 15 to 49 (compared to 613 for blacks and 455 for Anglos).

[9] The periods of largest immigration were 1920–29 (487,775) and 1955–64 (432, 573). A number of factors such as the elimination of the "bracero" program (post 1965) and the extremely rapid mechanization and automation of all industries, including agricultural, has severely reduced job opportunities for the unskilled and has considerably reduced more recent immigration.

[10] The 1960 census estimates that 87.2% of the Mexican origin population lives in the Southwest: California 40.1%, Arizona 6.0%, Colorado 1.2%, New Mexico 2.0%, and Texas 37.9% (Loyo, 1969, 35). They are primarily urban dwellers: 85.4% in California and New Mexico, 69.3% in Arizona, and 78.6% in Texas (Steiner 1969:142).

[11] This oral culture is now beginning to be collected and published in the Chicano press, especially such periodicals as Con Safos, La Raza, and El Grito. Steiner (1969:405-6) lists the addresses of 26 newspapers. Romano (1969) has recently edited a collection of native Chicano literature. One hopes the Chicano studies departments recently established at a number of colleges and universities will help in collecting and cultivating the community's "State-side" cultural and linguistic resources and not focus only upon varieties sanctioned and legitimized by foreign nation states whether contemporary or historic, e.g., Mexican, Spanish and pre-Columbian Indian.

[12] Only 4.6% of the Mexican-Americans were professionals (vs. 15.1% for Anglos) according to the 1960 census. Taking all white-collar jobs together (pro-

powerless,[13] sharply discriminated against and residentially segregated whether in urban or rural settings. Furthermore, Spanish is only a prestige idiom in the United States where there are irrelevant numbers of Spanish-speakers. Where Spanish-speakers are a relatively large group, it is an idiom held in considerable contempt.[14]

These few indicators only suggest some of the principal dimensions of the social context which must be kept in mind as we now consider first the pluralistic and then the assimilation models of bilingual education programs.

THE PLURALISTIC MODEL

This program is one initiated by a group of ethnic and non-ethnic community leaders in consultation with teachers and school administrators who form a continuing committee both to advise and control the program's operation. The bilingual program is a social issue around which the ethnic community becomes politically mobilized. The program's administration provides reciprocal control between the school and the community. Its reception and development are thereby tied into community decision-making and public opinion formation.

Before the program actually is begun, empirical research is conducted locally to ascertain: 1) the dominance configuration of the ethnic and non-ethnic languages for several social categories of speakers in the community, 2) the linguistic features of the specific varieties of ethnic language spoken locally, and 3) the attitudes of various social categories of community residents towards both the local and non-local ethnic language varieties. These investigations thus provide locally valid information which is utilized in the planning of the program components, such as the selection of linguistic varieties to be included in the classroom repertoire, choice of instructional materials, and determination of teacher in-service training components. These investigations additionally provide

<hr/>

fessional, managerial, proprietors, sales, and clerical) 19% of the Mexican-American population held such positions vs. 46.8% of the Anglos. Of all Spanish surnamed families in the Southwest in 1960, 34.8% were estimated as living at or below the "poverty level," meaning their annual family income was less than $3,000 in 1959 (Loyo 1969:78).

[13] For example, although one million Mexicans and Mexican-Americans live in Los Angeles, making it the third largest "Mexican" city in the world (after Mexico City and Guadalajara), districts have been so completely gerrymandered that they do not have a single representative on the city council (Steiner 1969:188-9).

[14] This might be formulated as "the Law of Anglo love of ethnic irrelevance," or the "Disneyland preference for symbolic ethnicity," i.e., the more locally irrelevant an ethnic language and culture is, the higher its social status, and the more viable it is locally, the lower its social status. Fishman (1966) has noted this attitude in the U.S. with respect to the most diverse ethnic languages and concluded that, "as long as these languages and cultures are truly 'foreign' our schools are comfortable with them. But as soon as they are found in our own back yards, the schools deny them." This amounts to honoring the dead while burying the living.

baseline data for later diachronic evaluations of the program's effects upon community language and language-related variables of both a behavioral and attitudinal nature.

The teacher(s) and aides in the bilingual program are of local, ethnic origin, newly appointed to the program, and receive special training to develop their communicative competence in using local and regional ethnic varieties of language and culture, their knowledge of ethnolinguistics (partly based on the pre-program community research), mother tongue instruction methods, and techniques for teaching English to speakers of other languages (TESOL).[15] The teachers live and are active in the local ethnic community and are members of the program's coordinating committee. Their cultural and linguistic ideologies favor, and their behavior manifests, stable biculturalism and bilingualism. In summary, the teachers are effective bilingual and bicultural role models for their students.

The bilingual program is "two-way," with members of both the ethnic and non-ethnic groups learning in their and the other's language (Stern 1963) and classes are ethnically mixed (non-ethnic on a voluntary basis) from the beginning or, if initially segregated they become mixed by the third or fourth grade (Gaarder 1967).

Initially the medium of instruction is dual, using the local ethnic and core group's dialects[16] and both are presented by the same teacher.

[15] Gaarder (1970) implies the desirability of separate teachers for each language. However, such a division would exemplify for the pupils a complete contradiction of the program's verbally stated goal of fostering true biculturals and bilinguals. In such a program pupils are enjoined to become what the actions of their teachers and aides manifest as impossible. Actions speak louder than words. Rosenthal and Jacobson (1968) have carefully demonstrated the impact of such nonverbal messages on pupils and their motivations. Naturally teacher and aide training is a serious problem. Equally important is the question, "what kind of training in which linguistic varieties of each language and with what level of literacy for specific grade level positions?"

[16] This option for beginning instruction in the medium of locally normative language varieties is predicated on the dictum that, "language teaching should be based on the resources that the child brings to the classroom" (Labov 1971:55). The American Association of Teachers of Spanish and Portuguese has recently recommended that, "Especially in the case of learners whose dialect differs markedly from world standard (Spanish), the first weeks, months—in some cases, the entire first year—should focus patiently on developing their self-confidence as speakers and writers and readers of their *own kind* of Spanish" (Gaarder 1971:5, emphasis in original). Note however that the everyday term "dialect"—as opposed to the sociolinguistic term "language variety"—always contains sociocultural and political judgments (Fishman 1972). Hence social conflicts often become manifest in decisions about whether or not a particular language variety is to be considered a "dialect" or not. It is a curiosity that Gaarder (1971) includes Barker (1971) in his references as she opens her book with a scathing condemnation of Pachuco Spanish—a widespread ethnic language variety spoken in the Southwest. Careful empirical research on intralanguage varieties and their educational significance has been conducted by Labov (1966), Stewart (1965, 1969), Dillard (1969), and Baratz and Shuy (1969) among others. Much of this work has

Each dialect receives equal time and equal treatment, initially through the presentation of a lesson in the student's strongest, or principal language variety followed by presentation of the same materials in the second language variety, i.e., in the principal language variety of the non-ethnic children.[17] Later when students have a better command of the second language variety, the class may alternate from one to the other without doubling or repeating the same materials in the other. Physical education and play periods permit the use of all language varieties. Some programs may later develop towards using the two linguistic varieties for separate but essential and socially significant subject areas without relegating either to unimportant purposes. Gradually the two standard varieties (ethnic and non-ethnic) are introduced but never completely supplant some use of the dialects[18] and do not disturb the overall ethnic to non-ethnic language balance. The developmental trend of the program, which lasts a minimum of nine years, is toward maintenance of both languages, i.e., all four varieties.[19]

The content of the bilingual curriculum stimulates ethnic community language planning efforts and includes considerable attention to the local and regional cultures of both the ethnic and core groups in such a way as to provide a natural context for alternate use of both dialect and standard varieties. The results of research on local attitudes toward language varieties, their speakers, and bilingualism,[20] as well as information on vocational opportunities in education, industry, commerce and government requiring or facilitated by bilingualism are presented first indirectly, and later directly.[21]

Demonstration classes are held for parents from all groups, both to

focused on the varieties of English spoken by blacks. Gumperz (1970a, 1970b, 1969a) has pioneered work on Chicano speech involving rapid Spanish/English switching and Kjolseth *et al.* (in preparation) are presently analyzing the grammar and social functions of such speech. Rayfield (1970) has analyzed similar switching patterns involving Yiddish and English.

[17] This is intended to facilitate the ethnic child's acquisition of a variety of the non-ethnic language which is *appropriate* (Hymes, 1966:22–3) in local peer level communication. Thus both ethnic and non-ethnic pupils initially add a language variety to their linguistic repertoires which is appropriate for local communication with their out-group peers, thereby favoring second language *use* by members of both groups in inter-group conversation outside the classroom.

[18] One place where "dialects" have an unquestionably appropriate place in classroom activities at all grade levels is that of creative writing, especially about relevant socio-cultural topics.

[19] Of course, as the pupil progresses, new stylistic levels in both languages (informal, careful, formal, ceremonial) are added to the classroom repertoire.

[20] A clear understanding of the content and social basis for local prejudices against different language varieties and their speakers is essential for "non-defensive cultural self-defense."

[21] Much more attention needs to be paid to presently non-existent occupational categories which are, however, necessary in meeting the needs of the local ethnic community's majority.

promote understanding of the bilingual program and its methods as well as to encourage interest in a parallel program of bilingual adult education. In general, the adult program is organized in ways analogous to that of the students but with materials adjusted to the age group: ethnically mixed classes, dual medium with equal time and treatment of the language varieties, an early emphasis on dialects, preferably the same teacher and similar content areas as in the children's program, information on bilingual vocational counseling, and local attitudes towards language varieties and their speakers.

A number of extracurricular activities involve both parents and children from both groups; for example a lending library might be established with a variety of materials such as comics, magazines, newspapers and books for a span of interests, social class levels, and age groups.

A series of public lectures and articles in local newspapers give information on the gamut of school and school-related programs, their rationale, organization, evaluation, and progress. Emphasis is placed on the program's interest in cultivating local varieties of language and culture for all groups. The community board of the bilingual program acts as the central controlling and coordinating body for this set of bilingual-bicultural activities in, near, and outside the school.

Evaluative research on the program considers not only changes in individual language skills and attitudes (as well as the traditional measures of academic achievement) but also tests for (sub-)*group qualitative and quantitative measures of the frequency of use of different language varieties in domains outside the school.* The emphasis is sociolinguistic.

The most important dimensions of the pluralistic bilingual program can be briefly summarized:

1) This program acts as a continuing stimulus to civic development and organization within the ethnic community and encourages a democratic and more transparent forum for the resolution of conflicts and differing interests within and between the ethnic and non-ethnic communities.

2) The teaching personnel are, on ascriptive, achieved, and behavioral grounds credible exemplifications for ethnic and non-ethnic students and parents of successfully operative bilinguals and biculturals.

3) Paralleling the composition of administrative control with its egalitarian distribution of power among diverse community interest groups, the linguistic and cultural content of the pluralistic program might be characterized metaphorically as "horizontally" articulated, emphasizing the complementarity of different varieties of situationally appropriate culture and language. This, along with an increased aware-

ness of ethnolinguistics, encourages the student to become active in a variety of settings, use a number of linguistic varieties, and become experienced in switching between them. Language skills and cultural perspectives are added without progressively destroying his home language and culture. Furthermore, these developments take place in *both* groups. The success or failure of this program is indicated most penetratingly by the degree to which it encourages, engenders, and insures norms of appropriateness for non-English language varieties in community domains other than the school.[22]

THE ASSIMILATION MODEL

This bilingual program is initiated by the school without any community-based advance planning. If a school-community advisory group is formed, it is without real powers to control the program. Community "involvement"[23] is encouraged and community control is avoided.

The teacher(s) is either a non-ethnic, or, if a member of the ethnic group, one who lives in a non-ethnic residential area and is either generally inactive in ethnic community affairs or active only in conservative elitist ethnic organizations and causes whose concerns and interests are distant from those which represent and speak to the basic everyday problems of the local ethnic majority. Transferred from some other class already within the school, this teacher will nevertheless have received some special in-service linguistic and cultural training for the position. This

---

[22] Any program's goals are reflected in three principal places: 1) the program's *statement* of goals, 2) the program's *structure* or design options, and 3) the teleology, hypotheses, and *research emphasis* of the program's evaluative component. The first is the weakest of the three as an indicator of what the program is, in fact striving for.

[23] "Community involvement" is presently a popular euphemism which veils non-reciprocal rights between professionals who "serve" and the laity who are "served." Lay members opine and recommend while professionals decide and execute. "Involvement" is a well known management technique long used in industry and designed to give those most directly affected by policy the feeling of influence rather than real influence itself. The U.S. Office of Education's Title VII Manual (USOE 1970:31–34, and Andersson 1970, Vol. 2: 7–20) *requires* community "involvement" and fails to make any recommendation concerning community control. It is interesting to note that only two existing programs funded by the federal government have anything like clear community control features built into them: Coral Way and Rough Rock (John and Horner 1971:28–31 and 17–20 respectively). Each is also quite unique in another, perhaps very relevant way. Coral Way serves a community whose ethnic members are primarily "middle" class, i.e., close in social status to the educational professionals. Rough Rock on the other hand serves an exclusively Navajo community which is geographically very isolated from any non-ethnic communities. For these reasons, neither provides a very relevant example because most programs are located in urban areas with a high concentration of "lower" class ethnics. Much more exemplary for having some community control features and a strong bilingual curriculum are Public Schools 25 and 155 in New York City (John and Horner 1971:52–56).

will not have included any significant concern for local ethnic culture, local language varieties (especially his or her competence in its *use*) or ethnolinguistics, but will have centered almost exclusively upon teaching a standard variety[24] of the ethnic language as a mother tongue (and as a medium of instruction) and the language's "high" culture. The teacher's attitudes with respect to language tend to be exclusive and purist, viewing "interference," whether from the ethnic dialect or English, as a major "problem" and local dialect as categorically improper and "incorrect."[25] Biculturalism of "high" culture and bilingualism of the "proper" variety

[24] This standard variety may be careful or formal "middle" class Mexico City Spanish, "world Spanish" (Gaarder 1971), or even academic Castilian Spanish. All are likely to be related to, but very distant from the locally appropriate and most frequently used ethnic language varieties of the Chicano community where a federally funded program is located, especially as the law requires demonstrating a concentration of ethnic families with annual family incomes below $3,000!

At a bilingual school in southern California in 1971 this writer was informed by a bilingual aid, who lived in the Mexican-American barrio, that she and the other first grade aids "envied" the "more correct" Spanish of the master teacher, who does not live in the barrio. One of the first grade readers being used (published in Madrid) was found to contain many vocabulary items (four on one particular page) which a "middle" class Mexican college graduate would not understand. The master teacher admitted having had to look up these terms in her dictionary —also published in Madrid. The terms were nevertheless justified as "better Spanish" although they are obviously inappropriate in any natural speech setting locally.

It should be added that we are notoriously ignorant about what actually transpires in classroom interaction and what language varieties are actually included in the classroom repertoire. Lewis (1970) offers a seminal exploratory study of problems of cross-cultural communication between teachers and students.

[25] The "high/low" metaphor in popular usage characterizing linguistic and cultural varieties as well as social classes is, unfortunately, often uncritically adopted into the working vocabulary of social science. As Goudsblom (1970) shows, "high" systematically implies "better," "freer," and "stronger." Descriptively it would be more responsible and useful to identify language *varieties* and conceive of them sequentially in the order learned.

The purist approach might be characterized as a kind of cultural and linguistic imperialism for it posits a single variety (of language or culture) as "correct" for all domains. Other varieties are felt to be in *competition* with the one they seek to impart in the school. These other varieties are a "problem." Herndon (1969:9) conveys the feeling of teachers toward such phenomena noting it is, "something which happens all the time . . . but which isn't supposed to happen. A problem. You were supposed to believe in, and work toward, its nonexistence." Rather than *adding* a linguistic variety to the child's repertoire (Gumperz, 1964a, 1964b, 1965, and 1969b, 1969c), it is felt that the school-approved "high" variety should *replace* the child's "low" variety. Steiner (1969:212–215) refers to this as "de-education," i.e., the belief that the "lower" class Mexican-American child "has to be de-educated before he can be re-educated," and adds that currently in the U.S., "the de-education of La Raza is indeed over achieved."

Sociolinguistic factors underlie these pervasive purist beliefs. Labov (1971: 52) points out that, "in a number of sociolinguistic studies it has been found that women are more sensitive to prestige forms than men—in formal style (. . .) and teachers in the early grades are women, largely from the lower middle class. This is the group which shows the most extreme form of linguistic insecurity, with the sharpest slope of style shifting."

is held to be a worthy goal attainable only with great effort by his students, who are held to suffer from "cultural deprivation." [26]

The program is one-way with classes only for ethnic students. It is held that there is no reason for non-ethnics to participate, or, if so, that one must bend to the insufficient interest or ingrained prejudices of non-ethnics and their parents.

The program, which lasts a maximum of three years, may begin with either the ethnic standard as a single medium, or with the ethnic and non-ethnic standards as dual mediums of instruction. However, as rapidly as is pragmatically deemed possible, the time and treatment of the non-ethnic standard is increased so that within a relatively short period of time the ethnic standard is used only for limited, non-essential subjects. Insofar as reading or writing skills in the ethnic standard are taught, it is the minimum considered necessary for establishing the base skills for their transfer to the non-ethnic standard. Basically the developmental trend in all the program's features is towards rapid and near complete transfer to the non-ethnic standard. The school's policy is essentially a "burnt bridges" approach: the ethnic language is seen only as a bridge to the non-ethnic language—one to be crossed as rapidly as possible and then destroyed, at least as a legitimate medium of general instruction, although some voluntary classes in it as a foreign language may be maintained.

Apart from some early consideration of distant, ethnic-related culture,[27] the content of the curriculum emphasizes non-ethnic, non-"lower" class interests and values. Ethnolinguistic matters are conspicuous by their absence and bilingual vocational counseling, if included, focuses upon traditionally stylized non-ethnic characterizations of vocations the exercise of which have been either antithetical or irrelevant to the

---

[26] Labov (1971:65) has affirmed that, "Linguists (. . .) without a single dissenting voice (. . .) concur that this (cultural or verbal deprivation) is a superficial and erroneous interpretation of the very data presented in support of it." Nevertheless, this brutal term of sociocultural coercion has become very popular among educators. "Middle" class ignorance of "lower" class culture and language is rarely recognized. This is hardly surprising in view of the non-reciprocal power relations (see footnote 23 above) between the groups involved. To this one can add the ethnolinguistic fact (Wolff 1964) that many teachers *will not*, and so *cannot* comprehend a linguistic or cultural variety which they hold to be "inferior" and "reprehensible." Hymes (1966:34) has suggested the need for a conference on the "cultural deprivation" of "middle" class teachers while noting its unlikelihood. Finally, economic deprivation is frequently (and conveniently) equated with "cultural deprivation."

The end result of these factors is a kind of "educational colonialism" with the "priests of education" busily "civilizing the savages."

[27] Emphasis is thus on "symbolic ethnicity" rather than upon existent persistent traditions. See also footnote 14.

existent culture of the ethnic majority, e.g., teaching, academic research, diplomacy, and positions with large supra-national corporations.

Demonstration classes and public lectures may be held for ethnic parents in order to convince them of the value of the program and to interest them in an adult education program.

If an adult bilingual education program is offered, its structure is in most ways similar to the children's program. Its goal is functional literacy in the non-ethnic standard via the ethnic standard if necessary. Almost all effort is focused upon the English as a second language (ESL) component.

Extracurricular activities, whether recreational or more serious, for young or old or both, tend to radiate a "high" and distant, ethnic-related culture.

Evaluation of the assimilation program is primarily focused upon testing the *quality of individual performances within the school setting* on a host of skill, aptitude and attitude measures. The bias is narrowly academic, linguistic, and psychological.[28]

Summarizing the essential dimensions of the assimilation program we see that:

1) Because originated from "above" by elites and administered in taken-for-granted, traditional ways by non-ethnic and supra-ethnic interests and forces, this program is likely to discourage ethnic community organization among the large majority and to stifle open appraisal of intra-, and inter-group conflicts.

2) The teacher exemplifies the ability of elite members of dominant cultures to master and propagate a "superior" brand of ethnic culture and language.[29]

---

[28] Some examples in each area are: *academic*; frequency of disciplinary problems, absenteeism, drop out rates, and academic achievement scores in all subject areas, *linguistic*; word re-call, translation, and sentence-completion performance measures as well as tests for phonological, morphological and syntactic "interference," *psychological*; attitudinal, interest, and "intelligence" test scores, etc. "Interference" and "intelligence" merit being enclosed in quotation marks in the opinion of this writer because, although originally developed in social science as neutral terms, they have both come to be frequently *used* by the educational establishment as symbolic justifications for crude and iniquitous methods of social control.

[29] Because pupils may more easily identify with an ethnic teacher, they may be even more effective than non-ethnic teachers in implanting in the pupils a sense of shame and inferiority with respect to the local varieties of ethnic language and culture. Steiner (1969:176–7) quotes one barrio leader as observing, "no one is more frightened, smug, and conservative, and harder on our people, than the typical schoolteacher (. . .) who has escaped from the barrios in a two-car port and a king-sized bed." Thus, for many, social mobility is up-and-*out* of the barrio. One's distance from the barrio is signaled geographically (suburbia), culturally ("high" ethnic culture) and linguistically ("correct" Spanish). In view of this it should be clear that local control and ethnic teachers are in themselves no panacea or guarantee of a pluralistic program. See also footnote 25.

3) The linguistic and cultural content of the assimilation program is metaphorically a "vertically" articulated one implying power and hegemony. It emphasizes the superiority or inferiority of different varieties of language and culture and encourages restricting use to correct forms of school-approved varieties in all domains of usage. This may be successful in alienating the student from the ethnic language and culture of his home and community if there are few or no extra-school domains where the careful "middle" class standard ethnic variety is appropriate. Pre-existent stereotypes on varieties of language and culture, their speakers and carriers held by youth and adults in both groups are unaltered or reinforced by these and other measures such as newspaper articles which describe the bilingual program as bringing "cultural enrichment" and a literate standard language to the "culturally deprived" and illiterate.

ANALYSIS

Which of these models do current bilingual programs approximate? To answer this question we now turn to the materials on bilingualism available through the Educational Resources Information Center (ERIC 1969) of the U.S. Office of Education (USOE) in order to examine the available reports and weigh their relevant structural features in terms of the two polar models.

This procedure presents two problems. First this file contains a collection of reports on existent programs (as of 1969) but cannot be taken to constitute anything like a representative sample of all bilingual educational efforts. A second drawback in using these materials is that reports currently present great problems of comparison because there is no adherence to even a minimal set of reporting categories such as numbers of hours of instruction in each language or materials taught in each language. In order to make such reports more useful for secondary analyses, the USOE should develop and sanction adherence to minimal reporting criteria such as the National Institute of Mental Health has encouraged with its program of model reporting areas for mental health statistics. This is an urgent need.[30]

Nevertheless, in spite of these two methodological problems inherent in the data used here, the results of this secondary analysis reveal such an overwhelmingly clear and one-sided trend that we can perhaps confidently assume it gives us a picture of what kinds of bilingual education programs are currently multiplying in the United States.

The finding is that *the great majority of bilingual programs (well over*

---

[30] Mackey (1970:80–82) has proposed a useful questionnaire which is an important step in the needed direction.

80%) highly approximate the extreme of the assimilation model while the remaining few are only moderately pluralistic.

Thus, in direct contradiction to the usual program's statement of goals, the structure of "typical" programs can be expected to foster not the maintenance but rather the accelerated demise of the ethnic mother tongue.

This is to say that in most cases the ethnic language is being exploited rather than cultivated—weaning the pupil away from his mother tongue through the transitional use of a variety of his mother tongue in what amounts to a kind of cultural and linguistic "counterinsurgency" policy on the part of the schools. A variety of the ethnic language is being used as a new means to an old end. The traditional policy of "Speak Only English" is amended to "We *Will* Speak Only English—just as soon as possible and even sooner and more completely if we begin with a variety of the ethnic language rather than only English!"

In light of this, the benefits to the ethnic language and culture optimistically supposed by many to be somehow inherent to any bilingual education program become not just questionable but suspect outright as one realizes that some (and today most) types of bilingual programs may achieve much more effectively what the earlier monolingual policy could not do.

The appearance of bilingual programs does indeed represent a new policy, but as currently structured, most may be best understood as being so designed as to represent a change from an earlier policy of simple repression to a more "modern" and sophisticated policy of linguistic counterinsurgency.

It is *not* assumed that those directly involved in bilingual programs consciously intend these consequences. On the contrary most are undoubtedly dedicated and well-intentioned. However, dedication and good intentions often manifest themselves in doing what comes naturally and the road to hell has not infrequently been paved with good intentions.

The relevant issue today is not simply monolingual vs. bilingual education but more essentially what *social* goals will serve the needs of the *majority* of ethnic group members and what *integrated set* of program design features will effectively realize them? Currently most programs are patchwork affairs, each searching for some distinctive gimmick and focusing its rhetoric and design towards the individual pupil in isolation from his family, peers, neighborhood, and community.

If this evaluation seems harsh, it may be important to the reader to know that since the above analysis of the ERIC data and its conclusion that most bilingual programs strongly foster assimilation and language shift, three important studies reviewing an even larger number of programs, many of which were more recently initiated, have all come to a similar conclusion.

For example, Gaarder (1970) has analyzed the official USOE program descriptions of all seventy-six bilingual education projects federally funded in the first year of Title VII operation and polled all project directors. He notes that, "the disparity between aims and means is enormous," adds that, "only six aim eventually to provide bilingual schooling at all grade levels, 1–12," and concludes, " 'bilingual education' . . . can serve the ends of either (Anglo) ethnocentrism or cultural pluralism."

The same trend again becomes clearly evident as one reads the many program descriptions reproduced by John and Horner (1971:15–100) and Andersson and Boyer (1970, Vol. 2, 241–291). John and Horner (p. 187) conclude with a warning: "Educational innovations will remain of passing interest and little significance without the recognition that education is a social process. If the school remains alien to the values and needs of the community, if it is bureaucratically run, then the children will not receive the education they are entitled to, no matter what language they are taught in."

More recently Andersson (1971:24–25), after noting a steady decline in the number of proposals for bilingual education programs received by the U.S. Office of Education (315 for 1970, 195 for 1971, and 150 for 1972), concludes that, "the obstacles to success are indeed formidable. Perhaps the greatest of these is the doubt in many communities that the maintenance of non-English languages is desirable."

Yet exactly this pervasive doubt that ethnic language maintenance is desirable might be an important reason for promoting more *assimilation* programs.

Again the more basic issue is, "*What type* of bilingual programs?"

All this is not even surprising when one considers that the assimilation program is essentially an expression of the existent social structures of most U.S. communities with sizeable ethnic populations. The school always has been an institution representative of the powerful community interest groups and their mainstream beliefs. The majority of Chicanos simply do not have presently either the sociopolitical power or the detailed and clear policy on language and culture necessary for their indigenous varieties of language and culture to be recognized in an institution for social *control* such as the school, which in all societies is one of the traditional sites where the results of overt and covert sociopolitical and cultural conflicts are operationalized in what, in English, we somewhat euphemistically call school "policies," rather than "cultural politics."

The difference between "policies" and "politics" is no idle matter of just words, but a consequential distinction implying two completely different modes of distributing power. "Policies" are generally understood to represent decisions appropriately made by professionals—in this case educators, administrators, and researchers. "Politics," however, directly implies the appropriateness of rights of influence and control (not just "involvement") in the decision-making process for lay or nonprofessional constituencies, especially those most directly affected—in this case the parents and children of the ethnic majority within the Chicano community.

To the typical Southwestern nonethnic American, the pluralistic program for Chicanos must sound radical for it seems to him to assume a host of factors which his social upbringing has taught him are absent. Where is the ethnic community ideology, interest, and consensus necessary for promoting an ethnic-based bilingualism and biculturalism? Where are there ethnics with the prerequisite basic training needed for recruitment into such a program? How can an "illiterate dialect" be considered appropriate for use in the school? What culture does a "culturally deprived" group have worthy of inclusion in an academic program? And many ethnic members, especially those of the elite, have adopted these same views, which makes even more understandable the tendency to propose only "high" cultural and linguistic varieties as acceptable for a program proposal.

Indeed the pluralistic program *is* one which in many ways runs against the tide and almost appears to present a dilemma.

If the assimilation program is an expression of the status quo social structures, the pluralistic program is an expression of planned social change, and its introduction itself presupposes some basic social changes in intra-ethnic ideologies and power relations.

Fishman and Lovas (1970:215) have suggested that, "bilingual education in the United States currently suffers from three serious lacks: a lack of funds (Title VII is pitifully starved), a lack of personnel (there are almost no optimally trained personnel in this field), and a lack of evaluative programs (curricula, material, methods)."

Realizing that these are real problems, let us nevertheless assume that more money, trained personnel, and evaluative programs *are* forthcoming in the future. Will this assure any change away from the community demise of the ethnic language?

This question lends greater weight to the principal concern of Fishman and Lovas, who emphasize that what is most needed is greater sociological understanding of the social consequences of bilingual programs.

While one cannot predict the types of bilingual education programs which are likely to appear should more funds, personnel, and materials become available, there would appear to be a strong possibility that the result will not be pluralistic programs. One possibility is of course the proliferation of more numerous assimilation programs.

However, some changes also may be expected. Because the progressive phasing out of the ethnic language as a medium of instruction, or what Mackey (1970) calls a "transfer" curriculum, transparently, achieves language shift *within* the school domain, and because a program in which the ethnic language continues to have a role as a medium of instruction throughout the progressive grades (a "maintenance" curriculum) obviously realizes ethnic language maintenance *within* the school domain, many influential proponents of bilingual education are coming to recognize the exploitation of the ethnic language inherent in the Transfer curriculum and are advocating the institution of more Maintenance curricula.

No sociological acumen is required to see this much.

However, if planners of new programs focus almost exclusively upon the "time and treatment" curriculum issue, the following may easily happen: one begins with what is essentially a near ideal-typical Assimilation program (which includes a school Transfer curriculum) and inserts in its place a Maintenance curriculum while retaining all the other features of the model. Such a change would be from a Transfer-Assimilation to a Maintenance-Assimilation program.

To call it a Maintenance-Assimilation program implies a contradiction, namely that while realizing ethnic language maintenance within the school it simultaneously promotes ethnic language shift within the community.

Is such a result possible? I would hypothesize not only that it is, but that there are sociological reasons for expecting that, in certain social contexts, a Maintenance-Assimilation program may be an even *more* potent, albeit less visible, instrument of linguistic counterinsurgency than the Transfer-Assimilation model.

A few reasons for such a possibility can be most concisely suggested by a schematic outline of postulates, assumptions, and hypotheses which, it is recognized, can only be confirmed or refuted by future empirical research. (It should be emphasized that from the value position of this writer most of the following hypothetical consequences are considered undesirable.)

The basic question is, "What are the diachronic effects of the Maintenance-Assimilation program on the local community dominance configuration?"

Postulate 1: Significant types of language shift may remain veiled unless in addition to the distinction between the ethnic and the non-ethnic languages, intra-ethnic language varieties are differentiated. For purposes of this discussion only two varieties will be distinguished: the informal local ethnic language variety (ELV_L) vs. a supranational world (Gaarder 1971) ethnic language variety (ELV_W).

Postulate 2: A speaker will view his stronger language in a more differentiated manner than he will his weaker language. That is, members of the ethnic speech community will be more aware of, and sensitive to differential competence in their command of distinct *intra*-ethnic language varieties than they will be to either their differential *inter*-language (ethnic vs. non-ethnic), or non-ethnic *intra*-language competence. For example, a member of the ethnic majority who is confident in his command of an informal ethnic language variety, may, when faced with a situation requiring "correct" usage (ELV_W), become painfully aware of his felt inability and therefore opt to switch into the variety of the non-ethnic language which he commands, although, for a native speaker of the non-ethnic language this variety may be felt to be far from formal. However, if fellow ethnic community members constitute his audience (see assumption 2 below), such an inter-language switch may be accepted as "more formal" than an intra-ethnic language variety switch because they hold similar norms highly differentiating varieties of their mother tongue and stereotyping the second language.

Assumptions:

1. The Maintenance-Assimilation program emphasizes ELV_W exclusively, i.e., either excludes ELV_L from the classroom repertoire completely or only tolerates it passively, e.g., the teacher does not overtly chastise a child for using ELV_L but will never use it herself.

2. The ethnic community is vertically stratified into a large "lower" class majority and a small "middle" class minority. Both tend to be residentially segregated from each other and from the non-ethnic population—the majority more so than the minority.

3. The ethnic majority has broad competence in ELV_L and very limited competence in ELV_W while the ethnic minority has more competence in ELV_W than in ELV_L.

4. Both the ethnic majority and minority subjectively distinguish ELV_L from ELV_W sharply.

5. Most members of the ethnic majority uncritically accept the ethnic minority's cultural and linguistic norms and their ethnolinguistic beliefs which characterize ELV_L as "low," "inexpressive," "incorrect," etc., and the ELV_W as "high," "eloquent," "correct," etc.[31]

---

[31] There is an impressive array of supporting evidence for assumptions 4 and 5. Only a few examples can be given here. Alvarez (1967) calls Spanish "calo" a

Hypothesis 1: The Maintenance-Assimilation program will tend to *increase the use of ELV$_W$* in those community domains which; a) play a secondary role in the ethnic majority's everyday communication networks, b) fulfill formal and ceremonial functions, c) tend to be governed by channel constraints or non-reciprocal rights firmly establishing one group as predominantly senders and another as predominantly receivers,[32] i.e., are domains which tend to be controlled by the minority elite and assign a passive-receptive role to the majority. Some examples of such domains would be the formal parts of festive, ceremonial and political gatherings, and mass media such as radio, television, and newspapers.

Hypothesis 2: The Maintenance-Assimilation program will tend to *decrease the use of ELV$_L$* in those community domains which; a) play a primary role in the everyday communication networks of the ethnic majority, b) fulfill intimate, casual, and informal functions, c) are governed by reciprocal rights of participants so that, d) all persons involved engage in the productive and receptive use of language which e) is mutually controlled by the partners to the speech event.

Hypothesis 3: The Maintenance-Assimilation program will tend to *decrease the overall use of ethnic language vis a vis the non-ethnic language* due to the greater prevalence and salience of informal over formal domains in the everyday life space of the ethnic majority. To use a quasi "evolutionary" metaphor, this result would amount to a sort of social "selection" of a "higher" species of the ethnic language—relegated however to a near vestigial or marginal role in community interaction. Ethnic language use in the community is thus "purified" and "elevated" while simultaneously isolated from the core functional concerns of the majority where it is replaced by the non-ethnic language which is more categorically approved without such fine or detailed distinctions between its various varieties as are made between those of the ethnic language as briefly sketched in Postulate 2 above. It is as if the ethnic language were gaining legitimacy through death and supporters of such a trend felt, "better a noble death than an ignominious life," that is, better the more restricted use of a "high" variety than a wider use of a "low" one.

The above hypotheses focus upon the ethnic majority. What might be the consequences for the ethnic minority?

Hypothesis 4: If the above postulates, assumptions and hypotheses are valid, the Maintenance-Assimilation program might be expected to *increase* the use of ELV$_W$ within the communication networks of the ethnic minority elite and increase their control over the ethnic majority

---

"snarl language." See also Barker (1971) and footnote 16. Even Haugen (1962) has characterized a number of normative dialect forms as "pathological."

[32] These terms are taken from Hymes (1964) etic paradigm of speech events.

in local affairs while at the same time increasing the ethnic minority's opportunities for social mobility beyond either local or ethnic boundaries. The ethnic minority elite would thus become more dominant over, while simultaneously less dependent upon and more divorced from the local ethnic majority. This might place them in a particularly advantaged position for being easily co-opted by supra-ethnic interests dedicated to a colonial policy of indirect rule and make more difficult any attempts on the part of the ethnic majority to form independent sources of power and influence.[33]

Summarizing this series of hypotheses, one might say that if the Transfer-Assimilation program represents the ethnocentric triumph of non-ethnic over ethnic values and interests, then in a sense the Maintenance-Assimilation program may bespeak a sociocentric victory of the ethnic minority elite over the ethnic majority's interests and values.

However, all these hypotheses, which suggest currently unanticipated consequences, must be put to empirical test.

As research can discover generally only what it sets out to find, adequate empirical tests only can be constructed by persistently holding on to the fundamental question: "What are the *social* consequences of particular bilingual education strategies upon the changing patterns of *community* language *use?*" And, as the four hypotheses above seek to make clear, even such studies are likely to cast a net too coarse to catch the most significant changes unless a finer net is spun which recognizes the internal heterogeneity of the ethnic community and differentiates between intra-ethnic language varieties, and their communicative roles, status, and consequences for intra-ethnic community social and political organization.

From the contradiction between current statements of goals for bilingual programs and their likely outcomes—given their present (and likely future) structures—it would appear that many if not most bilingual programs are being unintentionally, yet falsely, represented to those most directly affected by them, that is the pupils and parents of the ethnic majority.

CONCLUSION

From this one can conclude that future sociolinguistic research in this field has not only a scholarly but also an urgent democratic need to fulfill. Only by developing our knowledge of the longer range social consequences which specific programs have in their particular, heterogene-

---

[33] A recent example of such attempts at the development of independent sources of power is the formation of a third political party in 1970 and 1971 in several Southwestern states.

ous, and stratified community contexts, and by developing an awareness of the range of possible alternative bilingual education models, can
the real conflicts always involved in such projects become more transparent and the interest groupings affected have a basis for developing a
more enlightened stand towards the introduction and development of
desired programs.[34]

POSTSCRIPT

From the perspective of the above analysis it is particularly significant that at the time of the writing of this amended version (September
1971), after numerous communications with the U.S. Office of Education
and correspondence with Project BEST (in New York City) which is
engaged in a systematic review of the approaches used in every evaluative research component attached to each federally funded bilingual program in the United States, it has been possible to determine that *currently there is not a single study planned to determine program effects upon
community diglossia.*

Such a glaring absence presents a phenomenon which itself deserves
detailed investigation and should attract persons interested in the
sociology of science and knowledge.

Why does this notorious research lacuna exist? Will it persist?
Certain factors would seem to maintain it. Psychologists, educators, and
linguists far outnumber sociolinguists in the education research establishment. Also, the laymen, teachers, and administrators promoting
bilingual education programs have primarily been members of the ethnic
minority elite and non-ethnics who are generally disinterested in, or
directly opposed to many of the characteristics of the pluralistic model
presented here. Existent programs naturally have a built-in interest
in testing themselves on measures where they are likely to show "success"
and justify their expenditures in terms which will be persuasive and adequate for those who decide upon the continuation of programs and the
allocation of funds. On the basis of current trends, one could conclude
that for those who presently decide, community language maintenance

---

[34] The emphasis of this essay has been admittedly critical. The reader should
not lose sight of the fact that a few pluralistic programs do exist. Additionally,
many powerfully assimilationistic programs are admittedly very effective in re-
ducing disciplinary problems, drop out rates and absenteeism as well as promoting
higher levels of academic achievement. Also, a strictly Anglo-oriented "cost
analysis" of assimilation programs should show them to be a "good investment"
and even a "bargain": i.e., that they are effective in keeping youth off the streets,
out of juvenile hall (courts), and will result in fewer of them in the future appearing on welfare and unemployment rolls.
  The point, however, is that these traditional school-, and budget-oriented
goals can be achieved while simultaneously threatening or destroying community
diglossia and hence the future of the ethnic community as such.

in general and maintenance of the ethnic majority's cultural and linguistic varieties in particular is manifestly irrelevant or simply not considered desirable.

There are, nevertheless, some positive signs. Fishman (1966 and 1971a) has developed, applied, and refined the diglossic approach in several studies of different ethnic groups in the United States. Several centers for the preparation of sociolinguists have been developed in recent years. Gaarder (1971) has drawn attention to the significance of the relations between intra-ethnic language varieties and recommended the importance of giving local varieties a place in the classroom repertoire. And finally, within the Mexican-American community itself new political movements, leaders, and ideas more concerned with the future of the ethnic majority are being developed which are beginning critically to reexamine those of the ethnic elite minority.

Only one thing is certain. Not only do we not know what the major *social* consequences of different types of bilingual education programs are, but unless current trends and research priorities are altered basically, we are not going to know either—until too late, when the consequences have already been wrought and become sufficiently massive so as to be evident to all. Buth the important questions will then be of only historical interest.

Would it not be shamefully irresponsible to wait for such a *post mortem*?

REFERENCES

ALATIS, J. E., ED.
1970 Bilingualism and Language Contact: Anthropological, Linguistic, Psychological, and Sociological Aspects. *Georgetown Monograph Series on Languages and Linguistics*, No. 23. Georgetown University Press, Washington, D.C.

ALVAREZ, G. R.
1967 Calo: The 'Other' Spanish. *ETC* (Journal of the International Society for General Semantics) 24(1): 7–13.

ANDERSSON, THEODORE
1971 Bilingual Education: The American Experience. (A paper presented at a conference sponsored by the Ontario Institute for Studies in Education, Toronto, Canada.)

ANDERSSON, THEODORE AND MILDRED BOYER, EDS.
1970 *Bilingual Schooling in the United States.* 2 vols. United States Government Printing Office, Washington, D.C.

BARATZ, JOAN AND ROGER SHUY, EDS.
1969 *Teaching Black Children to Read.* Center for Applied Linguistics, Washington, D.C.

BARKER, MARIE ESMAN
1971 *Español para el Bilingüe.* National Textbook Company, Skokie, Illinois.

DILLARD, J. L.
1969 How to Tell the Bandits from the Good Guys, or What Dialect to Teach? *The Florida FL Reporter*, Spring/Summer: 84–85, 162.

Eric File on Bilingualism
A list of the materials in this file and information on how they may be ordered appears in *The Linguistic Reporter* 11: 3 (June 1969) 6–7. Center for Applied Linguistics, Washington, D.C.
Ferguson, C. A.
1959 Diglossia. *Word* 15: 325–340.
Fishman, Joshua A.
1965 Who Speaks What Language to Whom and When? *Linguistique* 2: 67–68.
1966 *Language Loyalty in the United States.* Mouton, The Hague.
1967 Bilingualism with and without Diglossia: Diglossia with and without Bilingualism. *Journal of Social Issues* 23 (2): 29–38.
1970 The Politics of Bilingual Education. In "Bilingualism and Language Contact: Anthropological, Linguistic, Psychological and Sociological Aspects." *Georgetown Monograph Series on Language and Linguistics*, No. 23. J. E. Alatis, ed. Georgetown University Press, Washington, D.C. pp. 47–58.
1972 The Sociology of Language: An Interdisciplinary Social Science Approach to Sociolinguistics. (Prepared for *Current Trends in Linguistics*, vol. 12. T. A. Sebeok, ed. Mouton, The Hague.)
Fishman, Joshua A. and John Lovas
1970 Bilingual Education in Sociolinguistic Perspective. *TESOL Quarterly* 4(3).
Fishman, Joshua A., R. L. Cooper, Roxana Ma, et al.
1971 *Bilingualism in the Barrio.* Language Sciences Series, University of Indiana Press, Bloomington.
Gaarder, A. Bruce
1967 Organization of the Bilingual School. *Journal of Social Issues* 23(2): 110–120.
1970 The First Seventy-Six Bilingual Education Projects. In "Bilingualism and Language Contact: Anthropological, Linguistic, Psychological and Sociological Aspects." *Georgetown Monograph Series on Languages and Linguistics*, No. 23. J. E. Alatis, ed. Georgetown University Press, Washington, D.C. pp. 163–178.
1971 Teaching Spanish in School and College to Native Speakers of Spanish. (A report commissioned by the Executive Council of the American Association of Teachers of Spanish and Portuguese.) Mimeographed.
Goudsblom, Johan
1970 On High and Low in Society and in Sociology: A Semantic Approach to Social Stratification. (A paper presented at the 7th World Congress of Sociology, Varna, Bulgaria.)
Grebler, Leo, Joan W. Moore, Ralph C. Guzman, et al.
1970 *The Mexican American People: The Nation's Second Largest Minority.* The Free Press-Macmillan, New York.
Gumperz, J. J.
1964a Linguistic and Social Interaction in Two Communities. *American Anthropologist* 66(2): 37–53.
1964b Hindi-Punjabi Code Switching in Delhi. In *Proceedings of the 9th International Congress of Linguistics.* Morris Halle, ed. Mouton, The Hague. pp. 1115–1124.
1965 Linguistic Repertoires, Grammars and Second Language Instruction. In "Report of the Sixteenth Annual Round Table Meeting of Linguistics and Language Studies." *Georgetown Monograph Series on Languages and Linguistics*, No. 18. Charles W. Kriedler, ed. Georgetown University Press, Washington, D.C. pp. 81–90.
1969a Communication in Multilingual Societies. In *Cognitive Anthropology.* S. A. Tyler, ed. Holt, Rinehart and Winston, New York. pp. 435–449.

1969b Theme. In *The Description and Measurement of Bilingualism*. Louis Kelley, ed. University of Toronto Press, Toronto, Canada. pp. 242–253.
1970a Sociolinguistics and Communication in Small Groups. (Working Paper No. 23). University of California Language Behavior Research Laboratory, Berkeley.
1970b Verbal Strategies in Multilingual Communication. In "Bilingualism and Language Contact: Anthropological, Linguistic, Psychological and Sociological Aspects." *Georgetown Monograph Series on Languages and Linguistics*, No. 23. J. E. Alatis, ed. Georgetown University Press, Washington, D.C. pp. 129–147.

GUMPERZ, J. J. AND E. HERNANDEZ
1969 Cognitive Aspects of Bilingual Communication. (Working Paper No. 28). University of California Language Behavior Research Laboratory, Berkeley.

HAUGEN, EINAR
1962 Schizoglossia and the Linguistic Norm. *Georgetown Monograph Series on Languages and Linguistics*, No. 15. Georgetown University Press, Washington, D.C. pp. 63–73.

HERNDON, JAMES
1969 *The Way It Spozed to Be*. Bantam Books, New York.

HYMES, DELL
1964 Introduction: Toward Ethnographies of Communication. *American Anthropologist* 66(6), Part 2: 1–34.
1966 On Communicative Competence. Mimeographed.

JOHN, VERA P. AND VIVIAN M. HORNER
1971 *Early Childhood Bilingual Education*. The Modern Language Association of America, New York.

KJOLSETH, ROLF, NORA MARGADANT, DAVID LOPEZ, AND ENRIQUE AND CARMEN LOPEZ
n.d. Chicano Talk. In preparation.

LABOV, WILLIAM
1966 *The Social Stratification of English in New York City*. Center for Applied Linguistics, Washington, D.C.
1971 The Place of Linguistic Research in American Society. In *Linguistics in the 1970's*. (Prepublication edition). Center for Applied Linguistics, Washington, D.C. pp. 41–70.

LANDMANN, SALCIA
1968 *Jiddisch: Abenteur einer Sprache*. (3. Auflage). Deutscher Taschenbuch Verlag, Muenchen.

LEWIS, LOUISA
1970 Culture and Social Interaction in the Classroom: An Ethnographic Report. (Working Paper No. 38). University of California Language Behavior Research Laboratory, Berkeley, California.

LOYO, GILBERTO
1969 Prólogo. In *El Inmigrante Mexicano: La Historia de su Vida*, Manuel Gamio, ed. Universidad Nacional Autonoma de Mexico, Mexico, D.F. pp. 5–80.

MACKEY, WILLIAM F.
1970 A Typology of Bilingual Education. In *Bilingual Schooling in the United States*, Vol. 2. Theodore Andersson and Mildred Boyer, eds. United States Government Printing Office, Washington, D.C. pp. 63–82.

MACNAMARA, JOHN
1967 Bilingualism in the Modern World. *Journal of Social Issues* 23(2): 1–7.

RAYFIELD, R., JR.
1970 *The Language of a Bilingual Community*. Mouton, The Hague.

ROMANO V., OCTAVIO IGNACIO, ED.
1969 *El Espejo/The Mirror: Selected Mexican-American Literature*. Quinto Sol Publications, Berkeley, California.

ROSENTHAL, ROBERT AND LENORE JACOBSON
  1968 *Pygmalion in the Classroom: Teacher Expectation and Pupils' Intellectual Development*. Holt, Rinehart and Winston, New York.
SCHMIDT-ROHR, GEORGE
  1933 *Mutter Sprache*. (2. Auflage). Eugen Diederichs Verlag, Jena.
STEINER, S.
  1969 *La Raza: The Mexican Americans*. Harper and Row, New York.
STERN, H. H., ED.
  1963 *Foreign Languages in Primary Education*. UNESCO Institute of Education, Hamburg.
STEWART, WILLIAM
  1966 Urban Negro Speech: Sociolinguistic Factors Affecting English Teaching. In *Social Dialects and Language Learning*, Roger Shuy, ed. National Council of Teachers of English, Champaign, Illinois. pp. 10–18.
  1969 On the Use of Negro Dialect in the Teaching of Reading. In *Teaching Black Children to Read*. Joan Baratz and Roger Shuy, eds. Center for Applied Linguistics, Washington, D.C. pp. 156–219.
UNITED STATES OFFICE OF EDUCATION
  1970 Manual for Project Applicants and Grantees: Programs Under Bilingual Education Act (Title VII, ESEA). Draft.
WOLFF, HANS
  1964 Intelligibility and Inter-Ethnic Attitudes. In *Language in Culture and Society*. Harper and Row, New York. pp. 440–445.

2. Bilingual Education for Mexican-American Children in California

RUSSELL N. CAMPBELL

Campbell suggests that educators and others may have grossly under-estimated the innate capability of all normal children to acquire a second language efficiently and completely and to succeed academically in that language. This pervasive attitude could have contributed to the persistent failure of Mexican-American children in our schools. Campbell also gives a bilingual education format for consideration.

THIS PAPER is presented with the hope that it will provoke discussion, perhaps even arguments, that will lead to some clarification of what will be required of our educational institutions if they are to provide the Spanish-speaking Mexican-American (MA) children in our midst the capacity to compete more successfully academically with their Anglo peers. To set forth a number of assumptions as to what seem to be the crucial aspects and what seem to be the highly desirable aspects of a success-oriented educational program for MA children, I shall rely heavily on my recent study of a number of articles and books on bilingual education, on observations of bilingual education and English-as-a-Second-Language (ESL) classes in this country and in Canada, and on discussions with many scholars who are seeking solutions to problems related to the education of minority groups.

I take it as given that the average MA child has not fared well in our public school system. It has been well documented that by the time he reaches the sixth grade he will perform two or three grade levels below the national norms on subject matter achievement tests. The drop-out rate of MA children who enter secondary schools is much higher than that of Anglos and the percentage admitted to college is, of course, much lower. The net result is that the possibilities for MA's to compete for prestige positions in business, education, government, and in the professions is minimal and his lower socioeconomic status is perpetuated.

This lack of success has not, of course, gone unnoticed. During the past decade or so, and especially during the last five years, a number of remedial plans have been put into action. I dare say that all such programs have resulted in some academic gains for these children. I cannot but believe that any special attention given to these children has resulted in raising their scholastic potential. For, as I shall argue later, perhaps one of the crucial factors that has been missing in the many classrooms, schools, and even, perhaps, in the homes, has been the strong conviction that MA children really can succeed in our schools. I am sure that those scholars and community leaders who have worked so diligently to establish special Head Start, ESL, or bilingual education programs, as well as those who have devised exciting new curricula for MA children in both Spanish and English, have been precisely those people who, *if proper conditions prevail*, have had the highest expectations for MA children. These conditions as defined and put into practice are extremely varied. A look at Gaarder's (1970) article on bilingual education, or at Andersson and Boyer's (1970) two-volume treatise on the same subject, or at Lesley's unpublished master's thesis (1971) will quickly reveal the multitude of solutions that have emerged in response to the problem associated with the education of children who come to our schools speaking a language other than English. As stated earlier, nearly any of the projects dedicated to the resolution of the problems are likely to result in some success. But, as suggested in a recent article by Tucker and d'Anglejan (1970:2):

> Diverse innovative approaches to bilingual education have been tried in many places, here in North America and abroad; but very few have been systematically evaluated or described. Longitudinal evaluations have been noticeably lacking. As social scientists with personal experience in both domestic and foreign bilingual programs, we believe that administrators and educators *must* begin to devote more of their attention to defining accurately the characteristics and objectives of their programs and to setting up long-term evaluation procedures. Parents as well as funding agencies should insist on accountability of this type.

I concur wholeheartedly with this admonition. Whatever tack we take, whatever program we put into effect must be definable in terms that can be measured so that the results of our efforts can be compared with other programs and any weaknesses in our plans can be identified and subsequently eliminated and any successes can be replicated.

It is inevitable that any considerations of the education of MA children should begin with a consideration of the roles of English and Spanish in their academic life in the United States. For the MA child to compete favorably with his Anglo peers, it seem to me that it is *obligatory* that he gain a proficiency in English equivalent to that of his Anglo peers. This is true as long as his ultimate success in high school and college depends upon his ability to comprehend and manipulate concrete and abstract concepts presented to him in English. However attractive it might appear, it would be folly to think that MA children in this country will ever have the opportunity to choose the language of instruction, either Spanish or English, for his higher education. Realistically, we must assume that his eventual academic and professional success is closely correlated to his ability to function in English much the same way as a native speaker of English does. That other factors in our society also might greatly influence his chances for success is not denied nor underestimated, but academic success in an English language educational system must require native-like facility with the English language.

On the other hand, for a number of compelling psychological, sociological, and political reasons, it is *highly desirable* and reasonable that MA children be given ample opportunity, in the school ambient, to maintain his first language and to become explicitly aware of his cultural heritage. The implications of such a statement are in sharp contrast to those times and places where the MA child was made to feel that his language, his customs, and his social values were beneath contempt and were not to be in evidence (subject to physical as well as mental punishment if violated) on the school grounds. There is even evidence now (Padilla and Long 1970) that MA students who have maintained these home traits are more likely to succeed academically than those who have, for whatever reason, been deprived of them. Therefore, I assume that any program designed for the education of MA children should include a component in Spanish and that they should receive instruction that permits them to maintain and develop their Spanish language skills and to see themselves in a positive historical and cultural perspective; namely, as heirs of the highly esteemed Hispanic and Amerindian cultures. One, perhaps controversial, note should be added to this paragraph, however. It would appear that all of the psychological, sociological, and political needs could be met and the child could still fail to compete successfully in our total school system if he were deficient in English. For this reason English has been given the priority rating of *obligatory* and Spanish the rating of *highly desirable*.

Let me now continue by making one huge, sweeping, complicated, quite "iffy" statement on which I shall later expand.

Five-year-old, Spanish-speaking, Mexican-American children, like all normal children of that age, are unquestionably capable of both acquiring native speaker competence in English (without special ESL instruction) and competing in subject matter areas in English (without any special adjustments to the current curricula being used for Anglo students) when taught by monolingual English-speaking teachers (who need no special training other than number four below) if a) they are taught as if they were English-speaking children and b) if the teachers, the school administrators and the children's parents *expect* that they can accomplish these goals.

If this statement were acceptable, and I doubt that it will be for many people, then the following suggestions for programs for MA children, insofar as we are concerned here with the students' acquisition of English and knowledge through English, might also be acceptable:

1. MA children should be immersed in an English curriculum precisely comparable to the curricula currently employed in Anglo schools and this should be done at the kindergarten age (assuming no prior Head Start program).
2. The teacher of the English curriculum should not use the children's language in their presence.
3. MA children should, when possible, receive their early instruction in classes made up entirely of Spanish-speaking MA children.
4. Teachers, school administrators, and parents should be given (by an instructional program or by means of group discussion sessions) every opportunity to understand their role in instilling and then, subsequently, sustaining in the children a strong, positive self-image and the understanding that the goals of the school are within their reach. (To some degree, this may mean convincing the teachers and parents that MA children can succeed even though they have considerable historical evidence to the contrary.)

Before discussing these assumptions and suggestions, let me say again that they are separate and, perhaps, for the first two or three years of elementary school, independent of the Spanish component which I have said is highly desirable and should be a part of the children's school experience but which I shall not discuss further here.

To return to the assumptions and recommendations made above, there is ample experimental and anecdotal evidence that children are innately capable of simultaneously acquiring a second language and gaining an education in that language. To do so has been a regular pattern in a large number of previously colonial states in Asia and Africa and it is still a common pattern in many multilingual countries where one language has come to be the national language of instruction. Furthermore, there have been an enormous number of non-English speaking students who have in fact accomplished these feats in our school system without fanfare and without special assistance. It has been assumed by many people around the world that to learn to function in another language is no heroic undertaking. What is surprising to many is that we consider it such a tremendous feat to learn to function in just two languages when they have had to learn four or five to carry out their personal and professional affairs.

Part of the experimental evidence that I use to support my assumptions comes from the extensive studies carried out in and around Montreal and reported on by Lambert et al (1970). It would take too much space to review their findings adequately here. For now, suffice it to say that Anglo-Canadian (AC) children who were taught, beginning in kindergarten, as if they were French (French teachers, books, tests, curricula) have acquired by the time they complete the third or fourth grades, near native-speaker competence in French and compete favorably with their French peers in all subject matter areas. It should also be noted that after receiving some instruction in English beginning in the second grade, these children compete favorably with their English peers in both language arts and in all subject matter areas. It is important to note that the French teachers of these AC children were not especially trained for this task, they did not teach French in some structured fashion that might resemble ESL instruction, and they did not use English at any time with the AC children. Nor did they use a specially designed curriculum for these children; rather, they used the same curriculum that is currently being used in French-Canadian schools in Montreal for French-speaking children. Finally, the children in these classes were all AC—they did not have to compete at any time with French-speaking children who had a common language with the teachers.

There is additional experimental evidence that can be brought into this discussion to both reinforce the notion of the feasibility of simultaneously learning a foreign language and learning in that language and the notion of beginning such instruction at the earliest possible time. The longitudinal studies performed in the Philippines and reported on by Davis substantiate both of these. Especially important is the evidence that those students who did not begin receiving instruction in English until their third or fifth years were put at a serious disadvantage in later years in junior high and high school where all instruction is in English. Davis said (1967:81), as a part of that report:

> Proficiency in English is directly related to the number of years in which it is used as the medium of instruction. . . . It is clear that any change in the number of years in which English is used as the medium of instruction will affect the facility and effectiveness with which the pupils can profit from instruction in English in secondary schools and colleges.

This point by Davis must be seriously considered by anyone who would recommend an all Spanish curriculum for MA children for the first several years of elementary school. However, it does not preclude the very common type of bilingual education program where both Spanish and English are used as languages of instruction.

As suggested above in the discussion of the Lambert studies, there may be great advantage for the MA child if all of the members of his class are having the same language switching experiences as he. That is, all of them are receiving instruction in a foreign language and the teacher is introducing new materials and new goals at the same rate for all students. I find it hard to believe that English-speaking teachers do not tend to pace the introduction of instructional materials to those who respond soonest. In a class where there are both Anglos and MA's, obviously the Anglos will respond quickest to instruction in English and the teacher will be inclined to react to their readiness for the next step in the program. The obvious results would then be that the MA very soon falls behind, appears slow to the teacher and to himself and in general finds himself in the unfortunate position of representing the slow group in the class—a position he may never be able to vacate. One need only read the study carried out and reported on by Rist (1970) to realize the frightening consequences of this possibility.

There are, of course, possible advantages for the MA who studies in mixed Anglo-MA classes—more opportunities to make friends with Anglos which will carry over to the playground, thus providing additional opportunity and need for English. But at the moment, I would suggest that these advantages are overshadowed by the disadvantages mentioned above. Perhaps the best of both worlds would be to have a number of integrated activities during the day, say, music, physical education, and manual arts classes, but for classes that depend heavily upon verbal communication for progress, then the MA children would benefit from the absence of competition with English-speaking children. The assumption here, again, is that under these conditions; namely, that in a situation where there is an honest, authentic need for English to communicate with the teacher, in a non-threatening environment, the MA child will efficiently and effectively learn English.

So far in this paper, I have ignored the obvious differences that exist between the experimental groups I have cited in Montreal and the Philippines and the MA children in California. It may well be that because of these differences there is little reason to hope that the assumptions and suggestions I have outlined above are appropriate for MA children in California. I do see that the students are different—the socio-economic status of their parents is different, the role of their home language in the greater community is different, the historical opportunities for success for members of their ethnic group in this predominantly Anglo society are different, and, perhaps, there are many others. Yet, in part for reasons discussed above, I am optimistic that in spite of these differences, MA children can successfully compete with their Anglo peers in our school system given that the teachers, parents, and school administrators *expect* them to. Perhaps the most urgent modification of our current practices would be the design and development of training programs that would result in dramatic positive changes in the expectations of success for MA children on the part of teachers, parents, and administrators. For it may well be that much of the lack of success in the education of MA children will be accounted for when we shift our attention from these differences in the children to the attitudes and stereotypes held by, above all, the teachers of MA children. Understanding the impact these attitudes and stereotypes have on teachers' expectations and students' performance may reveal that too little has been expected and therefore too little gained.

As suggested earlier, it would be unwise to put the assumptions and suggestions made above into practice without a carefully designed, long-term program that could be systematically evaluated. But that is precisely what I think should be done. If my assumptions proved to be correct, the implications are extremely important in terms of our current expenditure of effort as well as human and monetary resources. For example, if my assumptions, or better, if the results of implementing my assumptions, prove to be correct, it might suggest that the funds that are being invested in the development of special curricular materials may be largely unnecessary. Further, it might suggest that special English-as-a-second-language programs for very young children are superfluous and the resources spent on them might better be spent on, say, the Spanish component considered highly desirable above. This suggestion would be consistent with Rosenthal and Jacobson's statement (1968: 23):

> Our results suggest that yet another base line must be introduced when the intrinsic value of an educational innovation is being assessed. The question will be whether the venture is more effective (and cheaper) than the simple expedient of trying to change the expectations of the teacher. Most educational innovations will be found to cost more in both time and money than inducing teachers to expect more of "disadvantaged" children.

Futhermore, it might suggest that the selection and training of teachers might take on new dimensions. That is, it might suggest that what is crucial is that the teacher who is given the responsibility of teaching MA children must clearly understand that her attitude toward the MA child and her treatment of him in the classroom vis-a-vis other students must be such that the child is given every reason to believe that he can and will succeed. Given such a teacher, the success or failure, I hold, of the MA child will then not depend on the differences considered above but on the child's inherent capabilities as an individual rather than on the fact that he is a MA in California.

REFERENCES

ANDERSSON, THEODORE AND MILDRED BOYER, EDS.
    1970 *Bilingual Schooling in the United States.* 2 vols. Government Printing Office, Washington, D.C.

DAVIS, F. B., ED.
    1967 *Philippine Language Teaching Experiments.* Alemar-Phoenix Press, Quezon City, Philippines.

GAARDER, A. BRUCE
    1970 The First Seventy-Six Bilingual Education Projects. In "Bilingualism and Language Contact: Anthropological, Linguistic, Psychological and Sociological Aspects." *Georgetown Monograph Series on Languages and Linguistics,* No. 23. J. E. Alatis, ed. Georgetown University Press, Washington, D.C. pp. 163–178.

LAMBERT, W. E., M. JUST AND N. SEGALOWITZ
    1970 Some Cognitive Consequences of Following the Curricula of the Early School Grades in a Foreign Language. In "Bilingualism and Language Contact: Anthropological, Linguistic, Psychological and Social Aspects." *Georgetown Monograph Series on Languages and Linguistics,* No. 23. J. E. Alatis, ed. Georgetown University Press, Washington, D.C.

LESLEY, T.
    1971 Bilingual Education in California. Unpublished M.A. thesis. University of California at Los Angeles.

PADILLA, A. AND K. LONG
    1970 Evidence for Bilingual Antecedents of Academic Success in a Group of Spanish-American College Students. n.p. (Xerox)

RIST, R. C.
    1970 Student Social Class and Teacher Expectations: The Self-Fulfilling
          Prophecy in Ghetto Education. *Harvard Educational Review*, 40.
ROSENTHAL, R. AND L. JACOBSON
    1968 Teacher Expectations for the Disadvantaged. *Scientific American*, 218.
TUCKER, G. R. AND A. D'ANGLEJAN
    1970 Some Thoughts Concerning Bilingual Education Programs. McGill
          University, Montreal, Canada. Mimeographed.

3. Criteria for Cultural-Linguistic Subdivision in the Southwest

CHESTER C. CHRISTIAN, JR.

This article discusses internal and external criteria for identifying Mexican-Americans in the Southwestern United States: that utilized informally by in-group members dealing with degree of acculturation to the majority culture, and, that utilized by out-group people based on Spanish surname. Since internal criteria divide people with Spanish surnames into culturally significant sub-groups, social scientists should distinguish between types of criteria appropriate for specific research and action programs.

An earlier version of this paper was given at the joint annual meeting of the American Ethnological Society and the Southwestern Anthropological Association, April 29–May 1, 1971, Tucson, Arizona.

BOUNDARIES between language and cultural groups may be defined in terms of either internal or external criteria; that is, in terms of the criteria considered by members of a given group as essential in distinguishing them from members of other groups, or in terms of the differences between that group and others considered most important by those who are not members of the group characterized.[1]

Criteria which are considered extremely important by the members of a given group may be seen as of secondary or even negligible importance by others outside the group. For example, a particular rite of initiation into a given religious group may be considered of transcendental significance by members of that group, separating them from one moment forth from all other human beings. Nevertheless, it may be that this particular rite is of little or no significance to members of other groups, who may consider other criteria having nothing to do with rites of initiation as basic to the differentiation of the group in question.

Classifications of human groups may include both types of criteria: social scientists may, for example, question members of a group to discover what they consider their identifying characteristics, question non-members to establish the manner in which they define the group, then combine both sets of criteria in setting the limits of membership in the group for purposes of analysis.[2] Whatever the specific method used, however, the definition of boundaries between human groups is essentially arbitrary, and a definition which is satisfactory for a given purpose may be almost useless for another.

For the classification of human groups, continua would be more appropriate than discrete entities, since both language and culture are characterized by the clustering of phenomena on lines which represent gradations from one set of characteristics to another.[3] When languages and cultures are in contact, the result is an extension of the gradation between the languages and cultures as well as within them, with new clusters tending to form in the intermediate areas. This might be called the "continuum of acculturation," representing each of the unitary

---

[1] Discussions of the "in-group" and the "out-group" are frequent in sociology. Max Weber's (1965: 305) discussion of ethnic groups implies the recognition of both types of criteria: "Differences . . . give rise to repulsion and contempt for the bearers of these strangely different ways. . . . Seen from their positive aspect, however, the differences may give rise to a consciousness of kind. This consciousness of kind may then become the bearer of communal social relationships."

[2] The development of this combination of criteria has been most complete in relation to studies of social class, which usually have combined subjective with objective criteria. See Richard Centers (1949), Ralf Dahrendorf (1963), Harold M. Hodges, Jr. (1964), and the classic study by William Lloyd Warner (1949), for varying techniques and points of view, many of which are applicable to the study of ethnic groups in the Southwest.

[3] For a more complete outline of the approach proposed here, see Chester Christian (1970).

languages and cultures in contact, together with a line of points representing the transition between one and the other sets, and a cluster on the line representing those who speak both languages and participate in both cultures. As usually defined, "acculturation" also implies a direction from one area to the other.

LANGUAGE LIMITATIONS

We will deal shortly with the limitations of such a model as this in the differentiation of cultural groups in the Southwest, but these limitations probably are not as serious as the limitations imposed by the use of everyday language. With respect to terms referring to those who speak only English, those who speak only Spanish, and those who speak both languages, for example, each term used in either language has connotations which are inappropriate, these connotations are always in a process of change, and the connotations are not only different for each group, but may be different for the same person in different situations.

In El Paso, Texas a few years ago, for example, the words *chicano*, *pachuco*, and *pocho* were words used by an in-group to indicate various types and degrees of acculturation; they were used by members of the group of those whose ancestral or family language was Spanish to subdivide the group and to refer to themselves and to others of its members.[4] Outsiders—those whose native language was English—did not use the terms, and rarely even knew of their existence. They designated the members of the group as "Spanish," "Spanish-speaking," "Spanish-American," "Mexican-American," "Mexican," "greasers," "wetbacks," etc. When members of the in-group spoke with members of the out-group, they usually used the more prestigious terms accepted by the latter, often "correcting" them, as in stating that they were "Spanish-American" and not "Mexican."

These same persons, however, when speaking Spanish among themselves with no outsiders present, usually would use the terms *mexicano* or *chicano* in referring to themselves, and would refer to members of the out-group as *americanos*, *gringos*, or *gabachos*. The fact that these terms were based to a great extent on linguistic and dialectical forms is indicated by the fact that when the present writer acquired the local dialect of the Spanish-speaking group at the lower socio-economic levels he was introduced usually, in spite of blond hair and blue eyes, as *mexicano* or *chicano*, or even *más chicano que nosotros*, the latter due, presumably, to familiarity with the dialect of several of the different sub-groups, and the ability to introduce unfamiliar or little-used terms into a conversa-

---

[4] For a discussion of a variation of in-group terminology which focuses on another geographic area, see George C. Barker (1958).

tion, such as terms used by prostitutes in Mexico. The paradox of a *gabacho* speaking the language of the *chicano* apparently was much enjoyed.

Origins of words used sometimes give indications of the basis for subdivision of language groups, and it is interesting to note that the term "gabacho" is used in Spain to refer to the French (the Gabacho River is on the French side of the Pyrenees), and apparently many of the connotations have remained with the word for those who use it in the Southwest without knowledge of its origins.

A study made by the present writer in 1963, and one involving travel and interviews with Spanish-speaking persons throughout the Southwest, revealed that the above-mentioned words for different subgroups of the Spanish-speaking population were known in every major city, although connotations differed to some extent. *Pachuco*, for example, seems to be a word of fairly recent (early 1940s) origin, and to have been originally associated with Spanish-speaking youth from El Paso who went to work in defense plants in Los Angeles during World War II. They spoke a special dialect of Spanish/English, wore distinctive clothing, violated many social norms, and were aggressively self-assertive, often involved in gang fights with armed forces personnel. In the late 1950s, many young men of El Paso still followed similar cultural patterns, with distinctive dress, hair style, speech, etc., and called themselves, and were called, *pachucos*. The most common connotations of the word seem to be unapologetic delinquency, involving contempt for the home and the majority language and culture.

Some aspects of the *pachuco* attitudes, dialect, and subculture in general seem to have been adopted by those who now call themselves *chicanos*, and who accept neither the conventional standards of the mother culture or of the majority culture. It is possible that the term *chicano* became popular in preference to *pachuco* because of the relative specificity of the latter term. However, *chicano* formerly had more connotations of "resigned acceptance" than "aggressive defiance."

The meaning of a classificatory word may be relative and flexible as with the terms *blanco, negro, rubio*, and *moreno*, terms generally referring to shades of skin and hair color. A person may be *rubio* with reference to one group and *moreno* with reference to another, and the descriptive term used may depend more on language, dialect, or socioeconomic position than on skin color. In Mexico, however, the terms suggesting relative darkness of tone are not necessarily pejorative, and the reverse may be the case. The reference by Mexicans to persons of Mexican descent in the United States as *pochos* (discolored or faded) is pejorative, for example, as is the same reference by members of the Mexican-American group to other members who are relatively more

Anglicized, especially when the latter do not know or refuse to speak Spanish. The pejorative use of the term seems to derive from the renunciation of racial or national origins on the part of those designated by it, in a culture where such origins are considered normally an integral aspect of the person.

The term "chicano" seems to have been originally associated with Spanish-speaking persons of relatively low socio-economic position, and therefore has been a pejorative term when used by certain groups under specific circumstances. The origins of the term are not known, but in Mexico it seems to have had connotations similar to those of the term "Okie" in the United States, of poverty, ignorance, and provincialism. One guess is that it may be associated originally with residents of Chihuahua (Chihuahua plus *mexicano*); or it may be simply a shortening of the term "mexicano" (*xicano;* the *x* is sometimes pronounced in Mexican Spanish, from Náhuatl, as *ch* and was pronounced in early Spanish as French *ch*. Archaic influences persist, especially in New Mexico).

In recent years in the United States, the term has been adopted by a sub-group of persons of Mexican descent who emphasize aggressively not only cultural and linguistic differences between their members and the majority population of the United States, but also between them and citizens of Mexico. The members of this group call themselves "chicanos," although they may be identified more readily by their political aspirations than by linguistic or cultural characteristics. Their adoption of the term has had a strong influence on its current connotations and use.

PROVINCIAL STYLE OF GROUP

Perhaps the most adequate terms with which to characterize the new "chicanos" are aggressively political and defiantly provincial. Some of the leaders are not nearly so provincial as they pretend, though; they have adopted and adapted an ideology which many linguists, anthropologists, and other academicians promote, and are simply working out its logical implications, not only in the world of politics but, increasingly, in that of the university itself. There is enough sophistication in the way this is being done that institutions of higher education find the temptation to modernize, democratize, and create programs to increase the self-awareness of minority group members irresistible. The long-range cost of these programs probably will be paid by those who can least afford it: the more naive members of the minority group itself.

In contrast to in-group criteria for cultural-linguistic subdivision in the Southwest, we may consider the view from outside the group taken by social scientists, political leaders, and others who in recent years have been concerned with identifying and studying the characteristics of the group.[5] The criteria, we will find, have been in some ways more adequate and in other ways less adequate than the subjective criteria heretofore described.

It was not until social scientists began to study the members of this group that the term "Spanish-surname" came into fairly common use. The principal reason it was adopted was that it formed the basis for census counts, and census data showed that the group of "Spanish-surname" persons could be clearly differentiated statistically from the rest of the population.

The census report has divided minority groups in the Southwest into Spanish-surname, Indian, and nonwhite. The nonwhite group has been easily identified because of longstanding taboos against intermarriage. Navajo, Hopi, Apache, Papago and other Indian groups have been physically isolated from the remainder of the population, with rigid constraints on their way of life. Since there has been no prohibition of intermarriage of the Spanish-surname group with the majority population, and since the isolation and constraints on the way of life of the Spanish-surname population has been minimal in comparison with that of Indian groups, it is surprising that the former forms such a distinct group statistically, even when "Spanish-surname" (presumably, the *possibility* of Spanish representing the home language and culture) is the criterion for membership.

Significant differences between this group and the remainder of the population have been found with respect to education, income, trade or profession, family size, dependency ratio, age structure, and other important variables. This is all the more remarkable when we consider the fact that the Spanish-surname criterion lumps together all the different subcultural groups which have been discussed, as well as including non-Spanish-surname women married to Spanish-surname men, and all Spanish-surnamed persons who have lost their ancestral language and culture.

In spite of this, census data tended to confirm the appropriateness of considering the Spanish-surname group as distinct from the remainder of the population, with a cultural identity which shows statistical points of similarity to Mexico. For example, this population shows a natural increase almost twice that of other groups in the United States, and slightly higher than that of Mexico. One result is that it is a much younger population, with the median age 17.6 years in 1970 as opposed

[5] For an analysis of the 1960 census data, see Harley L. Browning and S. Dale McLemore (1964). It also contains data on the other Southwestern states. Some 1970 statistics, taken from a special report of the U.S. Census Bureau, were reported in the *El Paso Herald Post*, Feb. 17, 1971, p. 3B.

to 28 years for the remainder of the U.S. population. This signifies a higher dependency ratio (in 1960, 92 dependent persons per 100 of the remainder of the group, compared to the Anglo average of 63 per 100). In 1960, 30.1 % of the Anglo population, 44.4 % of the Mexican-American population, and 44.2 % of the population of Mexico was 14 years of age or younger.[6]

YOUTH OF POPULATION

The present tendency is for the Mexican-American population to grow progressively younger and the remainder of the population to grow progressively older. In essence, the problem of an older population is to provide support for those who no longer work, and that of a younger population to provide support for those who do not yet work. In a country where most young people do not begin to work until the age of 18, it begins to become a serious problem when more than half the population has not yet reached that age.

The aforementioned data must be taken into consideration to understand the full significance of data for the Spanish-surname group relevant to its socio-economic level. A report on the basis of the 1970 census indicates that the family income for this group was about $5,600 per year, with the average for the rest of the nation about $8,000.[7] The 1960 census data had shown that in the Southwestern states the income for the group was extremely low, with the average in Texas about half that of the remainder of the population of the state.

The statistics relative to income for Spanish-surname Americans represent a deceptively high figure. If we take into consideration the fact that the reported income for the entire group is about 30 % less per family than that of other U.S. citizens, together with indications that the Mexican-American family has about 50 % more members than the average for other families, their effective income is on the average less than half that of other families.

In addition to these statistics one considers that the lowest average incomes for the Spanish-surname group are found among the 55 % who are of Mexican origin, and that of these incomes the lowest are found in the Southwest, and that of these the lowest are found in Texas, one can see how the language and culture of the group comes to be identified with poverty.

Economic problems are reflected and aggravated by educational problems so that the Spanish-surname group also may be identified by relatively lower educational attainment than the remainder of the

---

[6] Browning and McLemore (1964, Table 3).
[7] *Herald-Post*, Feb. 17, 1971, p. 3B.

population, with the dropout rate increasing rapidly after age 15 and continuing throughout high school and college. For example, in 1960 about 90 % of Spanish-surname youth of 14–15 years of age were in school, but only about 70 % of those 16–17 years old, and less than 40 % of those 18–19 years old.[8] At the University of Texas at El Paso, where approximately 4,000 Spanish-surname students are enrolled, the freshman class contains about fifty percent Spanish-surname students, and the graduating class between ten and fifteen percent.

One surprising outcome of studies thus far is that the statistical differentiation of the Spanish-surname group does not indicate assimilation to the socioeconomic and cultural patterns of the majority group. Two studies, one in Texas and another in California, have indicated that third generation Spanish-surname persons have more education but less income than the second generation.[9]

These statistical indices may be considered indicative of the existence of sub-groups of the Spanish-surname population which differ much more radically from the majority population than does the Spanish-surname population as a whole. Categories of sub-groups which have been studied, such as those based on political or economic subdivisions, may have little relation to the most important factors in differentiating groups of Spanish-surname persons. If it were possible, for example, to devise indices which reflect language use and acculturation (as do the popular indices previously described), comparative data might become much more significant.

Studies made of the Spanish-surname population of the Southwest have tended to be either statistically or politically oriented, and in both cases linguistic and cultural considerations have been slighted. The statistical and the political aspects of the situation have in recent years become fused, with both providing a rationale for ignoring internal differences which have never been ignored by the Spanish-surname population itself.

CONCERN FOR WELFARE

On the basis of the 1960 census data, statistical reports gave cause for concern for the economic welfare of the Spanish-surname population, and one of the results has been the establishment of bilingual programs, especially in kindergarten and the elementary schools, designed to enhance the native language and culture, in a few cases giving the child literacy in his home language.[10] The criterion for cultural-linguistic

[8] Browning and McLemore (1964, Table 31).
[9] See the aforementioned study by Browning and McLemore, and the article by F. Peñalosa (1969).
[10] For a description of such programs, see Theodore Andersson and Mildred Boyer (1970).

subdivision of the Spanish-speaking population of the Southwest which has been most completely ignored is that of literacy in Spanish, yet this seems to be one of the most important criteria for subdivision and group identification in use among all other Spanish-speaking populations of the world. It has been ignored here because so few members of the population are literate in Spanish that statistical data on this group would seem insignificant. However, boundaries between the Spanish-surname group and the remainder of the population may retain their character as separations between hierarchical social and economic levels so long as there is an invidious distinction between the language and culture of those who speak Spanish and those who speak English at home, and this type of distinction is likely to remain so long as few members of the minority group read and write the home language.

The communities being served by the bilingual education programs would seem to represent at least potentially the most fruitful areas for research into subdivisions of the population of the Southwest both in terms of internal and of external criteria for subdivision of the population. There are such programs for speakers of Indian languages as well as for Spanish, population groups are identified which have retained a non-English language and culture, community representatives whose assistance could be requested are associated with the programs, school records are kept which would be useful in identification of sub-groups, teachers and administrative personnel could offer much useful information, etc.

For most of the members of this group, the "continuum of acculturation" mentioned at the beginning as a possible model presumably would terminate in the cluster representing those who speak both languages and participate in both cultures. As has been implied by the above discussion, however, this cluster may be expected to be much more complex than would be indicated by the concept of a simple transition from one language and culture to another. The model should include some principle lines of transition, each of which would contain its own system of continua. For example, language, family size and structure, educational objectives and attainment, employment and socioeconomic level, and perhaps others would be basic categories, each of which would contain a system of continua. Even within a given category, an individual, family, or social group might be moving in one direction with respect to a given continuum and in another with respect to a related one. For example, there might be a tendency for some parents to use progressively more English while their children use progressively more Spanish and at the same time more nearly standard English. There might be increased use of English and at the same time increased fertility. There might be higher educational attainment combined with lower family incomes.

In addition to this type of complexity, specific communities might differ, or even various groups within a given community. Some communities might be relatively homogeneous in the type and degree of acculturation, while others might be markedly heterogeneous. Some might be relatively stable, and others in a process of rapid change.

CULTURE AND LINGUISTIC CRITERIA

In summary, the in-group criteria (which have been used in the Southwest by those whose preferred family and informal language is Spanish) delineate groups on a linguistic and cultural basis which is more realistic than the "Spanish-surname" criterion which has become the basis for sociological analysis and political action. In view of the heterogeneity of this latter group, or even of that segment of it which is of Mexican descent, and the marked differences between it and the remainder of the United States population, the differences between that part of the group which remains linguistically and culturally different and that part of the United States population which represents most fully the middle class White Anglo-Saxon Protestant way of life and system of values must be of a much greater order of magnitude, both in terms of factual data related to it and in terms of its sociocultural orientation.

It also seems probable that many of those in the political world who wave most energetically the "chicano" banner are more closely related linguistically and culturally to the majority population than they are to that segment of the population which maintains a language and culture which has its roots in Spain, and which has points of similarity to the Indian languages and cultures of Mexico and the Southwest principally because it shares their poverty and illiteracy, and secondarily because Spain also left its imprint on the latter languages and cultures.

The power of this group does not ultimately reside in its influence on the course of events in Washington, but on its potential for reviving great linguistic and cultural traditions and joining them once again to the flourishing traditions of their linguistic and cultural brothers in the other countries of this hemisphere, while at the same time enriching the heritage of the United States. This is a service for which the United States should be willing to provide suitable and tangible rewards. It does not seem justifiable to solicit such rewards on the basis of surname alone; on the other hand, the provision of linguistic and cultural diversity may be of crucial significance in the immediate future development of U.S. society and culture, and there is much evidence that leaders are beginning to appreciate this type of contribution and to develop rewards for it.

REFERENCES

ANDERSSON, THEODORE AND MILDRED BOYER
1970   *Bilingual Schooling in the United States.* Southwest Educational Development Laboratory, Austin, Texas.

BARKER, GEORGE C.
1958   *Pachuco, An American-Spanish Argot and its Social Functions in Tucson, Arizona.* University of Arizona Press, Tucson, Arizona.

BROWNING, HARLEY L. AND S. DALE MCLEMORE
1964   *A Statistical Profile of the Spanish-Surname Population of Texas.* Bureau of Business Research, Population Series No. 1, University of Texas, Austin, Texas.

CENTERS, RICHARD
1949   *The Psychology of Social Classes.* Princeton University Press, Princeton, New Jersey.

CHRISTIAN, CHESTER
1970   The Analysis of Linguistic and Cultural Differences: A Proposed Model. In "Bilingualism and Language Contact: Anthropological, Linguistic, Psychological and Sociological Aspects." *Georgetown Monograph Series on Language and Linguistics*, No. 23, J. E. Alatis, ed. Georgetown University Press, Washington, D. C. pp. 149–162.

DAHRENDORF, RALF
1963   *Class and Class Conflict in Industrial Society*, 3rd edition. Stanford University Press, Stanford, California.

HODGES, HAROLD M., JR.
1964   *Social Stratification.* Schenkman Publishing Company, Cambridge, Massachusetts.

PEÑALOSA, F.
1969   Education-Income Discrepancies Between Second and Later Generation Mexican-Americans in the Southwest. *Sociology and Social Research* 53 (4): 448–454.

WARNER, WILLIAM LLOYD
1949   *Social Class in America.* Science Research Associates, Chicago, Illinois.

WEBER, MAX
1965   Ethnic Groups. In *Theories of Society.* Talcott Parsons et al., eds. The Free Press, New York.

4. The Local Colloquial in the Classroom

CHARLES OLSTAD

Olstad deals with one of his main interests: the Chicano student in the university classroom. He presents the case for bilingual education, including instruction through the non-English mother tongue, as being desirable and effective even if the mother tongue is non-standard or a "dialect." He outlines three areas of benefit deriving from school respect for, and study of, non-standard Spanish: (1) bridging the school-home barrier; (2) appreciating a rich and varied culture; (3) learning standard Spanish without losing linguistic self-respect.

An earlier version of this paper was given at the joint annual meeting of the American Ethnological Society and the Southwestern Anthropological Association, April 29–May 1, 1971, Tucson, Arizona.

IT HAS LONG been theorized that, when a child begins school speaking a language other than the national standard, his education is most efficiently accomplished via his own vernacular, whatever it may be. Over half a century ago, American teachers of Spanish were introduced to this basic tenet of bilingual education (Fitz-Gerald 1921). But although Fitz-Gerald cited examples from Africa, Great Britain and Canada, he balked at generalizing to include the American Southwest. So theory was seldom followed by practice, and decades passed before careful studies established the principle ambiguously suggested by Fitz-Gerald.

Much later, the well known UNESCO study (1953) stated flatly: "It is axiomatic that the best medium for teaching a child is his mother tongue." Drawing on the results of the Iloilo experiment in the Philippines, it indicated the superiority of bilingual instruction beginning with the child's mother tongue even when this mother tongue is a noncosmopolitan language in restricted use, a "dialect," in the layman's terms.

Peal and Lambert, in their now classic study (1962), destroyed the myth of the bilingual as mentally disadvantaged. On the contrary, they found that, where bilingualism is "balanced," students measured significantly higher in intellectual capacity and flexibility than a monolingual control group.

Recent experience in the Southwest tends to corroborate this study. Bilingual education, properly understood, can have beneficial effects for the Spanish-speaking child touching on both English competence and I.Q. In the El Paso Public Schools, for example, it was found (Saavedra 1969) that Mexican-American first-grade students receiving instruction in both Spanish and English scored as well on English language proficiency tests as the control groups who were instructed in English only. And obviously, their proficiency in Spanish was far superior.

A similar project involving 4,000 children in the San Antonio Independent School District has yielded even more impressive results (Arnold 1968). According to a summary published in pamphlet form, children receiving instruction in both Spanish and English made gains in English vocabulary and grammar *superior* to those children in the special English only program. Thus, bilingual instruction need not hamper the learning of the second language (here English); it may, paradoxically, even enhance it.

A landmark study (Modiano 1968) carried out in Mexico under near laboratory conditions clearly established the importance of the use of the native language in the classroom, even when the over-all objective may involve only the national language. The object of the study was to teach Indians of Mexico to read Spanish, a language in which they were not competent. Students in the state and federal schools studied only

[52]

Spanish, including reading. Students in INI (Instituto Nacional Indigenista) schools first learned to read in their own Indian languages; only later did they begin their study of Spanish. Tests showed the INI students to be *superior* in Spanish reading proficiency to the control groups, which had studied exclusively in Spanish.

Clearly, the above experiences substantiate the axiom of the UNESCO study. Bilingual instruction involving the child's mother tongue, far from being an upper-class luxury or an inefficient duplication of effort, is the preferred approach for children learning the national language as their second language. Not only can bilingual instruction give satisfactory results in both languages, it can—judging by the Peal-Lambert study—actually improve general mental ability. In the case of the San Antonio schools also, children receiving bilingual instruction not only tested higher in English proficiency, they made greater gains in I.Q. as well (Goodenough-Harris Draw-a-Man test) than those in the English only program.

In the Tucson Public Schools, unpublished findings suggest that part of the success of I.Q. testing in bilingual education may be due simply to the use of a language familiar to the Spanish-speaking child. Past experience with English-only I.Q. tests had shown Mexican-American children scoring consistently and significantly lower than national norms. But under the bilingual program, children were allowed to take a bilingual version of the test, choosing the language with which they felt most comfortable for each test item. Results showed the distribution curve for Mexican-Americans in the Tucson bilingual program to be significantly higher than the national curve. In this case, since sustained instruction via both Spanish and English had only begun, test score improvement was due presumably to the language option itself. Later measurements may be expected to show, as in San Antonio (Arnold 1968) and in the Peal-Lambert study, that sustained, balanced development of bilingual abilities can result in significant increases in general mental ability.

The implications are inescapable: bilingual education is essential where children begin school speaking little or no English (it is assumed that English is the *de facto* national language); further, the non-English vernacular is appropriate for school use at any level, even though it may be a colloquial of comparatively limited use. Thus, speaking now only of Spanish, in the beginning bilingual classroom the teacher should be familiar with, and may even use, whatever version of Spanish is the child's vernacular. "Whatever version" includes "Tex-Mex," "Spanglish," "border Spanish," "mexicano corto," "pachuco," and any other term devised by Anglo ethnocentrism or Hispano self-denigration. As

Anne Stemmler has pointed out (1966), almost in passing, with reference to the San Antonio experience:

> Intensive instruction in Spanish was originally included for two reasons: (1) to test the effect of instruction in the students' native language on the development of oral English and subsequent reading in English; and (2) to develop standard Mexican Spanish in place of limited local dialects. *Later, we became aware of the tremendous positive impact of according Spanish an accepted role in the traditionally English-speaking classroom.* Spanish all too often is considered a second-rate language in Texas and other border states, and to speak Spanish is a mark of low social status. The benefits of true bilingualism have generally been overlooked. In fact, a tacit and nearly general policy has been to punish children for using Spanish at any time in school. [Emphasis added.]

Objections to Spanish in the schoolroom and on the schoolgrounds have a long if inglorious tradition in the Southwest. In some of the more unenlightened districts, the "tacit and general policy" mentioned by Miss Stemmler is still in effect. Further, objections to all use of non-standard or inelegant dialects in the classroom is a part of the well-known stereotype of the English teacher. Martin Joos's legendary "school marm," Miss Fidditch, is perhaps the classic example (1962). More recently, objections to non-standard language—again English— have been buttressed by allegations of the supposed cultural disadvantage and linguistic deficit on the part of speakers of "black" English (Bereiter and Engleman 1966).

A similarly negative attitude toward non-standard Spanish, an attitude all too frequent among teachers, is revealed in a recent ethnological study.

> Nearly all the Barrio adults are Spanish speaking, but they use a patois nearly unintelligible to people who speak standard Spanish. In their vernacular, English words are liberally intermixed with local slang, with grammatically distorted and with poorly enunciated Spanish (Goodman and Beman 1968:84).

The cultural bias and linguistic naiveté implicit in the above statement are widespread in the world of school people (teachers, principals, supervisors, etc.), and must be dealt with forthrightly.

It is instructive to note the negatively charged terminology—hardly scientific—employed by Goodman and Beman in their one-paragraph incursion into linguistics. Barrio adults speak a "patois," they say; that is, a limited local dialect associated with uneducated villagers, which does not even exist in written form. It is supposed to be "nearly unintelligible" to people who speak standard Spanish, an assertion that will not bear the slightest testing.[1] The reference to the mixing of English

---

[1] Several times a year, both personally and through informants, I have occa-

words and local "slang" is no doubt true as a descriptive statement, over-brief and imprecise as it is. (Is "slang" the same as "patois" or a part of it? What about Hispanicized words on English roots? Etc.) But in the context of the other remarks, the statement clearly is meant as a value judgment to suggest adulteration, a departure from "pure" Span-ish. Finally, it is suggested that barrio adults are ignorant and slothful, ignorant in that they "distort" the grammar of their language, slothful in that they enunciate "poorly."

It is futile to argue that such concepts as distorted grammar, poor enunciation, or the supposed purity of the language (or dialect or patois), when applied to a given speech community, are simply so much linguistic nonsense. (The Anglo who insists, "Ah ain-a-gonna go," will be clearly understood, not only in his own speech community but in Boston, Mas-sachusetts or Jackson, Mississippi, as well. Likewise the Hispano who proclaims, "No me-vuair," will make his intent clear from El Paso del Norte to Tierra del Fuego.) The problem is not linguistic but rather at-titudinal, not in the language of the speaker but in the mind of the listener. Further, a negative attitude on the part of the listener, non-receptive or even disrespectful toward Spanish in general or non-stand-ard Spanish in particular, unfortunately serves to re-enforce the young Chicano's damaging suspicion that his home language is somehow im-proper in polite school society, and that the sooner he jettisons his lin-guistic—and cultural—heritage, the sooner he can make it in the Man's world.

In the balance of this paper I shall suggest how an attitude of open-minded respect for the local colloquial on the part of the teacher can have important and beneficial attitudinal effects for both teacher and student. I shall indicate, further, some linguistically based activities suitable for high school and college classes of Spanish where such an at-titude obtains.

1. An attitude of open-minded respect—personal and academic—can serve as one "entry" into the pupil's conceptual world, one means of circumventing or penetrating a barrier whose formation begins long before the school experience. Certainly many elementary school teachers recognize this barrier in the timid first-grade *chicanito* who never really participates successfully in classroom activities. High school teachers recognize the sullen imperviousness of the turned-off teenager who feels himself forced to remain in school. And university Spanish teachers are all too familiar with the Spanish-speaking students (those few who reach the university) fighting 12 or more years of school neglect while trying

---

sion to demonstrate the invalidity of this statement. Even where different dialect zones are involved, I have found that an educated speaker from Sonora, for ex-ample, can easily understand the "patois" of the lower Rio Grande valley.

to feel comfortable with the bookish Spanish spewing from the Anglo at the front of the room.

The linguistic and cultural barrier may have weak spots and even openings, but they must be discovered from both sides in order for contact, learning, and attitudinal change to occur. What follows is one small example of the importance of teacher attitude in a situation typical of a language class. The problem is to express in Spanish, "I wouldn't do that," a frequently used ellipsis in both English and Spanish involving only the conclusion clause related to an unexpressed hypothetical statement. The version usually given by a student of native speaking background is "Yo no hiciera eso," using a form of the imperfect subjunctive. The probable teacher responses are four: (1) "Wrong. Use the conditional form." (2) "Well . . . , yes, but . . . we are studying the conditional now." (3) "Possible, but not as good as the conditional." (4) "Correct."

Only the fourth response is appropriate in a class which includes native speakers of Spanish. But it is perhaps the response least likely from the average teacher. The fact is, that the so-called conditional is not frequent in this context (at least in spoken Spanish), is unusual in the spoken Spanish of Mexico, and is quite unknown to a good many less sophisticated speakers. The teacher who knows this, or at least suspects and respects it, can help shore up the sagging confidence of the Chicano in his language, while at the same time broadening the teacher's view of his subject. The insensitive, ignorant or rigid teacher will simply continue to re-enforce the barrier mentioned above.

2. An attitude of open-minded respect—personal and academic— can serve as an avenue of approach to the study and respect due a rich, but rapidly disappearing community culture. There follow two simple examples from recent experience, both of which involve the language teacher and the school situation.

a. A university student was questioning his father concerning legends of buried treasure in southern Arizona. Something in the discussion led him to ask me the Spanish word for 'stage coach.' I knew only *diligencia*, but his grandfather from Coahuila had known *conducta*. A quick check of the dictionaries revealed, among other definitions of *conducta* 'a pack train or wagon train used to transport money.' Under optimum school circumstances such a coincidence could easily lead into, or fit into, a unit on folklore (tales of lost treasure), linguistics (varieties of language usage), or history (the old West, the Butterfield Express, etc.).

b. A discussion of the language of children's games disclosed that in the state of Sonora, Mexico, a foot race is normally begun by the words, "Uno. Dos. Tres. ¡Santiago!" At the sound of the name of Saint James, patron of Spain, everyone charges headlong. Interestingly, in 10th century Spain, the shout of "¡Santiago!" was the battle cry for

Christian troops charging the Moorish infidel. Thus from an innocent, even frivolous, discussion of children's games, comes a noteworthy example of the persistence of Hispanic culture, in this case across 1,000 years of time, nearly half a globe of distance, and the competing cultures of several indigenous civilizations. Implications for learning are limited only by the imagination of the teacher and the fund of "raw data" of the students.[2]

3. An attitude of open-minded respect—personal and academic— can make possible a valuable contrastive model for aspects of world-standard Spanish. Here we are in the language teacher's paradise. In a classroom of some or all native speakers of Spanish, the teacher is surrounded by living, breathing dictionaries and grammar books of a language which he will be studying and learning all his professional life. As for the student, if his linguistic knowledge is respected for what it is, such knowledge can serve as a base for amplification and sophistication as he grows in the language.

There follow several concrete examples together with possible spin-off values related to language learning in general, but dependent on a teaching attitude which respects the local usage. It is profitable to begin with vocabulary, which is the most accessible aspect of language to the untrained and unsophisticated student.

A typical class activity might well be the gradual compilation of vocabulary lists in three columns headed perhaps (1) local Spanish, (2) textbook Spanish, (3) standard English. The resulting list could resemble the following in its initial stages.

Local Spanish	Textbook Spanish	Standard English
1. colorado	rojo	red
2. lumbre	fuego	fire
3. soquete	lodo	mud
4. sacate	hierba	grass
5. nomás	únicamente	only
6. trinches	cuchillos, etc.	knives; tableware
7. contimás	mucho menos	much less
8. amalhaya	ojalá	if only . . .
9. ubari	araña	spider
10. buqui	muchacho	boy
11. saquetines	calcetines	socks
12. troca	camión	truck
13. ahuitarse	enojarse	get angry

[2] For an example of the scholarly implications of such apparent minutiae, the academically inclined may wish to consult a careful study of a similar persistent cultural motif (Armistead and Silverman 1965–66). Certain types of Spanish language balladry current in twentieth century celebrations of Saint John's Day find their earliest known model in a twelfth century Andalusian refrain dedicated to the same occasion.

Local Spanish	Textbook Spanish	Standard English
14. ni modo (que)	es imposible (que)	it's impossible
15. me puede mucho	lo siento mucho	I'm very sorry
16. pararse	ponerse de pie	stand up
17. mois	hojuelas de maíz	corn flakes
18. jondear	tirar; mover?	throw; move?
19. mofle	silenciador	muffler
20. catotas	canicas	marbles
21. talaches	herramientas	tools
22. en	sobre	on; over
23. para	hacia	toward

Clearly this is a most heterogeneous list; words are tossed together with no apparent order. Further, there are real limits on how far one can go in language study with simple vocabulary. But such lists should be the beginning, not the end, of a process. And their very compilation should involve discussion and learning closely tied to the concerns— linguistic and possibly social—of the student.

Some areas for further class study might involve the words numbered 9, 10, and 20: *ubari*, *buqui*, and *catotas*. Discussion, research and/or exercises could center on, for example, the importance of Indian languages in new world Spanish, the problems of spelling new or nonstandard words, or the common confusion of "b" and "v" in spelling. Words 5 and 14, *nomás* and *ni modo (que)*, suggest a study of the standard spoken Spanish of Mexico as well as exercises in the use of the subjunctive and the written accent. Words 12 and 19, *troca* and *mofle*, open the vast area of Anglicisms, their extent and acceptability. Words 7 and 18, *contimás* and *jondear*, lead to areas that require the knowledge of cooperative local speakers. Are these words limited to a given region only? Are they considered provincial? Comic? Are they related in form or meaning to known dictionary forms? Words 22 and 23, *sobre* and *hacia*, are examples of apparently common words which, surprisingly to the outsider, are quite unknown to unlettered native speakers. Finally, word 8, *amalhaya*, suggests two topics. One is the limited topic of meaning and acceptability for various groups or regions. The other is the more difficult but more intriguing matter of taboo words, their identification, and people's reaction to them. (For some, *amalhaya* is a mild curse, improper in polite company. For others—in the same town—it is a common expression of desire.)

The compilation and study of simple word lists may lead naturally into related areas such as interjections and euphemisms, slang or ingroup talk, and the use of obvious Anglicisms. Here, as always, the native speaker of local Spanish is the most valuable informant, the most reliable source of words and expressions to study. The linguistically sophisticated student and the trained teacher can then help put things in order and generalize. (In the case of the examples below, for instance, it will be found that expressions thought to be local or "border" Spanish are in fact typical of informal spoken Spanish throughout Mexico.)

A short list of interjections follows:

(a) Úpale—while lifting something heavy
(b) Híjole—surprise, disbelief, annoyance
(c) Órale—encouragement
(d) Ándale—assent; encouragement
(e) Adió—surprise
(f) Vóytelas—exasperation; surprise
(g) Páscatelas—following a count to start a race

Since this list is of interjections or even "non-words," discussion must center on context of usage and on form, but seldom on conceptual meaning. *Ándale*, for example, seems to be based on the verb *andar* meaning 'go' or 'walk.' Yet as *ándale* it seldom suggests such movement. Further, the affix *le*, ordinarily classified as an indirect (or sometimes, direct) object pronoun in standard Spanish (as in *cuéntale*—'tell him'), here has no such function. Yet such constructions are perhaps the most frequently heard interjections in Mexican Spanish and constitute one of its hallmarks most easily recognizable to outsiders.

Students, after a glance at examples *a* through *d* above, can quickly begin to outline the model of this family of interjections: of three syllables, with stress on the first, *-le* being the last, and usually verbal in form. The grammatically sophisticated may look into the matter of transitive and intransitive verbs and the use of *-le* according to textbook norms. Those students closest to the living language may extend the list considerably. Those more comfortable with cultivated forms may wish to compile a parallel list, finding, in so doing, a new respect for the vigor and variety of the colloquial. Those more proficient in English can approach Spanish by seeking English equivalents approved by the most secure bilinguals. (That *ándale* means both 'OK' and 'you're welcome,' for example, can open up a most fruitful discussion, which may touch upon matters of language flexibility and ambiguity as well as on the importance of context in establishing meaning.)

Nowhere is the variety and vitality of the local colloquial more evident than among high school and college-age young people. The traditional linguistic inventiveness of youth is augmented by the bilingual situation and perhaps by the defensiveness of the minority. That is, just as the younger generation invents its own slang to differentiate itself and protect itself from its elders, so the young Chicano may develop a language, a bilingual argot, intelligible neither to his elders nor to the Anglo.

Whatever the causes, the Spanish of the student is no less worthy of study—and no less reducible to order—than any other speech system. Further, it is "relevant", it relates the classroom to the outside in the simplest and most direct possible way. If language is the expression of culture, perhaps the study of two languages in contact can give some insight into the fusion and confusion of our two cultures.

The following are some striking examples of basically Spanish structures formed on clearly English roots, perhaps deliberately or even playfully. They are not limited to student speech.

Ay lo guacho—The verb *guacho* is a calque on the English 'watch,' but made to fit the standard Spanish verb system: (yo) *guacho*, (tú) *guachas*, etc. The syntax is standard Spanish. The word *ay* is a normal phonological reduction of the adverb of place *ahí*. Curiously, in a bilingual setting it also suggests the English subject pronoun 'I.' An accurate English rendering might be 'I'll see you around.' Discussion points stemming from this and similar cases are legion. The persistence of Spanish verb forms even on outrageous calques (See *chirió* and *mistió* below). The verification of other tenses of such verbs. The origins of *guacho*—is it part of the rise of the *pachuco* dialect of the late 40s? The use of the formal or the familiar—*lo guacho* or *te guacho*. The persistence of standard Spanish syntax, even in non-standard Spanish or Spanish-English argot—(1) adverb *ay*, (2) object pronoun *lo*, (3) inflected verb *guacho*, (4) absence of subject pronoun [*yo*]. The function of out-group slang as defensive/selective, as a means of controlling membership and obliging recognition. The function of slang and discrimination by race, age, or status (student *vs.* non-student).

Whatever the origins of *ay lo guacho*, like a host of other expressions it is now firmly established in informal Spanish. Such is not yet the case of the peculiarly student calques *chirió* 'he cheated' and *mistié* 'I missed.' Products of the school environment of tests and grades as well as of the students' faulty knowledge of the appropriate standard Spanish, such inventions are perhaps both jocular and highly practical. They allow the speaker to use a truly Spanish sentence (thus selecting his audience), insert a well-known English word in "disguised" or Hispanized form (thus excluding even Anglo students of Spanish), and enjoy some rather sophisticated linguistic play.

In the language class, such words can yield to the same kind of study as *guacho* above. In the case of *chirió* the problem is compounded if the class tries to verify other forms of the verb. The preterite form *chirió* could derive from the hypothetical infinitive *cherir* (on the model of *herir, hirió*) or from *chiriar* (on the model of *lidiar, lidió*). If the students can verify the existence of other forms of the verb *chirió*, or if they can collect enough examples of other verb calques, they will probably decide on the second hypothetical infinitive—*chiriar*. To arrive at such a conclusion they will probably have to touch on not only the matter of verbal analogy within Spanish but also on the mechanism of borrowing and accommodating English words, *i.e.* giving them Spanish verb endings.

Languages and cultures in contact normally yield linguistic borrowings of all kinds, as we have seen. In most cases the borrowings are simply lexical and consist of a single step. That is, for our purposes, the Spanish speaker adopts an Indian or English word and adapts it to his already existing linguistic system. A more complicated and pedagogically more interesting two-step process is less frequent, but has recently been documented in Mexico and the Southwest (Olstad 1970; Galván 1971). Bilingual participants in our two cultures will doubtless contribute more examples.

In the cases under question, an originally Spanish word is borrowed by English, where it may undergo more or less phonetic and/or semantic change. This is the first step. Later the English form or usage finds its way back into Spanish, where it may co-exist with its ancestor. Thus Olstad (1970) has shown the Spanish noun *frito* has always been used generically to denote any fried food. In the last decade an American commercial interest has popularized the plural *fritos* as the trademarked English name of their product (step one). And more recently, at least one city in Mexico (Guadalajara) has seen the reentry of the word to designate—in Spanish—a similar product (step two). Here, it is clear, modern marketing methods, including packaging, advertising, and supermarket selling, have all had a hand in facilitating the double borrowing described here.

Galván (1971) describes, among several other examples, an older and more complex case. The Spanish word *cucaracha* names the well-known household pest. The English borrowing was first *"cacarootch"* and later the now standard cockroach. From these two English forms come the Spanish forms *rucho, roche* and *rocho*, unknown in the standard dictionaries but frequent in the Spanish of Texas.

The pattern of Spanish to English to Spanish is clear in these cases, although the acceptability of the end product may be open to question. The fate of *fritos* will depend on advertising and taste. *Roche* and its variants are perhaps limited to regional use.

Further examples and discussion can continue as time and interest permit. But always, of course, the data brought to bear on the linguistic issues raised should derive from students, parents, grand-parents, neighbors and peers, as well as from the teacher and his academic resources.

Another area of language which can be of interest is that of phonology. The untrained student may not be able to deal analytically with most of the phenomena. But he will distinguish variations in pronunciation and may even react to them with a socially oriented attitude. Thus the forms *pior* and *maistro* may be recognized as uneducated or "countrified" by contrast with the standard forms *peor* and *maestro*. If appropriate, such a class discovery can serve as initial examples of the insistent tendency in spoken Spanish—of 1,000 years standing—toward the reduction of hiatus. Thus *ahí* tends to become *ay*, *pasear* tends to become *pasiar*, etc.

Likewise, many students learning to read Spanish for the first time will recognize that the book forms *pared* and *ciudad* do not correspond to their versions *pader* and *suidad*. The phenomenon of sound transposition known as metathesis is common in all languages, of course. Here it may be explained as a tendency for sounds to seek out the most "comfortable" environment or expression. That is, for example, since in Spanish there are many thousands of words ending in "r" and considerably fewer ending in "d," popular speech tends to transpose sounds accordingly. Likewise, since the diphthong "-ui-" (as in *muy* and *fui*) is more frequent, *i.e.* easier, than "-iu-," again the transposition is perhaps normal. In both cases, however, the sophisticated speaker will recognize one form as preferable, the other as rustic or wrong. And the student who foresees himself in social or professional settings requiring "correct" Spanish will want to broaden his control of the language accordingly without, of course, losing the vivid expressiveness which is found in any local colloquial.

It is in morphology—the verb system especially—where contrastive study of local and standard dialects can become really interesting. Interesting to the teacher as he broadens his knowledge of the language; interesting to the student, hopefully, as he sees his previously scorned patois susceptible of systematic analysis; and interesting as a pedagogical device, since forbidding terms such as "subjunctive" and "radical change" and "third conjugation" can be related to the known local Spanish as well as the unknown bookish Spanish. A few examples must suffice. While watching a boring television program, a student may have noted a family member ask, "¿Cambeo la televisión?" Since *cambeo* differs from the standard *cambio* in both vowel pronunciation and stress pattern (*cambéo vs. cámbio*), it can be instructive to compare the verb system in a more systematic way. Conversation with native speakers, plus guidance from the instructors, will yield the following comparative chart of the present tense.

Standard		Non-standard
cambio	yo	cambeo
cambias	tú	cambeas
cambia	él, ella	cambea
cambiamos	nosotros	cambiamos
cambian	ellos	cambean

Further discussion may reveal other verbs which are considered to be members of the same (non-standard) verb class, such as *maniar* 'to brake' and *rociar* 'to sprinkle'.

Discussion points for more extended study could center on the matter of verb classes themselves and the confusion caused by their apparent arbitrariness. Thus, even within the standard language, similar infinitives from different classes yield dissimilar present tenses.

cambiar	enviar
cambio	envío
cambias	envías
cambia	envía
cambiamos	enviamos
cambian	envían

Similarly, the power of analogy throughout the verb system, while on the one hand working for uniformity and regularity, can by the same token give currency to non-standard forms. Thus *hacer* in the first person plural normally yields *hacemos*, as is standard for regular -*er* verbs. But by incorrect analogy, many native speakers derive *semos* from *ser*. Another example: in the imperfect tense *traer* often yields *traíba, traíbas*, etc. by incorrect analogy with *ir: iba, ibas* . . .and the entire class of -*ar* verbs.

Returning to *cambiar*, a look at the imperative forms gives the following contrast.

Standard	Non-standard
cambia	cambea
no cambies	no cambiés

The negative non-standard form is quite unlike anything in Mexican standard, yet it lends itself to discussion regarding other dimensions of the Spanish language. It is very close to the second person plural form standard in Spain (*no cambiéis*) and to the *voseo* form of Argentina, neither of which is used in Mexico. Thus, peculiarities of the language, even trivialities, can serve a double function. They can call attention, by contrast, to the standard or cultured version of the language. And they can suggest something of the range and variety— within a larger unity—of a language spoken by more than 200,000,000 people.

In all the preceding discussion of variety within the Spanish language, including specifically that variety occasioned by contact with English, one important feature stands out—the persistence of basically Spanish language features. That is, dialectical variations and loan features from English take on specifically Spanish characteristics. Even outrageous and deliberate calques on English—*sainear* for 'to sign'—are made to fit the Spanish verb system. Un-Spanish sound patterns are modified to fit Spanish phonology—'*mufflers*' with two un-Spanish vowel sounds and the impossible consonant cluster (-*rs* in final position) becomes *mofles*. And Spanish syntax patterns, by and large, determine the use of English sentence elements.

Nevertheless, there may exist at least one noteworthy exception to the predominance of Spanish syntax. Certainly, in an area where many speakers not only speak a Spanish influenced by English, but even routinely switch from one language to another in mid-sentence, new syntax patterns are to be expected. The basic sentence, in this case, is *Tengo que hacer park el carro* 'I have to park the car.' We might have expected rather the Anglicism *parquear* 'to park,' or possibly, in Spain, *aparcar*. But instead the un-Hispanized English verb is inserted in what seems to be a standard Spanish syntactic structure: verb phrase with *hacer* and dependent infinitive (in English) and complement. The utility of this structure is clear, since it obviates the need to Hispanize and even allows the bilingual to switch sound systems in mid-sentence, pronouncing *park* in English and the rest of the sentence in Spanish. The effect may be ludicrous to the outsider, or odious to the academic. But my informant assures me that the expression is, in fact, current, giving such examples as *tengo que hacer study, están haciendo shut down,* and even *vamos a hacer ir shopping.*

From the standpoint of the language student the expression is curious because its syntax is *not* basically Spanish. True, constructions with *hacer* and a dependent infinitive are normal in Spanish. But they imply separate subjects for the two verbs. Thus, if a Mexico City resident were to say *Voy a hacer estacionar el carro,* he would quite correctly be stating his intention to have someone else, such as the attendant, park the car for him. In the bilingual sentence the speaker clearly means to park the car himself. Apparently what has happened is that a Spanish syntactical pattern (*hacer* plus infinitive) has been changed in meaning to accommodate the English word. Or rather, a similar syntactical pattern has been generated—with a different meaning—under the influence of English.

Pending further study and further information from interested students, I suggest the following genesis of *hacer park el carro* 'to park the car'.

English makes extensive use of the auxiliary *do* to form negative and interrogative sentences. The following examples, all in the past tense, may suffice: I *didn't* park the car. *Did* I park the car? Where *did* I park the car? as well as the intensified form, I *did* park the car. Only the positive form (among the simple tenses) does not use the auxiliary: I parked the car.

A word by word comparison suggests one probable point at which the English pattern could help generate a Spanish equivalent.

Where	did-I	park	the car?
¿Dónde	hice	park	el carro?

Once such a syntactic calque is established parallel to its English origin, nothing prevents its behaving like a genuine Spanish sentence and appearing in all the inflective and periphrastic variations to which the Spanish verb is susceptible: *voy a hacer park el carro; haga park el carro; ¿y el carro, dónde lo hiciste park?* etc. Student informants can verify which of these expressions are in fact current, and which might sound strange or "wrong." Also, of course, they can establish the more formal or more standard equivalents.

* * *

Finally, let me refer directly to the title of this piece. The use of the term "local colloquial" suggests the existence of a single nonstandard dialect which can be contrasted to a single standard norm. Such a suggestion is surely misleading. Except perhaps in small isolated communities, students will soon become aware of the richness and variety even within a local colloquial. Any community recognizes, for example, that certain residents, perhaps a few of the older men, speak "better Spanish" and can be counted on for more formal occasions. Likewise any member of a given community recognizes that his own speech style must be adjusted—even though within the local colloquial—depending on circumstance. For example, a young man may take leave of his mother in the morning by saying simply, "Ya me voy" (I'm going now); he may leave his friends in the afternoon with "Ay nos vemos" or "Ay los guacho" (We'll see ya); and he may say good-bye to his future mother-in-law with "Con su permiso, señora" (a formal formula, roughly equivalent to: By your leave, ma'am).

Thus, as students compile their own word lists, verb charts and basic syntax models, they will not only construct progressively a grammar for the language they already know, they will also prepare a partial but highly relevant manual of style for everyday language use. Through constant comparison and contrast they will learn to move from the local colloquial to the standard and back, and to control the variety inherent in both aspects of the language to their own advantage. They may appreciate, in short, something of the notion that language is not simply "right" or "wrong," but that language usage is a function of time, place, and context.

REFERENCES

ARMISTEAD, S. G. AND J. H. SILVERMAN
  1965–66 La *Sanjuanada:* ¿huella de una ḫarǧa mozárabe en la tradición actual? *Nueva Revista de Filología Hispánico* 18: 436–43.
ARNOLD, RICHARD D.
  1968 1965–66 (Year Two) Findings, San Antonio Language Project, Thomas D. Horn, Director. The University of Texas, Austin.
BEREITER, C. AND S. ENGLEMAN
  1966 *Teaching Disadvantaged Children in the Preschool.* Prentice-Hall, Englewood Cliffs, New Jersey.
FITZ-GERALD, JOHN D.
  1921 The Bilingual-Biracial Problem of Our Border States. *Hispania* 4: 175–86.
GALVÁN, ROBERTO A.
  1971 More on "Frito" as an English Loan-Word in Mexican Spanish. *Hispania* 54: 511–2.
GOODMAN, MARY ELLEN AND ALMA BEMAN
  1968 Child's-Eye-Views of Life in an Urban Barrio. In *Spanish-Speaking People in the United States*, June Helm, ed. (Proceedings of the 1968 Annual Spring Meeting of the American Ethnological Society). The University of Washington Press, Seattle.
JOOS, MARTIN
  1962 *The Five Clocks.* Harcourt, Brace and World, Inc., New York.
MODIANO, NANCY
  1968 National or Mother Tongue in Beginning Reading. Research in the Teaching of English 2: 32–43.
OLSTAD, CHARLES
  1970 "Frito": An English Loan-Word in Mexican Spanish. *Hispania* 53: 88–90.
PEAL, ELIZABETH AND WALLACE E. LAMBERT
  1962 The Relation of Bilingualism to Intelligence. Psychological Monographs: General and Applied 76: 1–23.
SAAVEDRA, BARBARA HEILER
  1969 Applied Language Research Center, El Paso Public Schools. *Modern Language Journal* 53: 97.
STEMMLER, ANNE
  1966 An Experimental Approach to the Teaching of Oral Language in Reading. *Harvard Educational Review* 36: 45.
UNESCO
  1953 *The Use of the Vernacular Languages in Education.* (Monographs on Fundamental Education, 8). United Nations Educational, Scientific, and Cultural Organization, Paris.

5. The Acquisition of Lexicon in the Speech of Bilingual Children

RICARDO J. CORNEJO

The author's main interests deal with the development of bilingual curricula, and his article describes bilingualism from the standpoint of lexicography. His findings, conclusions, and recommendations should be of value in the preparation of teachers and teaching material for bilingual education in the Southwest.

The research study reported here represents a pilot project of a larger research project to record and analyze the language of five-year-old Mexican-American bilingual children in Texas. The recording was funded by the Southwest Educational Development Laboratory. The research, directed by Drs. Joseph Michel and Joseph Matluck of the University of Texas at Austin, was performed under a grant from the U.S. Office of Education, Department of Health, Education and Welfare.

THE COUNTRY is now passing through a period of acute awareness of the existence of the bilingual. The problem is being variously approached by the educator, the sociologist, the cultural anthropologist, the psychologist, the speech pathologist, and even by the politician, according to the particular focus which his discipline or interest imposes. In focusing on the problem, most research studies have left many problems unsolved. One of the most basic is the exact meaning of the term "bilingual." When reference is made to a bilingual individual, we do not really know the extent of the bilingual's knowledge of either of the languages he speaks, or his facility and fluency in them. Tests have been made in order to determine knowledge of a given language, but these are based mostly on assumptions regarding comprehension rather than expression.

It is therefore necessary to get as complete a picture as possible of the language and language ability of the five-year-old Spanish-speaking child of Texas when he is about to begin his formal schooling.

This study represents only a preliminary step in the recording of the speech of children in Arizona, New Mexico, and California, thus providing a composite picture of the Spanish-English speech of the Southwest.

One of the problems faced by people studying bilingualism has been that of defining bilingualism and determining who is bilingual. In the specific case of the Spanish-speaking children of Texas, the situation is such that their language skills go from almost 100 percent Spanish to almost 100 percent English, with degrees of compound, coordinate, and balanced bilinguality. This diversified speech pattern presents a serious challenge to the educators of these children.

The proximity to Mexico and the great number of people who have migrated constantly from that country have perpetuated a bilingual situation which is reflected in the difficulty which the children usually encounter in their mastery of both languages. As a result of this language contact, there is a high degree of linguistic transfer from language to language in this area.

The language research dealt with in this article had as an aim to collect an initial corpus of recorded material representing the speech of the Spanish-English bilingual children of Texas, in order to gather information concerning the lexicon of these children before they enter first grade.[1]

The analysis of the findings indicated that the language pattern of

[1] The recordings were done by Joi Kirwin, Mary Coats Ley, Gustavo Gonzalez, and Ricardo Cornejo, and took place in Austin, Del Valle, San Benito, and Harlingen. Approximately 100 children were interviewed. Of these, 24 were selected for language analysis: 6 from Austin, 4 from Del Valle, 7 from Harlingen, and 7 from San Benito.

the children presents some characteristics which correspond to a great extent to those expected in areas where two or more languages are in contact: significant evidence was gathered which shows a high degree of transfer, borrowing, and language mixture.

THE RESEARCH PROJECT

The purposes of this project were:

1. To collect a sample corpus of recorded material representing the speech of five-year-old Spanish-speaking bilingual children of Texas.

2. To start a collection of recorded speech which can be available for possible future studies.

3. To do lexical, phonological, and syntactical analysis of the findings, as well as a study of cultural patterns as shown in the language behavior of the children involved.

4. To develop techniques for eliciting speech.

5. To develop pictorial and other types of materials for use in collecting speech.

6. To evaluate different types of interview materials.

The criteria for the selection of informants and the areas of investigation were suggested by consultants in a meeting which was held before the recording began. The informants were to have the following characteristics: children between five and six years of age, of Spanish surname, of Mexican or Mexican-American parents, lifetime residents in the area, no previous schooling, bilinguality (responded appropriately in English and in Spanish during preliminary conversations with the interviewers. The recorded speech of children who spoke only English or only Spanish was not used for lexical analysis), and willingness to be interviewed.

The areas of investigation included both rural and urban elements from the Texas-Mexico "linguistic" border and the interior of Texas. For the purpose of this study, an urban community is any incorporated city of 25,000 inhabitants or more. A rural community is any incorporated or unincorporated town of 2,500 inhabitants or less that is not contiguous with an urban community.

The recordings in the "linguistic" border area were done in Harlingen, a city of about 40,000, and in a rural area near San Benito. Harlingen is twenty-five miles from the border; the San Benito area is about twenty miles from the border.

The recordings in the interior of Texas were done in Austin, which has a population of 250,000 inhabitants, and in the Del Valle area with a population of five hundred.

The questionnaire[2] used to elicit the speech of the children included

---

[2] The preparation of the questionnaires was carried out by Joi Kirwin and Ricardo Cornejo.

visual materials selected from the following sources: (1) a set of photographs from the *Illinois Test of Psycholinguistic Abilities*, *(ITPA);* (2) a set of black and white drawings from *See and Say;* (3) a set of four colored pictures from *On the Road to Reading;* (4) one colored picture from *Tom and Jerry Coloring Book;* (5) one colored picture from *Sylvester Coloring Book;* (6) one colored picture from *Batman;* (7) one colored picture from *Superman No. 190;* (8) a set of nine black and white pictures from *Pictorial Linguistic Interview Materials;* (9) a set of eight black and white drawings, entitled "I wonder," which was prepared by the author of this article for the purpose of eliciting spontaneous, imaginative speech; and (10) a set of toys; For English: marbles, crayons, drinking glasses, and water pistols; for Spanish: rubber ball, sponge, car, and baby bottle.[3]

The following steps occurred during the interview procedures.

1. The families of five-year-olds were contacted. This was done with the help of school principals, home visitors, and the families themselves, who would give names of people they knew.

2. Once the parents agreed to collaborate, the field recorders visited the homes to get acquainted with parents and children, and to fill out a Biographical Data Sheet, where personal information was recorded.

3. Those children who were bilingual were selected as subjects. Most of the interviews were done in the homes of the children, except the ones in Del Valle which were done in the school building where the children were beginning in a Head Start Program.

The interviews, which took place during April, May, and June, 1967, went through the following stages: individual interviews, dialog, and parent-child conversation.

An individual interview was one session conducted in English, and one conducted in Spanish. Each one lasted approximately fifteen minutes. The individual interview was comprised of: Auditory Vocal-Automatic, Visual Decoding, Visual-Motor Association, Auditory-Vocal Association, Descriptive Narrative, and Tactile Descriptive.

[3] These materials were obtained from the following sources: (1) *Illinois Test of Psycholinguistic Abilities*, *(ITPA)*, a booklet by James J. McCarthy and Samuel A. Kirk, Urbana, Illinois, 1961; (2) *See and Say*, a reader for Spanish-speaking children by Joseph Michel, Austin, Texas: W.S. Benson & Co., 1964; (3) *On the Road to Reading*, a prereader for kindergarten use by Sisters M. Marguerite and M. Bernarda, Boston: Ginn & Co., 1961; (4) *Tom and Jerry Coloring Book* by Loew's Inc., Racine, Wisconsin: Whitman Publishing Co., 1962; (5) *Sylvester Coloring Book* No. 2946 by Warner Brothers Pictures Inc., Racine, Wisconsin: Whitman Publishing Co., 1963; (6) *Batman* No. 191 (May, 1967), Sparta, Illinois: National Periodical Publications, Inc.; (7) *Superman* No. 190 (May, 1967), Sparta, Illinois: National Periodical Publications, Inc.; (8) *Pictorial Linguistic Interview Materials* (PLIM) by Stanley Sapon, Columbus, Ohio: American Library of Recorded Dialect Studies, Ohio State University, 1957; (9) "I Wonder" set prepared by the author of this article for the purpose of eliciting spontaneous, imaginative speech.

In the dialog, two children were paired together to elicit speech in a conversation mood. The dialogs were recorded in the speech of the child without prompting him to use either language. The parts of the dialog were: Descriptive Narrative, Interpretative Narrative, "I Wonder," Charade, and Inventive Games.

DESCRIPTION OF EACH STAGE

Individual

The Auditory Vocal-Automatic section was designed to cover the child's intuitive grasp of grammar. For example:

Here is one bed. Here are two ____. While stating the above sentence, the interviewer first showed the child a picture of a bed, and then another with two beds. The child was expected to complete the sentence, by providing the lexical element that was missing. In the Spanish part, the interviewer would say,

Ésta es una manzana. Éstas son dos ____.

The child was expected to say "manzanas."

The Visual Decoding section involved the child's ability to identify objects belonging to the same semantic category. For example, the interviewer showed the informant a picture of a table knife, followed by a picture of four assorted items, one of which was a pocket knife. The child was expected to indicate which object was "similar" to the one shown to him previously.

The Visual-Motor Association section was to determine the child's ability to identify objects that go together. For example, the child was shown a picture of a spoon; then he was shown a picture containing four items, including a cup and a saucer. He was then asked: "Which of these goes with this?" When the child responded, he was asked to elaborate on why a certain item went with another item.

The Auditory-Vocal Association section was to test the informant's use of analogies. A sentence-completion method was used here as in part one, but this time no visual materials were used.

Examples:

I sit on a chair. I sleep on a ____.
La pelota es redonda. La caja es ____.

In the Descriptive Narrative section the child was asked to describe the objects and people in a picture. The interviewer asked the child questions about what was happening in the picture, what the people were wearing, what objects were included in the picture, etc.

Dialog

In the Descriptive Narrative, the two informants talked about events depicted in visual materials.

In order to initiate the Interpretative Narrative phase, one informant was asked to describe what was happening in each of the pictures. The second child was asked to mention anything that the first might have forgotten, or to add to the narration. The interviewer acted as a catalyst by asking questions like "What else happened?", or "Did he leave anything out?"

Nonrepresentational pictures were used in the "I Wonder" phase. The informants were asked to interpret these pictures. No limit was set on the children's imagination; they could give any interpretation of the pictures they wanted.

In the Charade phase one of the children was shown the picture of an object such as a pencil sharpener, and was asked to pantomime the use of the object. The second child was directed to interpret the acting.

During the Inventive Game phase, the informants took turns assuming various imaginary roles while describing what they were and what they were doing.

Parent-Child Conversation

After the interviews were over, the interviewers invited the mother or father of the child to ask the child what he had been doing, what questions he had been asked, what things he had been shown, what he had liked best, etc.

ANALYSIS OF FINDINGS

Transcription

Out of approximately 100 children interviewed, 24 were selected for analysis of their syntax, phonology, lexicon, and semantics. The selection was based on their bilinguality as shown in conversations with the interviewers.

Each child was recorded three times: one interview with a Spanish-speaking interviewer who asked all questions in Spanish; one interview with an English-speaking interviewer who asked all the questions in English; and one dialog situation in which two children were paired together and the interviewer acted as a catalyst in the conversation.

A total of 60 tapes was gathered and transcribed by a team of analysts. This total was comprised of: 24 thirty-minute tapes of individual interviews in Spanish, 24 thirty-minute tapes of individual interviews in English, and 12 forty-minute tapes of dialogs. (The 60 tapes and 1,800 pages of transcriptions are filed in the library of the Foreign Language Education Center, University of Texas, 107 West 27th, Austin, Texas; and at the Southwest Educational Development Laboratory, 800 Brazos, Austin, Texas.)

The transcription and analysis of the tapes were done in 1968–69 by a group of graduate students in applied linguistics.

Lexical Items

The children used a total of 972 lexical items in English and 696 in Spanish.

The different lexical items recorded in English and Spanish are listed below in order of occurrence. This list included only those items used by the children more than twenty times.[4]

1. English

From 150 to 101

the	138	I	107

From 100 to 51

me	83	that	63
its	81	he	61
is	68	to	60
she	67	of	59
those	65		

From 50 to 41

in	48	toys	47
look	48	boys	47

From 40 to 31

a	40	boy	39
are	39	family	39
red	39	play	35
television	39	babies	35
this	39	you	35
black	37	father	33
does	37	mother	33
man	37	small	32
playing	37	with	31

---

[4] The complete list of lexical items is found in *Bilingualism: Study of the Lexicon of the Five-Year-Old Spanish-Speaking Children in Texas*, Ph.D. Dissertation by Ricardo J. Cornejo, University of Texas, 1969. This study has been published and is available from the Learning Disabilities Center, University of Texas, Austin, Texas.

From 30 to 21

big	29	made	24
marble	29	sofa	24
water	29	that's	24
brother	28	there	24
milk	28	yellow	24
no	28	houses	23
one	28	dog	22
school	28	gun	22
what?	28	spoon	22
children	27	apple	21
daddy	27	eyes	21
go	27	head	21
pen	27	horse	21
tell	27	my	21
ball	25	pass	21
buy	25	put	21
knife	25	shoes	21
time	25	sister	21
tree	25	so	21
T.V.	25	talking	21
door	25	town	21
Batman	24	visit	21
for	24	wolf	21

2. Spanish

More than 200

una	256	y	203
un	217	el (art.)	201
la (art.)	207		

From 200 to 151

a (prep.)	167

From 150 to 101

mamá	131
las (art.)	126

From 100 to 51

es	68	éste	62
los (art.)	67	en	59

From 50 to 41

aquí	49
mano	44
está	43

From 40 to 31

comer	39	para (prep.)	37
de	39	porque	37
unas	38	sí	35
con	37	mi (poss. adj.)	32
éstos	37	carro	31

From 30 to 21

ésta	30	pistola	26
al	29	agua	25
bebita	29	plato	23
bebito	28	traen	22
cosas	28	jugando	21
más	28	'amá (mamá)	21
no	28	muchachita	21
esa	27	pa' (para)	21

Comparison of Findings with Current Frequency Lists

The lexical items recorded in this study, when compared to frequency lists in English and Spanish, present the following correlation:

1. English

The lexical items are compared here to the first 1,000 words of Thorndike's (1921) *The Teacher's Word Book*.

The correlation indicates that out of the 972 items recorded in English, 270 of them appear in Thorndike's list. This correlation would have to be checked and tested by using a larger sample in order to account for its validity and reliability. It could also indicate that Thorndike's frequency list does not represent the spoken vocabulary of children today, since their language patterns have been highly influenced by mass media. There are quite a few lexical items used by the children which do not appear in Thorndike's count and whose rate of occurrence was very high in this study. Some of them are listed below.

Item	Frequency
aunt	12
barbecue	11
bathroom	7
birthday	17
bottle	12
candy	42
cartoons	20
cat	12
coffee	11
crayons	14
cream	12
daddy	27
didn't	19
dime	4
donuts	13
downtown	12
gun	22
hamburger	8

hungry	2
nickel	9
O.K.	9
pancake	7
peanut butter	12
pencil	18
penny	11
pies	7
potato	4
shirt	8
steak	8
telephone	3
television	39
tomato	4
T.V.	25

Since the majority of these items belong in the category of informal, familiar, oral language, it might be concluded that oral speech should be correlated with a frequency list which has been obtained from a sample where oral language was the basis of the count. Moreover, this study might yield a better correlation if it were compared to a frequency list of child language in English.

The lexical items listed in this research study (and those compiled from larger samples) eventually will be compared to more recent frequency lists for a better comparison and correlation.

2. Spanish

The lexical items recorded in the study were compared to the basic list of 554 items appearing in the *Spanish Idiom List* by Hayward Keniston (1938).

The comparison indicates that out of the 696 items recorded in the study only 76 appear in Keniston's list. The reason for this discrepancy seems to be the fact that Keniston's list was tabulated from the words used in literature (drama, fiction, prose, etc.). Consequently, many of the terms appearing in the list as very common words in Spanish are rather obsolete and rare. By the same token, Keniston leaves out quite a few items which are very common in Spanish. Some of them were used by the children interviewed in this study. They are listed below.

Item	*Frequency*
agua	25
azúcar	2
blanco	5
bueno	1
café (bebida)	3

café (color)	2
cama	19
cara	14
carne	3
caros	6
ciudad	1
comer	39
comida	17
cuchara	17
en	59
ése	14
ese	19
ésta	35
esta	18
está	43
mamá	131
primero	18
y	203

This lack of correspondence between the current frequency lists and oral language in Spanish seems to indicate that it would be advisable to prepare frequency lists of the written language and of the oral language as well. Only by comparing the results of research in oral language with frequency lists based also on the oral language of a large sample will it be possible to have reliable comparisons.

The lexical items listed here (and those compiled in subsequent phases of this research) eventually will be compared to the 700 most common words as they appear in *Recuento de Vocabulario Español* (Rodríguez 1952).

The analysis of this study also showed that it is of the utmost importance to compile a reliable frequency list of lexical items found in the Spanish language of the Southwest. This could be done starting from scratch or by comparison with studies such as the *Recuento de Vocabulario Español*, which is the most complete and reliable study to date.

Child Language (Baby Talk)

One of the most persistent and systematic features of the Spanish language of the children was the high frequency of words and expressions that would be considered "baby talk." It seems that their Spanish develops rather slowly because of a lack of reinforcement from everyday conversation and as a result of the English dominance in the surrounding environment (see Ferguson 1964). Examples of this are listed below:

abierta	— aberta	ie	>	e
abuelito	— abolito	ue	>	o
adentro	— arentro	d	>	r

agarras	— 'garas	rr	>	r
anda	— anna	d	>	n
anteojos	— ant'ojos	eo	>	o
así	— achí	s	>	č
bicicleta	— 'ticleta	s	>	t
bomba	— pompa	b	>	p
cafetera	— cafetela	r	>	l
carne	— ca'ne	r	>	ø
carrito	— ca'ito	rr	>	ø
clavando	— cavando	l	>	ø
colorado	— cololao	r	>	l
colorea	— colea	(reduction)		
comiendo	— comendo	ye	>	e
	comenno	ye	>	e
		d	>	n
	cumendo	o	>	u
		ye	>	e
comió	— comó	yo	>	o
comprando	— pompando	(mixture of phonemes)		
corren	— colen	rr	>	l
cosiendo	— cosendo	ye	>	e
cuando	— cuan'o	d	>	ø
cuatro	— cuato	r	>	ø
cucharo	— cuchala	r	>	l
	cutara	č	>	t
donde	— onne	d	>	n
dormir	— rormir	d	>	r
durmiendo	— rumiendo	d	>	r
		r	>	ø
entramos	— entamo'	r	>	ø
éste sí	— é'te tí	s	>	t
estufa	— 'tupa	f	>	p
flores	— fore'	l	>	ø
grande	— lande	g	>	ø
		r	>	l
ladrones	— lagones	dr	>	g
manzanas	— mantanas	s	>	t
mesa	— meta	s	>	t
mirando	— miranno	d	>	n
muchachito	— tatito	č	>	t
no sé	— no té	s	>	t
número	— númelo	r	>	l
Oscar	— O'ca	s	>	ø
		r	>	ø
para que	— pa' que			
se sienten	se senten	ye	>	e
parte	— palte	r	>	l
peleo	— pelo	eo	>	o
pera	— pella	r	>	ly
perro	— pelo	rr	>	l
	pero	rr	>	r

pies	— pes	ye	>	e
plantan	— pantan	l	>	ø
prender	— pender	r	>	ø
puede	— puere	d	>	r
puerta	— polta	we	>	o
		r	>	l
recto	— reto	k	>	ø
reloj	— leloj	r	>	l
rico	— 'ico	r	>	ø
suena	— sona	we	>	o
tazón	— sasón	t	>	s
tiene	— tene	ye	>	e
traía	— taía	r	>	ø
viene	— vene	ye	>	e
zapatos	— tapatos	s	>	t

Structural and Lexical Interference from English to Spanish

A large number of instances of interference from English to Spanish were recorded. Some of them are listed below:

al mushito (muchachito) lo cacharon los police

como mucho candy
con el baby
con my money

el bathroom
el boy se cayó
el dress
el grandfather
el grocery store
el monster
el sun se mete p'adentro
en el paper
en el twenty-first
en una white one
ésa tiene round patas
escribo las A B C's /ey biy siyz/
(es) 'tán con bathing suit

garas cabi (agarras cavidad)

hace el ice cream

iba trick or treating

la bottle
la doctor
la grandmother
la muchachita 'ta'a roller skating

la spongy
la river
las dishes
lavan el dishes
lavando los glasses
le quitó a la señora el baby
los tires (car tires)

mató a su wife
marti'o (martillo) para que le fasten it
mete the clothes en la box
mi daddy me da candy
mi daddy nos hace una casa pa' nosotros
mis brothers

pa' downtown y pa' México
pa' que le den un ride a la gente
pan y una taza y un ... fork y una mano y ... butter
pelea con people
porque es lovable
porque ésa tiene un longer dress
porque mata people

quedó sin la wife

se cayó de la fence
se ponen inside

té, agua, lemonade, hot juice, and ...
tiene un dress chiquito

un anything
un baby, hermanita y ...
un book
un clock y un penny
un crayon
un daddy
un desk
un hammer
un hat
un jewel bag
un marble
un mouse
un muchachito comiendo fried chicken
un pear
un pencil
un rocket
un sink

una axe
una bike

una bird
una blanket
una box
una butter
una chicken
una cup
una drum
una gown
una mother
una napkin
una roller skater que se quebró una pata

van a ir swimming
voy a downtown
voy p'al center

y popcorn
y tiene straight patas
y una star . . . y . . . glove
y un big one
y un sun . . . y una botona

One of the most fascinating aspects of the structural and lexical blending and mixture in the language of the children was the high degree of "grammaticalness" found in their structures. The mixture of English and Spanish followed a very systematic pattern of positive transfer, analogy and association. The "Spanglish" [5] idiolect of each child is an invitation to do more research in the area of language acquisition in bilinguals.

Some of these patterns are listed below.

1. Spanish Feminine Indefinite Article + English Noun

All the English nouns in this group are feminine nouns in Spanish. That is why the children used them in Spanish phrases preceded by a feminine article.

Child's Term	*Spanish Regular Term*
una axe	un(a) hacha
una bike	una bicicleta
una bird	un(a) ave
una blanket	una frazada
una box	una caja
una chicken	una gallina
una cup	una taza

[5] "Spanglish" is a general term used to refer to the mixture of English and Spanish. It doesn't have the derogatory connotation of "Tex-Mex" or other similar terms. It is similar to "Franglais," that is to say the mixture of "Français" (French) + "Anglais" (English).

una drum	una tambora
una star	una estrella
una gown	una bata
una mother	una madre
una napkin	una servilleta
una white one	una blanca
una roller skater	una (niña) patinadora

2. Spanish Masculine Definite Article + English Noun

The English nouns listed below are masculine nouns in Spanish. That is why the children used them preceded by a masculine article.

Child's Term	Spanish Regular Term
el baby	el bebé
el bathroom	el baño
el boy	el niño
al center (a el)	al centro
el dress	el vestido
el grandfather	el abuelo
el ice cream	el helado
el monster	el monstruo
el paper	el papel
el sun	el sol
el twenty-first	el veintiuno

3. Spanish Feminine Definite Article + English Noun

All of the English nouns in this group are feminine nouns in Spanish. That is why the children used them in Spanish phrases preceded by a feminine article.

Child's Term	Spanish Regular Term
la bottle	la botella
la fence	la cerca
las dishes	las vasijas (in Texas Spanish)
la doctor	la enfermera (the picture the child was looking at showed a nurse, not a doctor)
la grandmother	la abuela
la spongy (sponge)	la esponja

Borrowings from English to Spanish

A large number of English words were used in the Spanish of the children. On the other hand, very few Spanish words were used when the child spoke in English.

Borrowing in linguistics refers to "the process whereby one language absorbs words and expressions, possibly also sounds and grammatical forms, from another, and adapts them to its own use, with or without phonetic and semantic adaptation" (Pei 1966: 30).

1. Alien Words

"Alien words are borrowed words that still retain part of the phonemic pattern, stress, written form, etc., of the language of origin" (Pei 1966: 9).

Spanish	English
bisquete	biscuit
bos	bus
caite	kite
crismes	Christmas
daime	dime
lonche	lunch
nicle	nickel

2. Loan Translations

"Loan translations are compounds, derivatives or phrases brought into one language through translation of the constituent parts of the term in another language" (Pei 1966: 153).

lo puso p'atrás	he put it back
va para'trás	he goes back

3. Loan Shifts

"Loan shifts are the adoption from another language of a word similar to one that already exists in the borrowing language, with the form of the borrowing language and the meaning of the lending language" (Pei 1966: 152).

pelearla	fight her ("va a pelearla" instead of the Spanish "va a pelear con ella")
recado	wrecked
troca	truck

4. Loan Blends

"Loan blend is a new idiom which develops in a language as a result of borrowing, and of which one element is borrowed, the other native, but adapted to the loan original" (Pei 1966: 152).

suimear	to swim (swim + e + ar ending of Spanish verbs, by analogy with "golpear," "torear," etc.)

cachar	to catch (catch + ar ending of Spanish verbs, by analogy with "agachar," "marchar")
jailar	to jail (jail + ar ending of Spanish verbs)
/ĵeylar/	

Mexicanisms

Words found in the vernacular of Mexico (Santamaría 1959):

1. aguacate, from Aztec ahuacatl (avocado). In South America: palta
2. cacahuate, from Aztec cacahuatl (peanuts). In South America: maní
3. comal, from Aztec comatli (a kind of flat pan to make tortillas)
4. chamaco (niño) (boy)
5. chulo (simpático) (handsome, cute)
6. elote, from Aztec elotl (corn on the cob). In South America: choclo
7. guacamole, from Aztec ahuacamulli (avocado salad)
8. guajolote (pavo) (turkey)
9. güero (rubio) (blond, fair skin)
10. papalote, from Aztec papalotl (cometa) (kite). (Papalotl meant butterfly in Aztec.)
11. popote, from Aztec popotl (paja) (straw)
12. tamal, from Aztec tamalli (tamale)

Archaisms in Spanish

Archaisms are terms or expressions which have become obsolete in modern Spanish:

ansina	for	así
asina	for	así
mesmo	for	mismo
muncho	for	mucho
onde	for	donde
semos	for	somos
truje	for	traje
trujo	for	trajo

Archaisms such as the ones listed above are very common in certain regions of Central and South America, especially in rural areas.

"El vocabulario chileno tiene, igual que el de otros países hispanoamericanos, un apreciable caudal de palabras que dentro del español general se consideran obsoletas o están en vías de convertirse en tales" (Oroz 1966: 32).

Of the words listed above, "ansina," "mesmo," "onde," "semos," and "truje" are listed in Oroz's book as existing in the vocabulary of Chile and the Dominican Republic. These words and several others existing in the Southwest are commonly found in the literature of Latin

America in works such as *Martín Fierro*[6] and in the "novelas costumbristas" of most Latin American countries.

A research study intended to compare and correlate the archaisms in the Southwest and those found in South America would shed new light into the dubious myth of the so called "pocho" language of various regions in this area. It might be a pleasant surprise for many Spanish-speaking people to realize that the vocabulary they use in their everyday conversations dates back to *Don Quijote de la Mancha*[7] and *El Lazarillo de Tormes.*[8] Of course it is not modern up to date vocabulary, but it is not "incorrect" as people tend to label it. On the contrary, it is the vocabulary used by our ancestors.

Metathesis

Metathesis is the change of the order of the elements within the word:

clavar	becomes	cablar
cuchara	becomes	curacha
estómago	becomes	estógamo
pared	becomes	pader
tienda	becomes	teinda

Analogy

Analogy is the process of modifying words on the model of existing patterns, or of creating new words on the basis of such patterns.

puesto	becomes	pona'o (ponado) (from pon + er)
puso	becomes	ponió (from pon + er)
rota	becomes	rompida (from romp + er)
sé	becomes	sabo (from sab + er)
yo he	becomes	yo ha (from hab + er)
hemos	becomes	hamos (from hab + er)

English Phonology

Some of the significant features encountered in the speech of the children are:

1. Reduction of initial consonant clusters such as "sp, st, sl," and "sk."

---

[6] *Martín Fierro* is an epic poem written by the Argentinian poet José Hernández (1834–1886). It was written in two parts: "Ida" in 1872 and "Vuelta" in 1879 It is considered the most representative work of Argentinian literature.

[7] *El Ingenioso Hidalgo Don Quijote de la Mancha* was written in 1605 and is the most outstanding masterpiece of Spanish literature. It was written by Miguel de Cervantes Saavedra (1547–1616) and has been translated into most modern languages.

[8] *El Lazarillo de Tormes* of unknown author was published in 1554 and represents the maximum expression of the "novela picaresca" in Spanish literature.

Examples:

store	>	estór
straight	>	estréyt
slow	>	eslów
spoon	>	espúwn
sky	>	eskáy

This reduction of consonant clusters is to be expected since some double consonant clusters and triple consonant clusters do not exist in Spanish phonology.

2. Reduction of final consonant clusters. Examples:

diamond	>	dayəmən
elephant	>	éləfən

Final consonant clusters do not exist in Spanish either.

3. Elimination of the verbal copula. Examples:

he goin to play
that your car?

In some cases the "s" of "he's going" was an aspirated, diffused sound almost imperceptible.

4. Omission of a weak stressed syllable preceding the primary stress.

Examples:

because	>	kos
equipment	>	kwipmen

Both of these are found in dialectal varieties of English.

5. Shifting of primary stress. Example:

bicycle	>	biysíykol

Most tri-syllabic words in Spanish have the accent on the middle syllable: tricíclo, cabéza, ahóra.

6. Phonemic alternation.

a) $\theta > t$

three	>	triy
thank you	>	tank juw

The interdental voiceless "θ" does not exist in Hispanoamerican Spanish.

b) ḏ > d

father	>	fadər

The interdental "ḏ" becomes dental "d."

c) č > š

chair	>	šer
church	>	šərš
change	>	šeynǰ

Since "š" does not exist in Spanish, there seems to be a tendency to hypercorrection and the "č" becomes "š."

7. Vowel changes and glide simplification. Example:

bicycle > biysíykol

Some of the phonological patterns listed above have also been found in studies designed to record the language of English-speaking monolingual children speaking various dialectal varieties of American English (Shuy 1964).

English Structure

The English structure in the speech of the children showed the following features:

1. Nouns

a) Incorrect form of the plural noun: "The two man are here."

b) Omission of the apostrophe in the noun phrase of the genitive case: "Daddy car is outside."

2. Pronouns

Projection of the -n of "mine" to other genitives, as a result of analogy. Yours—yourn: "That machine is yourn."

3. Adjectives

a) Mixture of inflected comparisons, as a result of analogy. Beautiful—beautifullest: "My doll is the beautifullest."

b) Double comparisons: "This car is more prettier."

4. Verbs

a) Lack of agreement between person and number:
"You is a man."
"We was home."
"My father have a car."
"The one that have the rabbit."

b) Omission of the ed ending of regular verbs: "My daddy work at home yesterday."

c) Omission of the forms of "to be" in sentences with a predicate nominative and in sentences with a present participle:

is > φ

"He a boy." (He's a boy.)

"He going swimming." (He's going swimming.)

d) Omission of verb forms of "have" before the past participle "been":

has > φ

"Daddy been working."

CONCLUSIONS

The preliminary analysis of the recorded speech of this sample group of children showed the following characteristics in their language:

1. *English is the dominant language.* The majority of the children expressed themselves better in English than in Spanish. Whenever they were asked a question in Spanish which they could not answer in that language they would automatically switch to English. When they were asked in English and could not answer in that language they would tend to be silent or say, "I don't know," rather than to switch to Spanish. A larger sample incorporating children from large metropolitan communities compared to those from isolated rural communities will no doubt present a more accurate picture of the language domain.

2. *Spanish is used at home, but Spanish structure and phonology are influenced by English.* Examples of this phenomenon are the hundreds of phrases where English structural or lexical segments were used in sentences uttered while speaking Spanish. There were very few cases where Spanish terms were used in an English sentence.

3. In extemporaneous conversations with the children and their parents, the investigators noticed *a systematic pattern in their language domain.* The parents would speak Spanish among themselves, using quite a few English terms in their conversations; the children would usually speak English among themselves; the parents almost always addressed the children in Spanish and the children would answer in English mixing a few Spanish terms in their speech.

4. *There is significant interference from English to Spanish.* During the various conversations with the investigators, it was noticeable that the Spanish language of both parents and children was always influenced by English whereas the English of the children was more fluent and showed fewer instances of interference. English interference occurs at all levels of the speech of the children, being more preponderant at the lexical level.

5. *Interference from Spanish to English is highly significant at the*

phonological level; it is minor at the lexical and grammatical levels. It was observed that grammatical patterns in English show very few cases of Spanish structural influence. By the same token, only a few Spanish lexical items were recorded in the English interviews. The English phonology of the children showed a high degree of Spanish influence. The most relevant aspects of this influence were the many instances of reduction of consonant clusters, shifting of primary stresses, phonemic alternation, devoicing of consonants, and glide simplification.

6. *There was a below-age-level pattern in the fluency and articulation of common Spanish words.* Most of these words fall in the category of "baby talk."

7. *The homes in rural areas seemed to be more "literate" and more familiar with traditional children's literature than those in urban areas.* Most children in rural areas answered questions concerning fairy tales such as "Little Red Riding Hood" and others, whereas most children in urban areas either got them mixed up with modern tales such as "Batman" or did not answer at all.

The findings of this research stress the need for an accurate assessment of the speech development of bilingual children. For example, the "baby talk" situation in children who are almost six years old would present a serious problem to their success in school. In a bilingual education program, for example, it would be necessary to develop enrichment exercises in Spanish to help them improve and expand their proficiency in their mother tongue.

RECOMMENDATIONS

Some basic ideas and suggestions are given below.

Curriculum

1. Planning of bilingual curriculum to provide for all bilingual students.

2. A program flexible enough to provide for slow learners and bright students as well.

3. The language program should provide for positive transfer and reinforcement.

4. Emphasis on English as a second language in the initial stages.

5. Emphasis on Spanish as the home language and enrichment courses in the language.

6. The bilingual curriculum should be a whole-day curriculum rather than an appendix to the regular school day as it has been in most bilingual programs so far.

Teachers

1. All universities in the Southwest should offer a major in bilingual education.

2. Non-Spanish-speaking teachers who are in charge of the education of Spanish-speaking children should have at least six hours of college Spanish or its equivalent, and a minimum degree of fluency in the language.

3. The preparation of bilingual teachers should start with the identification of prospective teachers in the high school, and also in the freshman and sophomore years of colleges in the Southwest.

4. The training of bilingual teachers should include some basic knowledge of linguistics, psycholinguistics, and sociolinguistics, with special emphasis on the status of languages existing in linguistic borders.

5. Supervisors and instructors of bilingual teachers should have all the qualifications mentioned in No. 4 plus a good command of both languages and adequate training in supervision of instruction.

6. The whole faculty of bilingual schools should be trained in programs with a multidisciplinary approach to teaching, with emphasis on anthropological linguistics and related areas.

7. There should be a special course on the psychology of bilingualism and its implications in bilingual teaching.

8. Universities should start offering a major in counseling for bilingual children.

9. It would be advisable to found a bilingual teachers college to prepare educators, administrators, supervisors, and coordinators of bilingual schools all over the United States.

Materials

All elementary schools in the Southwest should have:

1. A good supply of bilingual dictionaries.

2. Bilingual textbooks where some consideration is given to the proficiency of the children in either language.

3. Audio-visual aids especially designed for bilingual instruction.

4. A good supply of books in Spanish with cartoons, tales, poems, riddles, and traditional stories from Spanish-speaking countries.

Needed Research

1. It is necessary to encourage investigators to study the area of language acquisition in bilinguals.

2. A survey of the psychological, emotional, and intellectual aspects influencing the learning process in bilingual students.

3. A systematic study of child language (baby talk) in order to find

out to what extent it perpetuates itself in the speech of bilinguals and in what way it affects learning.

4. A study of the validity and reliability of tests for monolinguals as applied to bilinguals.

5. An appraisal of the several tests for bilinguals that have been applied during the twentieth century, whose results have been contradictory.

6. A survey of tests being developed and the preparation of a battery of tests especially designed for bilinguals.

7. Study the language aptitude of bilinguals.

8. Study attitudes of bilinguals toward their mother tongue and the implications this may have in terms of bilingual education.

9. An appraisal of communication media, especially educational television and its possible application to bilingual education.

10. Study the effectiveness of pedagogical devices such as the audio-lingual approach, pattern practice exercises, substitution tables, etc., in the language instruction of bilinguals.

11. Survey the language situation in bilingual communities that are considered disadvantaged as compared to bilingual communities with a higher status.

Institutions

Considering the real "renaissance" of the Spanish language and culture in the Southwest, it might be advisable to found some institutions such as the ones listed below, in order to "pulir y dar esplendor al idioma español."

1. Instituto de Filología del Sudoeste. This institution would be in charge of research in the areas of: lingüística histórica, lingüística aplicada, bilingüismo, sicolingüística, sociolingüística, gramática transformativa (generativa), lingüística antropológica, and other related areas.

2. Instituto de Literatura del Sudoeste. This institution would be in charge of disseminating poetry, drama, novel, essays, short stories, tales, and other literary works written in Spanish. It could also disseminate information concerning the new developments of literature in other countries of Spanish-speaking America.

3. Academia Correspondiente de la Lengua. This would be an institution affiliated to the Real Academia Española. Its objectives would be to disseminate information on the Spanish language of the Southwest. It would not be a dogmatic normative institution, but rather a clearinghouse such as the Clearinghouse that exists in London for the English language.

It is necessary to make English-speaking and Spanish-speaking people aware of the fact that in an area like the Southwest, where two languages are in contact, it is bound to have transfer, borrowings, and structural interference from one language to the other. There seems to be a certain degree of scorn toward the Spanish-speaking person who uses words such as "lonche" (from "lunch"), "puchar" (from "to push"), and "mapear" (from "to mop") in his Spanish, and people refer to his language as "Tex-Mex", identifying this term with low quality.

Nevertheless, English-speakers use terms such as "lariat" (from "la reata"), "mustang" (from Mexican Spanish "mestengo", from Spanish "mesteño"), "barbecue" (from Spanish "barbacoa"), and absolutely no one refers to this as "Mex-Tex" (word coined by the author).

The same as the Spanish-speaker addresses the waitress and says, "Quiero un hot dog, por favor," the English-speaking person will enter the restaurant and say, "I'd like to have two tamales." There is no way for them to be able to find a word in English for "tamales" and a Spanish term for "hot dog." (The literal translation might be rather awkward.) This "Spanglish" situation is typical of communities where the local vernacular is highly influenced by two unrelated languages, in this case a Germanic and a Romance language.

Spanish itself has a lot of geographical dialectal varieties which are found in various places of the Southwest and Latin America. For example, the English word "pig" has the following Spanish equivalents, all of which are dictionary terms: puerco, cerdo, marrano, chancho, lechón, and cochino. When people mow their "lawn" in Mexico they cut "zacate;" in Puerto Rico, "grama;" in Cuba, "yerba;" in Chile, "pasto." Nevertheless, the word "césped" is also used in all of these countries, but it is a more sophisticated term. When one flies a kite it is a "volantín" in Chile, a "cometa" in Cuba, a "chiringa" in Puerto Rico, and a "papalote" or "huila" in Mexico and some areas of the Southwest. "Huila" also has other connotations which fall in the area of Spanish argot.[9]

The author believes that these findings, conclusions, and recommendations might be of value in the preparation of teachers and teaching materials for bilingual education in Texas and the Southwest. They could help in the design of curriculum for language instruction, especially in those programs which comprise areas of enrichment of the Spanish mother tongue in combination with English as a second language. They could also provide basic information for testing and evaluation.

[9] In 1962, the author wrote an article on "La Riqueza Lingüística de los Sinónimos en Nuestra Lengua." It will be updated and made available in mimeographed form to teachers in bilingual programs.

The results of the project point out the need to extend this type of research to the rest of Texas and the Southwest, and to other areas of language acquisition.

REFERENCES

FERGUSON, CHARLES
   1964   Baby Talk in Six Languages. In "The Ethnography of Communication." John J. Gumperz and Dell Hymes, eds. *American Anthropologist* 66 (6 pt. 2).
KENISTON, HAYWARD
   1938   *Spanish Idiom List.* The Macmillan Company, New York.
LEHMAN, WINIFRED P.
   1966   *Glossary of Linguistic Terminology.* Doubleday and Company, Garden City, New York.
OROZ, RODOLFO
   1966   *La Lengua Castellana en Chile.* Instituto de Filología, Universidad de Chile, Santiago, Chile.
PEI, MARIO
   1966   *Glossary of Linguistic Terminology.* Doubleday and Company, Garden City, New York.
RODRIGUEZ BOU, ISMAEL
   1952   *Recuento de Vocabulario Español, Consejo Superior de Enseñanza.* Editado por OEA y UNESCO. Universidad de Puerto Rico, Río Piedras, Puerto Rico.
SANTAMARIA, FRANCISCO J.
   1959   *Diccionario de Mejicanismos.* Editorial Porrúa, Ciudad de Méjico.
SHUY, ROGER, ED.
   1964   Social Dialects and Language Learning. Cooperative Research Project No. OE 5-10-148
THORNDIKE, EDWARD L.
   1921   *The Teacher's Word Book.* Teachers College Press, Columbia University, New York.
WEINREICH, URIEL
   1966   *Languages in Contact.* Mouton and Company, The Hague.

6. *The Development of Semantic Categories in Spanish-English and Navajo-English Bilingual Children*

RODNEY W. YOUNG

Young's paper deals with a basic question in cross-language research: whether the meaning system of a bilingual child is the same as that of a monolingual. He found that when bilingual children were tested for comprehension of semantic categories they showed patterns of difficulty that were different from those of English monolingual children but that were similar for their two languages. The Navajo-English case seems to reflect Navajo semantic factors while the difficulty pattern for the Spanish-English group reflects non-linguistic factors. These findings are in agreement with a theory of semantic markedness.

This paper was presented to the Conference on Child Language held in Chicago, November 22–24, 1971. The Conference was sponsored by the Association Internationale de Linguistique Appliquée, the Center for Applied Linguistics, and the American Council on the Teaching of Foreign Languages.

As CHILDREN acquire language, they gain control over an immensely complicated set of systems, and in acquiring the meaning or semantic system of a language, children come to recognize the many subtle differences in meanings of words and word relationships. For example, a child gradually realizes that not all motor vehicles are cars; some are pickups and some are trucks. As he gains in his perceptual capacity, his language reflects this increasing ability to differentiate and categorize (Lenneberg 1967). However, a meaning system of a language is considerably more complex than the labels of objects. The child must come to realize that *if* and *unless* are not the same in meaning (Hatch 1969), and that *more than* and *less than* are also not synonymous (Donaldson and Wales 1970). He must also acquire the subtle difference between expressions that are synonymous in one context but not in another, such as *return* and *take back*. It is permissible either to return or take back a book to the library, but it is not permissible either to return or take back a friend to the zoo (Bolinger 1968). The child further must realize that expressions of equality will be affected differently by negation. *Equal to* and *as many as* are quite similar in meaning, but *not equal to* and *not as many as* are obviously different.

Many of these subtleties of the meaning system of a language appear to be forbiddingly complex; nonetheless, almost all children eventually gain adequate control over the semantic level of their language. The current controversy over semantics in linguistic theory provides considerable motivation for investigation of this element, especially in a cross-language situation. Different languages exhibit their own particular semantic systems, and study of how the systems differ can throw light on what is universal to language and what is specific to a single language.

The interesting question and subject of this paper is whether children who learn a second language—English in this case—will develop the same semantic system as monolingual children or whether their semantic system will be different because of linguistic or cultural interference. A second, closely related question is whether the bilingual child develops separate meaning systems for his two languages or whether he operates by means of a single system.

This paper will present evidence from a study investigating these questions by comparing the relative difficulty of certain semantic constructions in comprehension tests for two groups of young bilingual children: Spanish-English bilinguals and Navajo-English bilinguals. A group of English monolingual children provide a basis for comparison. These two groups of bilingual children were chosen because Spanish and English are semantically similar languages, and Navajo and English are semantically dissimilar languages in the area being investigated.

In this study ten categories of numeric comparison (five positive and five negative) are used which express the three basic concepts of superiority of number, equality of number, and inferiority of number plus their denials. Each of these categories includes three syntactically different sentences, which are parallel in each category except that half the categories are negative. In this way syntax can be investigated as well as semantics. The sentences were translated into Spanish and Navajo when the categories were semantically equivalent, and each bilingual child was tested for comprehension of the thirty sentences in English and thirty sentences in his other language for accuracy and latency (response time). This methodology is an adaptation of the one developed by Kennedy (1970).

The following two tables illustrate the ten semantic categories in English used in this study and the three syntactic types established for each category.

TABLE 1

Semantic Categories of Numeric Comparisons

Semantic Category	Symbol	Linguistic Construction
1 Superiority	$>$	*more than*
2 Denial of Superiority	$\not>$	*not more than*
3 Inferiority	$<$	*less than*
4 Denial of Inferiority	$\not<$	*not less than*
5 Positive Equality	$=^+$	*as many as*
6 Denial of Positive Equality	$\neq^+$	*not as many as*
7 Negative Equality	$=^-$	*as few as*
8 Denial of Negative Equality	$\neq^-$	*not as few as*
9 Neutral Equality	$=^0$	*equal to*
10 Denial of Neutral Equality	$\neq^0$	*not equal to*

TABLE 2

Syntactic Types Within Semantic Categories

1 There are (not) more X than Y.
2 There is (not) a larger number of X than Y.
3 The number of X is (not) larger than the number of Y.

The translations of the sentences into Spanish and Navajo were done by native speakers and were verified by back translations. The Spanish paralleled the English in meaning and syntactic types and reflected the language of northern New Mexico. Two informants were used for the Spanish and both agreed that the meaning system of the ten numeric comparisons was the same as it would be for English. For example, the denial of positive equality (*not as many as*) and the Spanish equivalent (*no tantos como*) both unambiguously mean numeric inferiority of the first noun mentioned in relation to the second. For the

Navajo version three informants were used plus five back translations. The first difficulty was the absence of the desired syntactic variety. One informant provided different types but only through use of the English word *number;* two informants agreed fairly well on the single syntactic type that was used after certain exceptions had been resolved. The Navajo version was left with only one syntactic type rather than the three in English and Spanish. This is not to claim that the pattern used is the only one available; the claim is that the pattern was readily understood for the back translations and seemed compatible with Young and Morgan's (1958) explanation of the comparative construction in Navajo.

The concern over syntactic variety led to a more basic problem—directness of meaning. The relationship of numeric superiority can be expressed directly in English through the sentence *There are more X than Y.* The relationship also can be indirectly expressed by saying *There are many X; there are few Y.* Navajo informants produced comparative sentences that could be literally translated to parallel the indirect English expression just mentioned. They also produced constructions parallel to the English direct comparison, lending some support to a parallelism between the languages in directness of meaning for this category. The real concern came with the English construction *There are as many X as Y.* The Navajo equivalent would be parallel to an English construction *The X and the Y are equal and they are many.* A similar situation exists for constructions of *as few as.* The absence in Navajo of direct comparatives for equality which are built from adjectives of superiority and inferiority suggest that these categories (positive and negative equality) do not "directly" exist in Navajo. The clue comes when these expressions are modified by negation and they do not produce a parallel meaning. In English *not as many as* is not simple denial and unambiguously means less than. Negating the Navajo counterparts results in something like *The X and Y are not equal and they are many.* Four categories then could not be "directly" translated into Navajo and maintain a meaning system parallel with English and were omitted from the Navajo version.

The subjects were first and fourth graders recognized as bilinguals by their teachers and freely admitting to be so. All subjects were screened for knowledge of the lexical items used in the testing and general knowledge of the types of constructions in both languages. Subjects were not used without successfully completing the screening. The thirty sentences in English and the thirty in the other language were randomized and presented in blocks of ten sentences alternating between languages by blocks. The subjects were randomly assigned as to which language and which block of sentences they would begin with. They listened to tapes of the sentences which were recorded by native speakers and selected one of two pictures (rear-projected on two small screens in front of the subject) as a correct illustration of the meaning. In addition to accuracy, a latency measure was obtained. Figure 1 presents the type of illustrations used with an accompanying sample sentence. The letters represent drawings of common objects selected for their cultural neutrality. The relative positions of the compared objects were controlled experimentally.

From this testing came accuracy and latency scores for each semantic category. Each language group established a pattern of the relative difficulty of the ten semantic categories in English and these patterns were then contrasted without any quantitative comparisons. The bilingual's performance in his first language then provided an approach for explaining any differences. It would be expected that the Spanish-English group would parallel the English monolinguals but that the Navajo-English group would deviate from the pattern because of language differences.

The idea of patterns of difficulty of the ten semantic categories presupposes meaningful differences among them. These ten categories express the three basic concepts of superiority, equality, and inferiority plus their denials in subtly different ways. The concept of superiority can be expressed by *more than* and it can also be expressed by *not as few as*. Similarly, inferiority can be expressed by *less than* and *not as many as*. Equality can be expressed by *equal to, as many as*, and *as few as*. Of these last three only *equal to* can be denied simply. The previous examples show that negation of *as many as* and *as few as* unambiguously represent expressions of inferiority and superiority respectively. Denial of *more than* and *less than* is simple and direct and means no more than just that. In other words, *not more than* can be factually illustrated by either equality or inferiority. *Not less than* offers the two possibilities of equality and superiority. When these categories refer to the same basic concept, the point is that there is also a difference in semantic structure and

Figure 1

REPRESENTATIVE ILLUSTRATION FOR TESTING

"There are more Z than W."

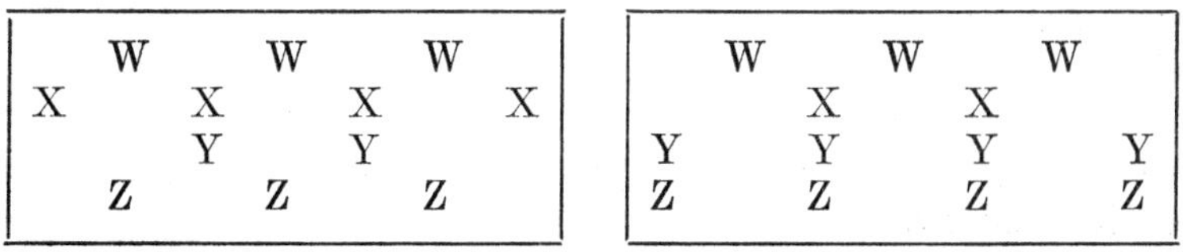

meaning. For example *more than* and *not as few as* both refer to the same basic concept. The linguistic form is obviously different and the semantic construction is also different. The semantic information contained in *more than* is less complex than semantic information in *not as few as*.

The semantic theory of Katz & Fodor (1963), Katz (1967), and Bierwisch (1967) offer an approach to explaining this by means of semantic features, which are considered universal for languages (although any particular combination of features is not). By means of features, each of the semantic structures for the ten categories can be represented and these features can also provide a way to account for the hierarchy of difficulty of these categories (the use of features and a theory of semantic markedness will be dealt with later).

The method of study that is used for this paper determines the hierarchy of difficulty of the ten semantic categories in English for each language group and then compares the hierarchies. The first significant finding is that first grade children do not sufficiently differentiate the categories to be able to establish a true hierarchy. There was little, if any, significant difference among the ten categories for first grade children; scores were generally low indicating that the younger children of all groups, regardless of language, were not comprehending the categories much beyond pure chance. However, the fourth graders sharply differentiated the categories on both accuracy and latency. This developmental finding strongly supports the notion that much of language acquisition is still going on after school age. With fourth grade performance strongly suitable for the technique of comparing hierarchies, the first analysis permitted a comparison of English monolingual children from two widely divergent areas. Kennedy's (1970) study was located in Los Angeles and the monolingual children for this study were in Albuquerque, New Mexico. The rank order correlation of the first eight categories (Kennedy's study did not include categories 9 and 10) was quite high in accuracy ($\rho = .958**$) and also significant for latency ($\rho = .786*$). This replication of Kennedy's study is in itself a significant finding. Two groups of monolinguals from distinctly separated areas found these semantic categories similarly difficult. This high degree of similarity suggests a certain degree of cognitive commonality in processing the information in the semantic categories. Certainly this finding supports the use of the English monolingual group as a base for comparing the two bilingual groups.

For the cross-language emphasis, the primary finding was that both groups of bilinguals established different difficulty patterns than the monolingual group. Figure 2 illustrates the relative pattern for all three groups in accuracy.

Figure 2
CATEGORY HIERARCHIES IN ENGLISH ACCURACY

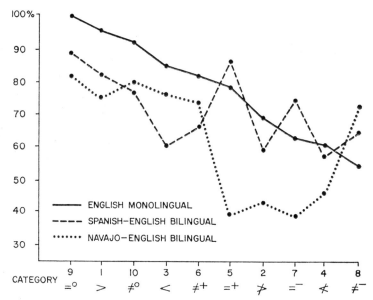

It is noticeable from this comparison that much of the deviation comes from categories 5, 7, and 8. For the Spanish-English group, positive equality, negative equality, and denial of negative equality (categories 5, 7, and 8) are relatively easier than the other categories in comparison to the English monolinguals. If one supports the notion of identical semantic structures for English and Spanish, this relative preference for these three categories must be explained on the basis of familiarity and preference rather than inherent complexity. This indicates that it is not only necessary to investigate language performance linguistically, but it is also necessary to investigate purely psychological factors as well.

For the Navajo group it was expected that positive and negative equality would be relatively more difficult because of the absence of these categories in Navajo. This prediction is upheld by the data. The interesting point is how negating these categories removes the relative difficulty. Generally negating a difficult category would be expected to increase its difficulty. However, if the sentence *There are as many X as Y* is being erroneously comprehended as superiority of X over Y because *many* is connected to X alone, then denial of the *many* removes the source of error. The sentence is interpreted as *There are not many X in relation to the number of Y.* Interpreting denial of positive and negative equality in this manner is much the same as what the deep structure of the construction would be. Roughly the deep structure of negative equality would be *There are few X/ there are few Y.* Negating the structure produces *NEG + There are few X/ there are few Y.* The first structure uses *few* (or *many*) for equality while Navajo would express the equality and then add the number sense. The denial, however, is similar to the Navajo which roughly translates *These X are not few/ these Y are few.* The Navajo child is used to a category that is expressed seemingly by both a positive and a negative. He puts the English sentences into this system and makes errors in comprehension. Navajo does not have positive equality that is built from *There are many X/ there are many Y.* This system is used only for meanings of superiority or inferiority. These data then would seem to suggest that the difference between the English and Navajo semantic systems is at the base of the Navajo-English bilingual's performance.

The latency measure (using right and wrong responses) generally supports the accuracy measure for the Spanish-English group as indicated by a significant rank order correlation ($\rho = .663^*$). However, the latency measure for the Navajo does not even differentiate the categories unless only the correct responses are used. Little difference exists for the Spanish-English group or the English group between latency of all responses and the latency of the correct-only responses. Time is not a significant variable for the Navajo unless he has some confidence in his understanding of the categories. The main finding from latency is that all three groups are quite similar in response time (correct-only responses for the Navajo) regardless of differences in accuracy. Latency seems to be a measure of confidence which is quite similar for all groups.

Examination of the three syntactic types in English reveals no particular preference or ease in comprehension of one type over another for the Spanish-English group or the monolingual group. However, the second syntactic type (*There is a larger number of X than Y*) was significant for the Navajo children. This unexpected showing is best accounted for by noting that the order of the comparison device and the nouns being compared is opposite from the order of the Navajo sentence where the comparison is last.

To answer the question of whether the bilingual child is operating with one or two meaning systems for his two languages, the hierarchies of difficulty from the child's two languages can be compared. For the Spanish-English group all ten categories can be used while only the six mutual categories can be used for the Navajo-English group. The rank order correlations for accuracy ($\rho = .821^{**}$ for the Spanish-English group and $\rho = .943^{**}$ for the Navajo-English group) strongly support the presence of a single meaning system at this level of development. This suggests a certain universality of semantics and even of some of the semantic categories in language comprehension. The latency index is similar ($\rho = .810^{**}$) for the Spanish-English group, but no correlation is possible with the Navajo group because correct-only responses are contributing scores in English, but total responses are in Navajo.

It seems apparent from the data that semantic categories are definitely significant factors in comprehension for all groups. These categories are sufficiently powerful in determining comprehension that absence of them in one language greatly increases their difficulty in another. The semantic system of one language forces interpretation of another language accordingly. The bilingual is eventually confronted with the task of acquiring a new semantic system to express the same basic meanings. However, at this state of development he definitely appears to be functioning with a single meaning system. Furthermore, presence of identical semantic categories in two languages does not guarantee the same hierarchy of difficulty as for the monolingual of the target language. Other factors are needed to explain these differences, such as preference and familiarity.

These results from analyzing comprehension by means of semantic categories can be formalized by extending a semantic theory based on features into a theory of semantic markedness on the same principle that Chomsky and Halle (1968) use with phonological features. The simple presence or absence of a feature fails to reveal whether that feature is intrinsic or natural to the meaning, hence not adding to its complexity. Clark (1969) establishes a principle of lexical marking to account for the extra difficulty of the negative half of a pair of polar adjectives. *More* is not as complex in meaning as is *less*. Clark uses features within a binary system to formalize this difference. Using Clark's basic principles but formalizing the use of features into markedness theory can account for this difference more realistically than the binary system. Both *more* and *less* contain the feature of "polarity," indicating their existence as polar pairs; however, *more* is unmarked or natural as to "polarity" and *less* is marked. This captures the asymmetrical nature of polar adjectives and formalizes that *less* exists in contrast to *more*, the basic member of the pair. For other examples, *equal to* can be differentiated from both *as many as* and *as few as* by being unmarked for a feature "equative" while both the positive and negative equality would be marked for "equative," indicating the unnaturalness of their use in expressions of equality. *As many as* would further be differentiated from *as few as* by the previously mentioned feature "polarity" which is unmarked for *as many as* and marked for *as few as*. The principle determining complexity is that only unmarked features do not add to the complexity of meaning.

Each of the ten semantic categories can be represented with features according to markedness theory and a hierarchy of difficulty predicted on the basis of the number of marked features. The English monolingual's hierarchy highly correlates in accuracy with the one predicted by the theory ($\rho = .870^{**}$). Also important is that this theoretical representation of semantic categories can be used to represent the categories from other languages. Positive and negative equality are marked for "equative" while neutral equality is unmarked for the same feature as are the Navajo categories of equality.

Although this theoretical representation is sketchily presented here, it is not difficult to imagine its usefulness in semantic analysis. Semantics, like phonology, may well be representable from a universal set of features when formalized within a theory of markedness.

In review, this study has shown that bilingual children do not parallel monolingual children in patterns of difficulty of semantic categories. Categories not present in their first language are appreciably more difficult in relation to the other categories than for monolingual children. Even when categories are present in the child's first language, factors such as preference and familiarity are also significant. Semantic categories do appear to be important determiners of comprehension especially when compared to syntax. A theory of semantic markedness can appropriately account for the relative difficulty of different categories and be quite suitable for use across language boundaries.

REFERENCES

BIERWISCH, MANFRED
    1967 Some Semantic Universals of German Adjectivals. *Foundations of Language* 3: 1–36.
BOLINGER, DWIGHT
    1968 *Aspects of Language.* Harcourt, Brace & World, Inc., New York.
CHOMSKY, NOAM, AND MORRIS HALLE
    1968 *The Sound Patterns of English.* Harper & Row, New York.
CLARK, HERBERT H.
    1969 Linguistic Processes in Deductive Reasoning. *Psychological Review* 76: 387–404.
DONALDSON, MARGARET, AND ROGER J. WALES
    1970 On the Acquisition of Some Relational Terms. In *Cognition and the Development of Language.* John R. Hayes, ed. John Wiley & Sons, Inc., New York.
HATCH, EVELYN
    1969 Four Experimental Studies in the Syntax of Young Children. Unpublished PhD dissertation. University of California, Los Angeles.
KATZ, JERROLD, J.
    1967 Recent Issues in Semantic Theory. *Foundations of Language* 3: 124–194.

Katz, Jerrold J., and Jerry A. Fodor
  1963   The Structure of a Semantic Theory. *Language* 39: 170–210.
Kennedy, Graeme D.
  1970   Children's Comprehension of English Sentences Comparing Quantities
         of Discrete Objects. Unpublished PhD dissertation. University of Cali-
         fornia, Los Angeles.
Lenneberg, Eric
  1967   *Biological Foundations of Language.* John Wiley & Sons, New York.
Young, Robert W., and William Morgan
  1958   *The Navaho Language.* Deseret Book Company (A publication of the
         Education Division, United States Indian Service), Salt Lake City.

7. A Kaleidoscope of Images: Mexicans and Chicanos as Reflected in American Literature

CECIL ROBINSON

This article demonstrates how creative writing reflects the realities of the cultural confrontations between two quite different societies in the borderlands of the Southwest. The negative stereotyped images that the American formed of the Mexican from the days of earliest contact have continued to influence Anglo-American and Mexican-American relationships to the present day, robbing the Mexican-American of his dignity and pride in a rich cultural heritage.

THERE ARE a number of tribal groups throughout the earth whose name for themselves is simply "the people." For example, the Navajo Indians in the Southwest of the United States call themselves *Diné* 'the People.' It is probably true of most self-assured cultures that their members, at least implicitly, think of themselves as being *the* people, and of others as being somewhat less so. But in a multicultural society such as ours, who are *the* people? Until quite recently one could have answered with little hesitation that Nordic Protestants considered themselves implicitly, and often quite explicitly, to be *the* people of the United States. Despite the evidence that WASP (White Anglo-Saxon Protestant) self-assurance has been somewhat shaken of late, the main stream of American culture is still considerably ethnocentric. It is a curious fact, for example, that despite the willingness of the English language to absorb a great number of foreign words, Americans have a pronounced aversion to learning other languages. The current agitation among students and some professors to have foreign-language requirements dropped in our universities can be taken to be a reassertion of our old provincialism. But of course, the time has distinctly passed when any one segment of our society can afford to act as though it were *the* people of the United States and as though Anglo-American culture were the only acceptable cultural expression within our borders.

Though the record of "the dominant culture" in its reactions toward other groups has undeniably been one of retrenchment, this record has not, historically, been a static one. Reverberations of the shiftings and rumblings that have occurred as our society has groped toward an understanding of its own nature are recorded in the seismograph of our literature. It is here that some of the most vivid impressions of the psychology of our cultural history can be found. An examination of the changing images or stereotypes of racial or cultural groups as they appear in our literature can serve to illuminate the cultural processes that we are still very much engaged in.

In the Southwest of the United States, the confrontation between Anglo-Americans and Mexican-Americans has produced one of the most persistent cultural storm fronts, and the cracklings of this collision, as heard in our literature, are particularly revealing. The westward-pushing Americans, advancing their frontiers into Mexican and Indian territories, could well have called themselves *Diné*—'the people'—and in effect they did. The doctrine of Manifest Destiny was the declaration of the divine right of the Anglo-Americans to subsume "the lesser breeds within the law" in order to fulfill their coast-to-coast destiny.

SELF-CONFIDENT LITERATURE

What impresses one about the early American literature of the borderlands is the immense self-confidence that it exudes. The writers of this literature seemed to have no doubt that Protestant American standards and attitudes represented the apex of civilized behavior and in effect constituted universal law, an absolute standard that others, unfortunately, fell too far short of. The culture of Mexico represented to these writers an affront to their major convictions. The ethic of thrift and hard work, the faith in progress through science and technology, the divine sanction upon meticulous personal hygiene, the "decencies" insisted upon in sexual matters, in sum, the Puritan culture as modified by frontier individualism and egalitarianism, seemed to run directly counter to the culture of the Mexico that the pioneers encountered, infiltrated, and finally overran. Here was a foreign country where the Romish priesthood seemed to rule as the foremost of several privileged castes in a hierarchical society. Furthermore, these priests in their unquestioned power and sybaritic way of life had clearly forsaken the true Christian mission. As for scientific enlightenment and modern notions of progress, these benighted Mexicans, according to our frontier writers, might as well be living in the Middle Ages. Subjected to tyranny and the rule of superstition, these people remained at the level of barbarism, sensuality, and lawlessness. And what more could be expected of a people who had lowered themselves to a state of general cohabitation with the Indians and had thus forfeited the right to be considered "white"?

These early writers of the frontier, unlike modern American novelists and poets, were in general accord with the society from which they had sprung. With a few exceptions, their productions were not, in the modern sense of the word, literary. They were the writers of diaries, letters, and journals. They were mountain men, soldiers, government officials, frontier traders, or just adventurers. The fact that they did not view themselves as literateurs makes their work the more valuable to modern students of American society. The social attitudes expressed by these writers were not those of a group set apart but were thoroughly characteristic of the American people of the mid nineteenth century.

One strain that is evident in this early literature is the missionary spirit, an enthusiasm still observable in aspects of our foreign policy. There seems to have been a corollary to the doctrine of Manifest Destiny. Not only was it to be the destiny of the United States to conquer all peoples who interposed themselves between the westward-pushing frontier and the Pacific coast, but it was also United States destiny to regenerate the heirs to the corrupted Roman Empire, namely the Mexicans. In fact, the God-given task of regeneration was used by North American orators and writers as a justification of the Mexican War, as in Justin H. Smith's monumental history of that conflict, which appeared as late as 1919. Expressions of this attitude can still be found in such popularized versions of the war as *The Story of the Mexican War* by Robert Selph Henry, 1950.

During the periods of the Texas Revolution and the Mexican War a literary genre arose known as the Texas Romances. These were hardback books, considerably more pretentious in style than the popular paperback Beadle and Adams' Dime Novels. When the Texan heroes of these "romances" were not slaughtering Mexicans they were lecturing them. In one of these books, *Mexico Versus Texas* by Anthony Ganilh, a Texan is explaining to a captain of the Mexican army why it has become the special mission of the United States to regenerate Mexico by means of military conquest. The Texan enumerates several points of character in which he claims the Northern nations to be superior to the Southern, but he puts his emphasis upon sexual morality. The following is an excerpt from his sermon:

> In point of chastity, also, the most important and influential qualification of Northern nations, we are infinitely superior to you—Lust is, with us, hateful and shameful; with you, it is a matter of indifference. *This* is the chief curse of the South: the leprosy which unnerves both body and mind. It is what caused the Roman empire to sink under the assaults of the Northern barbarians. Notwithstanding all the science, policy, and refinement of the *Queen of the Earth*, she was struck, as with moral consumption, by this vice; and all her strength was swept away by a deluge from the North. A mighty wave is again starting from the same point, and it will sweep even to the Equator. The Southern races must be renewed, and the United States are the *officina gentium* for the new Continent (Ganilh 1838: 205–206).

A modern Mexican historian, José Fuentes Mares, has emphasized this aspect of the historic conflict between the United States and Mexico. In his biography of Joel R. Poinsett, first U.S. minister to Mexico and a man accused by many Mexicans of having been a prime agent of North American subversion in Mexico, Fuentes Mares characterizes his subject as a man who "sought the indulgence of a healthy nation for a depraved one, of an enlightened people for an ignorant, of a Protestant toward a Catholic nation, of the Anglo Saxon toward the Spanish. Poinsett was, in Mexico, the advance guard of the Army of Salvation" (Fuentes Mares 1960: 88, translation mine).

There were several special circumstances which abetted racial and cultural tensions throughout the borderlands in the mid-nineteenth century. Of definite importance was the fact that the majority of the Anglo-American settlers in the Southwest came originally from the Southern states. Their long association with black slavery had instilled set attitudes toward people of darker complexion. The borderland chronicles are filled with examples of the most unabashed racism directed toward dark-skinned Mexicans. One of the Texas romances referred to Santa Ana as "that yaller nigger."

SOCIAL DIFFERENTIATION

Apart from racial differences, there existed in the borderlands a marked social difference which impeded compatibility between Mexicans and Anglo-Americans. The Mexico which the North American frontiersmen first encountered was in that period of its history known as the *criollo* era. These were the years following closely upon the wars of Independence. The hated Spanish bureaucrats, the *gachupines*, who had ruled Mexico under the colonial regime, were thrown out of the country after the establishment of Mexican independence. Into their former offices stepped the *criollos*, persons who claimed to be of purely Spanish blood but who were born in Mexico. The *criollos* formed the native Mexican aristocracy, and during the period encompassed by the Texas Revolution and the Mexican-American War the *criollos* held the important posts in the government, the army, and the church. Antonio López de Santa Ana represented the quintessence of *criollo* society.

When the Anglo-Americans first entered Texas under Mexican rule and first began to infiltrate into New Mexico, Arizona, and California, they encountered a society radically different from their own. As Frederick Jackson Turner has emphasized, North American frontier society was characterized by a considerable degree of egalitarianism. It was probably the most classless society that we have every known—with the ironic exception of the institution of black slavery along the southern frontier region. These frontiersmen found themselves living in a Mexican society which was rigidly structured along class lines. *Criollo* Mexican society, especially in its northern reaches, consisted of an elegant aristocracy supported by an ignorant and oppressed peasantry. There was very little that could be called middle class. The Anglo-Americans, therefore, who, if they had been challenged to identify themselves by class, would probably vaguely have identified themselves with the middle class, could not find among the Mexicans their opposite numbers. These frontiersmen disdained to associate themselves with the Mexican peons while at the same time they themselves were socially rejected by the *criollo* aristocracy.

One side of this social situation can be illustrated by a letter written to the president of Mexico by General Manuel Mier y Terán in 1828. This officer had been sent by the Mexican government ostensibly to survey sections of the northern boundary region. His real mission, however, was to observe and report on the North American colonists in Texas. Rumors of growing rebelliousness in Austin's colony had reached the Mexican capital. In his letter, sent from Nacodoches, Texas, Mier y Terán wrote:

> It would cause you the same chagrin that it has caused me to see the opinion that is held of our nation by these foreign colonists, since, with the exception of some few who have journeyed to the capital, they know no other Mexicans than the inhabitants about here, and excepting the authorities necessary to any form of society, the said inhabitants are the most ignorant of Negroes and Indians. . . . Thus I tell myself that it could not be otherwise than from such a state of affairs should arise an antagonism between the Mexicans and foreigners, which is not the least of the smoldering fires which I have discovered (Howren 1913: 395).

The other side of the social situation in the borderlands is also to be found in the literature of the Southwest. A notable example appears in one of the novels of the late Harvey Fergusson, *Grant of Kingdom*. Fergusson, mostly through the medium of fiction, brilliantly presented the complex social interrelations of Mexican and Anglo during the formation period of the American Southwest. The scene in *Grant of Kingdom* is the New Mexico of the 1830's. The situation is that of an American mountain man, Jean Ballard, who was attempting to initiate a courtship with Consuelo, the daughter of a wealthy and established *criollo* family, the Coronels. Fergusson describes the frustrations that Ballard encountered:

> For the first time in his life he felt the massive, inert resistance of old established things, of a people fortified by wealth and custom and tradition, by a way of life stronger than they were, a social pattern which was a power in itself. They did not hate him as a person but they hated anything alien. Family was everything to them. Their whole society was a great family and it was organized to repel intrusion. They did not have to insult him or reject him or even close a door to him. They could freeze him out and wait him out. He might come and sip chocolate for months and even for years and never pass any of the barriers of custom and manner that were set up against him (Fergusson 1950: 32–33).

One American who did manage to gain an entree into wealthy *criollo* households, perhaps because of his official position, was John Russell Bartlett, a boundary commissioner. In his *Personal Narrative*, published in 1854, Bartlett shows himself to be properly impressed by the Mexican aristocracy, but he uses his praise of the *criollos* as an occasion to excoriate lower-class Mexicans. Describing those who entertained him in Texas, he wrote: "These are a few respectable old Spanish families at El Paso, who possess much intelligence, as well as that elegance and dignity of manner which characterized their ancestors. ... A vast gulf intervenes between these Castilians and the masses, who are a mixed breed, possessing none of the virtue of their European ancestors, but all their vices, with those of the aborigines superadded" (Bartlett 1854, Vol. 1: 91). This view of the Mexican mestizo is echoed in many of the chronicles of the borderlands.

Given the polarization of Mexican society during the *criollo* era, the Anglo-Americans reacted with disdain for the masses and a mixture of resentment and grudging admiration for the classes. The result in the American literature of the borderlands was a procession of images, mostly unflattering, of Mexican types.

THE SPANISH LEGEND

The 1890s in California saw the rise of a curious phenomenon, "the California myth." That state, whose earlier record of cruelty and injustice toward Indians and Mexicans has been documented in a recent study (Heizer and Almquist 1971), suddenly decided toward the end of the nineteenth century that it had a priceless heritage in its "Spanish" past. This was the era in American history known as the gilded age, and the sudden appearance of the mirage of the Spanish legend in California was produced by a mixture of nostalgia and hucksterism. The legend found its literary voice in two novels which became immensely popular, Helen Hunt Jackson's *Ramona*, a book which had its serious side, and Gertrude Atherton's *The Splendid Idle Forties*. A literary gold rush ensued, and such writers as Bret Harte, Charles Warren Stoddard, Joaquin (a pseudonym) Miller, and even Mark Twain, were soon busily working through this rich vein. The nation was treated to a pageantry of splendid "Spanish" dons, displaying their magnificent horsemanship on gorgeous mounts, and of lovely señoritas in black mantillas who were the objects of the most courtly attentions. All of this was relatively harmless in itself, but it obscured some important social realities.

Two American writers in the 1940s, Ruth Tuck and Carey McWilliams, examined, with indignation and a certain wry amusement, the implications of the California myth as it extended into the twentieth century. In *Not With the Fist*, Ruth Tuck contemptuously exposed that aspect of the myth which maintained that there were certain fine old families of pure Spanish blood in California who were not to be confused with the later mongrelized immigrants that came up from Mexico. This myth allowed Anglos in California to associate on equal terms with a few wealthy descendants of the old stock on the grounds that they were "Spanish," while maintaining segregationist policies toward the great majority of Mexican-Americans. In refuting the myth, Ruth Tuck drew upon population statistics:

> By the time the colonization of the northern provinces began in earnest, racial and cultural fusion had been going on in Mexico for some three hundred years. It has been estimated that no more than 300,000 Spaniards ever came to Mexico and that most of them were men. The indigenous population of Mexico City alone was 300,000, and it was a small part of the total indigenous population. The most robust Castilian gene, in such a situation, could hardly be expected to survive, unchanged, to populate Texas, New Mexico, Arizona, and California with descendents of "pure Spanish ancestry." But such is the fiction the romantic tradition likes to maintain (Tuck 1946: 16–17).

Ruth Tuck then went on to assert that the real story of the settling of California from Mexico was much more interesting and remarkable than the gossamer tales of the "Spanish" legend. She named several of the early settlers who overcame great hardships. These people, she maintained, were mestizos. However, the publication of this fact "would do away with the convenient corollary . . . that any Mexican-American who is well-groomed, literate, and able must necessarily be from an 'old Spanish family'; and that others, being of less exalted genetic origins, cannot be expected to attain literacy and/or cleanliness" (Tuck 1946: 18–19).

In *North From Mexico*, Carey McWilliams makes a similar examination of the California myth. He reports on the results of his investigation into the backgrounds of the revered "Spanish" founding fathers of Los Angeles and their families. After giving their names and their ethnic backgrounds, he summarizes with the following conclusions:

> Thus of the original settlers of Our City of the Queen of Angels, their wives included, two were Spaniard; one mestizo; two were Negroes; eight were mulattoes; and nine were Indians. None of this would really matter except that the churches in Los Angeles hold fiestas rather than bazaars and that Mexicans are still not accepted as part of the community. When one examines how deeply this fantasy heritage has permeated the social and cultural life of the borderlands, the dichotomy begins to assume the proportions of a schizophrenic mania (McWilliams 1949: 36).

The analyses of life and literature in the Southwest made by Ruth Tuck and Carey McWilliams have served to make the point that the romantic treatment in literature of the Spanish borderlands, far from being a harmless exercise in nostalgia, has in fact helped to perpetuate a socially injurious hypocrisy. Though the works of these two writers are essentially sociological in content, the "savage indignation" which gives verve to their styles admits them to the honorable company of American protest literature. Furthermore, these works have established a precedent which is currently being followed. Recent books analyzing and supporting the Chicano movement in the Southwest are in this tradition. Among the better are *La Raza: the Mexican-Americans* by Stanley Steiner and *Sal Si Puedes: Cesar Chávez and the New American Revolution* by the gifted novelist Peter Matthiessen.

The works of Ruth Tuck and Carey McWilliams are symptomatic of a change that has taken place in the treatment of Mexican culture in American literature. Beginning in the first decades of the twentieth century, American literature showed itself disposed to treat Mexican and Chicano culture seriously. The images of the Mexican and the Mexican-American that begin to appear take on quite another focus. The stereotype of the dirty, thieving, cowardly, sensual, and backward mongrel, in sum the "greaser," that fills so many pages of the nineteenth century literature of the borderlands, is well on the way out. Also, the romanticized Spanish dons and señoritas of the California myth fade into the Western sunset, with Leo Carrillo of the movies representing, perhaps, the last flicker of this cult.

THE AGE OF PROTEST

There have been several developments in American culture, beginning at the turn of the century, which can explain the enlivened interest in the real Mexico and its cultural extensions into the American Southwest. Unlike the early borderland writers, the American novelists and poets of the twentieth century do not, by and large, feel themselves to be in general accord with their own culture. The late nineteenth and early twentieth centuries were to see the rise of the realistic and naturalistic novels which were to set the tone of much of the writing which was to come. Tough young writers began their careers determined to "tell it like it is." The object of their most persistent attacks was the "genteel tradition," that mellowed, latter-day puritanism which enjoined upon all writers that they treat only of the "smiling aspects of life" and be careful not to write anything which could be upsetting to the optimism or morals of carefully reared young ladies. However, even that genteel and well situated "dean of American letters," William Dean Howells, published in 1890 a bitter novel, *A Hazard of New Fortunes*, which was to depict the New York working class as poor, oppressed, and savagely intimidated by a burgeoning group of *nouveau riche* capitalists. Stephen Crane in *Maggie, a Girl of the Streets* and Theodore Dreiser in *Sister Carrie* were to challenge and reap reprisals from the genteel reading public by writing about women who were forced to seek survival by offering their bodies. Dreiser's performance was the more unforgivable because his heroine ended up triumphantly. American writing was becoming to a considerable extent a protest literature, and the literary artist in America was beginning to think of himself more and more in terms of that now overused word "alienated."

Certain aspects of this protest writing had their roots in earlier periods. By the mid nineteenth century, the puritan ethic had extended from purely personal to social-moral concerns. New England became the core of the abolition movement, and increasingly the protests against slavery went beyond condemnations of involuntary servitude to protests against racism per se. Just as the border writers had tended to extend their hostility toward the Negro to include a racial animosity toward the Mexican, so, conversely, did the New England writers begin to link their cause of abolitionism to their growing hostility to the Mexican-American war. Indeed, New England marshalled her greatest writing talents, those of Emerson, Thoreau, and James Russell Lowell, to launch a bitter, eloquent, and even witty protest against a war which was described as imperialistic, racistic, and designed primarily to aid the cause of the slave-holding South.

Thus the protest against racism, so familiar to us in current writing, has had a distinguished lineage in American literature. It was clearly one of the elements that went into twentieth-century writing about Mexico. Other elements of the American writer's disenchantment with his society also found their way into the new American writing about Mexican culture. In fact modern American writers were to discover Mexico as something of a perfect foil to modern urban American society. The technique of upbraiding one's own people by playing up the virtues of another has been serviceable ever since Tacitus in the First Century A.D. wrote his *Germania*, which contrasted the noble and simple virtues of the German tribes to Roman corruption, self-indulgence, and intrigue.

A NEW AWARENESS

It is, in fact, curious and significant that the very aspects of Mexican life which the early border chroniclers found appalling were those which the modern American writers have tended to look upon as salutary and bracing. As a counter to North American sexual repression, a vestige of the puritan heritage, these later writers prescribed the natural acceptance of sexuality inherent in Mexican culture. Against the cumpulsive work ethic of the Anglo-Americans, these writers cited the Mexican capacity to seize the moment's enjoyment. They also demonstrated the evident failure of salvation through "progress" and scientific technology and pointed out another way of living in the more earth-drawn life of Mexicans and Chicanos. They saw profit-hungry American farmers devastating the land with quick-money crops and contrasted them with the "paisanos" of New Mexico who have lived and died for generations nurturing a small area of beloved earth. To the Anglo-American's commercialized optimism and hurried avoidance or euphemizing of the subject of death they contrasted the Mexican's almost passionate embracing of death as the necessary and functional counterpart of life. The early border writers were horrified at the "frivolous" festivities carried on by the Mexicans during their feast of "the Day of the Dead." But to a number of the modern American writers the Mexican celebrations surrounding *El Día de Los Muertos* demonstrated a fearless, if fatalistic, sense of reality tinged with a profound mystical perception.

There is one subject upon which the early and later American writers seem to have been in general agreement. However grudgingly, the early border chroniclers conceded that the Mexicans had a superior sense of the aesthetic. This concept appears, for example, in an early account which achieved considerable popularity in its day, *The Narrative of the Texan Santa Fe Expedition* by George Wilkins Kendall, first published in 1847. The book deals with the author's experience as a member of a filibustering expedition which invaded Mexican territory from Texas. The attempt was a dismal failure ending with the capture of the entire expedition whose members were then marched as prisoners of war from Santa Fe to Mexico City. Kendall's prison was in the same building which lodged a hospital for lepers, and the author observed with fascination the ways in which these inmates accepted with resilience and sallies of black humor their special form of the death sentence. One passage in the *Narrative* describes the lepers decorating a hall in the hospital in preparation for the feast of San Lazaro:

> And here the Mexicans excel. Festoons, flags, and devices, cut in paper of all colours, were hung about the walls, and the lamps were decorated in the same way. The word "caridad"—charity—was also neatly cut in paper and pasted about on the different utensils and on places where it would readily strike the eye of visitors. The floor was stained with yellow tint, and on the ceiling long strips of red, white, and blue muslin were tastefully arranged in bows and different fanciful forms, giving relief and beauty to the general appearance. Flowers also were entwined about the cots, and, considering the material with which the lepers were provided, I doubt whether any other people under the sun could have given the room an appearance as beautiful (Kendall 1847: 147).

A number of modern American writers have used, by way of contrast to North American life, the theme of the pervasive aestheticism of Mexican culture. The modern American philosopher, F.S.C. Northrop, in *The Meeting of East and West*, has linked this concept with that of cultural imperialism. "What impresses as novel in Mexican culture," he writes, "is its highly developed appreciation of the aesthetic and its religion of the emotions; and what the Mexicans fear in the merging of their culture with that of the United States is that the latter, excessively pragmatic, economically centered culture will, in its zeal for its own values, overwhelm and destroy the cultural assets of the Indian-and-Latin world" (Northrop 1946: 436). The contemporary Mexican poet, Octavio Paz, has added as a wry postscript his belief that at the very time in which the culture of the United States, through the hippie movement and other counter cultures, is revolting against the pragmatism and commercialism of American culture, modern Mexico, in its current industrial and commerical emphasis, is naively taking on, anachronistically, that same faith in materialism.

The whole question of cultural imperialism has, in fact, run throughout North American writing about Mexico. It was noted earlier that the frontier writers, notably the authors of the Texas romances, proclaimed that it was the mission of the United States to regenerate Mexican society. Reference has also been made to the fact that Mexican intellectuals such as the modern historian José Fuentes Mares have been very conscious of this missionary aspect of the North American approach to Latin America. Modern American protest writers also have taken this strain into account. Toward the end of the nineteenth century, a note of wryness begins to appear when this theme is broached. "It seems," wrote Ambrose Bierce commenting on a speech by President McKinley, "that we have never gone to war for conquest, for exploitation, nor for territory; we have the word of a president for that. Observe, now, how providence overrules the intention of the truly good for their advantage. We went to war with Mexico for peace, humanity, and honor, yet emerged from the contest with an extension of territory beyond the dreams of political avarice" (Bierce 1912, Vol. XI: 95). Bret Harte reacted more with amusement than with indignation to the patriotic fanfare that went with the expansionist spirit of his age. In *Gabriel Conroy*, the following dialogue occurs between the American, Arthur Poinsett [a name which could hardly have been coincidental], and the Californian-Mexican priest, Padre Felipe:

> "Honesty is the best policy," as our earliest philosopher says.
> "Pardon?" queried the padre.
> Arthur, intensely amused, made a purposely severe and literal translation of Franklin's famous apothegm, and then watched Father Felipe raise his eyes and hands to the ceiling in pious protest and mute consternation.
> "And these are your American ethics?" he said at last.

"They are, and in conjunction with manifest destiny, and the star of empire, they have brought us here, and—have given me the honor of your acquaintance," Arthur said in English (Harte 1896: 142).

The late Jack Kerouac in *On The Road* combined the theme of North American pretensions vis-a-vis Mexico with another important theme, that of Mexico's strength through primitivism.

These people were unmistakably Indians and were not at all like the Pedros and Panchos of silly, civilized American lore—they had high cheekbones and slanted eyes, and soft ways; they were not fools, they were not clowns; they were great, grave Indians and they were the source of mankind and the fathers of it. . . . And they knew this when we passed, ostensibly self-important moneybag Americans on a lark in their land; they knew who was the father and who was the son of antique life on earth, and made no comment (Kerouac 1958: 229–230).

The occurrence of primitivism as a state of mind and inspiration for art in highly "developed" societies is an interesting and undoubtedly significant phenomenon. The *Germania* of Tacitus, referred to above, is an early example of this. The popularity of Arcadian and "golden age" literature in the Renaissance was part of the psychological response of the times to the growing complexity of life in Europe. In the late eighteenth century, Marie Antoinette, before losing her elegantly coiffured head, played, with her maids in waiting, at being farmerette, in frivolous response to the back-to-earth movement which Rousseau and his followers were beginning to make fashionable. And while the French Revolution and the consequent Napoleonic Wars raged in Europe, William Wordsworth was telling his countrymen and especially the inhabitants of London that, for their own salvation, they must cultivate the speech, manners, and way of life of shepherd boys. In fact primitivism was one of the most potent strains in the nineteenth century romantic reaction against eighteenth century rationalism.

When romanticism crossed the water to the New World the note of primitivism accompanied it and resonated the more powerfully against a virginal wilderness which seemed the very actualization of Rousseau's imagined Eden. Its notes are to be heard in the works of such diverse writers as Cooper, Emerson, Thoreau, Hawthorne, Melville, Whitman, and, in its wilderness theme, carries through into modern times with the works of Mark Twain and William Faulkner.

However, primitivism in twentieth century American writing is more than just a residue of nineteenth century romanticism. Specific conditions in American life brought forth new strains of it. If European industrialism, with its dislocations, its inequities, and its artificialities, was one of the causes of romanticism in Europe, the rise of this industrialism in the United States was both later and more virulent. It brought forth a new wave of primitivism which joined forces with the tough new realism and naturalism in American writing.

The industrial plant that was needed during the Civil War to supply armaments for the armies of the North arose almost overnight in the big cities of the North and on the prairies of the Middle West. After the war, these factories were converted to peacetime uses and went on expanding at an accelerated pace. This was the watershed period in North American life. Where the old rural and homogeneous society was to survive, it was to do so in isolated and "backward" areas. The exception, until recently, was the defeated and resentful South, which was to produce its own crop of talented and unreconstructed writers, who were bred to think of their region as being almost "another country."

As the factories of the North expanded and multiplied, more and more workers were needed to stoke the fires that provided the energy for the new behemoth. These came from two sources, principally, from the farmlands of America and from the superfluity of Europe's castoffs. These together were to produce the new sensibility upon which modern American literature has been developed. The two groups had at least one thing in common, the sense of separation from the past. European immigrants either welcomed or deplored the loss of contact with the mother cultures. The Americans who had left the land to flock into the cities became increasingly aware of their separation from a folk culture that had been nurtured over generations and had provided considerable spiritual sustenance and a confirming sense of community. After the first flush of exaltation over the greater freedom and cosmopolitanism provided by big city life, the old securities and sense of identity began to be missed. It was with this sense of loss that American writers began to look at their neighboring culture of Mexico with a feeling that more and more resembled envy.

A FOLK RELIGION

The old borderland writers were given to deriding Mexican Catholicism. Part of their aversion arose from the fact that their frontier egalitarianism was affronted by the undeniable power of the clerical hierarchy in *criollo* Mexico. But it went beyond that. These writers were constantly harping on the displays of primitivism, superstition, and frivolous festivity in Mexico's religion. These very aspects of a colorful and vital folk religion have been those which have elicited praise from modern American writers painfully aware of the cultural fragmentation and personal isolation in their own society.

In the justly celebrated *Death Comes for the Archbishop*, Willa Cather, an American writer who keenly felt the cultural impoverishment of modern American life, writes of her hero, Bishop Latour, a cultured Frenchman, as he entered a church in Taos, New Mexico.

> When the Bishop dismounted to enter the church, the women threw their shawls on the dusty pathway for him to walk upon, and as he passed through the kneeling congregation, men and women snatched for his hand to kiss the episcopal ring. In his own country all this would have been highly distasteful to Jean Marie Latour. Here, these demonstrations seemed a part of the high colour that was in landscape and gardens, in the flaming cactus and the gaudily decorated altars, in the agonized Christs and dolorous Virgins and the very human figures of the saints. He had already learned that with this people religion was necessarily theatrical (Cather 1951: 142).

To Willa Cather, a "theatrical" religion was a living one, a core expression of a culture which was very much intact.

Modern American writers in treating of the "primitive" aspects of Mexico's religion did not confine themselves to Mexican Christianity but displayed a lively interest in religious forms and ideas that derived from the Indian past. Some of these elements are in fact mixed with Mexican Christianity, and others survive in more or less a pure state. Frank Dobie, the Texan writer who has so skillfully converted folklore into literary art, delighted in Mexican popular religion for the exuberance of fancy it displayed. In *The Mexico I Like*, Dobie tells a tale about a *nagual*. According to Dobie, the concept of the *nagual* comes from the Indian side of Mexico's heritage. It was often a custom among certain Indians to name a son after an animal. The son, it was believed, would then grow up in great rapport with the animal, sometimes to the extent of being able to assume at will the animal's form. A person who had this power of transformation was a *nagual*. The story is about a young man, Chon, who tracked down a *nagual* who had been appearing in the form of a huge goat. Chon roped it, and one of the vaqueros with him hit it over the head with a machete. As blood poured out of the back of the head the *nagual* said: "Chon, you have killed your own grandfather." When Chon returned home, he found his family seated around the body of his grandfather who had apparently fallen and knocked his head (Dobie 1942: 46–53).

The poet Witter Bynner, one-time disciple of D. H. Lawrence, expresses in one of his poems the idea that Indian Mexico never really accepted the "foreign" god of Christianity. Instead, as expressed in the following lines, Indian religion is a religion of the earth.

No need of priests with knives for trespassers.
Let come who may with an estranging hand,
Let touch who will this earth so deeply yours,
None of it ever goes away from you.
Your gods are here, deeper than any spade;
And when you lie on the earth under the sun,
They whisper up to you ancestral spells
From your own roots, to rot these foreign hearts (Bynner 1930: 44–45).

The Mexican sense of a spiritualized relationship with the earth was seen by modern American writers as one of the most significant aspects of rural Mexican culture and was contrasted with a prevalent North American attitude toward the earth as an object for exploitation. In the early decades of the twentieth century, North American writers, in responding to this Mexican mystique of the land, were anticipating the current emphasis upon ecology and conservation. As early as 1919, the redoubtable Waldo Frank, ever the creative critic of American life, took up this theme. As he traveled through the Southwest, he recorded the impression that the Mexicans were the only people who had really left a cultural impress upon the land. All else seemed to him to have the flimsy impermanence which he considered to be the mark of the transient "gringo" with his materialistic and exploitative ambition. Not having this kind of ambition, the Mexican, according to Frank, was not "an ideal pioneer," for he was not the kind who "must for ever be ready to move on." Instead "he became attached to his soil and loved it and drew pleasure and drew beauty from it." The Mexican's adobe house "gives us his inner life. Here a man has settled down and sought happiness in harmony with his surroundings: sought life by cultivation, rather than exploitation" (Frank 1919: 94).

Harvey Fergusson has elaborated this concept in his discussion of the villagers in the small New Mexican communities in the Sangre de Cristo mountains between Santa Fe and Taos. The case for primitivism against the American faith in progress is made quite explicitly.

The wide-hatted men and the black-shawled women are figures little changed. And here is an atmosphere, too, that belongs unmistakably to another age, before hurry began or machinery was invented. It is profoundly quiet but with a quiet that never seems dead. One gets from the faces and movements of the people and from their voices an impression of indolent vitality—of life that is never driven or frantic as it is wherever machines set the pace and the hopes of progress is an ever-receding goal.

These owners of tiny farms were sometimes called paisanos—men of the country, men of the soil. And true peasants they are, perhaps the only ones that ever existed within our borders. For the peasant is a lover of the earth who asks nothing better than to live his whole life on one patch of soil, scratching it for a living, laying his bones in it at last. And there has never been much of this resigned sedentary spirit in the American farmer of the Anglo Saxon breed. He was originally a wanderer and always an exploiter. He settles down only when there is no place else to go. He does not cherish the earth, he loves to conquer it. Always he tends to exhaust the soil and move on, whether in a few years or a few generations, as did the tobacco planters in Virginia, the cotton planters farther south. His interest is always in a "money crop." He believes in progress and longs for change.

No wonder he has always despised these men in whom the blood of an ancient European peasantry mingles with that of sedentary Indians. They ask of the earth only a living and imitate the past because it has seemed good (Fergusson 1933: 107–108).

Another author writing in this same early part of the century— and in a similar vein which seems so pertinent to us now—was Robert Herrick. An English professor teaching in Chicago when that city was the "stormy, husky, brawling City of the Big Shoulders"—as Carl Sandburg put it—Herrick wrote several fine novels, but his voice was lost in the din. Both an idealist and a realist, Herrick was very much a protest writer, and his works are beginning to find the recognition that they deserve. The protagonist of one of his novels, *Waste*, was an engineer who had worked for a private power company tapping the resources of the West. He had become disgusted with the policy of the company which had an eye only to profits and was totally disinterested in his own project for developing the area in terms of the public good. His professional advancement, despite a high degree of competence, was always frustrated by his own nonconformity and social idealism. In New Mexico, which he was visiting for the first time, he licked his wounds and tried to think his position through.

He liked the country immensely. Something in its stark indifference to man soothed him like the touch of a large, firm hand. The Indians blended with the background whether cultivating their fields along the river bed, or living their family life in the pueblo, or driving their little horse teams through the winding cañons. The Mexicans, living much the same sort of life as their Indian predecessors, even mixed with them in blood, in the same sort of indistinguishable mud houses, clustered in unobtrusive hamlets harmonized with nature, the strange practices of the Penitentes seeming but a natural barbaric rite in this primitive arid land . . . Only the "tourist" crossing the plains for his beloved heaven of California brought the smell and the ugliness of dollar civilization, and for the most part, luckily the tourists passed by the great highway to the south through Santa Fe, only stray specimens of the tribe occasionally venturing into the Santa Cruz district in search of "color. . . . " There were few human beings in this immense area of land and sky, untouched by the hand of man save along the river bottoms, or by a road blasted indistinguishably from the sandstone cliffs of a cañon. So few! and so impotent! With irony Thornton thus summed up the fascination of this mountain region—Man had been able to do little harm in it, to spoil it! (Herrick 1924: 405–406)

These quotations from Harvey Fergusson and Robert Herrick make clear why northern New Mexico, from Santa Fe through Taos and northward, has become a haven for a new wave of protesters who are seeking to work out a "counter culture" in their "communes." Ironically, their arrival has been greeted with surprise or displeasure by the descendents of those ancient settlers whose way of life the newcomers are trying to imitate.

INFLUENCE OF LAWRENCE

American writers dealing with Mexico responded to the attraction of the man who was perhaps the most influential "primitivist" writer in modern literature. During an important period of his writing career, D. H. Lawrence made his home in Taos, New Mexico, where he held forth as the central figure of a group of artists and writers who clustered around him. The impress of his ideas can be found in the work of a number of American writers who have dealt with Mexican culture, and Lawrence's influence here is not confined to the members of his inner circle. Such diverse talents as those of Witter Bynner, Hart Crane, Conrad Aiken, Selden Rodman, Katherine Anne Porter, and Paul Horgan have been impressed by Lawrence's interpretation of Mexican culture. When he was most pleased with it, D. H. Lawrence saw Mexico as a country whose people had not lost the primitive élan, who were closer to the earth and the rhythms of nature than were the people in his own industrialized England or in most of Western Europe and North America.

His famous injunction to modern man was to "live in the blood," and in his campaign against the abstract mentality and emotional anemia, which he claimed to be the condition of modern technologized man, he developed his mystique of sexuality. Contemporary American writers, engaged in a frontal attack on the Puritan tradition in the United States, found Lawrence an effective reenforcer of positions that they already held. They too looked to Mexico for an antidote to the sexual repression which they insisted was pervasive in American culture.

An egregious example of this attitude in fiction is to be found in John Steinbeck's *Tortilla Flat.* The reckless paisanos of the novel, Danny and his cohorts, romp throughout their days drinking red California wine and making love as it comes their way. Their friend Teresina is constantly having children by different fathers, whom she can't begin to sort out. Written in a similar vein is *Dark Madonna* by Richard Summers. The theme of Mexican naturalness in sex as contrasted to North American puritanism has been utilized by a number of other

American writers, a list of whom would include Bret Harte, Robinson
Jeffers, Frank Dobie, Frank Goodwyn, Tom Lea, Paul Horgan, Harvey
Fergusson, John Houghton Allen, Wright Morris, and Jack Kerouac.

The theme is handled with considerable subtlety by Katherine
Anne Porter in the collection of masterful short stories, *Flowering
Judas*. The story that bears that title concerns an American girl, Laura,
who, though of a conventional, puritanical background, has become a
Communist party worker in Mexico City. Her work brings her in contact with a Mexican party leader, Braggioni, a highly-sexed, shrewd,
fierce, and totally opportunistic man, who exploits the Communist
cause for his own advantage. Braggioni stalks her hungrily, and Laura,
a woman who recoils compulsively from sex, dreads the inevitable
sexual demand. Avoiding him as much as possible, she devotes her
time to teaching school to Mexican youngsters, whom she loves but
cannot come close to, and giving herself unstintingly to party work.
When a friend, Eugenio, an agitator who has been imprisoned, dies
from taking an overdose of the sleeping pills which Laura has given
him to be taken sparingly, the event registers itself in her dream the
following night. Eugenio, in the dream, offers her the ripe blossoms of
the Judas tree to eat. When she greedily swallows them, he accuses
her of eating his own flesh and blood, crying "Murderer! Cannibal!"
She awakens shouting "No! No!" Though the interpretation is left to
the reader, the dream apparently represents Laura's subconscious
awareness that in her own way she, as much as Braggioni, has been
exploiting the political cause for which she works, seeking in it a substitute for the sexual expression she cannot permit herself and for the
love she craves (Porter n.d.). Sexuality in Mexico is treated in quite a
different way in another story in the collection, "Maria Concepción."
In this most skillful and effective tale, the principal characters are all
Mexican. The story deals with sexual desire, waywardness, jealousy,
and violence, but all in the frame of reference of a rural code which can
enforce its own sense of propriety.

Katherine Anne Porter, in her sophistication, is able to detect the
naiveté in aspects of the cult of the primitive as practiced by American
writers, and she is not beyond satirizing them. One of the stories in
Flowering Judas, "That Tree," deals with a young American who first
went to Mexico to become a poet and had gone native with much de-
liberation. One evening he took his midwestern, school-teacher wife,
Miriam, to a cafe in Mexico City. While they were dancing, one of four
quarreling generals got to his feet and grabbed for his gun. Immedia-
ately the Mexican girls on the dance floor, in a gesture which seemed
to the American to display a magnificently primitive instinct for self-

preservation, swung their partners' backs toward the generals as shields. Miriam simply dove under the table. This action struck the American as "the most utterly humiliating moment of his whole, blighted life." Later he accused Miriam of having "instincts out of tune." She glared at him, and "when she tightened her mouth to bite her lip and say 'instincts!' she could make it sound like the most obscene word in the language" (Porter n.d.: 103–104).

A consideration of Katherine Anne Porter's satirical treatment of "primitivism" in American writing leads to the observation that some modern American writers, though their intentions have been vastly different, have been as guilty as the early border chroniclers in dealing in stereotypes when it comes to depicting Mexican character. In fact those who have been making this very accusation quite emphatically, of late, are the interesting new crop of Mexican-American, or Chicano, writers. The Mexican-American of the Southwest is no longer simply being written about, he himself is doing the writing, and the American reading public is now able to see how the Chicano looks upon himself.

BEHIND THE CHICANOS

Though the principal thrust of this article is to examine how Anglo-American writers have viewed Mexican and Mexican-American culture, some observations about the Chicano movement and its literature are relevant here. In the first place, the cultural situation which has produced the movement was accurately analyzed over fifty years ago by one of the American writers whom we have been discussing, the perceptive Waldo Frank. In *Our America* he wrote of the sense of moral defeat which the Mexican-American was apt to feel in the presence of Anglo arrogance and commercialism.

> For the Mexican is cowed, and is beaten. He moves about like one who feels himself a dog among men. He bends the neck to the steel-mill and to the hard, keen masters who are the makers of steel. The Americans live in ugly houses, so he comes to despise the intimate temper that made him beautify his own. The Americans go to the Machine for their pleasure as well as for their food. So he comes to despise the labor of his hand. Nothing that is his meets the approval of the "gringos." He is a "greaser," a half-breed, a "nigger." The Americans are stronger and the Americans do not respect him. What then will it gain him to respect himself? (Frank 1919: 95–96).

The Chicano movement is an eleventh-hour surge to throw off the long endured incubus of this cultural overlordship and to assert once again a pride in and identity with a rich cultural heritage that is one's own. The rapidly increasing literature of the movement expresses itself in all the forms: the novel, short stories, drama, and poetry. Also,

Chicano spokesmen make use of such media as the magazine *El Grito* and the Chicano press to publish essays defining their positions.

One of the most frequent complaints made by articulate Chicanos is that even academicians and the literati are guilty of dealing in stereotypes in the various images of the Mexican-American that they present to us in print. Clearly a number of the Mexican figures that appear in modern American literature are tailored to fit message-bearing roles that are more expressive of the inner needs or ideological campaigns of the "Anglo" writers than they are of the complex reality of Mexican or Mexican-American culture. As a result, some Chicano intellectuals are saying that only Mexican-Americans should be writing about Mexican-Americans. While it is undoubtedly true that members of a given culture have a certain feel for it that outsiders cannot duplicate, the creative imagination of any literary artist, Anglo, Black, Chicano, or Amerind, will trespass where it feels the urge to go. It is, nevertheless, an important addition to American literature that talented Chicano writers are speaking out for their culture. In this way literature in the United States gets the increased benefit of a double vision, the view from within and the view from without.

With the recent rise of literatures giving tongue to specific cultures within the general framework of American society, the American voice in literature is becoming considerably less ethnocentric. Though some writers, crossing cultural boundaries, may still slip into stereotypes, the animus behind serious current writing in the United States is vastly different from that which promulgated the caricatures of the Mexican in the chronicles of the early literature of the borderlands. Nevertheless, the question may still be posed as to whether the American populace at large, with its remaining tendencies toward ethnocentricity and its aversion toward learning other languages, will follow the lead of its more cosmopolitan writers. Part of the answer to this question seems already to have been given. Avant-garde movements of our time do seem to have had the effect of increasing general sensitivity to racial, social, and cultural issues. In all of this, the creative literary imagination has, as often before, set the pace for the more literal formulators of ideas.

REFERENCES

ATHERTON, GERTRUDE
  1902 *The Splendid Idle Forties.* Macmillan Company, New York.
BARTLETT, JOHN RUSSELL
  1854 *Personal Narrative of Explorations and Incidents in Texas, New Mexico,
        Sonora, and Chihuahua.* 2 vols. Appleton and Company, New York.
BIERCE, AMBROSE
  1912 Antepenultima. In *The Collected Works of Ambrose Bierce.* 12 vols. The
        Neale Publishing Company, New York.

BYNNER, WITTER
1930   *Indian Earth*. Alfred A. Knopf, New York.
CATHER, WILLA
1951   *Death Comes For the Archbishop*. Alfred A. Knopf, New York.
CRANE, STEPHEN
1960   *Maggie: A Girl of the Streets*. Fawcett Publications, Greenwich, Connecticut.
DOBIE, FRANK
1942   *The Mexico I Like*. University Press, Dallas.
DREISER, THEODORE
1959   *Sister Carrie*. Dell Publishing Company, New York.
FERGUSSON, HARVEY
1933   *Rio Grande*. Alfred A. Knopf, New York.
1950   *Grant of Kingdom*. William Morrow and Company, New York.
FRANK, WALDO
1919   *Our America*. Boni and Liverwright Publishers, New York.
FUENTES MARES, JOSÉ
1960   *Poinsett, Historia de una Gran Intriga*. Libro Mex Editores, S. de R. L., Mexico City.
GANILH, ANTHONY
1838   *Mexico Versus Texas*. M. Siegfried, Philadelphia.
HARTE, BRET
1896   *Gabriel Conroy*. Riverside Edition of Works, XIII and XIV. Houghton, Mifflin and Company, Boston.
HEIZER, ROBERT F., AND ALAN J. ALMQUIST
1971   *The Other Californians*. University of California Press, Berkeley.
HENRY, ROBERT SELPH
1950   *The Story of the Mexican War*. The Bobbs-Merrill Company, New York.
HERRICK, ROBERT
1924   *Waste*. Harcourt, Brace and Company, New York.
HOWELLS, WILLIAM DEAN
1960   *A Hazard of New Fortunes*. Bantam Books, New York.
HOWREN, ALLEINE
1913   Causes and Origin of the Decree of April 6, 1830. *The Southwestern Historical Quarterly*, Vol. XVI.
JACKSON, HELEN HUNT
1935   *Ramona*. Little, Brown and Company, Boston.
KENDALL, GEORGE WILKINS
1847   *Narrative of the Texan Santa Fe Expedition*. Henry Washbourne, London.
KEROUAC, JACK
1958   *On The Road*. Signet Books, New York.
MATTHIESSEN, PETER
1969   *Sal Si Puedes: Cesar Chávez and the New American Revolution*. Random House, New York.
McWILLIAMS, CAREY
1949   *North From Mexico*. J. B. Lippincott Company, New York.
NORTHROP, F. S. C.
1946   *The Meeting of East and West*. The Macmillan Company, New York.
PAZ, OCTAVIO
1969   México: La Última Década. 1969 Hackett Memorial Lecture. Institute of Latin American Studies. The University of Texas, Austin.
PORTER, KATHERINE ANNE
n.d.   *Flowering Judas and Other Stories*. The Modern Library, New York.
ROBINSON, CECIL
1969   *With the Ears of Strangers: The Mexican in American Literature*. The University of Arizona Press, Tucson.

SMITH, JUSTIN H.
1919   *The War With Mexico.* 2 vols. The Macmillan Company, New York.
STEINBECK, JOHN
1935   *Tortilla Flat.* Corvici Friede Publishers, New York.
STEINER, STANLEY
1970   *La Raza: The Mexican-Americans.* Harper and Row, New York.
SUMMERS, RICHARD
1952   *Dark Madonna.* Bantam Books, New York.
TACITUS, CORNELIUS
1935   *The Germania of Tacitus: A Critical Edition.* Rodney Potter Robinson,
       ed. American Philological Association, Middletown, Connecticut.
TUCK, RUTH
1946   *Not With the Fist.* Harcourt, Brace and Company, New York.
TURNER, FREDERICK JACKSON
1920   *The Frontier in American History.* Henry Holt and Company, New York

8. *Bilingual Onomastics: A Case Study*

LURLINE H. COLTHARP

Coltharp deals with some specific problems that a bilingual city has in naming streets. She examines the influence of English and Spanish in the street names of El Paso, Texas, and illustrates how these local names are a record of past and present interaction between two languages and cultures.

The author expresses appreciation to those who helped in establishing an accurate list of street names: Ashley T. Wagnon, chief of current planning, and David A. Garcia, planning technician. Additionally, she is grateful for assistance rendered by Dr. Eugene Porter and Dr. John Sharp of The University of Texas at El Paso, Mrs. Robert Chapman, Mrs. W. W. Lake, and Cleofas Calleros.

THE REVEREND ISAAC TAYLOR (1865: 1) wrote, "Local names . . . are never mere arbitrary sounds, devoid of meaning. They may always be regarded as records of the past, inviting and rewarding a careful historical interpretation." Names, Reverend Taylor continued, "may indicate—emigrations—immigrations—the commingling of races by war and conquest, or by the peaceful processes of commerce: . . . " To some degree, the street names in El Paso, Texas, show traces of all of the influences cited by Reverend Taylor with emphasis on a peaceful commingling; they reflect the bilingual character of the city.[1]

El Paso had its beginning in recorded history as one of the nation's oldest international crossroads in June, 1581, when the first European visitors, Father Agustín Rodríguez and Captain Sánchez Chamuscado, crossed the river which now forms the boundary between the United States and Mexico. The *entrada* was motivated by a combination of missionary zeal and greed for gold, two opposing aims ever-present in Spanish expansion. The *Relación* of Hernán Gallegos (1927) told about the expedition. As the Spaniards followed the trace of an old Indian trail across the river, they laid the first Spanish name upon the site. They dubbed the crossing *El Paso del Río del Norte*, 'the Ford of the River of the North,' a name that was to wear well.

In 1598, emigration northward to New Spain became a reality as colonists under Juan de Oñate crossed the river and claimed the land on behalf of King Philip with much pomp and ceremony. The old Indian trail used by earlier *conquistadores* became a *Camino Real*— "Royal Road" or "King's Highway." The term was comparable to "U.S. Highway" as a designation; the road was now in use by an expedition sponsored by the crown and—theoretically—subject to maintenance and protection with funds from the royal treasury (Simmons 1968: 73).

As settlement of the new land quickened and commerce began,

---

[1] Several limitations were imposed on this study. The first applied to the corpus itself. The card file of the City Planning Board was used as the final arbiter. The decision to use this file involved several minor decisions. Only official city streets would be used, thus excluding private roads. This eliminated street names within Fort Bliss, Biggs Field, and William Beaumont General Hospital—three Federal military installations surrounded by the city. A procedural limitation was applied to dividing the street names between those of English and those of Spanish origin. First, the influence of other languages was investigated. There are names of Indian tribes from Algonquin to Zuni, but the actual influence of Indian languages as well as of other languages was deemed negligible. This reduced the problem to a binary division. A word was considered to be English unless it could definitely be established as Spanish (Velazquez de la Cadena 1967; Tibon 1961). Along geographical lines, names of Spanish-speaking areas were included as Spanish. Orthography was used to decide some classifications. Arrollo Road is spelled with two *l*'s as in Spanish and was so classified. Carlotta is spelled with two *t*'s and consequently was put with the English. If there were any questions about the legitimacy of a Spanish classification, the word was put into the English file.

travelers often had to camp south of the ford to wait for the flood-swollen river to subside. A community formed, El Paso del Norte, serving travelers over the road between Santa Fe and Chihuahua. In practical usage, the name was variously shortened to "Paso del Norte," "El Paso," or simply "Passo" (Thomlinson 1945: 1).

It was more than two centuries before a scattering of Americans began to come along down the Camino Real, the first in 1806 (Sonnichsen 1968: 101). The Mexican War brought United States' troops, the Treaty of Guadalupe Hidalgo established the river as the boundary between the two nations, and American traders and businessmen came to the north bank of the river. As C. L. Sonnichsen put it in his history of El Paso (1968: 123): "After this there were two El Pasos, one Mexican and one American, but in spite of irritations and misunderstandings, the relations of the two peoples after 1846 were on the whole good, and sometimes warm and close." Actually, in the beginning, most of the settlements on the American side were called after those who lived there, names like "Smithville," "Coons' Ranch," "Hart's Mill," and "Magoffinsville" (Strickland 1963).

Then gold was discovered in California; a military post was established. As a way station on the southern route to the gold fields, the fledgling community attracted gold-seekers, traders, the Butterfield Overland Mail and its stagecoach drivers, rumors of a coming railroad, and real estate promoters. Six of the latter employed Anson Mills, a surveyor, to draw up a "Plat of the Town of El Paso". He finished it in 1859, complete with street names (see Table I). (Anson Mills 1921: 49–55).

As was common with stagecoach towns, streets leading out of the village were named for the destinations of the stagecoach line. Decorative illustrations on the map indicated the nature of the traffic with, appropriately enough, an oxcart on El Paso Street pointing toward the ferry to the Mexican village across the river. (The confusion over town names was ended once and for all in 1882 when El Paso del Norte was officially changed to Ciudad Juárez to honor Benito Juárez.) In 1859, the town-to-be had little history to commemorate in street names. Juan María Ponce de León had formerly owned much of the land occupied by the new town plat. His memory was kept green by Ponce and Leon streets. However, most of the remainder of the original twenty street names were after political subdivisions in Mexico and the United States.

NAMES OF LITTLE USE

Street names were of little practical use; in a place where there was so little, everybody knew where everything was. "The business

TABLE 1

First El Paso, Texas, Street Names

Spanish Names	Origins
Chihuahua Street	Mexican place name
Durango Street	Mexican place name
El Paso Street	Road destination: Mexican place name
Leon Street	Early Mexican settler
Ponce Street	Early Mexican settler
Santa Fe Street	Road destination: old Spanish capital
San Antonio Street	Road destination: former Mexican town
Sonora Street	Mexican place name

English Names	Origins
Franklin Street	Early local settler
Kansas Street	U.S. place name
Main Street	Ubiquitous bow to U.S. tradition
Missouri Street	U.S. place name
Oregon Street	U.S. place name*
Organ Street	Nearby mountain range*
Overland Street	After mail and stagecoach line
St. Louis Street†	Road destination: U.S. place name
San Francisco Street	Road destination: U.S. place name
Stanton Street	Early local settler
Texas Street	U.S. place name
Utah Street	U.S. place name

* Some have maintained that present Oregon Street was the former Organ Street, a name no longer in use. However, both names appeared on the original plat, on parallel streets a block apart. The error obviously originated because Organ Street was in the center of Anson Mills' map and was hidden by the binding when published in his book, *My Story* (1921: 54–55).

† St. Louis Street was changed to Mills Street to do honor to Anson Mills, the surveyor.

houses, with one exception, were on El Paso street and around the little plaza. . . . The postoffice was on the west side of El Paso street, facing the head of San Antonio street, and in this same large room there was also a whiskey saloon, a billiard table, and several gambling tables." (W. W. Mills 1962: 7–8). By 1881 the need for street addresses had not increased measurably. Nineteen local display advertisements appeared on the front page of Volume I, Number 1, of the *El Paso Times* on April 2, 1881. Only five of the nineteen advertisers thought it necessary to state their street addresses. Nine more used the simple designation El Paso, Texas, while some located themselves by juxtaposition to a building, by reference to some other commercial establishment, or by adjacency to the plaza.

Eight of those original twenty street names were Spanish language designations—40.0 per cent. El Paso's first census, the Federal Census of 1860, revealed that 61.45 per cent of the population had Spanish surnames. There were only seven Anglo women in the village (W. W. Mills 1962: 5n). Those women of Mexican extraction who were married to Anglo males did not show in the Latin percentage. It is interesting to note that over the next century the increase in Anglo population was only 17.85 per cent. The 1960 census tallied 43.6 per cent of the city's population with Spanish surnames.

For the most part, street names are selected by real estate developers and promoters during the process of laying out a new subdivision. Historically, more selections have been made by people with English names because more subdivision-sized tracts of land have been in the hands of Anglos. Names are assigned under rules administered by the City Planning Board. They are usually chosen to create a favorable theme or atmosphere for the subdivision and, consequently, to aid and abet the sale of homes and homesites. One who wishes to honor a person or an event with a commemorative street name usually contacts a developer. Sometimes action is taken directly by the city council. For example, recently a Lee Treviño Day was promoted to honor El Paso's golfing hero—1971 winner of the U.S., Canadian, and British opens. The city council named a soon-to-be-completed street Lee Treviño Drive for the occasion.

This study takes up, first, the English names; second, the Spanish names; and, third, the interaction between the two.

The English street names follow fairly predictable patterns (Stewart 1958: 244–249). There are numbers and there are letters, but these have not been used as a basic pattern. In fact, at one time there were four sets of streets which started numbering, "First, Second..." The use of letters has been restricted to alleys with Alley A through Alley R.

BASIS FOR NAMES

Streets have been named for people, local and national; they have been named along geographic lines, local and national; they can show specific influences; and they can be grouped into various categories. First, there are streets named for local dignitaries, such as Magoffin Avenue for Joseph Magoffin who was mayor of El Paso from 1881–1885. And there are some named for men who perhaps would have been forgotten were it not for the street names such as Hills, Hammett, and St. Vrain for early realtors. There are streets with women's names such as Florence, Myrtle, and Octavia—commemorating the wives of early residents (Porter 1968: 33–34).

In addition to the names of local residents, names of nationally famous men were used; as an example, twenty-one of the thirty-seven Presidents of the United States had streets named for them.[2]

Second, geography continues to play its part: countries, states, cities, mountains, bodies of water, landmarks, and others. Twenty-one of the states in the United States are present. Utah, one of the original twenty streets, was lost in a name change. It was deemed advisable to change the name when Utah Street became synonymous with sin because of the many bawdy houses that clustered along the southern end during El Paso's roaring frontier era. It became Mesa Street, since it leads to the mesa or upper level of the city.

Local Western influence can be illustrated by such terms as Cactus Place, Rodeo Avenue, Mustang Avenue, and Lariat Street. Note that the last three are Anglicizations of Spanish *rodear*, *mesteño*, and *la reata* respectively. The fact that El Paso is in a mining region has influenced street names with rocks and minerals such as Granite, Gold, Silver, Copper, Bauxite, and Graphite.

Two specific instances of special influences have been chosen for presentation, one a positive influence and the other almost negative. On the positive side, the army has made an impression on civilian streets with such names as Pershing Drive for General John J. Pershing. To show impartiality, there is Villa Way, commemorating Pershing's quarry in the abortive Punitive Expedition into Mexico. Recalling an earlier officer is Doniphan Drive named for Colonel Alexander W. Doniphan who led his First Regiment of Missouri Mounted Volunteers into Paso del Norte in 1846. But the leader of the Mexican forces may be represented by Santa Ana Way.

On the negative side, the fads of the nineteenth century had very little effect on street names in El Paso even though in other places, "The charm of these names for that generation was manifold. They were 'poetic.' They brought to mind English country estates—and our more cultivated people, in spite of two wars, remained ardently Anglophile." (Stewart 1958: 273). The early imports of -ville, glen-, and -vale were not used. Of imports current in the second half of the nineteenth century—-hurst, -mere, and -meade—none was used in that century. It is only in the last twenty years that there have been

---

[2] It was necessary to use care in attributing a name to a national figure. Grant Avenue was not named for President Grant but for Judge Walter B. Grant of Boston, Massachusetts, who is credited with obtaining a large endowment for the local college (Porter 1968: 33).

three uses of these suffixes: Elmhurst, Pinehurst, and Edgemere. Of those that have been used, -dale, an early import, has been used in seven names and -mont appears in sixteen compounds. However, on the treeless desert, -wood has been used in thirty-seven combinations. "Americans had always said *woods*, and so the word came to suggest any bit of second-growth forest, neither grandly primeval nor prettily park-like. But without its *s* the word suggested the romantic outlaws of Sherwood, and any number of English country estates." (Stewart 1958: 272).

Street names can be grouped into many different categories. Only three have been chosen to illustrate the process. One is the category of flowers: Azalea, Rose, and Pansy. A second is fruit: Apple Lane and Pear Lane; and finally trees: Ash, Cedar, and Elm give a sampling.

Spanish names have been used from the beginning. According to the U.S. Post Office Department *Street Directory to 1908*, El Paso was the only town in the United States with a street named Porfirio Díaz and one of four in the entire country that had a Mesa Street.

The Spanish names reflect practically the same categories as the English: people, geography, special influences, and various categories. On the local level, there are streets named for early dignitaries, such as Martínez Street for Felix Martínez who was influential in getting Elephant Butte Dam built on the Rio Grande above El Paso. There are streets named for later dignitaries such as Raymond Telles Drive for the man who was mayor of El Paso from 1957 to 1961. Famous or almost forgotten: Rodolfo Ramón Way commemorates a man whom I have not been able to trace. Women's names are present: Elena, Juanita, and María among others. National figures of Mexico have been used. Six of the presidents of Mexico have streets named for them in El Paso, which has served as a staging area for, and a considerable influence in, Mexican political activity (Sonnichsen 1968).

Geography affected the Spanish names chosen. Terms used in the West are Arrollo and Corral. Spanish also uses rocks and minerals: Piedras, Plata, and Galena. A wider use of geography can be illustrated by the names of Mexican states such as Chihuahua and Durango; and there are cities: for example Acapulco, Guadalajara, Guaymas, Mazatlán, Vera Cruz, and Zaragosa.

Only one special influence which is present in the use of Spanish names will be isolated. It is the use of explorers' names. There are Balboa, Cortez, De León, De Soto, and others—all in a subdivision called Coronado for the leader of the first organized Spanish exploration expedition into the Southwest.

The same categories that were chosen for English can also be used in Spanish. First, there are flowers: Mimosa, Rosa, and Ocotillo. There is fruit: Durazno, Manzana, and Pera; and trees: Alamo, Mesquite, and Tornillo.

NAME DUPLICATION AVOIDED

This indicates a parallelism which might mask the fact that bilingualism places some strains on the naming of streets. The City Planning Board's directive for checking proposed new names contains a general statement that "a proposed new name must not directly duplicate any known name in the County of El Paso." In addition, a special section is included which reads: "Spanish-English: Due to the bilingual character of this area, no street name should be allowed which, when translated, duplicates an existing Spanish or English name." (City Planning Board n.d.: 2). Examples that this has been followed are numerous. To cite only two pairs: There is a Conejo Street, but no Rabbit; there is a Durazno Avenue, but no Peach. The instances where a word is used in both Spanish and English are very few indeed. One example is the pair Algodón and Cotton. Another pair, Campestre Road and Country Club Road, is an overlap according to the local usage of the word *campestre*. A third pair is Avenida de las Americas and Avenue of the Americas.

Sometimes a signal is carried over from one language to another "and then duplicated by an essentially equivalent signal within the second." (Gleason 1965: 110). In the past, this has been avoided in El Paso. When a street has been given the word *camino* in the name as in Camino de la Vista, Camino del Fuego, and Camino Real, the one mention of *camino* 'road' was enough. Similarly, the three uses of *calle* 'street' in Calle Santa Rosa, Calle Santiago, and Calle Visnaga, also avoided duplication of signals. However, in 1968 two new adoptions were Camino Alto Road and Camino de la Paz Court. The first has the duplication of the word "road." The second contains the incompatible "road" and "court."

The City Planning Board has a rule about types of words, requiring that "whether Spanish or English," the word be "a proper, respectable word" and cites Manteca 'lard' and Hog as offensive. It even rules against comical words; however, a few have been accepted, such as Tonto 'stupid' or 'foolish'.

A further complication arises in the printing of the names. Street signs are printed in capital letters, and Ñ and accent marks are not economically practical. Additionally, local commercial printing establishments and newspapers do not customarily use diacritical marks. This results in names such as Espana instead of the orthographic España and Onate instead of Oñate, both on street signs and in most printed material. Lack of understanding of Spanish sometimes results in humorous errors in printed lists of street names such as in the telephone directory or on city maps. For example, one such list began with a series of names which used *La* 'The' as in La Jolla, La Junta, and La Luz. The word *Laguna* 'lake' was separated into *La* and *Guna*.

There have been problems with spelling. One is the b-v problem, the [B] of *burro* or the [B] of *vaca*. Tobar is officially spelled with a *b* instead of a *v*. The spelling of the proper name Cortez—with an *s* or with a *z*—became a major hurdle to a citizens' committee that assisted with renaming El Paso streets in 1958. Also there are problems of word divisions. One of the officially accepted names is the word for 'little mountain'—*montecito*—which is written as two words, Monte Cito.

As could be predicted, many pronunciation problems arise. Words like *Hueco* or *Tornillo* are difficult for the newcomer who does not speak Spanish and has not yet become familiar with Spanish pronunciation. However, most border residents are familiar with the common mispronunciations of both Spanish and English, and nobody has yet found the body of the tourist from Boston or New York or Cincinnati who starved because he could not pronounce the name of a street on which a restaurant was located sufficiently well to find it. And the story of the traveler from the interior of Mexico who called a taxi to the corner of Right Turn and No Parking is undoubtedly likewise apocryphal.

The interaction of the two languages has shown problems with translation, duplication of signals, printing, spelling, and pronunciation. These problems are slight and should not overshadow the "peaceful commingling." In El Paso, speakers who are conversant in only Spanish or English recognize each other's problems with a tolerance born of experience.

A picture of bilingualism has been shown in that the street names have been drawn from both Spanish and English and can be placed in parallel classification in both languages. It also has been shown in the problems caused by the interaction of the two languages. These present true reflections, but the depth of the interaction of the two languages is shown best in the hybrid forms. There are separate words put together in phrases such as Lost Padre Mine Road and Old Pueblo Road. There are proper names that show hybridization such as Willie Barranza Way and Willie Martinez Way. In addition, there are compounds with morphemes taken from both languages to form single words. These are Lomaland, Verdeland, and Yermoland. Thus, bilingual onomastics can be shown in the intimate joining of the two languages in street names. However, none of this seems particularly strange in a community where a friend may use the greeting, *"Usted okay?"* And the reply may be, "Oh, I'm *bueno. Y usted?"*

REFERENCES

CITY PLANNING BOARD
n.d.   Street Names—General Information. El Paso, Texas.

GALLEGOS, LAMERO HERNÁN
1927   *Gallegos' Relation of the Rodríguez Expedition to New Mexico.* George P. Hammond and Agapito Rey, trs. and eds. Publications in History, Vol. 4 New Mexico Historical Society, Santa Fe.

GLEASON, H. A., JR.
1965   *Linguistics and English Grammar.* Holt, Rinehart and Winston, Inc., New York.

MILLS, ANSON
1921   *My Story.* Press of Byron S. Adams, Washington.

MILLS, W. W.
1962   *Forty Years at El Paso, 1858–1898.* Introduction and notes by Rex W. Strickland. Carl Hertzog, El Paso.

PORTER, EUGENE
1968   El Paso Streets and How They Were Named. *Password* XIII: 2.

SIMMONS, MARC
1968   *Spanish Government in New Mexico.* The University of New Mexico Press, Albuquerque.

SONNICHSEN, C. L.
1968   *Pass of the North, Four Centuries on the Rio Grande.* Texas Western Press, El Paso.

STEWART, GEORGE RIPPEY
1958   *Names on the Land.* Houghton Mifflin Co., Boston.

STRICKLAND, REX W.
1963   *Six Who Came to El Paso, Pioneers of the 1840's.* Southwestern Studies, Vol. 1, No. 3. Texas Western College Press, El Paso.

TAYLOR, ISAAC
1865   *Words and Places.* George Routledge and Sons, Ltd., London.

THOMLINSON, A. H.
1945   *The Garrison of Fort Bliss, 1849–1916.* Hertzog & Resler, Printers, El Paso.

TIBÓN, GUTIERRE
1961   *Onomástica Hispanoamericana.* Editorial Intercontinental, S.A., Mexico, D. F.

U.S. POST OFFICE DEPARTMENT
Street Directory of the principal cities of the United States, embracing letter carrier offices established to April 30, 1908.

VELAZQUEZ DE LA CADENA, MARIANO
1967   *Spanish and English Dictionary.* Follett Publishing Company, Chicago.

PART II

AMERICAN INDIANS

9. *Assumptions for Bilingual Instruction in the Primary Grades of Navajo Schools*

ROBERT D. WILSON

This article is a review of some of the assumptions the author has made in the development and implementation of bilingual-bicultural curriculum for Navajo students in the early primary grades. It provides a brief characterization of some of the ideas of Piaget and Bruner that underlie the assumptions under review and offers suggestions about the possible effects of a second language and culture.

Adapted from a presentation originally made to the Conference on Child Language held in Chicago, November 22–24, 1971 sponsored by the Association Internationale de Linguistique Appliquee, the Center for Applied Linguistics, and the American Council on the Teaching of Foreign Languages.

THE NAVAJO CURRICULUM[1] is unlike any other curriculum in its design, in the breadth of its comprehensiveness, and in the depth of its integration; yet in some way or another it is like many other courses of study both recent and ancient.

My original assignment was to develop an ESL course similar to *Starting English Early*, (Wilson, et al, 1967) one that would be appropriate to the Navajo situation. I soon realized however that what was needed was a total curriculum (all day, all subject areas, plus learning itself), needed not only for teaching English more effectively[2] but also to provide the Navajo student with the abilities for coping with the school situation, with the two cultures, and with change—the one predictable feature of the future. This realization resulted in a change of assignment: develop and implement a total curriculum—with no restrictions on the design.[3]

Simply stated, the curriculum set out to develop and expand the students' abilities for learning, teaching them how to learn, so they could

[1] The original invitation by Allen Yazzie, former education officer of the Navajo Tribe, for me to participate in what is now known as the Rough Rock project eventually led to the decisions by Dr. William Benham of the Navajo Area Office of the Bureau of Indian Affairs for me to design and direct a thousand-participant workshop, two workshops for academic administrators, and the development and implementation of the bilingual-bicultural curriculum (one of a number of curricula available to his teachers) discussed in this paper.
    CITE (Inc.), for Consultants In Total Education, was formed to facilitate the legal and financial processes required in undertakings such as this. Materials and services from CITE include the following: (1) Planned programs for 160 effective teaching days (approximately 1000 separate lessons) per school year for each grade level. These are produced in approximately 30 manuals. Each lesson is essentially a complete plan for the teacher and aide, including specifications of materials to be used, staging, and a brief explanation of the theory behind the instruction. Specific visuals (picture materials) and other realia are also furnished. (2) In-service training of teachers and aides. Planned in the context of specific objectives, this training provides the teacher/aide team with appropriate practice in the use of the curricula and supplies evaluation of post instruction behavior of the team as learners. Training takes the form of a summer workshop and a midyear workshop as well as clinical supervision by CITE staff and CITE-trained BIA supervisors.
    [2] "In the Rizal statistics there are strong implications that the degree of mastery of a language (be it Filipino or English) that a pupil achieves depends much more on extensive use of the language than on direct language instruction. The evidence is particularly clear with regard to the mother tongue, which is, of course, almost the only language the average pupil uses outside of school hours. Conclusion 2 of the Rizal experiment states: 'The average level of literacy in Tagalog (Filipino) *is not* closely related to the number of years in which it has been used as a medium of instruction.' In other words, the pupil learns his mother tongue largely by using it to satisfy his normal non-academic needs for communication. With regard to the second language, Conclusion 1 states: 'Proficiency in English *is* directly related to the number of years in which it is used as the medium of classroom instruction.' A little reflection seems to resolve the apparent contradiction. It is in his subject-matter classes that the Filipino child gets his best opportunity to use English for communication purposes." (Prator 1967:vi)
    [3] Except for the limitations due to the level of funding; but this was adequate if not generous.

cope with change. It set out to sensitize them to the two cultures, teaching them to be aware of the underlying human nature shared by the two cultures, so they could cope with the two cultures. It set out to structure what the teachers taught and to generalize how they taught, tailoring the curriculum to the children's needs as humans and as Navajos, so they could cope with the school situation. And it wove all three objectives into one design so that in the process of achieving one objective, the students were getting ready to achieve another objective; for example, cultural and human awareness predisposed them to learning, learning how to learn predisposed them to schooling, structured (alternating with unstructured) schooling predisposed them to more learning, generalized teaching methods taught them how to learn, how to learn predisposed them to learning the new culture and understanding their own, etc., etc., etc.

Making students aware of how to learn assumes their innate abilities for learning. Making them aware of the human condition that underlies the two cultures assumes a common humanity, theirs and everybody else's. Making them aware of structure in subject matter assumes their basic predisposition towards pattern—for pattern takes less storage space (than lists) and generates knowledge (deBono 1969). Innate abilities, common humanity, structure in subject matter are all inherent qualities.

This is the basic heuristic of the curriculum, to find the inherent and make them pervasive like growing veins in the organism. The inherent generates. Innate learning abilities process knowledge into structure. Structured knowledge accommodates knowledge beyond itself. (Bruner 1960:Ch. 2) Humanity makes room for all cultures. And the inherent regenerates. Awareness of one's innate learning abilities, if appreciated and used, consciously used, brings about a stronger grasp of one's innate learning abilities. Awareness of structured knowledge, if appreciated and used, consciously used, brings about a greater familiarity with structured knowledge. Awareness that humanity makes room for more than one culture, the two cultures, if appreciated and (given the opportunity) used, consciously used, brings about a deeper sense of humanity. It is what the curriculum considers inherent and what the curriculum has done with the inherent that will characterize the assumptions reviewed in this paper.

One of the suspicious exercises of program writers is to claim assumptions without specifying how, specifically, they are made manifest in the program. (What, in other words, the curriculum has done with the inherent.) I will avoid this by giving examples from the methodology of the curriculum, but two things should be kept in mind. First, that one example of how an assumption is expressed in the curriculum does not list all of the ways in which the assumption is expressed in the curriculum. Second, that the derivation of a curricular expression of an assumption from the assumption is not an exercise in logic, where an expression is the only necessary derivation from a particular assumption. Rather, such derivation is the bold act of an intuition, a decision based on insufficient evidence. This second caveat is the motivation for the following section.

CLARIFICATION: THE TERMS OF A SCHEMA FOR INSIGHTS

It took quite a while for practitioners of TESL to detach themselves from absolute faith in pattern practice. The growing concern with pattern practice finally succeeded in breaking with the faith when Clifford Prator saw pattern practice as manipulation, pointing out at the same time that all that practice was not altogether appropriate practice for a terminal objective of language, communication (Prator 1965). Prator's insight was based on implicitly seeing two levels of the pedagogical schema: manipulation as a term in a learning assumption and pattern practice as a term in an instructional hypothesis. Insights like his are more easily come by when a proper schema is explicitly available. It is the purpose of this section to propose a schema that will provide the analytical clarity needed for generating insights into pedagogical issues and, consequently, for efficiently developing curriculum, any curriculum—and provide, as well, the terms and framework for discussing a few of the assumptions for instruction in the primary grades of Navajo schools.

The schema has four terms: learning assumption, instructional hypothesis, teaching technique, and teacher performance. A learning assumption postulates that an interpretation on the part of the learner will generate learning of some kind. An instructional hypothesis predicts the condition under which the learner's (appropriate) interpretation is likely to be secured. A teaching technique determines and projects the condition-corresponding behavior on the part of the teacher that is likely to trigger the intended interpretation on the part of the learner. A teacher's performance actualizes the technique and makes it believable, like an actor makes a role believable.

There are two theses to the schema. First, that it is the teacher's creative act in making the performance of the technique believable that triggers the intended interpretation, and the interpretation—itself a kind of learning—generates the learning promised by the assumption. Second, that each level of the schema (i.e., each term) is a system: a system of assumptions, a system of hypotheses, a system of techniques, and, even, a "system" of performance.[4]

The caveat from the preceding section bears repeating. The chain of events from the teacher's creative act to the learning promised by the assumption is as strong as the weakest link in the derivations from term to term in the schema. A derivation, say of an instructional hypothesis from a learning assumption, is not an exercise in logic, where one instructional hypothesis is the only necessary derivation from a particular learning assumption. Rather, derivation is the bold act of an intuition, a decision based on insufficient evidence.

Learning Assumptions vs. Instructional Hypotheses

The confusion of learning assumptions with teaching hypotheses is apparently quite common in education, taking the form of doctrinaire instructional hypotheses. This happens because it is apparently presumed that the derivation of instructional hypotheses from learning assumptions is an exercise in logic, where one instructional hypothesis is the only logical derivation from a particular assumption. This is well exemplified in statements that inform both assumption and hypothesis as one and the same claim. For example, it is claimed that learning increases with the increase of individual attention provided in smaller classes, in smaller groups within a class, or ideally in a one teacher-one pupil ratio in a tutorial situation. The assumption: learning increases with the increase of individual attention. The hypothesis: this increase in individual attention is effected through smaller classes, smaller groups within a class, or a tutorial situation. The doctrine: only this hypothesis will bring about the increased learning promised in the assumption.

One source of the confusion between learning assumptions and instructional hypotheses is the failure to take note that while a learning assumption is, as a rule, held true for an individual, an instructional hypothesis, in the social context of today's education, is predicted to hold true for a classroom full of pupils. So, learning increases with increase of individual attention—for the individual so attended, according to the instructional hypothesis that opts for, say, small groups in a class, in which individual attention is expressed as something physical or geographical. Thus, in a classroom full of pupils where a teacher has sub-

---

[4] The level of performance is also systemic, requiring a coordination of skills and a recurring pattern of such coordination in order for the performance to be effective and consistently effective. This is implied in the section, "the task of improving performance." The reason for discussing performance separately from the other levels is that the others are more amenable to analytic systematization while performance is more amenable to synthetic systematization.

divided his class into five smaller groups, group A is getting more of the teacher's attention at any given time. Presumably, group A is increasing its learning. However, groups B, C, D, and E are meanwhile not getting the teacher's attention as implied by the hypothesis. Presumably, these groups do not profit increased learning. Indeed, these four groups profit less learning than if the teacher attended to the class as a whole, distributing what little of his attention is available to each in such a large class.[5] An important question is raised. Is the increased learning in group A alone greater or less than the increased learning for the whole class if attended to as a whole? The point here is the question, not the possible answer to the question. The question suggests that the proposed instructional hypothesis, teacher-pupil ratio, might not be adequately expressing the assumption of increased learning from increased individual attention. It implies that there might be another instructional hypothesis which would be adequate.

If individual attention is not to be expressed as something physical or geographical in the specific form of teacher-pupil ratio, how else might individual attention be expressed? Note, first, that attention implies attention felt by the students (since ineffective attention would promise no increase in learning). Note, second, that individualized attention implies attention felt by each and every student as applying to himself. Given these two observations, individual attention might simply mean that each and every child in the class believes that he has a secure place in the mind (and heart?) of the teacher. Secure . . . a guarantee that nothing, but nothing, will threaten that security, not failure to succeed, not failure to behave, not failure to conform, nothing. Such a feeling of security does not occasion remarks like "The teacher doesn't like to call on me" nor the compulsive "Teacher likes to call on me first." Appreciate the challenge of these remarks, considering that even some of the best intentioned teachers fall into patterns of calling on mostly one category of pupils in the class. For example: mostly the brightest pupils or mostly the slowest ones because the teacher likes to provide challenge; mostly the best behaved ones or mostly the most troublesome because the teacher means to keep control; mostly the well-adjusted or mostly the maladjusted because the teacher wishes to be a parent. The challenge: "Call on me to participate on the same chance that anyone and everyone of my classmates has. Do not select among us, not even me, on the basis of any criterion whatsoever. Don't make me dependent on any criterion for a place in your mind and heart. Such dependency

---

[5] Perhaps, if the children in group B through E are self-teaching rather than simply keeping out of the teacher's way with busy work, some amount of increased learning can be claimed, that is, if.

makes me insecure, distracting me from the objective of the lesson, from learning, and eventually from caring about learning—caring, and attending, only to the criterion you have set up."

To meet such a challenge, I have provided the curriculum with an instructional hypothesis: *randomization* of pupil participation assures individual attention for all members of the class. Randomization of pupil participation means that every child in the class has equal chances of participation, equal to every other child, virtually all the time.[6] It means, further, that every child in the class believes he has an equal chance of participation because he recognizes randomization for what it is, a game of chance. If the hypothesis is found to hold true, then, on the basis of the learning assumption that increased individual attention brings about increased learning, it may be inferred that to the degree that the pupils feel assured of individual attention, they will profit increased learning. The difference between this instructional hypothesis and that of teacher-pupil ratio is the degree to which they can assure individual attention to each and every child in the class. Whatever the difference and whichever assures greater individual attention, it has been demonstrated that more than one instructional hypothesis can be derived from one and the same learning assumption.

Instructional Hypotheses vs. Teaching Techniques

However, neither the teacher-pupil ratio nor the randomization hypothesis is a hypothesis in the sense of testable, at least not by current experimental methods in pedagogy. Both of them need to be behaviorally defined. And both of them should be placed in very specific contexts, also behaviorally defined. If they are to be compared, their contexts should be identical or near identical, depending on the rigor required.

The behavioral form of an instructional hypothesis is a teaching technique, and the technique is tested in a specific teaching situation which, itself, includes other teaching techniques.

An experiment attempts to determine the effect of the teaching technique in the teaching situation. Confusion arises when the experiment is believed to have determined the effect of the instructional hypothesis rather than of the teaching technique. This is generally due to the behavioral orientation of interpreters of experiments: disinclined as they are to recognize a more general, nonbehavioral, yet insightful instructional hypothesis underlying the more specific, behavioral, also insight-

---

[6] No one instructional hypothesis can dominate all of the class time; otherwise, other useful hypotheses would have to be excluded. The effectiveness of an instructional hypothesis often depends on the presence of another instructional hypothesis (or more) in the same teaching situation. In this case, Randomization is related to Volunteering (to be discussed on p. 152).

ful teaching technique, they make the teaching technique the underlying principle itself. This confusion of technique for the more general hypothesis reveals itself among some educators in their obsession with particular media—either for or against them—for example, color coding, workbooks, primers.

The confusion of teaching technique for instructional hypothesis is sometimes traceable to the presupposition that there is only one technique for an instructional hypothesis. But this is just not the case. For example: one technique for effecting the instructional hypothesis of randomization is to have the teacher select students for participation by picking out a card from a deck of cards (like an honest card dealer would), each card with a pupil's name on it; another would be to pull out a slip of paper from a paper sack full of slips of papers with the pupils' names on them; still another would be for a blindfolded student in the middle of a circle of his peers to turn several times with one hand outstretched, stopping to point, unpredictably, to one of them; and why not a crap game between each pupil of a pair, the winner of each pair playing against another winner, and so on until only one winner remains. All of these techniques but the last one have the advantage of brevity, leaving enough time in the period for the objective to be learned. The last one, however, will take most of the class period, leaving very little time for learning. Should the last technique be the one used in a pedagogical experiment, the effect of randomization on learning would be minimal, that is, nonsignificant. Should such an experiment be interpreted as a demonstration of the ineffectiveness of the instructional hypothesis? Or of the teaching technique?

On the other hand, a technique that is demonstrably effective in an experiment elicits a degree of confidence in the underlying instructional hypothesis—but not to the exclusion of other representative techniques that may also be demonstrably effective. The exclusion of other techniques as representative of one and the same instructional hypothesis when one technique has already been demonstrated effective probably arises when the experiment is believed to be generalizable to other contexts: that is, the same technique that proved more effective[7] in a specific context is applicable, unchanged, to another context. The same technique may prove effective in the next context, but then again it may not. Stated this way, hypothetically, the non-generalizability of a technique elicits academic agreement to the thesis. For example, the demonstrable effectiveness of the technique of written texts for the instruc-

[7] The notion of inference from sample to population (parameter) in experiments on human behavior is currently being debated; cf. Denton E. Morrison and Ramon E. Henkel (eds.), *The Significance Test Controversy* (1970).

tional hypothesis of programmed instruction among able readers does not turn out as effective a technique among weak readers, for example, beginning ESL learners in high school classes where number systems are taught through programmed texts in English.

The Tasks of Formulation and Reformulation

One can begin to appreciate the tasks of formulating and reformulating teaching techniques, instructional hypotheses, and learning assumptions by realizing the implications of the thesis that there is more than one possible derivation from term to term in the schema. This is the thesis that has been argued so far in this paper. An example of the implications of this thesis in the formulation of a teaching technique from an instructional hypothesis is here presented to plant the seed of appreciation.

The example. The questions below are relevant to the formulation of a technique (or set of techniques—depending on one's unit of behavior) for the instructional hypothesis recommending a smaller teacher-pupil ratio in a classroom, specifically, smaller groups within a class.

(a) Will the class be divided into two, three, four, five, or more groups?

(b) What criteria will be used to determine the groups?

(c) Will the pupils be informed of the criteria for the grouping? If so, how will the criteria be presented?

(d) Which subgroup will the teacher attend to first on any given unit of time, say during a day, which second, which third (etc.)? Will different groups be attended to first on different days? if so, how will this be determined?

(e) Will the teaching differ for each group or only for some of the groups, or not differ at all?

(f) Will the groups not directly attended to by the teacher at any given time be self-teaching? Or will busy work be allowed? How will self-teaching be distinguished from busy work?

Still more questions come to mind should the division of the class into small groups be changeable:

(g) Will the different groups be formed daily, weekly, or monthly? Or will some particular behavior, like a symptom, signal the need for a new division of the class?

(h) Will the same criteria to determine the groups be used each time a new division is formed? Or different criteria?

(i) Will the time taken to determine the groups at different times be significant enough to affect, negatively, the promises of increased learning? If so, how can this be avoided?

(j) Will teaching change as different groups are determined according to different criteria?

Appreciation of the tasks of formulating and reformulating the components of each level (i.e., each term) of the schema deepens with a consideration of a second thesis of the schema, that each level is a system—a system of techniques, a system of hypotheses, and a system of assumptions. For example, take questions (e) and (j) above, both of which ask about teaching itself. If the teaching will differ for the different groups or if the teaching will change as the groups change, how will the teaching change? An entire spectrum of teaching techniques becomes a kaleidoscope of questions. And the answers to these questions, a specific set of techniques, can make or break the previously determined technique (whatever it was) for implementing the teacher-pupil ratio hypothesis. Thus, the formulation of a technique requires the formulation of other techniques related to it, that is, the task is one of formulating a system of techniques. It is easy to believe that if the teaching techniques are all of a system, the instructional hypotheses from which they are derived are quite likely to be all of a system themselves— *pari passu* for learning assumptions.

On the level of instructional hypotheses, relatedness between hypotheses can also be shown. Take the instructional hypothesis of randomization explained earlier. It gives everyone in class an equal chance to participate, yes, those who feel ready as well as those who do not feel ready. When the latter are called to participate, an important learning assumption is violated: a student must feel ready to participate if he is to improve his learning, perhaps even, if he is to learn at all. What is needed, then, is an instructional hypothesis derived from the learning assumption of felt readiness. So, I have provided the curriculum with an instructional hypothesis that purports to reflect that assumption: *volunteering* to participate. This hypothesis requires the teacher to permit a student to refuse to participate when, as a result of randomization, he is expected to participate. (It also requires the teacher to call on only those students who are volunteering to participate in the situation where only the teacher's sense of randomization is the means of selection—but this aspect of volunteering is not relevant here.) On the other hand, volunteering without randomization would make boldness a criterion for belonging, violating the learning assumption that learning comes more readily when the student feels like an individual: that he belongs simply because he is he.

The learning assumptions are systemic in that they form a hierarchy of categories. First, there are those learning assumptions which postulate the interpretations that make it possible for learning to take place: its initiation, its continuance, and its termination. Learning might be said to be initiated by interpreting a phenomenon, say something heard, as having a particular feature, for example, a car engine with a noise pattern like that of a neighbor's. The learning might be said to be continued by evaluating the feature as worthy of checking, for example: if it is the neighbor's car, he is home earlier than usual. The learning might be said to be terminated by checking the hypothesis that it is the neighbor's car or by deciding not to check the hypothesis. The latter decision leaves the individual with only an hypothesis, the former with a conclusion; in either case, learning has occurred.

Then there are those learning assumptions which postulate the interpretations that make it possible for learning of a certain kind to take place. For example, what interpretation might be postulated for product-learning that is capable of generating more learning of the product, for example, for counting 1, 2, 3, 4, etc.? Possibly, it might be assumed that the interpretation of the product, the subject matter, as having structure, a principle, a generalization (and a particular one at that) is the interpretation that would make product-learning capable of generating more learning of the product; for example, to interpret counting 1, 2, 3, 4, etc. as an instance of addition by 1 (or, even more generally, of addition) would make the student capable of counting with numbers he is not familiar with, say 194,328,576.

There is a relationship between the two kinds of learning assumptions above. Learning assumptions that postulate interpretations which make it possible for learning to take place are prerequisites to the learning assumptions that postulate interpretations which make it possible for learning of a certain kind to take place. This seems like an obvious relationship, and it is, but it is apparently not kept in mind by some practicing educators when formulating (implicitly, probably) their instructional hypotheses (and the condition-corresponding techniques). Take the professor who describes structure XYZ of his subject matter in a lecture but fails to point out that he is describing structure XYZ or at what point in his lecture he is describing it—to initiate learning. Or take the professor who does point out structure XYZ but fails to justify, interest, or motivate the students to consider structure XYZ as worthy of checking out—to continue learning. Or the professor who does both of the preceding but fails to provide an opportunity for checking out the accuracy of the students' understanding of the structure, say by providing examples which the students have to identify as having or not having structure XYZ—to terminate learning. In any case, the relationship suggests the systemic character of the learning assumptions.

The reformulation of the components on each level may start with the learning assumptions. A new assumption may suggest itself, an established assumption may be seen in a different light, a former and rejected assumption may now appear valid. What follows is a reexamination of the system of instructional hypothesis, sometimes resulting in a modification. This, in turn, prompts a reexamination of a specific technique and the rest of the system of techniques, sometimes resulting in a new design. Or the reformulation may start with an instructional hypothesis. A particular hypothesis may be inadequate, failing to provide the stated interpretation. Or it may be superfluous, another instructional hypothesis already supplying the stated interpretation. Or one instructional hypothesis may be inconsistent with another, one nullifying the effects of the other. What follows is a reexamination of the system of assumptions and the system of techniques.

The motivation for reformulating techniques is empirical, or should be. This is the level of the schema which is testable. As the techniques of a curriculum get tested, whether rigorously or loosely, a pattern for modification may be revealed. The key to discovering a pattern and selecting the most promising new design of techniques is a familiarity with the system of instructional hypotheses from which the system of teaching techniques has been derived. Modifying the system of techniques means a reexamination of the system of instructional hypotheses, making it, in turn, subject to possible modification itself. With possible ramifications for the system of learning assumptions.

The Task of Improving Performance

Awesome as the task of formulating and reformulating is in the development of a curriculum, even more challenging is the task of training teachers (or of teachers training themselves) in the performance of the techniques. It is obvious, but the parallelism should be noted, that just as there may be more than one instructional hypothesis to express a learning assumption and more than one teaching technique to give form to an instructional hypothesis, there may be more than one teacher performance for implementing a teaching technique.

Teaching performance varies from teacher to teacher and from day to day for the same teacher. It is dependent on the teacher's ability to act, to play a role more challenging than that of an actor or actress on a stage if only for the fact that the teacher's acting involves audience participation, demanding that the teacher prepare (with the help of the curriculum design) for a variety of situations. And the teacher must do this before and with an audience that must be more than entertained, an audience that must be taught so that it learns—as in the finest forms of play making. Like an actor or actress, the teacher must practice and perfect techniques, learn and identify with the role (instructional hypotheses), as well as understand and believe in the play (the curriculum). Like a Burton or a Bancroft, the teacher is a creative artist—at the performance, leaving (*qua* teacher) plot and script to the playwright (curriculum designer), direction to the director (curriculum supervisor) and production to the producer (school principal).[8]

Teacher performance, like acting performance, must be credible and consistently credible in order for the pupils, like an audience, to be willing and able to interpret the act of teaching for what it is: a learning opportunity. *Willingness* to make learning the interpretation of the teaching act ultimately depends on the credibility of the teacher's performance. Does the manner belie the words? Does the frown belie the smile? Does even the overjoyed surprise at a pupil's unexpected correct response belie the low esteem for this particular pupil? On the other hand, the *ability* of the pupils to make learning the interpretation of the teaching act ultimately depends on the consistency of the credibility of the teacher's performance. Does correction always provide individualized instruction—or does it sometimes express disappointment at the pupil for the mistake? Does the presentation of the lessons' objective always imply its importance and inherent interest—or are some lessons' objectives not really to be taken seriously as learning tasks? The recurrence of inconsistency increases the probability of error, the error of giving an interpretation other than learning to an act of teaching.

The seriousness of inconsistency is difficult to overestimate. As inconsistency repeats inconsistency in teaching, inconsistency begins to infect related areas like discipline, affection, esteem . . . and eventually inconsistency repeats inconsistency on all levels of communication between teacher and pupils . . . until finally mood and feeling alone dominate. The effect on the pupils? Anxiety.

Or, worse, as inconsistency repeats inconsistency, the importance of the teaching act, and its intended product—learning, becomes suspect: "What does teacher really want? Not learning. Not all the time anyway. Sometimes teacher just wants me to speak up loudly. Sometimes to make mistakes . . . when I get something right, teacher finds some

---

[8] A similar comment was made by Bernard Spolsky in "An Evaluation of Two Sets of Materials for Teaching English as a Second Language to Navajo Beginners," Final Report, BIA Contract No. NOO C 1420 2415, June 13, 1969. The comment:

> To what extent does a precise curriculum free a teacher, and to what extent does it bind her? A difficult question to answer in the abstract, but in practice much simpler than it appears. An excellent teacher with unlimited preparation time will be more creative with less guidance, but the average teacher, with a full teaching day, performs best when she is called on to "perform" rather than "compose". The musical analogy is reasonable: one senses individual interpretative creativity in a performer of a piece of music rather than in an improviser. In practice, I felt more individual variation, more evidence of teacher personality, in those using the Wilson than in those with . . . materials.

other mistake I've made . . . I guess I'm stupid. Sometimes to behave
. . . calling on me when I'm not paying attention . . . what I say is not
important so long as I start paying attention again." Learning as the
meaning of class activities loses importance and other meanings for the
school experience gain importance. Eventually, the primacy of learning
loses its hold on the students and the primacy of conformity to teacher's wishes takes over. Only the teacher's personality can hold the class
now, and if that loses its attraction (as is likely with inconsistent per-
sonalities), the pupils' chances of maturing into self-learners are those of
a poker addict playing against a crooked dealer. But, unlike the poker
addict who can't quit playing poker, the learning addict (he is born an
addict) may very well decide to quit the game of learning when he
realizes the odds against inconsistent teachers. If he is blessed with wis-
dom, appreciating the high stakes involved, he only quits school, not
learning.

On the other hand, a consistently credible teacher, especially one
so confident in his techniques that he consistently expects learning as the
appropriate interpretation of his teaching, emphasizes the importance of
learning, underlining it with talent, effort, time, and sincerity. There is
no better way to keep students hooked on learning.

DEFINITION: THE INTERPRETATION OF LEARNING

The title of this section is intentionally ambiguous. First, it suggests
the activity of the learner in learning, as in the definition of *learning
assumption* in the preceding section. Second, it suggests an understanding (mine) of the learning process: its bases, its stages, its uses. Together,
the first as subject and the second as predicate, they form the proposi-
tion: "The learner learns." This is by way of saying that the purpose of
this section is to provide an appreciation of the independence of the
learner from teaching. (The dependence of the learner on teaching is the
theme of another paper.)

Rather long quotes from the writings of Jean Piaget and Jerome
Bruner will have to be made; as a pedagogue, I can only select and take
the views (of psychologists) which I consider to be promising learning
assumptions, promising in that they will provide me with a fertile
source of effective and efficient instructional hypotheses.

The Learner

The interesting thing about learning is that it occurs. It doesn't
have to. Take learning as simply a changing. Changing occurs. Hit a
glass bottle with a hammer and the bottle shatters. The bottle is pieces
of glass. But changing does not have to occur. Hit a brass bottle with a

hammer, and the bottle does not shatter. It remains a bottle. Point out a bird a child has never seen and the child learns about the bird in some visual way; but point out a bird a blind child has never seen and this child does not learn about the bird in any sense visually. Learning does occur, but it doesn't have to.

For learning to occur, there must be an organism that can learn. For specific learning to occur, there must be a learner capable of such specific learning. If learning in a specific *manner* is to occur, say visually, then there must be a learner capable of learning visually. If learning about *something* specific is to occur, say a visual image of a bird, then there must be a learner cabable of learning in such a manner that learning about the something specific is possible (visually about the bird).

For learning to occur, there must be an organism willing to learn. A rat is willing to press a lever to get food, or avoid a passageway to prevent shock. For learning to occur in a specific manner, e.g., play the piano by reading notes (i.e., visually) rather than by ear (i.e., auditorily), there must be a learner willing to learn in just such a specific manner rather than the other. And if learning about something specific is to occur, then there must be a learner willing to learn about that specific something. The blind child is unable to see the bird; the child unwilling to see the bird is just as blind. (Bruner 1968: chapters 6 & 7).

Able and willing—and both inherent in the organism. The rat is able to press a lever though it may not know enough yet to do so; and the rat is willing to press a lever though it may not know enough yet to want to nor hungry enough to do so. The pupil is able to read though it may not know enough yet to do so; and the pupil is willing to read though it may not know enough yet to want to nor interested enough to do so. These two classes of potential functions are not learned, not from the experimenter by the rat, not from the teacher by the pupil. To say inherent of these is to say innate: in the genes.[9]

What *is* the pupil able to do?

> ... all such behavior that has innate roots but becomes differentiated through functioning contains, we find, the same functional factors and structural elements. The functional factors are *assimilation*, the process whereby an action is actively reproduced and comes to incorporate new objects into itself (for example, thumb sucking as a case of sucking), and *accommodation*, the process whereby the schemes of assimilation themselves become modified in being applied to a diversity of objects. The structural elements are, essentially, certain *order relations* (the order of movements in a reflex act, in a habitual act, in the suiting of means to end), *subordina-*

---

[9] "Having solely a genetic basis. This is what I, and I believe most geneticists and psychologists, ordinarily understand by the term (innate). According to this definition, only the genes are innate." (Braine 1971:184)

tion schemes (the subordination of a relatively more simple schema like grasping to a relatively more complex one like pulling) and *correspondences* (recognition, invariance, causality as in getting at things by using a stick—RDW). (Piaget 1970:63)

This is the way the pupil begins his life as an organism. He grows, develops, matures, i.e., "becomes differentiated through functioning," by means of these very same functions and structural elements; for example:

> As soon as the semiotic function (speech, symbolic play, images, and such) comes on the scene and with it the ability to evoke what is not actually perceived, that is, as soon as the child begins to represent and think, he uses reflective abstractions: certain connections are "drawn out" of the sensori-motor schemata and "projected upon" the new plane of thought; these are then elaborated by giving rise to distinct lines of behavior and conceptual structures. The *order relations*, for example, which on the sensori-motor plane were altogether immersed in the sensori-motor schema, now become dissociated and give rise to a specific activity of "ranking" or "ordering." Similarly, the *subordination schemes* which were originally only implicit now become separated out and lead to a distinct classificatory activity; and the setting up of *correspondence* soon becomes systematic: one/many; one/one; copy to original, and so on. (Italics mine— RDW) (Piaget 1970:64)

What is the pupil willing to do? In other words, if the Piagetian view of the ability to generate structures and behavior is all that the organism begins with, what explains an organism's willingness to generate specific sorts of structures and behavior and not others, human language by humans, flying by birds, and neither by horses, for instance? As Piaget puts the question to himself: "Why does it look 'as if' the results were 'predetermined'?" (1970:62)

> The behavior of the living subject depends upon quite explicit meanings; instinctual structures, for example, function in terms of all sorts of hereditary "clues"—the IRM's, "innate releasing mechanisms," of the ethologists. But meanings are implicit in all functioning, even the specifically biological distinction between normal and abnormal conditions depends on them; for example, when at birth, there is danger of suffocation, the coagulation of the blood immediately gives rise to regulation through the nervous system. (Piaget 1970:48)

He is apparently unwilling to view as innate the underlying structure of behavior even while criticizing empiricism's view that all learning is dependent on the environment:

> ... what is no less essential is that contemporary ethology tends to show that all learning and remembering depend upon antecedent structures (conceivably the DNA and RNA themselves). Thus, the contacts with experience and the fortuitous modifications due to the environment on which

empiricism modeled all learning do not become stabilized until and unless assimilated to structures; these structures need not be innate, nor are they necessarily immutable, but they must be more settled and coherent than the mere gropings with which empirical knowledge begins. (1970:51)

What Piaget proposes is an innately guided (by the meanings, the clues, the IRM's) process of construction that of necessity generates species-specific structures of behavior (Piaget 1970:67, 90). It is instructive to have Piaget elaborate on this:

> In the construction proposed . . . the function (in the biologist sense of the word) chiefly credited for the formation of structures was "assimilation" . . . Biologically considered, assimilation is the process whereby the organism in each of its interactions with the bodies or energies of its environment fits these in some manner to the requirements of its own physico-chemical structures while at the same time accommodating itself to them. Psychologically (behaviorally) considered, assimilation is the process whereby a function, once exercised, presses toward repetition, and in "reproducing" its own activity produces a schema into which the objects propitious to its exercise, whether familiar ("recognitory assimilation") or new ("generalizing assimilation"), become incorporated. So assimilation, the process or activity common to all forms of life, is the source of the continual relating, setting up of correspondences, establishing of functional connections, and so on . . . (1970:71)

Note in particular the phrases, "fits these in some manner to the requirements of its own physico-chemical structures" and "produces a schema into which the objects propitious to its exercise, whether familiar or new, become incorporated," for they lead to the next question.

What is the pupil willing to do that he is able to do? For example, which of the thousands of languages he is capable of learning will he learn? Or, what does the pupil become? Piaget's view is that the organism particularizes not by itself alone but by interaction with the environment while reaffirming again the influential role of the organism's responses, influential on itself and on succeeding generations. He remarks on C. H. Waddington's work (1957):

> Waddington has shown that environment and gene complex interact in the formation of the phenotype, that the phenotype is the gene complex's response to the environment's incitations, and that "selection" operates, not on the gene complex as such, but on these responses. By insisting on this point, Waddington has been able to develop a theory of "genetic assimilation," i.e., of the fixation of acquired characteristics. Roughly, Waddington views the relations between the organism and its environment as a cybernetic loop such that the organism selects its environment while being conditioned by it. (1970:49–50)

> Waddington, by reestablishing the role of the environment as setting "problems" to which genotypical variations are a response, gives evolution

the dialectical character without which it would be the mere setting out of an eternally predestined plan whose gaps and imperfections are utterly inexplicable. (1970:50)

Piaget is insistent on taking the learner as the controlling agent of the learning process:

> Everyone grants that structures have laws of composition, which amounts to saying that they are regulated. But by what or by whom? If the theoretician who has framed the structure is the one who governs it, it exists only on the level of a formal exercise. To be real, a structure must, in the literal sense be governed from within. So we come back to the necessity of some sort of functional activity; and, if the facts oblige us to attribute cognitive structures to a subject, it is for our purposes sufficient to define this subject as the center of functional activity. (1970:69)

Piaget has been suggesting that the pupil brings with him all the processes and all the structural elements—the innate ability (as well as the innate willingness)—to learn species-specific behavior like language and thinking and sensory-motor skills, needing only contact with the environment, i.e., needing only experience, to particularize the language, groove the thinking, and sharpen the sensory-motor skills. Remember that Piaget's pupil brings with him only the structural elements (order, subordination, and correspondence), not structures themselves; structures (that is, particular structures, like a particular language) are constructed by means of the processes of assimilation and accommodation regulated by the pupil himself on the basis of his nature. In short, species-specific particularized structures and behavior are learned; they are not given, but they are inevitably learned. The learner learns.

The Learning

The purpose of this subsection is rather ambitious: to provide a model of learning that takes Piaget's stages of intellectual development as the given rules of a race and Jerome Bruner's modes of representation as the tactics for running the race. It is not an explanatory model for it does not provide data about behavior needing explanation. It is not a hypothetical model for it does not provide hypotheses about behavior for testing. It is simply a heuristic model in that it has helped me to organize the learning assumptions that underlie the instructional hypothesis of the curriculum. And it is limited, providing only for the intellectual domain of the curriculum.

Piaget's work of the last thirty years has produced a description of the intellectual development of children that is consistent with the behavior of Swiss children and shows promise of being consistent with the behavior of children in other cultures, allowing for accelerations and delays. (Piaget 1970: 37). It is only a promise, but it will do. I now quote Piaget, letting him describe his theory in his own words and in the least technical language I could find. (Each of the four stages will be named for later reference; they are not part of the quote.)

Sensorimotor

> With perceptions and movements as its only tools, without yet being capable of either representation or thought, this entirely practical intelligence nevertheless provides evidence, during the first years of our existence, of an effort to comprehend situations. It does, in practice, achieve the construction of schemata of action that will serve as substructures for the operational and notional structures built up later on. At this level, for example, we can already observe the construction of a fundamental schema of conservation, which is that of the permanence of solid objects . . . Correlatively, we can also observe the formation of structures that are already almost reversible, such as the organization of the displacements and positions of forward and backward or circling movements (reversible mobility). We can watch the formation of causal relationships, linked first of all to the action proper alone, then progressively objectified and spatialized through connection with the construction of the object, of space, and of time.

Semiotic

> The onset of this second period is marked by the formation of the symbolic or semiotic function. This enables us to represent objects or events that are not at the moment perceptible by evoking them through the agency of symbols or differentiated signs. Symbolic play is an example of this process, as are deferred imitation, mental images, drawing, etc., and, above all, language itself. The symbolic function thus enables the sensorimotor intelligence to extend itself by means of thought, but there exist, on the other hand, two circumstances that delay the formation of mental operations proper, so that during the whole of this second period intelligent thought remains preoperational.
>
> The first of these circumstances is the time it takes to interiorize actions as thought, since it is much more difficult to represent the unfolding of an action and its results to oneself in terms of thought than to limit oneself to a material execution of it: for example, to impose a rotation on a square in thought alone, while representing to oneself every ninety degrees the position of the variously colored sides, is quite different from turning the square physically and observing the effects.
>
> In the second place, this reconstruction (to interiorize actions as thought—RDW) presupposes a continual decentering process that is much broader in scope than on the sensorimotor level . . . the child must not only situate himself in relation to the totality of things, but also in relation to the totality of people around him, which presupposes a decentering process that is simultaneously relational and also social, and therefore a transition from egocentrism to those two forms of coordination, the sources of operational reversibility (inversions and reciprocities).
>
> Lacking mental operations, the child cannot succeed during this sec-

ond period in constituting the most elementary notions of conservation, which are the conditions of logical deductibility. Thus he imagines that ten counters arranged in a row become greater in number when the spaces between them are increased . . . that a quantity of liquid in glass A increases when poured into the narrower glass B, etc.

Concrete operations

. . . there begins a third period in which these problems and many others are easily resolved because of the growing interiorization, coordinating, and decentering processes, which result in that general form of equilibrium constituted by operational reversibility (inversions and reciprocities). In other words, we are watching the formation of mental operations: linking and dissociation of classes, the sources of classification; the linking of relations A B C . . . the source of seriation; correspondences, the sources of double entry tables, etc; synthesis of inclusions in classes and serial order, which gives rise to numbers; spatial divisions and ordered displacements, leading to a synthesis of them, which is mensuration, etc.

But these many budding operations still cover no more than a doubly limited field. On the one hand they are still applied solely to objects, not to hypotheses set out verbally in the form of propositions (hence the uselessness of lecturing to the younger classes in primary schools and the necessity for concrete teaching methods). And, on the other hand, they still proceed only from one thing to the one next to it, as opposed to later combinative and proportional operations, which possess a much greater degree of mobility. These two limitations have a certain interest and show in what way these initial operations, which we term "concrete," are still close to the action from which they derive, since the linkages, seriations, correspondences, etc, carried out in the form of physical actions also effectively present these two types of characteristics.

Formal operations

. . . there begins a fourth and final period . . . characterized in general by the conquest of a new mode of reasoning, one that is no longer limited exclusively to dealing with objects or directly representable realities, but also employs "hypotheses," in other words, propositions from which it is possible to draw logical conclusions without it being necessary to make decisions about their truth or falsity before examining the result of their implications. We are thus seeing the formation of new operations, which we term "propositional," in addition to the earlier concrete operations: implications ("if . . . then"), disjunctions ("either . . . or"), incompatibilities, conjunctions, etc. And these operations present two new fundamental characteristics. In the first place, they entail a combinative process, which is not the case with the "groupings" of classes and relationships at the previous level, and this combinative process is applied from the very first to objects or physical factors as well as to ideas and propositions. In the second place, each proportional operation corresponds to an inverse and to a reciprocal, so that these two forms of reversibility, dissociated until this point (inversion of classes only, reciprocity of relationships only) are from now on joined to form a total system in the form of a group of four transformations. (1970b:30–33)

The four stages are not to be associated with actual age groups; Piaget only claims that they occur in the sequence given (1970:37). He provides approximate ages as guidelines, ages based on his observation of Swiss children. The sensorimotor stage begins at birth, the semiotic at about the age of two, the stage of concrete operations at about the age of seven or eight, and that of formal operations at about eleven or twelve of which the plateau coincides with adolescence (1970:30–33). The Navajo children participating in the curriculum at present are six and seven years old, and they will be ten when the planned five-year curriculum is completed. My (informal) observations permit me to estimate cautiously that they begin the curriculum when they are in the last mile of the semiotic stage and are well into the concrete operational stage by the end of the second year of the curriculum.

The heuristic model of learning takes Piaget's theory as constituting the rules of a race. There are just three rules. One, that there are always to be these four stages: perhaps more by a finer classification. but not less, i.e., no skipping. Two, that the four stages occur in the sequence given: sensorimotor first, semiotic second, concrete operational third, and formal operational fourth. Three, that the bottom rung of each stage is a *sine qua non* for beginning that stage: purely verbal hypotheses for the fourth stage, operational reversibility and internal representation of action (interiorization) for the third stage, language for the second, and perception and movement for the first. On the other hand, there are no rules against acceleration or deceleration, as Piaget himself has pointed out (1970:37), nor are there rules against using a preceding stage as basis for acceleration in the following stage, as implied by Piaget's view of each stage being a preparation for the next in his description and discussion above.

Bruner, too, has developed a view of intellectual development, which he calls instrumental conceptualism:

> . . . that is organized around two central tenets concerning the nature of knowing. The first is that our knowledge of the world is based on a constructed model of reality . . . that rests on what might be called an axiomatic base . . . That is, the physical requirements of adaptive action "force" us to conceive of the world in a particular way, a way that is constrained by the nature of our own neuromuscular system. So, too, are we constrained by the primitive properties of visual, auditory, and haptic space in our effort to represent our knowledge in terms of imagery. Finally, our representation of reality in terms of language or symbolism is similarly constrained by what again seem to be our native endowment for mastering particular symbolic systems, systems premised on rules of hierarchy, predication, causation, modification, and so forth.
> . . . the second is that our models develop as a function of the uses to which they have been put first by the culture and then by any of its mem-

bers who must bend knowledge to their own uses . . . Our instrumentalism is inherent in this double emphasis on the role of use . . . one cannot separate (except analytically) cultural instrumentalism and individual instrumentalism. (Bruner 1966:319–320)

The parallel with Piaget and Waddington is evident: the innate necessity of choosing and performing species-specific behavior in a certain way yet modifying that behavior in a particular way in interacting with the environment; for example, the innate necessity for humans to choose to communicate through (human) language and inventing—performing it in a certain universal manner yet modifying it so that it becomes the particular language needed for a particular environment.

What distinguishes Bruner's theory from Piaget's that is of interest to the heuristic model are the three techniques Bruner posits man has for constructing a model of reality: the enactive, the ikonic, and the symbolic. Briefly, and in his words:

> . . . the means by which growing human beings represent their experience of the world; and how they organize for future use what they have encountered. There are striking changes in emphasis that occur with the development of representation. At first the child's world is known to him principally by the habitual actions he uses for coping with it. In time there is added a technique of representation through imagery that is relatively free of action. Gradually there is added a new and powerful method of translating action and image into language, providing still a third system of representation. Each of the three modes of representation—enactive, ikonic, and symbolic—has its unique way of representing events. Each places a powerful impress on the mental life of human beings at different ages, and their interplay persists as one of the major features of adult intellectual life. (Bruner 1966:1)

To understand how these three techniques of representation serve as available tactics for running the race of learning according to Piaget's rules, one must understand representation as *act* (as Piaget would prefer) or as *medium* (as Bruner would have it) towards some *objective*. It is uninstructive to make an issue between act and medium; since Bruner infers medium from behavior (as he must, methodologically), one might agree to see the act/behavior as creating the medium/representation in the mind.[10] In explaining the three modes of representation, Bruner begins by viewing each as external:

> With respect to a particular knot, we learn the act of tying it and, when we "know" the knot, we know it by the habitual pattern of action we have mastered.
> Representation in imagery is just that: the picture of the knot in

---

[10] Though Piaget reportedly "doubts whether . . . enactive representation ought to be called representative at all." (Bruner 1966:10)

question, its final phase or some intermediate phase, or, indeed, even a motion picture of the knot being formed. It is obvious . . . that to have a picture before one (or in one's head) is not necessarily to be able to execute the act it represents, as those who have invested in books called "Skiing Illustrated" know all too well.

The representation of a knot in symbolic terms is not so readily stated, for it involves at the outset a choice of the code in which the knot is to be described. For symbolic representation, whether in natural or mathematical "language," requires the translation of what is to be represented into discrete terms that may then be formed into "utterances" or "strings" or "sentences," or whatever the medium used to combine the discrete elements by rule . . . it is also necessary to specify whether one is describing a process of tying the knot or the knot itself (at some stage of being tied). There is . . . a choice . . . whether to be highly concrete or to describe this knot as one of a general class of knots. (Bruner 1966:6–7)

But it is as "internal" that the three techniques of representation must be understood if they are to serve some objective; they must be understood as *plans* (Miller et al, 1960) by which objectives may be reached, if the individual is willing. The characteristics of internal representation are only beginning to be understood; but they show promise of being in the right direction. It is only a promise, but it will do. So, in Bruner's words (the headings are not part of the quote):

Enactive Representation

When motor activity becomes "regularized" or "steady," is it converted from a "serial" to a "simultaneous" form? . . . In order for behavior to become more skillful, it must become increasingly freer of immediate or serial regulation by environmental stimuli operative while the behavior is going on. I believe that this "freedom" is achieved by a shift from response learning to place learning—in effect, the placing of the behavior in a spatial context or "layout" that makes possible detours and substitutions to meet changed conditions . . . For example, over time all hammering behavior becomes translatable into a common schema, even though the different hammering acts may each involve different muscle groups.

(Earlier in the same chapter, page 10, Bruner provides two examples of "substitution:")

What is at first a habitual pattern for using sensorimotor activity to achieve some end later becomes a program in the sense that various "substitutes" can be inserted without disrupting the over-all act. Even a chimpanzee who is unable to get a hand into an opening to extract a desired object can substitute a stick in place of reaching. Or in skilled tool-using by humans the carpenter who forgets his plane can substitute a chisel in the smoothing routine, a pocket knife, or the edge of a screwdriver, if need be.)

It is of some comfort to quote . . . Leeper (1963, pp. 404–405) on the relation of motor activity to underlying representational process . . . "Maybe the whole point can be summed up by saying that movements often are like symbols or actually are symbols. Their significance is determined by the relations of those movements to a larger context of the situation. A person blows on his hands to warm them, he blows on his soup to cool it." (Bruner 1966:18–21)

Ikonic Representation

Perception in young children can be characterized by the following features, according to Gibson and Olum (1960): (1) it is "stuck" or non-transformable; (2) it is "autistic" or subject to the influence of effect; (3) it is "diffuse" in organization; (4) it is "dynamic," in the sense of being closely related to action; (5) it is concrete rather than schematic or abstracted; (6) it is "egocentric," in the sense of having a central reference to the child as observer; and (7) it is marked by an unsteady attention. To this interesting list we would add one more entry: (8) the young child's perception is organized around a minimal number of cues, and these cues are usually the ones to which the child can most readily point.

... —all suggest a system that, unlike the serial ordering of action and enactive representation, is labile (subject to change) and highly lacking in ... economy ... It is as if the young child, having achieved a perceptual world that is no longer directly linked to action, now deals with the surface of things that catch attention rather than with deeper structures based on invariant features. Or, to put it another way, it is as if the child has as its next principal task to find precisely a way of getting to the base structure of the world of appearance. In one experiment after another ... we ... see the younger child failing to solve problems by virtue of using surface cues while the older child succeeds by learning to respond to such "invisible" or "silent" features as relations, hierarchies, etc.

... the inferior conceptual performance of children with imagery preference is a result of their use of surface features in grouping.

Ostensive definition (e.g., pointing), as we shall see again and again in later chapters, is critical to the child's thinking in ikonic representation. It is only when he can go beyond this "match by direct correspondence" that he comes to deal with such "nonsensory" ideas as the relations between quantities, invariance across transformations, and substitutability within a conceptual category. (Bruner 1966:21–29)

Symbolic Representation

... symbolic activity stems from some primitive or protosymbolic system that is species-specific to man. This system becomes specialized in expression in various domains of the life of a human being: in language, in tool-using, in various atemporally organized and skilled forms of serial behavior, and in the organization of experience itself. We have suggested some minimum properties of such a symbolic system: categoriality, hierarchy, predication, causation, and modification. We have suggested that any symbolic activity, and especially language, is logically and empirically unthinkable without these properties.

What is striking about language as one of the specialized expressions of symbolic activity is that in one of its aspects, the syntactic sphere, it reaches maturity very swiftly. The syntactical maturity of a five-year-old seems unconnected with his ability in other spheres. He can muster words and sentences with a swift and sure grasp of highly abstract rules, but he cannot, in a corresponding fashion, organize the things words and sentences "stand for." This asymmetry is reflected in the child's semantic activities, where his knowledge of the senses of words and the empirical implications of his sentence remain childish for many years, even after syntax has become fully developed.

One is thus led to believe that, in order for the child to use language as an instrument of thought, he must first bring the world of experience under the control of principles of organization that are in some degree isomorphic with the structural principles of syntax. *Without special training in the symbolic representation of experience, the child grows to adulthood still depending in large measure on the enactive and ikonic modes of representing and organizing the world, no matter what language he speaks.* (italics mine—RDW)

In view of the autonomy of the syntactic sphere from other modes of operating and of its partial disjunction with the syntactic sphere, one is strongly tempted to give credence to the insistence of various modern writers on linguistics that language is an innate pattern, based on innate "ideas" that are gradually differentiated into the rules of grammar. (Bruner 1966:47-8)

One of the striking observations Bruner makes regarding these instruments of intellect, these plans, these techniques of representation, is that—except perhaps for enactive representation—they could possibly not "occur." Ikonic representation would begin but could remain locked in by the strategy of attending only or mostly to surface features in grouping. Symbolic representation, too, would begin—language certainly—but could remain locked in by the strategy of attending only or mostly to the goals of communication and conformity that language makes possible, but not to the goal of thinking. It is this observation that makes Bruner's techniques of representation something like decision-making acts, strategies, tactics, for intellectual development. The wrong tactics can knock a pupil out of the race. The right ones help him win the race. If the rules are obeyed, Piaget will permit the runner to go faster:

> The development of intelligence, as it emerges from the recent research just described, is dependent upon natural, or spontaneous, processes, in the sense that they may be utilized and accelerated by education at home or in school but that they are not derived from that education and, on the contrary, constitute the preliminary and necessary condition of efficacy in any form of instruction. (Piaget 1970b:36)

As plans, modes of representation are put to use to serve certain purposes, the most important of which, for the heuristic model, are the translation or transformation of one mode of representation to another.

(Bruner 1966:11, 48–49) This is a two-step process. A mode of representation guides behavior: doing, sensing, and symbolizing. The behavior in turn, creates a representation. When a mode of representation guides behavior other than the behavior specific to it, then the new kind of behavior creates the representation specific to *it*. Suppose the teacher says, "Point to the ship" or "Point to the sheep," the student's looking is guided by language and the looking creates an ikonic representation.

It should be evident that the transformation of one mode of representation to another is a combination of tactics that could just possibly accelerate the pace of a student in the race of learning. All possible transformational combinations are available to the child of school age, to the bilingual learner as well as to the monolingual. Indeed, the Navajo child has a potential advantage: he can combine the awareness of the structure of the second language (specifically, its syntax) that comes from his deliberate learning of it with an awareness of thought processes as isomorphic to that structure—*if the curriculum provides him with "special training in the symbolic representation of experience."*

From all this, from Piaget and Bruner (as I understand them), the pupil is to be taken as central: his is the ability and the willingness to initiate and incorporate learning; his are the acts that initiate and incorporate learning; his is the culture or cultures that measure his learning. Thus, that the *learner* learns is one of the assumptions. Also, that the learner *learns*.

But does the learner learn *enough*? Or, does the learner learn *well enough*? That is, on his own? In other words, can he construct a model of his experience with *all* three modes of representation? Put differently, can he reach his full intellectual potential as *homo sapiens* on his own?

> Then, if the child lives in an advanced society . . . he becomes "operational" (to use the Genevan term for thinking symbolically), and by age five, six, or seven, given *cultural supports* (italics mine—RDW) he is able to apply the fundamental rules of category, hierarchy, function, and so forth, to the world as well as his words. Let it be explicit, however, that if he is growing up in a native village of Senegal (Chapters 11 and 13), among native Eskimos (Chapter 13), or in a rural mestizo village in Mexico (Chapter 12) he may not achieve this "capacity." Instead, he may remain at a level of manipulation of the environment that is concretely ikonic and strikingly lacking in symbolic structures—though his language may be stunningly exquisite in these regards. (Bruner 1966:46)

(Whether one of the "cultural supports" needed, even in an "advanced" society, is teaching, and specifically teaching that provides "special training in the symbolic representation of experience," is the theme of another paper.)

STIPULATION: THE CONDITIONS FOR LEARNING[11]

A learning assumption, one remembers from section II, postulates that an interpretation on the part of the learner will generate learning of some kind. The interpretation on the part of the learner is input in a learning assumption but output in an instructional hypothesis, which, one remembers, predicts the condition under which the learner's (appropriate) interpretation is likely to be secured. This section of the paper reviews those interpretations of the assumptions of the curriculum that are derivable from the learning theories discussed in the preceding section. How the interpretations from these learning assumptions are made manifest in the curriculum will be phrased as instructional hypotheses.

It will help at this point to observe that Bruner's term, "representation," and my term, "interpretation," are equivalent. Also, Piaget's view of the learner as the "center of functional activity," i.e., as the source of learning acts, constitutes a representation the learner has of himself; otherwise, it would not be within him to be willing to learn. In my terms, the learner interprets—sees, feels, intuits—himself as the agent of learning.

The first learning assumption, then, is that the learner who sees himself as a decision-making agent of learning is willing to learn. (His willingness to learn is actualized into learning when other conditions for learning are present, but these other conditions are not relevant here except as they appear below in the explanation of the instructional hypotheses.) Two of the instructional hypotheses that express this learning assumption in the curriculum are *volunteering* and *breaks*. Volunteering was explained in section II under the heading, "The tasks of formulation and reformulation." *Breaks* predicts that pupils who are given an opportunity to decide whatever they want to do or to choose among several activities will see themselves as decision-making agents of learning. The curriculum provides for *break* time after each and every

---

[11] The title of this section refers to the conditions stipulated in instructional hypotheses. It is intended to emphasize the importance of converting learning assumptions into instructional hypotheses, even in a paper on learning assumptions if the paper is intended as a paper in education. A remark by Bruner is appropriate here:

One might ask why a theory of instruction is needed, since psychology already contains theories of learning and of development. But theories of learning and of development are descriptive rather than prescriptive. They tell us what happened after the fact; for example, that most children of six do not yet possess the notion of reversibility. A theory of instruction, on the other hand, might attempt to set forth the best means of leading the child toward the notion of reversibility. A theory of instruction, in short, is concerned with how what one wishes to teach can best be learned, with improving rather than describing learning. (Bruner 1968:40)

lesson. The children's decisions fall into two classes: problem-finding, i.e., deciding whatever they want to do, and problem-solving, i.e., choosing among several activities much like those independent problem-solving tasks found in Montessori classrooms. The realia for the *breaks* fall into the same two classes. For example, in the problem-solving category, a jigsaw puzzle may be chosen instead of a pair of cubes with matching equivalent number sentences. If a child chooses the jigsaw puzzle, he obligates himself to put the pieces together and form the expected picture. On the other hand, if the jigsaw puzzle is in the problem-finding category, a child who chooses that may also put the pieces together to form the expected picture, or he might stack them up to see how high they will go (or for whatever reason he may have in mind), or he might deploy them on the floor, imagining them to be horsemen on a hunt, etc.

Another assumption stems from the learner's actions, a basic concept in Piaget's theory:

> ... the essential fact ... is that knowledge is derived from action, not in the sense of simple associative responses, but in the much deeper sense of the assimilation of reality into the necessary and general coordinations of action. To know an object is to act upon it and to transform it ... To know is ... to assimilate reality into structures of transformation, and these are the structures that intelligence constructs as a direct extension of our actions.
>
> The fact that intelligence derives from action ... leads up to this fundamental consequence: even in its higher manifestations, when it can only make further progress by using the instruments of thought, intelligence still consists in executing and coordinating actions, though in an interiorized and reflexive form ... intelligence, at all levels, is an assimilation of the datum into structures of transformations, from the structures of elementary actions to the higher operational structures, and that these structurations consist in an organization of reality, whether in act or thought, and not in simply making a copy of it. (Piaget 1970b:28–29)

What this implies is that a pupil need not actually participate in the condition-response situation of a lesson himself but that he participate in such wise that the "condition-response" fact is acted upon and transformed by him. This provides the curriculum with the learning assumption that the pupil who accurately interprets the response of another pupil as either correct or incorrect himself assimilates the response. The mental transformation consists in rendering the expected response in the form of an evaluation. Observe that this rendering need not occur overtly and needs only to be intended for some sort of transformation to take place and make the response a part of the evaluating pupil. The instructional hypothesis that expresses this learning assumption in the curriculum is *evaluation*. It predicts that pupils who have been taught to expect to be asked to evaluate the response of another will interpret the response of the other pupil as correct or incorrect. It should be noted that this instructional hypothesis effects the promise of the learning assumption only for those pupils who evaluate accurately. For those who do not, another instructional hypothesis (actually a subsystem of instructional hypotheses), *correction*, provides the desired learning. One of the teaching techniques for implementing *evaluation* is simply to call on another pupil, selecting on a random basis, to evaluate the response of the (overtly) participating pupil by saying, "Is that right?" Because this is done virtually all the time, day in and day out, the procedure becomes an accepted convention to the point of being taken for granted. Any use of the procedure to embarass an erring child would not be due to the procedure as such but to the deliberate lack of charity of the abuser—if it ever happens. Notice, too, that such a convention gets all the pupils in the class to expect to evaluate at any time, making them participate vicariously as evaluators until one of them is chosen (randomly) to overtly evaluate: everyone learns.

Bruner's three modes of representation are classes of representations, taking their form in the curriculum in many different ways. The enactive mode is particularly useful in the *pronunciation* and *rhetoric* (in the first level, dramatics) strands. The ikonic mode is itself the objective of the *visual* strand. The symbolic mode is a major objective of the entire curriculum. To explore their systematization and implementation in the curriculum is too formidable a task at present. Suffice it to say that they constitute a major portion of the system of learning assumptions on which the curriculum is based.

However, one learning assumption from Bruner's theory is too interesting to ignore. And that is: the pupil who interprets language as an instrument of thought becomes a willing builder of symbolic representation. Bruner motivates this assumption with:

> Once language is applied, then it is possible, by using language as an instrument, to scale to higher levels. In essence, once we have coded experience in language, we can (but not necessarily do) read *surplus meaning* into the experience by pursuing the built-in implications of the rules of language. (Italics mine—RDW)   (1966:51)

In other words, language is not necessarily applied as an instrument of thought, that is, language is not necessarily used to read surplus meaning into an experience. But, because the rewards are so great and inherent in the act itself and because symbolic representation is a natural ability available to *homo sapiens*, a realization of language as an instrument of thought should succeed in persuading the student to use language to structure his world in terms of symbolic representation.

One instructional hypothesis that grows out of this learning assumption is the prediction that pupils who are constantly expected to verbalize their school-learning experience will interpret language as an instrument of thought. Obviously, this does not prevent the children from interpreting language as a means of communication or a form of conformity. The deliberate implementation of this instructional hypothesis in a technical society might not seem too useful to Bruner:

> What has become much plainer to us in the course of our work is that there are important institutions and pressures that develop within societies of the technical type, which lead to the demand for confirmation between the three modes of knowing. Whenever learning occurs outside the context it will be used, outside the range of events that are directly supportive in a perceptual way or indirectly available for pointing, then language enters as a means of conveying the content of experience and of action. Under these circumstances, there is more often than not a requirement of developing correspondence between what we do, what we see, and what we say. It is this correspondence that is most strikingly involved in reading and writing, in "school learning," and in other abstract pursuits. The confrontation may not always work its way to correspondence, to be sure. (1966:321–322)

Still, his last statement, the risk of not achieving the correspondence between enactive or ikonic representation and language, is enough motivation for the instructional hypothesis. The odds may be good, but the stakes are high. An even more important motivation for the instructional hypothesis, however, is to effect another related learning assumption as well: the pupil who constantly interprets language as an instrument of thought learns to prefer symbolic representation over the other two modes of representation. (Other instructional hypotheses maintain a sense of importance for the other two modes of representation: for the enactive mode in strands requiring performance, e.g., *music* and *rhetoric*, and for the ikonic mode in strands requiring visual structure, e.g., *geometry*, *rhetoric* (stage layouts with make believe props), and art activities.

The implementation on this instructional hypothesis in the curriculum is thorough. Virtually every lesson presents its objective perceptually with very carefully selected sentences to express it. The lessons that require action also provide the necessary language. Many lessons need to set up situations and the teachers use imperatives to direct the students in the set up. Most of the lessons expect the students to generate questions about actions or scenes previously associated with language of their own so that transformation from imperatives or statements to questions are the order of the day. Most importantly, this instructional hypothesis is supported by another instructional hypothesis, *correction*, which gives priority to semantic errors over grammatical or phonological ones. In other words, the correction procedure is primarily aimed at structuring experience, and structuring it symbolically, I might add.

LIMITATION: THE SITUATIONS OF LEARNING

Situation is context. It is a limitation only in the sense that a general theory of instruction needs to be transformed to be effective and efficient in a particular situation. Changing a situation can be one of the objectives of a theory of instruction, for example, the design of a school building could be changed to better serve learning. Still, changing the situation is but a preliminary step if and when it can be done. Very soon, and in some cases at once, attempts to change the situation cease. At this point the situation is a given. And it is neutral. Wailing and complaining about the situation may be effective for the long run, but for the here and now it is inefficient.

Situation is not always a handicap. In the case of Navajo children in American schools, creating a bilingual and bicultural situation, the situation provides opportunities for the Navajo pupil that are not available to his monolingual-monocultural fellow American. The bilingual situation provides the Navajo pupil with the opportunity to better develop symbolic representation. The theory of instruction should take advantage of this opportunity by providing the already predisposed pupil with an ESL course of study that elicits a *deliberate* learning of the second language. And it should take the same advantage of the opportunity in the other areas of the curriculum, emphasizing even more the deliberate learning of the semantics of the new language. L. S. Vygotsky, in his impressive work, *Language and Thought*, remarks:

> Specifically, our experiments brought out the following inter-related facts: The psychological prerequisites for instruction in different school subjects are to a large extent the same; instruction in a given subject influences the development of the higher functions far beyond the confines of that particular subject; the main psychic functions involved in studying various subjects are interdependent—their common bases are consciousness and deliberate mastery, the principal contributors of the school years. (1962:102)
>
> (Our) chief purpose was to test experimentally our working hypothesis of the development of scientific concepts compared with everyday concepts ... Analysis of the data compared separately for each age group ... showed that as long as the curriculum supplies the necessary material, the development of scientific concepts runs ahead of the development of spontaneous concepts. (1962:106)
>
> ... though he can correctly answer questions about "slavery," "exploitation," or "civil war," these concepts are schematic and lack the rich content derived from personal experience. They are filled in gradually, in the course of further schoolwork and reading. One might say that *the development of the child's spontaneous concepts proceeds upward, and the development of his scientific concepts downward, to a more elementary and*

concrete level. This is a consequence of the different ways in which the two kinds of concepts emerge.

> In working its slow way upward, an everyday concept clears a path for the scientific concept and its downward development. It creates a series of structures necessary for the evolution of a concept's more primitive, elementary aspects, which give it body and vitality. Scientific concepts in turn supply structures for the upward development of the child's spontaneous concepts toward consciousness and deliberate use. (1962:108–109)
>
> The influence of scientific concepts on the mental development of the child is analogous to the effect of learning a foreign language, a process which is conscious and deliberate from the start. (1962:109)

The bicultural situation provides the Navajo pupil with an even more impressive opportunity. Consider what one culture does for an individual: "Insofar as man's powers are expressed and amplified through the instruments of culture, the limits to which he can attain excellence of intellect must surely be as wide as are the culture's combined capabilities." (Bruner 1966:326) Imagine what two cultures could do for the individual. Consider further the rare opportunity of perceiving not just the differences between the two cultures but the deep similarities as well. In so doing the Navajo child might wonder if the similarities aren't accidental, that perhaps, just perhaps, the similarities reflect genuine human values. And one day someone will make a chance remark like "We are all brothers under the skin," a cliche, nothing more; but the Navajo child, now a little grown, will read surplus meaning into it.

REFERENCES

DeBono, Edward
  1969   *Mechanism of Mind.* Simon & Schuster, New York.
Braine, Martin D. S.
  1971   On Two Types of the Internalization of Grammars. In *The Ontogenesis of Grammar. A Theoretical Symposium* Dan I. Slobin, ed. Academic Press, Inc., New York.
Bruner, Jerome S.
  1960   *The Process of Education.* Harvard University Press, Cambridge.
  1968   *Toward a Theory of Instruction.* W. W. Norton & Co., Inc., New York.
  1971   *The Relevance of Education.* W. W. Norton & Co., Inc., New York.
Bruner, Jerome S., Rose R. Olver, Patricia N. Greenfield, et al.
  1966   *Studies in Cognitive Growth.* John Wiley & Sons, Inc., New York.
Chomsky, Noam
  1968   *Language and Mind.* Harcourt, Brace & World, Inc., New York.
Lenneberg, Eric H.
  1967   *Biological Foundations of Language.* John Wiley & Sons, Inc., New York.
Miller, George A., Eugene Glanter, and Karl H. Pribram
  1960   *Plans and Structure of Behavior.* Henry Holt & Co., New York.
Morrison, Denton E. and Rama E. Henkel, eds.
  1970   *The Significance Test Controversy.* Aldine Publishing Co., Chicago.
Piaget, Jean
  1970a *Structuralism.* Basic Books, Inc., New York.
  1970b *Science of Education and the Psychology of the Child.* Orion Press, New York.

PRATER, CLIFFORD H.
   1965   Development of a Manipulation Communication Scale. In *1964 Conference Papers, National Association for Foreign Student Affairs*, R. Fox, ed., Washington, D.C.
   1967   Foreword to *Philippine Language Teaching Experiments* by Frederick B. Davis. Alemar-Phoenix Press, Quezon City, Philippines.
SPOLSKY, BERNARD
   1969   An Evaluation of Two Sets of Materials for Teaching English as a Second Language to Navajo Beginners. Final Report, BIA Contract No. NOO C 1420 2415, June 13.
VYGOTSKY, L. S.
   1962   *Thought and Language*. The M. I. T. Press and John Wiley & Sons, Inc., Boston and New York.
WILSON, ROBERT, EVELYN BAUER, EDDIE HANSON, JR., DONALD MEYER, AND LOIS M. MICHAEL
   1967   Teaching English Early. ERIC Accession Numbers: ED 018 801 and ED 081 802.

10. *Bilingual Education for Navajo Children*

ELIZABETH W. WILLINK

Willink stresses the need to use and teach the Navajo language in the classroom as English is used and taught in Anglo schools. Such instruction for Navajo children may be essential for the development of the thought and learning processes that are needed for success in school and adult life. English also should be taught from the beginning, she maintains, but only gradually should English be used for the intensive development of the cognitive skills of Navajo children.

THE EDUCATOR'S CONCERN is with providing the conditions, including the guidance of learning activities and materials, under which the individuals in his care may optimally develop. Historically, the first educational task assigned to the school was to teach certain skills. The tasks of teaching a certain body of knowledge and of certain attitudes and appreciations soon followed. They are mainly thought of as utilitarian tasks: society needs educated people and therefore society pays the bill for the schools. It is true that, particularly in America, the responsibility of the school is understood to be to equip the student with such skills, knowledge, and attitudes that he will have the widest possible range of choices for the way he may choose to lead his adult life in the American society, rather than keep his choices limited to just a few alternatives by dint of ignorance, lack of ability, and too early specialization. Yet, this worthy goal does not detract from the basic assignment to the school: to deliver citizens who can be productive in society, satisfactory and useful to themselves, but decidedly also to society. This aspect of utility to society definitely is subsumed under "optimal" development of the students.

The educator then, pondering the best conditions for his students' optimal development, should listen to the social philosopher who will tell him nowadays that in the American society minority groups should be favorably regarded and respected as such—by everyone, including themselves. He should listen to the psychologist and the sociologist who will tell him that the attitude toward one's mother tongue, including one's own attitude, affects one's self-acceptance. The educator had better listen to this, for he knows that self-acceptance is a strongly favorable psychological condition for learning whatever one has to learn.

The arguments for bilingual education that derive from such social philosophy and these findings of psychology and sociology are therefore important to the educator. In a sense they are basic to his task of providing optimal conditions for optimal development of his students. Nevertheless, they are peripheral to the educator's central task, which is to concern himself with curriculum, method, and materials.

SCOPE OF DISCUSSION

This paper will limit itself to a discussion of bilingual education for Navajo children who come to school with no, or hardly any, English at all (by conservative estimate 1,500 to 2,000 every year). The discussion will stay within the narrow focus of the educator's concern for the development of skill by his students in those cognitive processes that are most suited to learning in school and to leading a useful adult life. With our world changing more and more rapidly, the emphasis in education is shifting—perhaps expanding—to include not merely content, but also process; to include not merely a certain body of knowledge and such skills as reading and writing, but also learning how to think, learning how to learn, cognitive skills; to include making the students not only informed but also smart—smart problem-solvers—for change tends to create problems.

In the narrow focus of the educator's concern for the development of useful cognitive skills, bilingual education looks as appealing to the educator as it does to the social philosopher, the psychologist, the sociologist. The problem of implementing a bilingual program for Navajo children, however, is complex and difficult to solve. The difficulties are in the realm of practice, not of theory. They bear on materials, personnel, scheduling, cost. These will not be dealt with in this paper.

BILINGUAL EDUCATION DEFINED

For a clear discussion of theory it seems necessary, first of all, to qualify and specify what is meant by "bilingual education." Together these terms mean that education—teaching and learning—should take place and that, language being what it is, education should take place *in* and *through* two languages.

This implies then, first, that it is not enough that two languages are *used* in the classroom. If merely usage were the criterion, it could be said that bilingual education has been a fact on the Navajo Reservation ever since the first school opened, as the students use Navajo, and continue to use it, among themselves, for years, even after they have learned some English.

Second, it means that it is not enough either that one language, English, is taught as such, and that it is also used to teach other school subjects (as far as this is possible), while the other language, Navajo, is used for explanatory purposes. In this sense today's Bureau of Indian Affairs schools could be said to use bilingual education in many classrooms.

Third,—and this point is made here with emphasis—it is not even enough when one language, English, is taught as such, and also used to *teach*—not merely explain—the so-called "content" subjects and mathematics. Even this is not enough.

In order to be attractive to the educator—at least to this educator—bilingual education should mean that both languages are taught, are "developed," in educational jargon, to the same extent that we teach English to our Anglo children, that the French teach French to their French-speaking children, that the Germans teach German to their German speaking children, etc. In all countries with the institution of formal education, the mother tongue is taught in school with the highest priority among the many subjects that vie for a place in the curriculum. Even though the children already speak their mother tongue when they come to school, their language is taught, is developed, through the teaching of vocabulary and syntax, and through the development—the teaching and much practice—of the language arts, with a heavy emphasis on reading. This kind of language teaching, it is here posited, also should take place in the Navajo bilingual classroom, in both languages, if it is to serve the sought goal. For Navajo, the method should be the traditional method of native language teaching. For English it should be TESL, since English *is* the second language to our Navajo children. English, of course, initially will lag a long way behind Navajo in development.

The point that the native language should be taught with and through all four language arts, might seem too obvious for statement for bilingual education for Spanish-speaking children in America, because literacy in Spanish is an established tradition for millions of people. For Indians the point may not be so obvious, hence the emphasis it is given here.

As far as other school subjects are concerned, both languages should be used to teach them, to the extent of the learners' command of the languages, and to the extent that the teacher has developed sufficient command of the language for such teaching. The last qualification pertains to the Navajo teachers, who, though fluent in Navajo, have never used their language for teaching purposes, having gone to school before the time of bilingual education. These teachers' Navajo has remained undeveloped. They often find it difficult to use their own language for school-educational purposes, for which they themselves have heard and used only English.

School subjects other than English or Navajo should be taught for their own sake, of course. But teaching them in two languages has two important side effects. First, there is the practice it provides in the two languages themselves. Second, not any less important, there is the practice it provides for functioning in two languages, for functioning as a bilingual. This is important, for smooth bilingual functioning is quite an accomplishment. It requires a mental agility of a particular kind; it usually requires, or is accompanied by consciousness or near-consciousness of concepts that monolinguals can afford to leave alone in the subconscious; it requires effort and much practice to learn it. So, we should provide this practice. Subject matter other than the languages themselves should be dealt with in both Navajo and English.

"ECHOING" OPPOSED

This does not mean that every lesson should be "echoed" as some seem to assume is implied in this advocacy of having the students deal with the same subject matter in both languages (Wilson 1968–1970). By "echoing" is meant that the same lesson is taught in identical manner in the two languages. This is clearly a waste of time and effort as far as the content is concerned. Strictly speaking, it is a contradiction in terms. If the students have learned what the first lesson was supposed to teach, then the second lesson, if of the same format as the first one, could not possibly "teach" the same content again, as "teaching" presupposes the acquisition by the learners of new skills or ideas. If the second lesson is identical in format to the first one, it could teach the language for the already learned content. It would then be a language lesson, however, maybe a useful one, but not a lesson in the content area. Almost all lessons, however, need follow-up lessons in which the content is made more familiar, closer delineated, practiced with. Such follow-up lessons, in the second language, can teach the language of the subject matter as well as more of the subject matter itself. The students will then get practice in bilingual functioning, the rationale of the recommendation to deal with the same content in two languages, but from the standpoint of learning content, there is no waste of time and effort.

LANGUAGE-THOUGHT RELATIONSHIP

The deliberate development—not merely the use—of both languages' in and through all the language arts, has been emphasized here because we have known for a long time the intimate relationship that exists between language and thought, between language development and thought development. The relationship is complex, dynamic rather than static. A great deal about it is still unknown.

Summarizing what seems to be the consensus to date among the investigators of this relationship (Piaget 1959; Vygotsky 1962; Liublinskaya 1957; Amster 1965; Taba 1965), we could define thinking as structuring reality, i.e. "making sense" out of the continuous stimulation to which we are submitted by virtue of being equipped with our senses. For this structuring, that is, for thinking, actual sensory perception is used, which itself can be characterized as an active and selective mental process. In addition, the memory of previously received stimuli, and the thoughts and concepts derived from those, are used in thinking. Concepts find their expression in language, in vocabulary as well as in syntax. But besides expression language has another important function. The child "learns the world" along with, and through, his first language.

The mother tongue greatly aids in *forming* concepts in the growing child. And the importance of the role of language in concept formation increases as the child grows older.

Language then not only expresses, but also forms concepts in the learner. Language learning, mother tongue learning, and conceptual development, however, don't appear to take place along neatly parallel lines and at the same rate. There is prelinguistic conceptualization and there is also a period, apparently, until about the age of twelve or thirteen, on the average (in the children of the investigators' culture, that is), during which language competence runs ahead of true concept acquisition. Yet, even this discrepancy is believed to be aiding the child in acquiring the concepts for which he already has learned the language (Vygotsky 1962:126,127).

Whatever light further investigations may shed on this complex relationship between thought and language, the educator, who cannot wait with his teaching until all the answers are in, knows, and has known for a long time, that when he speaks of his pupils' language development, he implicitly means their general mental development. One need not even turn to schoolteachers for this common knowledge. Many a concerned mother of a "big-word-using child", about to enter school, has heard the reassuring comments from non-schoolteacher friends: "Don't worry about him. He is bound to do well in school. Just listen to his vocabulary!" For once a folk notion that does not seem likely to be contradicted by scientific findings!

To summarize the argumentation thus far presented: language development, and particularly mother tongue development where the mother tongue is the child's dominant language when he comes to school, is extremely important for thought development, and thought development is what education is about. Once the child has better learned how to think, and thereby how to learn, he is better equipped to learn anything that he may need to learn—including the second language, English. This theory is now beginning to be confirmed in some recent studies (e.g., Modiano 1966).

The implication seems obvious: we should not be satisfied with letting the native language merely be used in the bilingual classroom in a haphazard and undirected way. We cannot expect Navajos to develop thought processes at the rate and of the quality that Anglos develop them, without giving the Navajos the same help in the form of deliberate native language teaching and practice that we give Anglo children.

LANGUAGE/LANGUAGE ARTS

Any language program should take into account the distinction between language and the language arts as well as the relationship between them. Development of language-mediated thought, of language-mediated cognitive skills, takes place through the practice of the language arts. When the child comes to school, he already has learned a great deal of his own language. He also has already acquired some skill in listening and speaking when he comes to school. Reading and writing are taught in school with the help of the already acquired competence in listening and speaking. Also, all four language arts or skills are 1) further developed in activities that have this development as their purpose, 2) utilized and practiced in the teaching and learning of more language, 3) utilized and practiced in the teaching and learning of subject matter other than language. Clearly, the relationships among language, the language arts, thought, and learning—in whatever subject area—are complex and interacting. Whatever the complexity, it is certain that language helps, and greatly forms, thought; that language and thought find their connection in the language arts, and that thinking and learning—in whatever subject area—are highly correlated, perhaps, it could be argued, identical.

A tool cannot be used profitably for its purpose until the user has developed a certain familiarity with it and at least some skill in using it. A language cannot be used profitably for cognitive purposes, either by the user privately or in communication, until the language itself, its structure as well as its content vocabulary, has become familiar, has become "known" to a certain extent, and, secondly, until the user has developed at least some skill in the language arts. This explains why the conceptual range and thought processes cannot really be expanded very much to include concepts on a higher than the concrete level of organization in small Navajo children through the medium of English during the first few years of school. It is futile to hope for this. English, the language itself, the tool, must first be learned. This takes time. Especially under the prevailing conditions in most schools attended by young Navajo children—the "beginners" year that the B.I.A. and some public schools have allowed before the first grade, is not enough. The English that the first grade curriculum assumes the first graders to have learned before they come to school cannot be learned by Navajo children in one year under the prevailing conditions. Our whole experience to date with Navajo education attests to this conclusion. (It is interesting to note that one year does not seem to be enough for the young Maoris in New Zealand either, judging from Ashton-Warner's (1963) anticipation that with better reading materials the young Maori might no longer have to spend three years in the infant room.) Only when the learner has acquired a familiarity with, a knowledge of, the English that he is assumed to have acquired by the curricular materials, is he ready for the intensive development of the psycho-motor techniques that reading and the productive language arts require, i.e., only then is the learner ready for being taught by these curricular materials. Only then can he begin to draw upon his knowledge of English and his growing skill in the English language arts for his general mental development. This means that there should be a period of several years in the school program during which the language itself, English, should be taught intensively and as efficiently as possible with great emphasis on listening comprehension. This comprehension should include comprehension of structural signals, which signify the more difficult to understand abstract relationship concepts, as well as comprehension of easier to grasp content vocabulary. The skills of speaking, reading, and writing in English also should be taught, but the student should not be asked to express or read meanings in English that he has not learned to understand in spoken English. (With older students, well versed in all the language arts in their native language, the methodological sequence for learning a second language might be different.)

The above may answer the skepticism of many towards bilingual education: why mental development in such a roundabout way—first through the development of Navajo and then through English? Why add to the learning load? Why not forget about Navajo, teach reading in English early and let that take care of mental development as is done with Anglo children? It cannot be done. One cannot improve one's mind through reading in English unless one has first learned to read in English, and one cannot learn to read in English unless one has first learned English. It is just one of those cases where the roundabout way is the most efficient way, as when the longer, but paved, road over the Navajo Reservation is clearly the better choice over the shorter dirt road where one is likely to get stuck in the sand or mud, or break an axle on the rocks.

For people with an established and well developed tradition of literacy, the emphasis in language arts instruction is on reading. Navajos do not have such a tradition. Very few reading materials are now available. It is uncertain whether they will ever become available in bulk. That will depend on whether the Navajos who may become literate in their own language will choose to offer a market, to create a demand, for materials written in Navajo. Yet, even though printed Navajo is in relatively short supply, it would seem preferable to start reading instruction in Navajo rather than in English. If a child learns to read in the language in which he is proficient rather than deficient, it would seem much more likely that he will, from the onset, understand that reading is receiving a message. Once he has thoroughly understood this, he can transfer this important understanding to reading in English. He is likely to bring the expectation of a message to whatever reading he will be asked to do, in whatever language. He will understand the purpose of exercises in reading skills, and he will be able to transfer acquired skills to reading in English. In November, 1971, in response to an informal inquiry, all of the Navajo classroom personnel, about twenty adult Navajos, at Rock Point Boarding School in the Chinle, Arizona Agency of the Navajo Reservation, declared that only close to the junior high school level, or even later, had they been able to read independently some of the assigned material with some real understanding. All frankly admitted to still finding that "reading is difficult." Each of these people's knowledge of English was still rudimentary, even though adequate for communication about day to day routine affairs. All of them are products of monolingual education in English. All of them said that they remember the first three years of school as one blur of confusion (not necessarily unpleasant as a whole, but not enlightening). It is the author's experience with these people that they still conceive of reading as looking for a fact here or there, a name perhaps, a bit of information; not as being on the receiving end of the writer's communication of a line of thought a reasoned commentary, a detailed description. What mental stimulation, what cognitive growth can be expected to take place from reading in English by people with such a limited command of English and such an unfortunately, but inevitably, acquired conception of the purpose of reading? What is to persuade them that reading is worth the trouble, that the written page may carry a message that is stimulating, reaction provoking, mind expanding?

For the early development of language-mediated cognitive skills we are, fortunately, not entirely dependent on the availability of reading materials in Navajo. We can capitalize on the potentialities of the already possessed language arts of listening and speaking in Navajo by our Navajo children. We can devise specific listening and speaking activities in which the already available language, Navajo, is used to have the children practice such mental processes as memorization—probably greatly aided by deliberate visualization—induction, inference or deduction, hypothesizing (all very useful in problem solving), analysis, synthesis, critical thinking, classification, creative thinking, etc. In Anglo middle-class homes and in good Anglo schools a great deal of such activity goes on in the form of puzzles, riddles, jokes that play on sounds and words, thought or question games, giving specific oral instructions the execution of which is then closely supervised, etc. There are now a great number of materials on the market that are designed for just such mental exercises, either for use at home or at school. They can be used in Navajo.

QUALITY NEEDED

The above might simply be summarized by stating that the education that takes place in the bilingual classroom in Navajo should be quality education. It should be remembered then that quality education has always put great emphasis on the language arts, the manipulation of symbols. Of the three R's, two refer to the natural language, the third to mathematics, which is the language, the symbolic system, for our experience of quantity.

A good educational program then, heavily relies on the language arts as the aid *par excellence* for thought development. Cognitive skills can, and should, be developed in, and with, the dominant language, Navajo. Once developed, as is possible with any skill, such language-mediated cognitive skills can, and should, be capitalized on for transfer in the learning of other subject matter, including English. It is of course true that such transfer, as any transfer, is not likely to be done spontaneously by all students. It will need the help, the encouragement, the "teaching for transfer" by the teacher. But an acquired, well-developed skill has at least the potential for being transferred, while, on the other hand, a Navajo child whose language-mediated cognitive skills have been left underdeveloped can, at best, transfer only just such rudimentary skill to situations in which he is expected to use English as his medium.

It is not known whether the Navajos give their children a great deal of deliberate language-and-thought practice at home in the way of language involving games, puzzles, closely supervised specific instructions, etc. It does not seem likely that they do. The school should do it—in the bilingual classroom, in Navajo, from the beginning of school. Parents visiting such classrooms might get the idea, because they, too, for the first time in history, would be able to understand—because it is in Navajo—what the school is after. They might then give their children a better preparation for school than they are now able to do.

At the rate that English is being learned, the same deliberate utilization of the language arts for cognitive development should be striven for in English. At first, as has been explained, the possibilities will be extremely limited, for the rate of learning English under the prevailing conditions is extremely slow. This means that—it might be repeated—the English monolingual classroom for Navajos has, for all practical purposes, to give up on the idea of using English as a serious means of general mental development for quite some time, for years. A break of years in mental development is too serious to be compensated for later as we know from our disappointing experience of the past century. Bilingual education, as roughly outlined here, would seem worth an honest try.

WHEN TO BEGIN

With regard to instruction in English in the bilingual classroom, there is a conflict between the recommendations of the child psychologist and the second language teacher. Caution has been recommended by some child psychologists against the early introduction of a second language. Not before the age of nine, or eight at the earliest, should the second language be introduced, they advocate (John 1967). The reasons for this caution are based on this very relationship between language—the mother tongue—and thought development that has been mentioned above. This relationship should not be interfered with, warns the child psychologist, until it has had time to become firmly established. Too early instruction in the second language might mean interference, resulting in confusion to the detriment of harmonious cognitive development, it is feared.

The second language teacher, on the contrary, urges starting as early as possible, because the second language apparently is learned with less conscious effort, frustration, or outright disgust, and better learned at a young age rather than later in life.

How is the educator to decide with such contradictory recommendations? It would seem that the second language teachers have strong arguments. Just the practical implications of a delay of the introduction of English would constitute enormous difficulties. Besides, and more convincing from a theoretical point of view, there are millions of people who grew up from a very early age with two languages, who had to learn a number of other languages in school, and who yet do not seem to suffer from any damage to their mental development or mental health. It would seem that the kind and the extent of the use that the child is expected to make of the second language he is learning in school has a great deal to do with the occurrence or non-occurrence of interference with general mental growth. A strong English program from the very first day of school would seem indicated, whether this be grade school, kindergarten, pre-school—as early as parents can be persuaded to bring their children to school. The nature of the English program and the use that the child is expected to make of the English he is learning should differ from the kind and the initial purpose of the English program that is now used in schools for Navajo children. Bilingual education does not mean that we should relax in our efforts to teach English, nor that we should postpone these. We can be somewhat relieved of our worries, though, in a bilingual program. We can be relieved of our worries as far as they pertain to our learners' conceptual development and their badly needed language-mediated cognitive skills. Instead of being interrupted, their mental growth can continue, if their Navajo is well developed. Aural-oral English should be learned as a subject first. Only gradually should the English thus learned be used and practiced in the teaching of other subject matter, including the language arts of reading and writing in English. Such an English program, complementing a solid instructional program in Navajo, far from being likely to interfere with general mental growth, may even contribute to it. No interference with mental growth need be feared, for there will not be the arrest of the development of the mother tongue—a condition for harmonious mental growth. There will not be the *exclusive* necessity to receive and transmit ideas with the limitations and the distortions that are inevitably caused by the clumsy use of a not fully mastered medium of communication. Since these two interfering conditions are not present in a bilingual program—arrest of the mother tongue and exclusive deficient communication—there would seem to be no reason to fear such interference with harmonious, continuous, and vigorous mental growth.

WHO CAN TEACH BEST?

Of all the practical questions pertaining to the implementation of a bilingual program for Navajo children, only two very briefly will be discussed here. The first one has a theoretical as well as a practical aspect: who shall teach in Navajo and who in English? One bilingual teacher, or two monolingual teachers? The latter is the preferable solution from a theoretical standpoint. The theory has to do with the concepts of compound and coordinate bilingualism, as defined by Ervin and Osgood (1954). The compound bilingual needs his dominant language to arrive at meaning. He translates, in effect. The coordinate bilingual decodes and encodes meanings directly from and into the language that is used. In the process of translation, meaning elements tend to get lost, added, or distorted. Moreover, the compound bilingual is slower than the coordinate bilingual when he functions in his weaker language. The educational goal, therefore, should be to establish in the minds of the learners a coordinate system for using the languages, rather than a compound system. This seems to be best achieved by keeping the stimuli that are most likely to elicit a response in one language as separate as possible from those that tend to elicit responses in the other language. The strongest stimulus for the use of one language or the other seems to be the person one is communicating with. The often cited classical example is the case of the non-English speaking grandmother from Germany living with her English-speaking children. Her grandchildren, knowing that she does not speak, nor understand English, will grow up as coordinate bilinguals. If Grandmother picks up some English, and lets her grandchildren know this, a kind of pidgin language is likely to develop for their communication, a mixture, convenient and adequate for what they want to communicate, but not wholly intelligible for either Anglo or German monolinguals. Pidgining is detrimental to learning either language well as it tends to foster interference from one language with the other. Moreover, pidgin languages are limited in their potential for expressing concepts on the higher levels of organization of experience, which invariably deal with abstractions. For cognitive development then, mixing of languages should be avoided as much as possible. It is true, of course, that languages incorporate elements from other languages; the English language itself is an outstanding example of this phenomenon. But such "borrowing" seems to take place mainly with vocabulary items, not with structural devices.

Though there is no consensus on the validity of the idea that individuals could be neatly classified as either compound or coordinate bilinguals, nor on the exact sequence of learning stages in learning a second language under conditions such as are present for our Navajo children, it would seem preferable from experience as well as theory to avoid the inducement of mixing Navajo and English in our pupils as much as this is possible. Therefore, it would seem best to set up bilingual classrooms in which a Navajo teacher teaches in Navajo, and exclusively in Navajo, expecting the children to use only Navajo with her (or him), and in which an Anglo teacher teaches in English, and exclusively in English, expecting the children to use only English with her (or him). This set-up would certainly increase the cost of such classrooms, but they might cost far less than the expensive remedial programs that are now in existence in great numbers.

The other practical question that is to be discussed here, briefly, pertains to the daily schedule—where to find the time to teach and learn the extra load of the bilingual classroom.

The answer to this question is that the time in the classroom must be used more efficiently than is currently done in most classrooms. There appears to be a considerable amount of time that is not used to its best learning advantage in the average American classroom. This circumstance gives the bilingual classroom a chance to teach and learn more and yet keep up with the general curriculum. If well planned and executed, the extra learning load will not be to the detriment of the children's mental health. Examples in other countries seem to show this; besides there is the now famous Coral Way School in Miami, Florida. Children can carry a greater learning load than they normally do in the United States and thrive on it. Careful planning and scheduling would seem to be then another condition for the successful bilingual classroom.

REFERENCES

AMSTER, H.
     1965   Concept Formation in Children. In *Elementary English* XLII, May: 543–552.

ASHTON-WARNER, S.
     1963   *Teacher.* Simon and Schuster, New York.

ERVIN, S. M. AND C. E. OSGOOD
     1954   Second Language Learning and Bilingualism. In *"Psycholinguistics,"* a Supplement to *Journal of Abnormal and Social Psychology* XLIX. Charles E. Osgood and Thomas Sebeok, eds. October: 139–146.

JOHN, V.
     1967   In a conversation with the author.

LIUBLINSKAYA, A. A.
     1957   The Development of Children's Speech and Thought. In *Psychology in the Soviet Union*, B. Simon, ed. pp. 197–204.

MODIANO, N.
     1966   *A Comparative Study of Two Approaches to the Teaching of Reading in the National Language.* University of New York, New York.

PIAGET, J.
     1959   *The Language and Thought of the Child.* Humanities Press, New York.

TABA, H.
     1965   The Teaching of Thinking. In *Elementary English* XLII, May: 534–542.

VYGOTSKY, L. S.
     1962   *Thought and Language.* Massachusetts Institute of Technology Press, Cambridge.

WILSON, R. D.
     1968-1970   In a number of conversations with the author.

11. *Bilagáana Bizaad*[1]: $E\{^S_F\}L$ *in a Navajo Bilingual Setting*

WAYNE HOLM

This article maintains that English should be taught at Rock Point as a foreign language rather than a second language. As such, one devotes more time to structural-sequential English and less time to situational English. The aim is coordinate bilingualism with an English-speaking teacher and a Navajo-speaking aide teacher working as a team to effect a separation of languages by person. Some of the problems inherent in such a program are noted and some of the changes in the role of the EFL teacher are mentioned.

[1] In Navajo, 'the Anglo, his speech,' i.e., 'the English language.'
This paper was presented at the TESOL (Teachers of English to Speakers of Other Languages) convention, New Orleans, March 1971.

THE NAVAJO RESERVATION is comparable in size to the entire state of West Virginia. Most of the c. 130,000 Navajos on the reservation speak Navajo. The largest percentage and the largest number of non-English-speaking Indians are found on the Navajo Reservation. The number of Navajo speakers actually continues to increase. There are on the reservation any number of communities like Rock Point which are a hundred miles or more from the nearest non-Navajo centers of population—in excess of 10,000 population, say. In such communities, the 'Rock Points' of the reservation, Navajo is *the* language of wider communication. One can, in such communities, satisfy almost all one's needs in Navajo. Navajo interpreters, or semi-bilingual Anglos, can be found or recruited in those non-Navajo institutions of the community: the mission, the clinic, the trading post, and the school. And this same situation also is found in a number of the institutions in the reservation-peripheral non-Navajo towns with which community people have most frequent contact. Even in the school, an essentially non-Navajo institution, Navajo is *the* language of wider communication.[2] Most of the staff members are Navajo and Navajo-speaking. Navajo is the language spoken by the children on the buses, in the dormitories, and in the dining room. Navajo is spoken by the children before, during, and after classes. Indeed, although there are individual and domain exceptions (both of which seem to be on the increase) the only place one consistently hears students speaking English is in response to their non-Navajo speaking teachers.[3] Such teachers, then, despite whatever feelings they may have of participation in a 'psychological majority' are, at the school and community level, a rather small linguistic minority.

The situation I'm describing is the one William Mackey (1970:73, No. 3) diagrams as follows: Here the language of the home (Navajo) *is* that of the immediate area (the Rock Point community) but *not* that of formal instruction in the school or of the nation as a whole.

[2] An extensive survey of the teacher-perceived language abilities of six-year-old Navajo children entering school in school year 1970–71 indicated that only about 1% of the children entering BIA (Bureau of Indian Affairs) schools and about 3% of the children entering public schools were considered to be English monolinguals; only about 10% of the children entering BIA schools were considered to be English-dominant; about 20% of the children entering public schools were considered to be English-dominant (Spolsky and Holm 1971).

[3] Similar observations of Sioux schools are made by Wax, Wax, and Dumont (1964) and of Oklahoma Cherokee schools by Dumont and Wax (1969). There are, I think, some differences in the Rock Point situation. At this time, and in a community elementary school, it's my impression that the children talk to one another mostly (but not entirely) in Navajo more because of less conscious notions of "ease" than of more conscious notions of "in-group solidarity." The latter tends to come when the children go into the public junior and senior high schools outside the community. The situation at a community elementary school probably reflects the greater insulation from Anglo society—the children just do not feel as threatened.

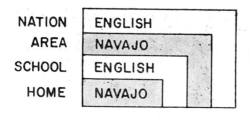

NATION	ENGLISH
AREA	NAVAJO
SCHOOL	ENGLISH
HOME	NAVAJO

Figure 1.

In a paper Albert Marckwardt (1963:25) advocated a British distinction between the then often synonomous terms "ESL" and "EFL" which seems to have laid that particular terminological controversy to rest.

> By *English as a Foreigh Language* they mean English taught as a school subject ... solely for the purpose of giving the student a foreign language competence ...
> When the term *English as a Second Language* is used, the reference is usually to a situation where English becomes a language of instruction in the schools ...

The essential distinction, if I understood it aright, was that of school language environment. An EFL situation was one in which the "foreign" language (English) was taught, and used, only during a given, relatively small, portion of the school day; the remainder of the school day was conducted in the native language of the students. (Thus, at the elementary school level, an EFL program was the mirror image of a FLES (Foreign Languages in the Elementary School) program; English was the "foreign" language.) An ESL situation was one in which the "second" language (English) was not only taught as a subject but also was used throughout the school day as a, or the, language of instruction.

Our situation on the reservation, that of both teaching English and teaching in English, seemed to us an ESL situation. And yet, in visiting ESL programs elsewhere, we found our situation, and our program, rather unlike those we found outside the reservation. In visiting programs for urban Chicano children we found a much higher degree of what we came to call "second language pressure" than we found on the reservation. There was, we felt, considerably more English "in the air": in the communities themselves, in the mass media, in public transportation, and in the schools. There seemed to us to be considerably less such pressure on the reservation, particularly in such communities as Rock Point.

Here it may be useful to relate the ESL—EFL distinction to another sort of program distinction. We have found it useful at Rock Point to make a distinction between what we call "structural-sequential" and what we call "situational" English (Willink 1968). We see the situation of the Navajo child attempting to learn English at school as being quite different from the situation in which that same child learned Navajo. The same language-learning processes may be involved but the situation itself is quite different. A truly *foreign* language—foreign in that it is seldom heard outside the classroom—simply does not, in a classroom setting, teach itself. We assume, then, that in such a situation *some* attempt to present an ordered, developmental, program of English structure, one which tends to move from simpler to more complex structure, is *more* likely to enable these children to learn to use English structure for their own purposes than is a program of random or topical English use. Hence the notion "structural-sequential" English.

On the other hand, in a setting such as ours, situations do unfortunately arise which require the child to understand or to produce English the child has not been taught and may not know. A child needs to go to the toilet from the first day of school on. Most teachers do not talk Navajo. One cannot very well say that since yes-no questions with modals are not introduced until, say, the second year that the child must wait until then. One gives the child the phrase needed to enable him to cope with the situation here and now. To the child the phrase may very well be an unanalyzed whole, outside of or beyond that English he has learned to date. But it works. It may be that only when he begins to learn that particular structure will the previously unanalyzed phrase become "grist" for his own language "mill." "Situational" English, then, is English out of sequence. As a child progresses through a developmental program of English, he should encounter relatively less "situational" English each year.

Here it should be noted that "situational" English is not just the language of classroom control but that, particularly in the lower grades, much if not most of the language of instruction is, in effect, "situational" English. Most teachers apparently find it very difficult, particularly at the lower grade levels, to keep the language of instruction within the structural means the children have mastered to date. To the extent that the teacher fails to do so, "situational" English is (albeit often unknowingly) involved.

The child entering such a program of education can be seen as having a dual English-language need: one, for an orderly presentation of English structure in such a way as to enable him, as efficiently as possible, to master the sentence-making machinery of English for his own purposes; the other, for a presentation of that English which will enable him to cope with the here-and-now of school life and instruction in English. In an adequate English language program for non-native speakers, *both* types of instruction are necessary. The "mix" is a function of how much English, and what English, is being learned elsewhere. (From our point of view, one of the main reasons apart from language similarity, that many essentially "situational" programs succeed with urban Chicano children to the extent that they do is because considerably more English is being "taught" outside the classroom than in. This is the "second language pressure" I referred to earlier.) In our situation, where almost all of what English is taught is taught in the classroom, we must devote considerably more time to the "structural-sequential" aspect of the program.

In terms of these two aspects or components, EFL programs can be seen as devoting more time to the "structural-sequential" component. ESL programs can be seen as a more balanced presentation of the "structural-sequential" and the "situational" components.

THIRD APPROACH NEEDED

For communities such as the one described earlier, *neither* the usual ESL nor the usual EFL programs seem appropriate. Somehow, where Navajo is so strong, and English comes so slowly, we must begin to try to make use of the child's and the community's Navajo. This is the direction in which some of us at Rock Point have been moving these past four years.

We have for some years advocated, and tried to implement, a rather intensive ESL program at Rock Point. We experimented briefly in 1965 and 1966 with a few modest Navajo-language activities but simply did not have the staff for anything more ambitious. In school year 1967–68, receiving Title monies for the first time, and encouraged by the Modiano (1968) study to think that perhaps bilingual education could be justified on pragmatic grounds, we ventured rather cautiously into bilingual education. In a paper given at San Antonio (Holm 1968), I discussed some of the problems and possibilities of that initial venture.

Ours has been perhaps a somewhat amateurish and homegrown program. Certainly, financed for only nine months at a time with Title I (not Title VII) funds, it has been a financially precarious program.[4] With uncertain funding, temporary personnel, and limited materials, it has been, of necessity, a "transitional" rather than a "maintenance" program.[5] But in these last four years, the program has grown slowly

---

[4] Since this paper was written, the community School Board's Title VII proposal has been approved. Non-public schools on the reservations were not originally entitled to Title VII funds.

[5] Mackey (1970) makes a distinction between "transitional" programs of bilingual education where, as in our case, Navajo is used as a means to the end of enabling children to go-to-school-in-English. In a "maintenance" program, the

from two, to three, to five, and now six, classrooms. And the more I've seen of some of the more ambitious, but essentially imposed programs off-reservation, the more I think there is something to be said for the "home-growing" of programs.

SEPARATE EFFORTS

If there *is* any reality to Ervin-Tripp's earlier notions of "compound" and "coordinate" bilingualism, then we feel we're more likely to enable the children to achieve something like "coordinate" bilingualism by separating the language stimuli—by striving for a measure of excellence in both languages but, at least at the lower grades, separately (Ervin and Osgood 1954).[6] In practice, this has meant having *two* teachers in the bilingual classrooms: an *E*nglish-*l*anguage *t*eacher and a *N*avajo-*l*anguage *t*eacher, hereafter referred to as the EL and the NL teacher respectively. The two share responsibility for the children in that room: they might be thought of as "team-teaching in two languages." The two teachers plan together, quite closely. But, once the children have arrived in the classroom, the two teachers teach separately but "parallel-ly." They attempt to avoid translation. Inasfar as is reasonable, the NL teacher talks to the children only in Navajo and the EL teacher only in English.

The school is on a modified Saratoga split-schedule which allows, in the lower grades, four half-hours when only half of the children are present. The bilingual classrooms are laid out in such a way that the two teachers conduct activities at opposite ends of the rooms simultaneously. The children sit in the middle to do independent work and go to one or the other ends of the room for group activities. Most activities involve half-class (12–15 children) or quarter class (6–8 children) groups; few activities last longer than half an hour.

The NL teacher puts major emphasis on reading or reading-readiness

---

maintenance and development of Navajo would be seen as an end in itself. In a "transitional" program, the use of Navajo as a language of instruction is phased out at some point in time; in a "maintenance" program, some such use of Navajo would be continued throughout the child's school career. While we do feel that a "maintenance" program may be more desirable, we're also aware that we're desperately short of the wherewithal for even an adequate "transitional" program. Without an established body of written material one can "hook into" (as is the case with Spanish), anything beyond a token "maintenance" program is beyond our means at this time. It is to be hoped that successful "transitional" programs may make "maintenance" programs feasible and desirable.

[6] There has been considerable discussion in the literature as to the reality of these constructs. Macnamara (1970:36) sums up his thinking on the controversy:
    . . . I do not believe that there is any evidence that there are at least two different sorts of bilinguals, coordinate and compound, at least as these have been described in the literature . . . I want to add one other disclaimer to these: I am not sure that the pair of concepts which are disassociated . . . are essentially unrelated. In other words, I am not even sure that any negativisim is justified.

(for initial literacy in Navajo) and on mathematics-and-logic. Social studies and science, to the extent that activities are drawn from these areas, are taught in Navajo. The EL teacher puts major emphasis on the teaching of English as a *foreign* language and on mathematics-and-logic. All concepts in mathematics-and-logic are first developed in Navajo; extensive use of manipulative materials is made in both the Navajo- and the English-language mathematics-and-logic activities.

No millennium has arrived. Classes still average 30. Materials are scarce or non-existent; most of the materials are being put together locally at night and on weekends. And one could say that our NL teachers are but classroom aides by another name. Most of them are but high school graduates. But they are called, and, more importantly, *are functioning* as, teachers. And, as teachers, they are probably more effective than all but a handful of non-Navajo teachers teaching at the same levels elsewhere. Our thesis, bluntly put, is that it is easier to learn education than it is to learn Navajo. It is easier for alert and concerned high school graduates who already know Navajo to learn something of the relatively little we really know about the teaching of initial reading and mathematics than it is for college-trained non-Navajos to learn Navajo. Easier, not easy.

There *are* real problems. Planning is difficult. EL teachers often don't know enough about Navajo, nor do NL teachers know enough about curriculum. There are personal and situational problems. EL teachers can feel quite threatened by some "little slip of a girl" who has better control of, and communication with, the children than she does. NL teachers can feel quite "put down" by an EL teacher who, despite her relatively recent arrival and her difficulties in understanding or communicating with the children, draws considerably more money than she (the NL teacher) does. True team-teaching and shared responsibility require not only considerable ability and stamina but also mutual trust. Training is also a problem. No NL teacher was ever taught by a NL teacher when he or she was a child. Nor has the NL teacher received any training in how to teach in Navajo. He or she must learn from, and with, others who are still exploring the role. Terminology is another problem. Considerable discussion is required to reach consensus on basic terms. Sometimes time is inadequate and no such consensus is arrived at. And materials are a problem. There are some early reading materials available. Almost everything else must be adapted or made locally.

WAITING FOR TEACHERS

This is *not* the way we would wish things to be. We would like to see true team teaching with equally well-trained teachers. And there are some hopes that this might, in time, come about. One of our most promising NL teachers has gone on to college; others are taking summer courses or workshops and/or are taking part in a new Career Opportunity Program. But a cadre of local, college-trained Navajo-language teachers is still somewhere in the future.

But perhaps it is just here, if nowhere else, that this program might suggest a solution for other areas where college-trained native-speakers are not available or are not available in sufficient numbers. If one of the primary purposes of a "transitional" bilingual educational program is to "talk education to the children in their own language," then is it necessary to wait until there are college-trained native-speakers to do so? I am *not* saying that anyone who talks the language can teach in it. I think I am more aware than most that this is not the case. *Nor* am I saying that partially trained native speakers should be used in place of college-trained native-speakers. What I am trying to say is that reasonably sensitive native-speakers, with reasonably good on-the-job assistance, may very well do a far better job of reaching the children, personally and academically, than all but a handful of college-trained teachers who do not speak the children's language—at least at the lower grades.

Such a program, with all of its self-admitted difficulties, offers a great deal of hope. We have done relatively little even semi-formal testing. Due to lags in funding, the program has not run long enough continuously to allow us to assess the results formally. What semi-formal testing has been done by Dr. Willink and others seems extremely promising.

One area of achievement should be of particular interest here. It's our very distinct impression that the children are learning more English than ever before. This may seem at first a bit paradoxical: the children seem to be doing better in English *despite* spending only half as much time in English-language activities. But perhaps not so paradoxical. First, there's the matter of attention. Most of us have had the experience of listening, on the radio say, to a language we only partially understand. After awhile, and perhaps even despite our best efforts, we realize we've been hearing only "static" for some time. It is as if we had some sort of "circuit-breaker" to protect us from an "overload" of novelty. One's system simply "cuts out" in self-defense. I can't help feeling that something very like this must happen to many young Navajo children much of the time in an English-only classroom situation. It may well be that in the coordinate bilingual classroom, with its relatively short periods of English-language activity, interspersed with periods of independent and Navajo-language activity, less English may be being "sent"—but that considerably more of what is being "sent" is being "received." Second, there's the matter of participation. In situations where only half- or quarter-class groups are being taught, the teacher may be able to know and to challenge the children, to pace a lesson so as to keep the group's interest and attention, to be more flexible in her responses to the children, and to allow or require more participation by the children. Third, there's the matter of preparation. A teacher who's teaching only EFL and mathematics-and-logic in the English the children have been taught to date, *should* be better prepared than one who attempts to teach all things to all children. Assuming that she is supposed to use only the English the children already know, she is more likely to be able to do so than one who may be talking over the children's heads in a foreign language most of the day and who after awhile begins to assume that this is a 'normal' state of affairs. So . . . perhaps the apparent paradox—that the children may be learning more English in a coordinate bilingual setting than they did in a reasonably good English-only setting—is not so paradoxical after all.

Such a program is not meant to "teach in Navajo *instead* of teaching English." Even in the more remote communities of the reservation, twentieth (and twenty-first) century America is, perhaps unfortunately, inescapable. Most parents insist on "good" English programs. Rock Point's children will have to know English and know it well if only to cope. We *would* wish to see them acquire excellence in both languages. But, for the time being at least, we see only the means for "transitional" bilingual educational programs. Such a program hopes to teach English more successfully by delaying the transition to reading-in-English. Such a program hopes that, while teaching English, we can at the same time, begin to get at teaching "how to learn" in Navajo. This is perhaps one of the most exciting aspects about such a program. Navajo-language instruction, at its worst, can be a caricature (as it might well be) of some of the poorer English-language instruction this reservation has seen. (We all tend to teach as we were taught.) But, at its best, Navajo-language instruction is something altogether different. One sees children and teacher working together in the very mature, very workmanlike, very Navajo manner one often sees in good Navajo homes—but relatively seldom in English-only classrooms. This, with the increased possibilities of parental participation in the child's education, offers very real hope for Navajo education.

There have been of late several papers seriously questioning the presumed advantages of initial literacy in the vernacular—a key component in most bilingual programs. Venezky (1970) shows that no existing bilingual project has shown "demonstrably superior results." Wilson

(1970) seriously questions any easy notions of "transfer". In response to Venezky, I think that one can say that for those three projects he cites for which test data is available, these same tests also could be interpreted to say that the experimental groups have done *at least as well* as the control groups *in the state language*—and that they have learned *more* in other content or social areas in the vernacular. This, to me, is not an insignificant claim. In response to Wilson, I can only say that we must avoid any exaggerated claims for easy or automatic transfer. In fact both papers can be taken as serious warnings that bilingual education is not "the answer." But neither is ESL alone. To me, the two papers seem to presume the existence of far more rapid and effective in-school English-language-learning programs than any I've seen. Wilson's may well be the best materials available today. But I'm not convinced that even with his materials can Navajo children move into English fast enough to avoid the 'learning-gap' that now occurs. Until or unless the language situation itself changes quite a bit, it would seem to me that the bilingual approach is the more reasonable of the two approaches.

PROGRAM PROPOSED

We are proposing, then, not an English as a Second Language program nor an English as a Foreign Language program but a program of English as a foreign language within a bilingual setting. In such a program, the English-language teacher might play a rather different role than she has in past English-language programs on the reservation.

1) To begin with, the NL teacher would be in charge. If both teachers are college-trained, it would seem rather ridiculous that the one who communicates least effectively with both the children and their parents should be in charge of the classroom.

2) The EL teacher's basic responsibility would be to teach English. i.e., there would be a frank admission on everyone's part that she *is* teaching a *foreign* language. She must be better prepared to do so than are most teachers now—with education, not just some training, in the field of English-language teaching. And as more and more of the teachers are Navajo-speakers, school boards can be much more selective in appointing the fewer, if any, non-Navajos they want as English-language teachers. These teachers must be able to plan much more closely, and teach much more effectively, than do most teachers, who must be jacks-of-all-trades, do now.

3) To the extent that the English-language teacher does teach content in English, that instruction must be set up primarily to achieve English-language, not just content, goals. Content will be taught, at

least at the lower grades, in Navajo. Again, this will require much better planning and preparation; it also will require much better awareness of, and control of, the English structure used in classroom interaction.

4) To the extent that she attempts to teach Anglo-style classroom culture—how to cope with Anglos in their own schools—the teacher will have to be much more aware of just what that culture is and what it isn't.

In such a setting, the English-language teacher would be seen as a specialist in an admittedly foreign language. And, as such, he or she must renounce a number of much more extensive but more poorly defined areas of activity. She must concentrate on doing one thing and doing it well: of making it possible for Navajo children to cope successfully with education-in-English. She need not renounce "creativity." But "creativity" in foreign-language activities is of a different order than that in first- or non-language activities. The English-language teacher must be "creative" in finding ways to enable children to be "creative" in a foreign language. That is creativity within a much smaller, and much more disciplined, compass. Good intentions are absolutely necessary. But good intentions alone will not suffice.

REFERENCES

DUMONT, ROBERT AND MURRAY WAX
 1969   Cherokee School Society and the Inter-cultural Classroom. *Human Organization* 28(3): 217–227.
ERVIN, SUSAN AND CHARLES OSGOOD
 1954   Second Language Learning and Bilingualism. In "Psycholinguistics: A Survey of Theory and Research Problems," supplement of *Journal of Abnormal and Social Psychology*. Charles E. Osgood and Thomas Sebeok, eds. 49(4): 139–146 (Part 2).
HOLM, WAYNE
 1968   The Possibilities of Bilingual Education for Navajos. Unpublished.
MACKEY, WILLIAM
 1970   A Typology of Bilingual Education. In *Bilingual Education in the United States*. Theodore Andersson and Mildred Boyer, eds., vol. 2. Government Printing Office, Washington, D.C.
MACNAMARA, JOHN
 1970   Bilingualism and Thought. In *Report on the Twenty-First Annual Round Table Meeting on Linguistics and Language Studies*. James Alatis, ed. Georgetown University Press, Washington, D.C.
MARCKWARDT, ALBERT
 1963   English as a Second Language and as a Foreign Language. *Publications of the Modern Language Association* 78(2): 25–28.
MODIANO, NANCY
 1968   National or Mother Language Teaching in Beginning Reading: A Comparative Study. *Research in the Teaching of English* 2(1): 32–43.
SPOLSKY, BERNARD
 1970   Navajo Language Maintenance: Six-Year-Olds in 1969. *Language Sciences*, no. 13.

Spolsky, Bernard and Wayne Holm
1971 Literacy in the Vernacular: the Case of Navajo. In *Studies in Language and Linguistics*. Jacob Ornstein, ed. Texas Western Press, The University of Texas at El Paso.

Venezky, Richard
1970 Nonstandard Language and Reading. *Elementary English* 47(3): 334–345.

Wax, Murray, Rosalie Wax, and Robert Dumont
1964 *Formal Education in an American Indian Community*. The Society for the Study of Social Problems, Kalamazoo, Michigan.

Willink, Elizabeth
1968 A Comparison of Two Methods of Teaching English to Navajo Children. Unpublished PhD dissertation. The University of Arizona, Tucson.

Wilson, Robert
1970 How Indian Indian Education. In *Workpapers* IV. University of California at Los Angeles.

12. The Role of American Indian Linguistics in Bilingual Education

KENNETH HALE

The author has been actively involved in making linguists of American Indians and using linguistics in bilingual education. His article makes a number of suggestions about how linguistic games can be a part of education in bilingual schools. The examples come from the Navajo language but are applicable to any comparable linguistic situation and illustrate how a person's innate knowledge of his native language provides a valuable resource for linguistic insights and teaching strategies.

This work was supported by the National Institute of Mental Health (Grant No. MH-13390-04).

I am honored to be able to dedicate this paper to the late Professor Edward P. Dozier who, both as a friend and as a colleague, was in many ways responsible for my current interest in exploring ways in which American Indian linguistics might be of use in education.

[203]

A NUMBER of American Indian communities are developing programs around the concept of bilingual education according to which the American Indian languages spoken natively by their children and young adults play an important role throughout the period of formal schooling.[1] That is to say, educators and parents in these communities have taken the extremely reasonable position that the American Indian languages spoken by themselves and by the pupils in their schools should constitute an important vehicle of learning and a serious subject of study at all levels of formal education—they, therefore, reject the idea that their languages should function merely as an educational bridge, to be burnt once students have acquired English.

In order to maintain this conception of bilingual education, it is necessary for the communities involved to give serious consideration to the precise role which their languages should play in education, particularly in those phases in which a substantial portion of formal instruction is conducted in English. This means, among other things, that decisions must be made regarding a reasonable division of labor between the two languages used in a particular school and, of great importance, a body of materials must be developed in the American Indian language involved.[2] In seeking answers to some of the questions which arise in this regard, a number of American Indian educators are exploring the possibility that the field of linguistics might be relevant to their needs. One of the possibilities that suggests itself for a school in which an American Indian language is used is that the study of that language might itself constitute an integral part of the curriculum at all levels. Along this line of thought, I would like to present some ideas that seem to me to be promising. My discussion will be restricted to an actual example, that of the potential use of Navajo linguistics in a school curriculum. The suggestions which I will pursue derive in large part from my brief participation in summer workshops conducted by Diné Bi'ólta' Association, based in Chinle, Arizona, and from discussions with staff and students of the Rough Rock Demonstration School.[3] Although I will be using the example of Navajo,

---

[1] In my judgment, this is one of the most important developments in education in this country. I have attempted to present some of my reasons for believing this in my Navajo Linguistics: Parts I, II (Hale 1970, 1971a).

[2] These considerations have been addressed in a variety of ways—to cite one example, the Diné Bi'ólta' Association in the Navajo community conducts summer workshops designed specifically to help Navajo-speaking teachers to develop materials and courses dealing with aspects of Navajo culture and language, and the Navajo Curriculum Center has been established to produce materials in physical form.

[3] I wish to express my gratitude to these organizations for the opportunities they have given me. The present paper is drawn in large part from the material I prepared for the Diné Bi'ólta' Association workshops (Hale 1970, 1971a).

I intend the discussion to be applicable *mutatis mutandis* to any bilingual situation.

EARLY LANGUAGE EXPERIENCE

It makes extremely good sense to engage school-age children in the study of their own language—it is perhaps, one of the very best ways of enabling them to become familiar with certain basic principles of scientific inquiry. It has an advantage over other sciences in that the school-age child comes prepared with an extremely large body of data (in the form of intuitions about the sentences of his language) which are readily accessible to him. In other words, he comes equipped with the primary data of linguistics, the science which seeks to explain the fantastically complicated ability which human beings have which enables them to speak and to understand the indefinitely many sentences of their native languages. Since primary linguistic data are so readily available, they provide an excellent opportunity for teachers to engage their students in the process of making observations about language, observations which are similar in nature to the kinds of observations that any scientist makes in relation to the phenomena he studies. I do not mean to imply that it would be appropriate for teachers to have their students do precisely the things that a linguist does when he studies a language, but it is nonetheless quite possible, using much the same resources as the linguist, to involve students in the discovery of patterns and generalizations which inhere in the data at their immediate command. Not only does this provide an opportunity for students to develop skills of observation, but it also provides them with an opportunity to use language in novel and creative ways—the mere act of reporting (i.e., formulating verbally) a linguistic generalization which he has discovered, involves the student in the kind of creative activity which is basic to sciences of all kinds; and in general, skills which are developed and exercised in making and reporting linguistic observations are of a kind which can be of great use to students in many phases of their lives, both academic and non-academic.

One can begin to make conscious discoveries about one's own language at an extremely early age—before school-age, in fact. Moreover, there is no real reason to suppose that a person is ever too old to make discoveries about his language. In other words, language is an appropriate subject of study at all ages. I will be concerned here primarily with the study of language at an early age.

Fortunately, or unfortunately, depending on one's viewpoint, we do not know enough about language to make it possible to set out in absolute terms the grammar of any given language. This means that it is quite appropriate to take the position that the task of a particular language study program is to attempt to uncover the principles which underlie the competence which the speakers of the language possess, rather than to force students to learn pre-established (and, in all probability, false) rules of grammar, or the like. In other words, instead of teaching rules of grammar, it is more appropriate to enable students to discover the rules for themselves—i.e., to bring to consciousness the principles which underlie their own ability to understand and speak the sentences of their language. Nor is it necessarily appropriate to teach students a prescribed vocabulary of technical terms for talking about language—an efficient linguistic terminology can be developed, by the students and teachers involved, in the course of making linguistic observations. In the case of languages for which no conventional linguistic jargon or grammatical doctrine exists, the students themselves can be directly involved in the process of creating a linguistic tradition and of developing language-related materials for use in the schools of their community.

There are many ways in which students can be encouraged to use their language in a manner which reveals its structure and internal richness. One of the best methods, for young students particularly, is the use of *language games*. In the remainder of this paper, I would like to present some possible language games for Navajo and to indicate the kinds of linguistic competence they explore.

MAKING GENERALIZATIONS

An important task of the linguist is to discover generalizations about the language he studies—i.e., to capsulize in a single statement something that is true about the way the language works. It is relatively easy to construct a language game which will bring out this ability in students. Navajo is particularly well suited for this, because of its rich system of classificatory verb stems. The way this might work is as follows. The teacher might write on the blackboard a sentence like:

beeldléí shaa níłtsóós.
Give me the blanket.

The teacher might then erase the first word, replacing it with a blank

_____ shaa níłtsóós.
Give me the _____.

and then ask the students in the class to think of as many words as they can which could fit into this frame. The students might then give a list like the following:

naaltsoos paper
naak'a'at'ą́hí cloth
éé' clothes, shirt, etc.
akał leather
tł'aakał skirt

Once a list of this type has been volunteered, the students might be asked
to make a generalization about the nouns in the list—i.e., to state the
property which is shared by all the members of the list. The point, of
course, is that the verb . . . -ł tsóós requires that its object be a noun
which denotes an object which is flexible and flat, like paper, a blanket,
or so. It is important that the teacher not make the generalization for the
students; rather, the students should try to figure it out for themselves.
Another way to bring the generalization out is to ask the students why
a sentence like, say,

*tsé shaa níłtsóós

with *tsé* 'stone' as object, sounds wrong (unless it is a *sack* of stones). This
will help to refine the generalization and make it more accurate.

When the students have arrived at a generalization, the students
should be asked to state it *in Navajo*. The reason for this is that it will
give the students experience in actually making statements about language—i.e., making a conscious statement of what they already know in
a more or less subconscious way. It also helps the student think of ways
of talking about language in Navajo and to begin to develop a Navajo
vocabulary for discussing linguistic subject matter.

It is quite easy to construct frames like the one above in Navajo,
because a great many verbs have the property that they select nouns
denoting objects with specific characteristics. All of the verbs meaning
'to handle, give, etc.' are of this type.
Thus, the frame

_____ shaa nítįįh.
Give me the _____.

for a slender, rigid object, and the frame

_____ shaa nílé.
Give me the _____.

for a slender, flexible object. And so on. The verbs meaning 'to eat' are
similar in their behavior. Thus:

_____ deeshchosh.
I will eat the _____.

for foods like lettuce, herbs, and the like,

_____ deeshghał.
I will eat the _____.

for meats, and

_____ deeshkił.
I will eat the _____.

for bulky and roundish foods; and so on. And similarly for the verbs meaning 'to drop it':

_____ nááłdéél.
I dropped the _____.

for a slender, flexible object;

_____ nááłne'.
I dropped the _____.

ror a bulky or roundish object, and

_____ náá'ah.
I dropped the _____.

for a flat, flexible object; et cetera. Navajo is extremely rich in this area, as is well known, and provides an extremely useful tool for developing and exercising a student's ability to formulate general statements.

The classificatory verb stems of Navajo can also be used in another way to involve students in the novel and imaginative use of their language. Under normal circumstances, it would be incorrect to say something like

∗ashkii nídiilá
I picked up the boy.

because the verb stem which is used implies that the boy is long and flexible, like a rope. The proper way to say it is

ashkii nídiiłtį.

using the verb stem which is appropriate for animate objects. One might, however, create an imaginary world, as in a science fiction story, in which the beings are totally unlike the human beings of our planet. One could then ask the students to describe an imaginary encounter with these beings. An intelligent but rope-like being might assume a stance more aptly described as silá 'a long flexible object is in position' than as sidá 'he is sitting', or as sitį 'he is lying down', or as sizį 'he is standing'; his method of taking hold of an object might be described as *yiyiiloh* 'he lassoes it' rather than as *yiyiijih* 'he grasps it'; he might fall the way a rope does *naadeel* rather than the way a human does *hadaatłíísh*. A student might even allow himself to imagine that the being's gait should be described by the otherwise nonexistent verbal form *naalé* 'he "ropes" around' of *naaghá* 'he walks around'. In any event, imaginary play of this sort could provide ample opportunity for students to give and to defend their various opinions about the proper linguistic usage in an entirely novel situation and, thereby, to come to grips in a rather direct way with certain semantic capabilities of their language.

WHAT IS WRONG WITH THIS SENTENCE?

The ability to speak a language means not only that one can speak and understand *correct* sentences, but one also can determine when a sentence is *incorrect*. Often incorrect sentences are perfectly understandable, but they are wrong for *grammatical* reasons. The study of why incorrect sentences *are* incorrect is another way to discover generalizations about a language. Thus, for example, noticing that sentences like

*shí naalnish
*I is-working

are incorrect helps one to discover the rule according to which *the verb of a sentence must agree in person with the subject of the sentence*. This suggests another linguistic game. The teacher writes an incorrect sentence on the blackboard (or presents it orally if the students are not yet reading) and asks the students why it is wrong. The students try to explain it and to express, in as general a way as possible, what general fact about the language is at work. It is very easy to construct ungrammatical sentences to focus on almost any area of grammar. For example, number agreement:

*ashiiké yilwoł.
The boys is-running.

in which the verb *yilwoł* is singular and the subject *ashiiké* is nonsingular. And tense agreement:

*adą́ą́dą́ą́' na'nízhoozhígóó deesháál.
*Yesterday I will go to Gallup.

in which the verb *deesháál* is in the future, while the adverb *adą́ą́dą́ą́'* refers to a time in the past.

A rule which is specific to Navajo is the one whereby a transitive sentence of the form

SUBJECT OBJECT yi-VERB

can, by a process not unlike the passive of English, be converted to the form

OBJECT SUBJECT bi-VERB

This operation is illustrated by the pair of sentences

łį́į́' dzaanééz yiztał.
The horse kicked the mule.
dzaanééz łį́į́' biztał.
The mule was kicked by the horse.

Now, it is a fact about Navajo grammar that this rule cannot apply freely to all transitive sentences. Thus, for example, the sentence

łééchąą'í łeets'aa' yiłnaad.
The dog is licking the plate.

is of the form SUBJECT OBJECT yi-VERB, but it cannot be converted to OBJECT SUBJECT bi-VERB. In other words, the "passive" counterpart

*łeets'aa' łééchąą'í biłnaad.
The plate is being licked by the dog.

is unacceptable in Navajo. And sometimes, the rule must apply—thus, the sentence

ashkii tsís'ná bishish.
The boy was stung by the bee.

of the form OBJECT SUBJECT bi-VERB has no acceptable "active" counterpart of the form SUBJECT OBJECT yi-VERB:

*tsís'ná ashkii yishish.
The bee stung the boy.

The point is, there are conditions on the application of the Navajo rule of subject-object inversion—under some conditions, it can apply optionally; under others, it cannot apply; and under still others, it must apply. Very roughly, the principle is as follows. Navajo nominal concepts are ranked, with humans highest and inanimate and abstract entities lowest. The rule applies optionally where the subject and object are equal in rank, it blocks where the subject outranks the object, and it is obligatory where the object outranks the subject.[4] This fact of Navajo provides a

---

[4] This rule is discussed briefly in Hale 1971b. Mary Helen Taptto is currently doing research on the rule and has been able to refine the principle which governs its application, based on her own Navajo usage.

coherent problem which students could attempt to solve. They could be presented with well-formed and ill-formed transitive sentences illustrating the rule and asked to try to uncover the principle which governs its application.

The grammar of any language provides many opportunities to play this game. Again, the point of the game is to develop the ability to make general statements and to exercise the ability to talk *about* a language *in* the language.

DEFINING MORPHEMES

One very good way to develop the ability to talk about language is to formulate definitions of morphemes. This is something which is very natural for people to do, since it is often necessary to explain to a child, or to an outsider, the meaning of a word or expression which he has never heard before. But this activity can become quite interesting, and difficult, when one attempts to define morphemes whose meanings are either so obvious that they are taken for granted or so elusive as to require a great deal of introspection.

Concrete nominal and verbal concepts are relatively easy to define; the teacher might begin with these and, perhaps, engage the students in the construction of a monolingual dictionary of basic vocabulary items. The skills which could be learned in this way would be of considerable benefit to students in later phases of their careers when the use of dictionaries becomes important.

At a more advanced level, students could be involved in defining morphemes whose semantic content is somewhat more difficult to characterize—like that of the particle *hanii*, which distinguishes

> doo hanii yáníłti' da.
> You are not speaking, contrary to expectation.

from

> doo yáníłti' da.
> You are not speaking.

The definition of morphemes of this latter type requires a great deal of skill in observation, in order to determine the semantic content, and a great deal of verbal dexterity in order to formulate a definition which can be understood by others. In fact, an adequate and understandable semantic description of a particle like *hanii* requires what amounts to an essay.

A number of games can be constructed which will exercise a student's ability to formulate definitions. For example, the teacher might pretend ignorance of the meaning of a particular Navajo word and ask the students to teach her how to use it by constructing a strictly verbal definition, in Navajo. Or a game might be constructed according to which a student is required to elicit a particular word from his classmates solely by means of a verbal definition.

The dictionary project also can be done in the form of a game, of sorts. The vocabulary of Navajo might be explored within the framework of domains, or semantic fields—each class session might be devoted to a particular domain (e.g., animals, plants, landscape, fire, water, time, or the like), and the students could be given the task of volunteering as many lexical items as they can think of which belong to that domain. Quite apart from the pedagogical usefulness of the dictionary project, it also serves as a data base by means of which it will be possible for teachers to gain some appreciation of the Navajo vocabulary which students of different ages command. Furthermore, it provides a basis for further study of the language—for example, particularly appropriate for a bilingual situation, the principles of Navajo nomenclature can be compared and contrasted with the principles employed in English. Ultimately a project of this type could lead to an extremely rich and valuable monolingual encyclopedic dictionary of Navajo language and culture, a resource which does not now exist but which would be tremendously useful for schools attended by Navajo-speaking students.

TAKING WORDS APART

Navajo words are rarely monomorphemic, and the verb word in particular is extremely complex in its internal structure. Thus, for example, the verb form

> nanilnish.
> You are working.

consists of an adverbial prefix *na-*, a subject person marker, *ni-*, a classifier *-l-*, and a verb stem *-nish*.[5] One of the primary concerns of Navajo linguistics has been the analysis of the verb, and this area of Navajo grammar offers a rich variety of problems to which Navajo-speaking students could address themselves.

As a beginning, students could be given the task of analysing Navajo words into their meaningful subparts, starting with relatively simple and perspicuous cases, like the possessive forms of nouns, for example, proceeding then to the more complex and often extremely difficult

---

[5] For a discussion of the internal structure of the Navajo verb, see Sapir and Hoijer 1967 pp. 85–101.

subanalysis of verb forms. As students become skilled in the morphemic analysis of words, they can be presented with a number of other tasks— e.g., that of making generalizations about the purely formal, or internal syntactic, make-up of verb words according to which a stem is preceded by certain classes of prefixes which appear in a fixed relative order, and the problem of identifying the semantic content of prefixes and stems. They can also come to grips with the fact that the phonological rules of Navajo often obscure the proper morphemic analysis of verb words, making it appropriate to view a Navajo verb word as having an abstract representation, at which the morphological constituency is clear, as well as a surface (i.e., actually pronounced) representation at which the morphemic constituency is sometimes greatly masked.[6] Morphemic analysis of this type is by no means simple, but it is an exciting area of study and one which is of the greatest importance to the student who wishes to gain a conscious understanding of the structure of Navajo. Furthermore, this is one of the many areas in which Navajo-speaking students can make a contribution to our general understanding of Navajo grammar.

Most of the verbal prefixes of Navajo are monosyllabic; in fact, most are of the abstract canonical shape CV, although this canonical pattern of individual prefixes can be greatly modified by the operation of phonological rules. Verb stems are also monosyllabic, exhibiting the canonical patterns CV(V)C and CV(V). These facts of Navajo morpheme structure provide an opportunity to create a game based on the abstract structure of verb words. The game would be a form of "scrabble" in which chips are made for the syllables of high frequency in the prefixal portion of verbs. Each player could be given a number of such chips; his task would be to create the maximum number of possible prefix sequences using the chips in his hand; and for each such sequence, the player would be required to supply an appropriate stem. The object of the game would be to use as many as possible of the chips—the player who uses all his chips wins over the player who is unable to exhaust his supply. In the case of a game in which all players are able to exhaust their supplies, different values might be assigned to the hands which players produce— e.g., the hand with the lowest number of verbs, and hence greater internal complexity for each one, might be valued the highest, and so on.

This game would be a highly abstract one, and therefore somewhat advanced in the student's career. The abstractness of the game derives from the fact that the prefix shapes written on the chips may well be

---

[6] Roger Higgins (1971) has given a discussion of this aspect of Navajo phonology, designed particularly for the Navajo-speaking layman, in the form of a dialogue on the so-called classifier.

different from the surface representation of prefixes in the actual pronunciation of verb words. Thus, the players will be producing the underlying phonological representations of verb words, and they must be prepared to defend them by reference to phonological rules which apply to them to derive surface representations. Students who are able to play this game well are without question potential linguists.

All definitions of morphemes should be given in Navajo, for the reasons mentioned before—to exercise the student's skill in talking about language in Navajo. The teacher might also go on to a much more difficult problem—i.e., the definition of *classes* of morphemes. For example, students might be asked to explain what kind of word *dibé* 'sheep' is, and what kind of word *nanilnish* is. This will, hopefully, suggest ways of talking about nouns and verbs, i.e., the parts of speech. Similarly for the other kinds of meaningful elements which appear in words—person marking prefixes (as: na-*ni*-l-nish), adverbial prefixes (as: *na*-ni-l-nish), and so on. Eventually, it will be necessary to talk about the classes of morphemes and about the parts of words, *in* Navajo. It might be wise to begin developing a suggestive technical linguistic vocabulary in the classroom itself—the students will be thoroughly familiar with this way of talking when they go on to study Navajo grammar in a more formal way.

The next game which I would like to suggest can be done at a much earlier stage in a student's career, before literacy, in fact; and it might provide an appropriate prelude to the more complex game just described.

MAKING UP NEW WORDS

An interesting way to make people aware of the structures of words is to invent totally new morphemes and to use them in sentences. The Navajo verb stem provides an excellent opportunity in this regard. The teacher might, for example, make a new verb stem, say *-baash*, give it a meaning like 'to walk around stooped over swinging one's arms from side to side, like a monkey.' The meaning might be presented orally by defining the form *njíbaash* as follows: *mogí nahalingo njígháago óolyé* 'It means to walk around like a monkey.' Alternatively, the stem could be presented to the students in a sentence, like:

k'ad naashbaash.
Now I am walking around stooped over swinging my arms from side to side.

And the meaning of the new verb could be illustrated by the teacher actually performing the action in front of the students. The students could then be asked to say what the teacher is doing. This will require the students to use the verb in a new way—i.e., in the second person:

> nanibaash.
> You are walking around stooped over . . .

And the students could be asked to make up other sentences using the new verb. For example, assuming that the new verb stem conforms to a common pattern of stem alternations:

> adą́ą́dą́ą́ kingóó nishébáázh.
> Yesterday I went to the store stooped over . . .

A lot could be done with this game. It would give the teacher an opportunity to point out that a verb has many forms, depending on how it is used, and that the verb has a stem—it is only the stem which is new in this word; the prefixes are the same as those which appear in a great many Navajo verbs. The new verb could be compared with real verbs the students already know:

> naashbaash.
> I am walking around stooped over . . .
> naashá.
> I am walking around.
> naashbé.
> I am swimming around.

And their attention can be drawn to the fact that all of these verbs share the adverbial prefix *na-* 'around, about'. They can be asked to attempt to state the meaning of this prefix, and furthermore to contrast its meaning with other prefixes which might be combined with the new stem:

> naashbaash.
> I am walking around stooped over . . .
> ch'íníshbáásh.
> I am walking out horizontally, stooped over . . .
> haashbáásh.
> I am walking out upwards, stooped over . . .
> dishbáásh.
> I am starting to walk stooped over . . .
> ninishbáásh.
> I walk to a certain point and stop, stooped over . . .

In addition, stem alternations can probably be observed in the students' usage of the new verb—e.g., *-baash* for continuative imperfective, *-báásh* for momentaneous imperfective, *-bash* for progressive and future,

-báázh for perfective, and so on. If this happens, i.e., if the students do not simply regard it as a stem which lacks alternations, then this fact can also be pointed out to them, and the stem can be compared with others which alternate in the same way. In other words, most of the essential facts of Navajo verb morphology can be studied by means of this game.

Many verb stems could be made up to illustrate various facts of Navajo grammar. Another example might be a transitive verb . . . *-l-jash*, and its meaning might be, say, 'to grab someone by the cheek and twist gently'. The teacher might say

> díí ashkii deeshjash.
> I will grab this boy by the cheek and twist gently.

and actually do it to one of the students. Then the teacher might do it to herself (or himself) and ask the students to say what she (or he) is doing. They would then be required to use the verb in a new way:

> ádíljash.
> You are grabbing yourself by the cheeks
> and twisting gently.

This may not be the actual form which they will use, but in any event, if they understand the game, they will use the verb in one way or another to describe the action. In this particular case, the verb could be used to point out to the students how the reflexive is formed—or rather, to bring to their conscious attention the form taken by the reflexive, which they already know how to use as speakers of Navajo. In short, the game can be used in this way to study virtually any aspect of the Navajo verb.

ANALYZING SENTENCES

The next game is, in some ways, a much more advanced one. What the students are asked to do is to break sentences down into their main parts. For example, the students might be given a sentence like

> awéé' yicha.
> The baby is crying.

and asked to say what the primary constituents of the sentence are. It is quite easy in this case, because the two words *are* the two parts:

> awéé' / yicha.

But when the sentence has more than two words, the task is more difficult. The sentence

> díí awéé' yicha.
> The baby is crying.

is probably to be analyzed as

díí awéé' / yicha.

And the students will probably do it correctly. But then the thing to do is to ask them why they do it this way—why does the word *díí* go with the word *awéé'*; and why would it be wrong to break the sentence up in the following way

díí / awéé' yicha.

or

díí / awéé' / yicha.

This kind of exercise is important both in teaching students about the structure of sentences and in teaching them how to talk about language— when they give their reasons for analyzing a sentence in a particular way, they are required to think of appropriate ways of talking about the structure of sentences. Primarily, however, this exercise enables students to become aware of the fact that sentences have a structure—sentences are not merely strings of words; rather, they are words in a particular structural configuration. This can be brought out clearly by observing that the interpretation of a sentence depends in part on the structure which is assigned to it. Thus the string

ashkii bilįį' yizloh.
boy his-horse he-roped-it.

is ambiguous, depending on whether the subsequence *ashkii bilįį'* forms a single constituent or not—if it does, the sentence means 'he roped the boy's horse,' and if not, then the sentence means 'the boy roped his horse.' It can be further pointed out to students that this structural difference can be demonstrated syntactically. Thus, the negative particle *doo* is more likely to be placed either before or after the subsequence *ashkii bilįį'* in negating the first meaning:

doo ashkii bilįį' yizlohda.
ashkii bilįį' doo yizlohda.
He didn't rope the boy's horse.

While in negating the second meaning, the negative particle is more likely to be placed after the word *ashkii*, reflecting the fact that the subsequence *ashkii bilįį'* forms two separate constituents:

ashkii doo bilįį' yizlohda.
The boy didn't rope his horse.

The analysis of sentences is similar in its purpose to that of parsing or diagramming sentences, an activity which finds little favor in modern education. However, the point of the exercise is to allow students to discover for themselves the structural relationships among words in a sentence; the point is not to force them to learn the rules for diagramming sentences which some authority has established in advance. The fact is, sentences do have structure, and it is important for students to become consciously aware of it, for it plays a central role in language.

A related exercise is the analysis of complex sentences. Here students might be given a complex sentence, like

shizhé'é łį́į' yik'i dah aznilę́ę yóó' eelwod.
The horse my father saddled ran away.

and asked to state what simpler sentences it is composed of.

The exercise can be done in reverse, also. In this case, the students are given pairs of sentences and asked to make a single sentence out of the two. For example, the students might be given the sentences

dibé yóó' eelwod.
The sheep ran away.
dibé biya hodéłhiz.
I frightened the sheep.

and asked to combine them into a single sentence in as many ways as possible. Among the ways in which these sentences can be combined are:

dibé biya hodéłhizę́ę yóó' eelwod.
The sheep I frightened ran away.
dibé biya hodéłhizgo biniinaa yóó' eelwod.
The sheep ran away because I frightened it.

When students become skilled at this, their attention can be drawn to the various ways in which complex sentences are formed in Navajo, and they can begin to consider some of the rules that would have to be postulated in order to accommodate such structures in a generative grammar of Navajo. The same is true of the other games suggested earlier—all of them relate in one way or another to the grammar of Navajo. The observations which emerge in the course of these exercises must somehow be represented in an adequate theory of Navajo grammar.

PHONETICS

The phonology of any natural language recognizes an inventory of distinctive phonological segments, corresponding in a specifiable way to the alphabetic symbols used to write the language, provided the writing system is in some sense "phonemic". However, the grammar of any language reveals that the phonological segments are not unanalyzable units; rather, they are composed of features which play a direct role in phonological rules. Thus, for example, the most general statement of the alternation between "ł" and "l" in such comparisons as

absolute	prefixed
łid smoke	shi-lid my smoke
łį́į' horse	shi-lį́į' my horse
łóód sore	shi-lóód my sore

is one which mentions specifically the phonological feature of voice—i.e., the stem-initial continuant is voiceless after word boundary but voiced after a prefix ending in a vowel. The reason why this is the most appropriate statement is that it applies not only to the lateral continuant, but to other continuants as well—there is an identical alternation between "s" and "z", between "sh" and "zh" and between "x" and "gh." In other words, the generalization has to do with voicing in continuants, and it cannot be expressed adequately as an alternation between individual segments without reference to their phonetic properties.[7]

Phonological features can be divided conveniently into two large classes: those relating to the position which the major articulators (tongue, lips) assume during the production of a particular sound, and those relating to the manner of articulation (i.e., roughly, the particular way in which the lung air is manipulated during the production of a sound). Thus, a sound segment can be characterized as a particular combination of position and manner features—e.g., Navajo "b" is a bilabial unaspirated stop; "m" is a bilabial nasal; "s" is an apico-alveolar voiceless continuant; and so on. And the sounds of a language comprise natural classes on the basis of phonological features which they share—e.g., the Navajo sounds "s, ł, sh, x" share the manner features [continuant] and [voiceless] and, therefore, belong to the class of voiceless continuants; and the sounds "j, ch, ch', sh, zh" share the position feature [lamino-alveolar] and, therefore, belong to the class characterized by that feature.

An awareness of the articulatory phonetic properties, or features, of the sounds of one's own language is of considerable potential usefulness

---

[7] This point of view is lucidly presented in a pair of papers by Morris Halle (1964a,b). The phonological features which I employ here are not the same as those developed by scholars working within the framework of generative phonology—rather I use the conventional, non-binary, terms of articulatory phonetics; I intend only to introduce the subject of articulatory phonetics by means of games and expect that the principles of binary phonological oppositions can be introduced at a more advanced level.

to students, not only as preparation for a formal study of the phonological rules which exist in the language, but also as preparation for an intellectual understanding of the principles which underlie writing (particularly where the writing system reflects the feature composition of sounds to some degree) and as preparation for the acquisition of the phonology of a second language.

I will assume that it makes sense to begin developing an awareness of how Navajo sounds are produced in the earliest phases of education—perhaps even before the students have learned to represent sounds alphabetically. The first step is to identify, or rather, help the students identify, the most obvious organs of speech and their Navajo names—i.e., the lips, the tongue, the tip of the tongue, the back of the tongue, and so forth; this, in fact, is the foundation of a Navajo phonetic terminology which could be amplified and perfected as students proceed through their elementary schooling. It is reasonable to involve the students themselves in the creation of this terminology. It will be of value, as the study proceeds, to let the students become familiar with representational drawings of the speech organs. This involves, at the beginning, teaching them to identify the lips, teeth, tongue, tongue-tip, etc., in "x-ray" drawings of the type used by phoneticians. It may take some time to get younger children to the point where they can interpret such drawings with ease, but it can be done; and once this ability is acquired, it will prove to be of tremendous value as their study of phonetics continues.

While this basic foundation is being developed, it is possible at the same time to have students begin to pay attention to, and attempt to describe verbally, the movements of the primary articulators (lips and tongue) in speaking. For example, the students could be asked to describe exactly what happens to the lips when one begins to pronounce such words as *mą'ii* 'coyote', *máazo* 'marble', *bááh* 'bread', and other words in their vocabulary which begin with bilabials. Once they are able to describe what happens—i.e., to observe that the lips articulate against one another (*hadaa' ahininílá* or *hadaa' ałch'į' át'é*, or however they choose to express it), they can be taught to recognize this position of articulation in a drawing. And similarly for the other positions of articulation—e.g., the tongue-tip placed behind the upper front teeth, as when one begins to pronounce words like *naadą́ą́* 'corn', *dibé* 'sheep', and so on. The students should be helped to suggest an appropriate description of the articulation for themselves—in this way, a phonetic vocabulary with which they feel comfortable will be developed.

I suggest that, in the beginning, particularly with the youngest children, only three basic positions of articulation be presented, together with their x-ray pictures: bilabial, apico-alveolar, and dorso-velar. These basic types should be exercised until the students are thoroughly familiar with them and can correctly associate the x-ray pictures with the corresponding initial sounds in words like *maʼii* and *bááh* for the bilabials, *naadą́ą́ʼ*, *dibé*, and *tin* ʻiceʼ for the apico-alveolars, *gah* ʻrabbitʼ and *ké* ʻshoeʼ for the dorso-velars. After this, the lamino-alveolar position, represented by the initial consonants of such words as *jį́* ʻdayʼ and *chaaʼ* ʻbeaverʼ, can be presented; the corresponding x-ray picture is only subtly different from that for the apico-alveolars, and it may take some time for young students to recognize the difference. It may be helpful to have the students themselves suggest an appropriate way to draw the x-ray pictures.

A SIMPLE GAME

Once students are familiar with the four basic positions of articulation, it is possible to construct a simple card game which will help them to become thoroughly comfortable with the idea of thinking of sounds in terms of their production. The game involves two sets of cards—one set consists of x-ray pictures for each of the four positions of articulation (say 5 cards for each, giving a deck of twenty); the other set consists of pictures of objects whose initial consonants represent the positions of articulation (say thirty to fifty cards). The players (a small number) sit in a circle; each player is dealt a hand of four x-ray cards from a shuffled deck (or each player might be dealt five instead, but in that case, one card would be a duplicate, since only four positions of articulation are represented by x-ray pictures in the Navajo game); the picture cards are placed face-down in a pile at the center of the circle. One of the players is chosen to start the game. This player turns the top picture card face-up and places it beside the pile; he then consults his hand of x-ray cards, and if it contains an x-ray picture corresponding to the position of articulation of the initial consonant in the word which the picture card represents, he takes it from his hand and places it face-up next to the picture card. If there are two x-ray cards which correspond to the initial consonant of the picture word, the player can place both of them down; if three, all three; and so on. When he has done this, the next player goes through the same procedure. The object of the game is to get rid of all the x-ray cards in one's hand—the winner of the game is the first player who gets rid of his hand. One can imagine several variations of this game—the students will undoubtedly think of ways of changing it.

Perhaps the most productive way to introduce this game to younger students is to teach it first to older children, around ten years of age, and have them teach it to the younger ones. This is a particularly good way to establish a terminology for talking about phonetics to younger children. The older group will, in all probability, have an efficient way of giving oral instructions to the younger group, and a great deal can be built upon the terminology they use.

This game (and variations on it) not only helps students to become familiar with the positions of articulation and the role which the articulators play in speech production, but it also helps to teach the fact that sounds belong to classes—e.g., that "b" and "m" belong to the class of "lip-sounds", that "t", "d", and "n" all belong to the class of "tongue-tip sounds"; and so forth. Once these observations are made, it is possible to begin to introduce the idea of *manner* of articulation. Students can be asked to think about, and to attempt to describe, the differences between sounds belonging to the same position of articulation—e.g., the difference between "b" and "m"; the difference between "d" and "n", and between "t" and "d", and so on. Their descriptions of these differences will suggest an appropriate Navajo terminology to be used in reference to the manner of articulation. It is possible to represent the manners of articulation in the form of x-ray pictures as well, by using an arrow to represent the flow of breath. When this dimension is added, and students become familiar with its role in speech production, the card game can be appropriately modified to incorporate it. And when the students have learned the alphabetic symbols, and have begun writing, the game can be further modified by replacing the picture cards with letter cards—The game would proceed as before, but now the players associate an x-ray card with letters. This will help to teach the association between sounds, thought of in terms of how they are produced, and the conventional letters used to represent them.

Once these basic points of the system of phonological features and something of their role in classifying sounds are understood, it is possible to construct another sort of game. Five letter cards can be dealt out to each of the players, the remainder being placed face-down in the center of the circle. Each player consults his hand and attempts to classify the letters into "families"—i.e., into groups according to shared phonological features. The object of the game is to have the most complete family of sounds possible (i.e., a hand which has all stops wins over a hand which has, say, a dorso-velar stop, an apico-alveolar continuant, a glide, and the two nasals). Each player has two chances to improve his hand by drawing a card from the center deck (and discarding one from his hand). A game of this sort will help to teach the natural classes which exist in the sound system.

By proceeding in this way, from the relatively simple to the more complex, developing a familiarity with the phonological properties which characterize the sounds of Navajo, it is possible to elaborate, in cooperation with the students, an appropriate Navajo usage for speaking and writing about this aspect of the language. Out of this will come an appropriate set of names for the phonological features. When this is available, it is possible to construct more sophisticated games. For example, a set of feature cards could be made—each card would have the name (in Navajo) of a phonological feature on it; five, or so, cards could be made for each feature. Each player would be dealt a certain number of cards (say, seven or ten). The object of the game is, again, to have the most highly valued hand—the best hand is the one which comes closest to defining one or more complete sounds (i.e., functioning feature combinations). Thus, a hand which has cards for the features

1. stop
2. bilabial
3. unaspirated
4. continuant
5. voiceless
6. apico-alveolar
7. lateral

wins over a hand which has the following cards:

1. stop
2. continuant
3. nasal
4. glottalized
5. voiceless
6. glottalized
7. nasal

The first hand wins because it has two nearly complete feature combinations in it—one for "b", and another for "ł":

$$
\begin{array}{cc}
\text{b} & \text{ł} \\
\left[\begin{array}{c} \text{bilabial} \\ \text{stop} \\ \text{unaspirated} \end{array}\right] &
\left[\begin{array}{c} \text{apico-alveolar} \\ \text{continuant} \\ \text{lateral} \\ \text{voiceless} \end{array}\right]
\end{array}
$$

The second hand loses because it only has two very incomplete feature combinations:

$$
\left[\begin{array}{c} \text{stop} \\ \text{glottalized} \end{array}\right] \qquad
\left[\begin{array}{c} \text{continuant} \\ \text{voiceless} \end{array}\right]
$$

The complexity of this game could be increased by allowing certain features to function as "wild cards"—e.g., the feature [glottalized] might be allowed to stand as the complete feature combination for a glottalized stop provided the hand also contains a feature combination which represents, say, an aspirated or unaspirated stop. Thus, with [glottalized] as a wild card, the hand

1. consonant
2. stop
3. apico-alveolar
4. lateral
5. unaspirated
6. glottalized
7. nasal

can be judged as having two complete feature combinations in it:

<table>
<tr><td align="center">dl</td><td align="center">tł'</td></tr>
<tr><td>
consonant
apico-alveolar
stop
lateral
unaspirated
</td><td>
consonant
apico-alveolar
stop
lateral
glottalized
</td></tr>
</table>

The number of possible card games which could be constructed on this model is enormous. Such games help to reinforce the student's understanding of the principles of classification which underlie the sound system of Navajo. The same game could, of course, also be applied to English, once the phonological features of that language have been studied.

The familiarity with phonetics which could be gained in this way also would provide an opportunity to explore new linguistic possibilities —i.e., to introduce sounds which do not occur in Navajo or English; this would be of great value to students who wish to specialize in the study of language and to investigate languages other than their own. This type of exploration could be begun by combining features in ways which depart from the principles of combination which are basic to the Navajo system. For example, a student might be asked to attempt to produce the sound characterized by the feature combination

$$\begin{bmatrix} \text{dorso-velar} \\ \text{nasal} \end{bmatrix}$$

i.e., "ŋ"—the conventional phonetic symbol could be introduced to the student as well. Or a student might try the combination

$$\begin{bmatrix} \text{bilabial} \\ \text{stop} \\ \text{glottalized} \end{bmatrix}$$

i.e., the glottalized bilabial stop /p'/, found in such languages as Tewa—
e.g., Tewa *p'o* 'water'. And so on. The possibilities here are many.

I have presented only a few of the language games and language-based tasks which might be used in teaching students certain properties of the Navajo language. Many more games could be conceived to accomplish the same purpose. The aim is to get students involved in using their language in ways which will bring out its wealth of structure.

REFERENCES

HALE, KENNETH
    1970   Navajo Linguistics: Part I. Unpublished.
    1971a   Navajo Linguistics: Part II. Unpublished.
    1971b   A Note on Subject-Object Inversion in Navajo. Unpublished.
HALLE, MORRIS
    1964a   On the Bases of Phonology. In *The Structure of Language.* Jerry A. Fodor and Jerrold J. Katz, eds. Prentice Hall, Englewood Cliffs, New Jersey. pp. 324–333.
    1964b   Phonology in Generative Grammar. In *The Structure of Language.* Jerry A. Fodor and Jerrold J. Katz, eds. Prentice Hall, Englewood Cliffs, New Jersey. pp. 334–352.
HIGGINS, ROGER
    1971   A Dialogue on the Navajo Classifier. Unpublished.
SAPIR, EDWARD, AND HARRY HOIJER
    1967   *The Phonology and Morphology of the Navajo Language.* University of California Press, Berkeley and Los Angeles.

13. English Loan Words in the Speech of Young Navajo Children

AGNES HOLM, WAYNE HOLM, AND
BERNARD SPOLSKY

This article is an outgrowth of a two-year study of the vocabulary of six-year-old Navajo children which is itself part of a study of the feasibility and effect of teaching Navajo children to read their own language first. The article indicates that there has been a major change from the absence of loan words in Navajo thirty years ago to the situation today. These findings provide support for Dozier's argument that socio-cultural factors are more important than structural ones in language borrowing.

The work reported herein was supported in part by the United States Department of the Interior (Bureau of Indian Affairs, Navajo Area Office, Contract No. NOO C 1420 3462), and in part by the Ford Foundation. It appears also as Navajo Reading Study Progress Report No. 16.

[227]

In a survey of studies of linguistic acculturation in the Southwest, Dozier (1967) points out the importance of socio-cultural rather than structural factors as an explanation of whether a language will be likely to accept loan words. There is, he says, no "neutral contact situation where the speakers of two distinct languages meet as cultural equals" and so no way of testing the influence of structural characteristics.

Most earlier comments on Navajo followed the structural view propounded by Sapir (1921:196):

> The Athabaskan languages of America are spoken by peoples that have had astonishingly varied cultural contacts, yet nowhere do we find that an Athabaskan dialect has borrowed at all freely from a neighboring language. These languages have always found it easier to create new words by compounding afresh elements ready to hand.

He goes on to speak of a "psychological attitude" of a language, structural characteristics that affect its willingness to accept foreign words.

The dictionary (Young and Morgan 1945) and works by Harrington (1945), Liebler (1948), Reichard (1951) list fewer than forty words borrowed from Spanish, and this after more than three centuries of contact. Young and Morgan list even fewer loan words from English.

As an admittedly extreme example of a tendency to coin a descriptive term to avoid borrowing, they cite for 'tank'

chidí naa'na'í bee'eldǫǫhtsoh bikáá' dah naazniligíí,

literally, 'the automobile that crawls about (tractor) upon which they set big things by means of which explosions take place (cannons)!

Haile (1941) writes that there are very few loan words in Navajo: "Pueblo contact has not influenced Navajo to a noticeable degree, while Spanish elements in the language are comparatively few, and English elements practically none." (Haile 1941:1). Reed (1944) explains this as part of the make-up of the Navajo whose "highly independent spirit" involves "a definite disinclination to learn and speak the languages of other peoples."

But in the thirty years since Haile wrote, there would seem to have been a serious change. This change involves the social factors, for the language is still basically as before, capable of elaborate coining of new words from native elements. The amount of contact with English has increased tremendously. A large number of young Navajo men served in the armed forces during World War II. An even larger number left the reservation to work in war-related industry. Since then, contact with the outside world has continued to increase. As late as 1949, fewer than half of school-age Navajo children were in school, but by 1955, attendance figures were close to 90%. The children now beginning school are the first generation, most of whose parents were educated in English-medium schools. (Spolsky 1971).

As a result, while both absolutely and proportionately the Navajo are the largest group of non-English speaking Indians in the United States, and while over two-thirds of six-year-olds still come to school unable to do first grade work in English, the language situation on the reservation has changed markedly in the last thirty years. These socio-linguistic changes have, as Dozier argued, evidently led to an increased receptivity to loan words.

The present study presents some preliminary data on English loan words in the speech of six-year-old Navajos. In the course of a study of the speech of six-year-old Navajo children (Spolsky, Holm, and Embry 1971), we analyzed taped interviews with over 200 children, preparing among other things a spoken word count. In looking over the data, we noticed early the occurrence of a number of English words in otherwise Navajo conversations. In the first interview, a child asked *Díkwíish niná-hai?* 'how old are you?', replied, 'Five,' and continued to speak in Navajo.

To investigate the extent and nature of this phenomenon, we went through the complete text of all the interviews and listed all English words. A computer program prepared a concordance of these words, printing them in alphabetical order and giving the sentence context in which they occurred. In this study, we have considered only words that appear in the speech of children, ignoring in the meantime the speech of the adults interviewing them.

There are a number of limitations that need to be mentioned. First and foremost is that our study is based on a corpus, with all its limited relevance to linguistic competence. Further, most of the interviews were conducted in school by school personnel. Generally, the interviewer was known to the child, which led to fuller responses, but the school orienta-tion tended to influence the topic and style of talk.

We generally omitted from consideration most personal names: the widespread use of English first names and surnames among the Navajo is a topic in itself. (Holm, ms.) Only personal names that show strong Navajo influence, like *Cháalátsoh*, are included. Similarly, we have not taken into account English place names (e.g. Rock Point) except when they occur with Navajo enclitics (Rock Pointdi 'at Rock Point').

Within the corpus, then, we found 508 different words we classified as loan words, representing 9 % of the different words children used in the corpus. Loan words occurred 1549 times, 3.6 % of the 33,580 words used by the children in all. These two figures show the great change since Haile's (1941) statement that there were practically no English loan words in Navajo.

It must be stressed that our evidence of the occurrences of a word in the speech of one or more children is not conclusive evidence of integration in the lexicon, but it is certainly highly suggestive. In the rest of this paper, we analyze the words that occur from a number of points of view.

Classifying the words by their parts of speech in English, the overwhelming number are nouns. This confirms Young's observation (1948:87):

> Navajo does not commonly borrow terms from foreign languages . . . True, Navajo has borrowed a handful of Spanish and English nouns. . . But Navajo has not borrowed verbs and other parts of speech.

Dozier (1967:396) points out evidence of how general is their tendency for loan words to be almost entirely nominal forms.

Of the 508 different words, then, 453 are English nouns, 26 verbs, and the rest other parts of speech. The nouns occur isolated, embedded in Navajo, or within English phrases. Almost all the verbs, articles, and pronouns, occur within English phrases which themselves may be isolated as complete utterances or embedded within Navajo.

A number of the words occur in Navajo sentences with affixes attached. A few occur with Navajo possessive pronouns: *shilittle sister* 'my little sister' (the treatment of this as a single element possibly reflects the fact that Navajo requires age distinction in siblings), *shipant* 'my pants' (the singular is used probably because most Navajo nouns are unmarked for number).

Many of the words were used with Navajo suffixes: more than twenty different suffixes occur in the text with English loan words. Postpositional enclitics are freely used:

> schooldi 'at school'
> dormitorygóó 'towards dormitory'

Some English nouns are made into yes-no questions: *bookísh?* 'is it a book?' Some English nouns are marked as no longer present or functioning: *record playeryéé'* 'the late record player' (the suffix *yéé* is added to the names of people who are deceased, or to objects no longer present or working). When loan words are included in lists, they are not marked by intonation: instead *dóó* 'and' is used: *dóó coyote dóó ma'ii dóó ná'áshjaa'* 'and coyote and coyote and owl'.

A considerable number of the loan words, and almost all the verbs, occur embedded in English phrases. Many of these are set phrases:

> Ready, set, go.
> Hide and go see (sic).
> Are you sleeping.
> We wish you a merry Christmas.

The phrases are often marked as quotations: *spank you, níi łeh* 'he usually says "spank you" '; *get in line, shi'di'niih* 'someone says to me "get in line" '.

One especially interesting case involves use of an English verb together with a Navajo verb: *jump íyiilaa* 'he made a jump'. The more usual way of saying this in Navajo would be *dah neeshjį́į́d*, 'he jumped', using a *si*-perfective form of the verb. But there is an awkward but acceptable circumlocution: *dah ná'ńljį́į́h íyiilaa*, using an agentless passive iterative form, where the content verb is nominalized. This is what appears to happen in the example: this structure permits using an English verb as thematic and still mark the verb for number, mode, etc.

To sum up, then, almost all the loan words are nominal in form; there is good evidence of morphological integration, and some interesting hints of syntactic modification.

In meaning, the loan words cover a wide range of domains or centers of interest. The appendix lists the words according to a semantic classification. In general, as might be anticipated, the words generally refer to non-Navajo objects or concepts, reflecting the culture from which they are borrowed. Objects and concepts associated with the domain of school—school equipment and supplies, numbers, time, events, schoolbook animals—are prominent. A second major grouping are non-Navajo foods. More surprising perhaps are the kinship terms and some of the animal names. But it is reasonable to generalize that the terms generally represent new or alien concepts or objects, and give evidence of acculturation.

Occasionally, interviewers made an effort to see if children knew the Navajo equivalent of the loan words. This happened especially with numbers, and the following translated excerpts show what happened.

1) Int.   How old are you?
   Child. 'Seven' (in English)
   Int.   How do you say that in Navajo?
   Child. Seven (in Navajo)
2) Int.   How old are you?
   Child. 'Six' (in English)
   Int.   I don't understand English. How old?
   Child. 'Six'
   Int.   How do you say it in Navajo?
   Child Six (in Navajo)
3) Int.   How old are you, Vic?
   Vic.   'Seven' (in English)
   Int.   How do you say that in Navajo? How do you say that? I don't understand English. Let's count in Navajo: you say it after me. One, two, three, four, five, six, seven. Now, how old are you.
   Vic.   Six (in Navajo)
   Int.   You're six?
   Vic.   Yes.

In considering the status of these loan words in the lexicon of Navajo, we were interested to find out if they had Navajo equivalents. As a rough check, four bilingual Navajo college students were asked the Navajo equivalent for the loan words: we also checked Young and Morgan for its translation. There is actually a continuum, ranging from those words for which all could agree on an equivalent, to those for which no equivalent is generally known. Five general classes may be identified within this continuum. In the following list, the Young and Morgan translation is given first.

I. Loan words that occur in the text for which all agreed easily on a Navajo equivalent: 'ribbon' *lashdǫ́ǫn*, 'purse' *béeso bizis*, 'airplane' *chidí nat'a'í*.

II. Loan words occurring in the text for which there was general agreement, but minor etymological or pronunciation variants: 'peach' *didzétsoh, didétsoh, jidétsoh*; 'table' *bikáá'adání, bik'i dah adání*; 'chair' *bikáá' dah asdáhí, bik'idah'asdáhí, bik'i dah asdáhí*.

III. Loan words occurring in the text where there was considerable variation in the equivalents offered: 'apricot' *didzétsoh yázhí, altsé nit'ánígíí, bégáashii, tsįįlgo nit'ánígíí*; 'ice cream'—(no Young and Morgan form), *tin abe' yistiní, abe' sikazí*.

IV. Loan words occurring in the text where some of the informants knew a Navajo equivalent but others used the loan themselves: 'bus' *chidí diné bee naagéhí, dlchíní neeghéhe, dlchíní bee naagéhí*; 'salad' (no Young and Morgan), *ch'il, ch'il altaanáshgiizhii*; 'lettuce' *ch'il, ch'il ligaií*.

V. Loan words for which none of the four informants could offer an equivalent: 'alligator' (Young and Morgan gives *bitsee' yee 'adílhalhi*, but it was not known by any of the four); 'math', 'pickle', 'raccoon'.

In general, there were few words for which the informants could not think up an equivalent or translation; on the other hand, they agreed that they themselves would have used most of the loan words when speaking to someone whom they knew understood English. More study will be needed before more definite statements are possible about the integration of these words into the lexicon: their presence in the speech of six-year-old children, and their acceptability to college-age bilinguals are, however, quite suggestive.

As Dozier's study of Yaqui and Tewa makes clear (Dozier 1956), linguistic borrowing is an excellent area for the study of acculturation. In the case of Navajo, a change of social contacts has in thirty years led to a major change in receptivity to borrowing. Further study of English loan words in Navajo will cast valuable light on the changing linguistic and cultural situation.

APPENDIX
Loan Words Classified by Domains and Centers of Interest
NOUNS

ANIMALS

Large Wild Animals:

Bears	Kangaroo
Bears-dó'	Fox
Buffalo	Giraffe
Buffalo-léi'	Lion
Camel	Magí 'monkey'
Coyote	Magí-yéé
Deer-léi'	Monkey
Elephant	Tiger
Jumbo Elephant	Wolf

Small Wild Animals:

Chipmunk	Raccoon
Mouse	Squirrel
Rabbit-dó'	

Domesticated Animals:

Calf	Horse
Cat	Kitten-léi'
Cow	Lamb
Dog	Pig
Donkey	Pony
Gídí	Puppy
Gídí-dah 'kitten'	Sheep
Gídí-Yázhí	

Birds:

Bat	Chicken
Bees	Crow
Bees-dó'	Duck
Bird	Owl
Butterfly	Rooster

Reptiles:

Alligator	Snake-dó'
Fish	Spider
Frog	Turtle
Snake	

PLANTS AND TREES

Flowers	Tree
Gardens	Christmas Tree
Grass	Apple Tree
Leaf	Tree-di
Leaves	Trees

FOODS

Fruits:

Apple	Grapes
Apple-dó'	Orange
Apricot	Peach
Banana	Plum

Vegetables:
  Beans   Potato
  Carrot   Potatoes
  Carrots   Potatoes-léi'
  Corn   Tomato
  Lettuce
Meats:
  Bacon   Chicken
  Beef
Grains:
  Cereal   Oatmeal
Dairy Products:
  Butter   Ice Cream
  Egg   Milk
  Eggs   Manidigíyaa-dah 'butter'
Pastries:
  Cake   Doughnut-dó'
  Cake-dó'   Pie
  Cookies   Pie-dó'
  Cookies-dó'
Sweets and Others:
  Candy   Bubble Gum
  Candy-dó'   Kool Aid-léi'
  Sugar   Raisin
  Juice   Raisin-dó'
  Pop   Chips, potatoes
  Gum-dó'
Miscellaneous:
  Bread   Salad
  Pickle   Sandwich-dó'
HOUSEHOLD ITEMS
Furnishings:
  Bed   Picture
  Chair   Rug
  Couch   Stove
  Door   Table
  Heater   Toilet
  Mattress   Mouse trap
Dishes and Containers:
  Basket   Glass
  Can   Pan
  Cup   Knife
  Cups   Spoon
Miscellaneous:
  Clock   Tape recorder
  Gun   Tape recorder-léi'
  Keys   Telephone
  Record Player-dó'   Tooth Brush
  Record Player-yéé   TV
  Record-yéé   Wash Cloth

CLOTHING

Boots

Clothes

Coat

Diaper

Dress-dó'

Hat

Pant

Purse

Rainhat

Ribbon

Shirt

Sweater

TRANSPORTATION

Airplane

Boat

Bus

Car

Trailer

Train

Truck

SCHOOL SUPPLIES

Bulletin Board

Book

Chalk

Check

Color

Comic Book

Desk

Envelope

Eraser

Paper

Pencil

Rubber Band

TOYS

'aswing

Ball

Ball-dah

Ball-go

Balloon

Bike

Bingo

Blocks

Bomb

Checkers

Doll

Drum

Ghost Balloon

Jacks

Kite

Marble

Merry-Go-Round

Puzzle

Sand Box

Roller Skate

Swing

Swing-dah

Tank

Teeter-Totter

Toys

Whistle

NUMBERS-AGE-TIME

Ten Cents

Five Dollars

Eighty

Fifty

Five

Five-go

Four

Four-go

Hundred

Nine

Nineteen-jí

Numbers

One

One-jí

Seven

Six

Ten

Ten-jí

Three

Three-go

Thirteen-gi

Thirty-go

Twenty

Two

COLORS

Black

Blue

Brown

Green

Orange

Red

White

Place and Place Names

Towns (off reservation):

Albuquerque-di	Farmington-di
Blanding	Gallup-di
Bloomfield	Phoenix-di
Cortez-di	Phoenix-déé'
Cuba	Town
Denver-di	Town-góó
Denver-góó	

Reservation Communities:

Ch'inlį́įdi	Rock Point-di
Cottonwood	Crownpoint-di
Crystal	Rock Point-góó
Many Farm-jí	Shiprock-di
Mexican Water-di	Shiprock-góó
Mountain (Lukachukai)	Whitehorse-di
Round Rock-di	Window Rock Lodge-di

Places within a Community:

Boarding School	Mission
Church-di	Step
Church-jíígíí	Upstairs-góó (di)
Church-góódó'	West Mesa-jí
Dormitory-di (jí)	Preschool-di (jí)
Dormitory-góó	Railroad-di
Farm-jí	School-di (jí) (góó)
Foodway	Public School-di
Hiway-góó	Store-jí (góne')
Hospital	Water-di
Jail	Window-gi
Junction	Zoo-di (gi) (góó)
Junior High-jí	
Lake-di	
Line-gi	

Places in the School:

Activity Room-góne'	Hall-góó
Classroom-di (góne')	Room
Class-góne'	Toilet room-di
Dining Room	

Directions

East	Northwest
North	South

Names

Kinship:

Blackie (name of a dog)	Brother
Buddy (name of a dog)	Father (shi) (Davis) (Bear)
Peter Rabbit	Grandmother
Cháalá 'Charles'	Grandma
Cháalátsoh 'big Charley'	Mama
Auntie	Mother
Baby	Niece
Baby-dó'	Sister

People, Position:

Babysitter	Man
Beginner(s)	Midget
Boy (Ginger Bread)	Miss
Chief-léi'	Mr.
Christian	Mrs.
Clown	name (nihi)
Cowboy	Navajo
Fireman	Police
Girl	Policeman
Grade (first)	Soldier
Group (A, B)	Principal
Indian	Snowman
Indian-go	Teacher
Jesus	

NATURAL PHENOMENA

Earth	Sun
Moon	Sunshine
Ocean	Water
Rainbow	Water-go
Snow	

EVENTS

Birthday	Meeting
Easter	Party
Halloween	Trip-góó
Halloween-léi'	Valentine Party

SEASONS

Snow-go	Spring

DAYS OF THE WEEK

Friday	Thursday
Monday	Thursday-go
Sunday	

MONTHS

April	March

TIME OF DAY

Afternoon-go	O'clock
Noon-go	O'clock-go

HOLIDAYS

Christmas	Holiday

MISCELLANEOUS

Arithmetic	End
Arrow	Flag
Barn	Head
Bedroom	Highway
Bi-chair	Fire
Bi-Church	Hair
Bi-teacher	Hand
Box	Home
Bridge	House
Bridge-lá	Light
Brownie	Line

MISCELLANEOUS—*continued*

Math
Money
Nest
Number
Paint
Present
Rock
Seeds
Skeleton

QUESTIONS

Book-ish

Sleeping
Snowball
Trail
Trash
War
Wood
Work-shíí
Window
Wire

VERBS

Are
Call
Check
Clean
Close
Come
Feed
Get
Go
Help
Hide
Jump
Mash

Mashed
Reach
See
Send
Spank
Take
Telephone
Use
Wait
Wash
Watch
Wish
Work

PRONOUNS

I
Me
My

We
You

ADJECTIVES

Bushy
Dirty
Little
Merry

New
Old
Shiny
Wild

ADVERBS

Fast
Read

Set

PREPOSITIONS

In
Of

To
Up

ARTICLES

A

The

MISCELLANEOUS

And	Don't
Back	Hello

SOUNDS

Moo	Ding

REFERENCES

DOZIER, EDWARD P.
1956 Two Examples of Linguistic Acculturation: the Yaqui of Sonora and Arizona and the Tewa of New Mexico. *Language* 32: 146–157.
1967 Linguistic Acculturation Studies in the Southwest. In *Studies in Southwestern Ethnolinguistics*. Dell H. Hymes and William E. Bittle, eds. Mouton and Co., The Hague.

HAILE, BERARD, O. F. M.
1941 *Learning Navaho*, Vol. 1. St. Michaels Press, St. Michaels, Arizona.

HARRINGTON, JOHN
1945 Six Common Navajo Nouns Accounted for. *Journal of the Washington Academy of Sciences* 35(12): 373.

LIEBLER, H. BAXTER
1948 Christian Concepts and Navaho Words. *Utah Humanities Review* 2(2): 169–174.

REED, ERIK
1944 Navajo Monolingualism. *American Anthropologist* 46: 147–149.

REICHARD, GLADYS
1951 *Navaho Grammar*. J. Augustin, New York.

SAPIR, EDWARD
1921 *Language*. Harcourt, Brace and Company, New York.

SPOLSKY, BERNARD
1971 Navajo Language Maintenance II: Six-Year-Olds in 1970. Navajo Reading Study Progress Report No. 13.

SPOLSKY, BERNARD, WAYNE HOLM, AND JONATHAN EMBRY
1971 A Computer-assisted Study of the Vocabulary of Six-Year-Old Navajo Children. Navajo Reading Study Progress Report No. 9.

YOUNG, ROBERT
1948 What's in a Name? *El Palacio* 55(3): 86–89.

YOUNG, ROBERT, AND WILLIAM MORGAN
1945 *The Navaho Language*. United States Indian Service, Phoenix.

14. *Problems of Southwestern Indian Speakers in Learning English*

MARY JANE COOK

Cook takes a different position than that held by many linguists who believe that work in teaching languages should be based on a contrastive analysis between the first and second languages of the learners, with separate materials for speakers of each language background compared with the language being learned. Her study of the writings in English of speakers from a number of Southwestern Indian language backgrounds indicates that there is a commonality of errors in English among these speakers that should be of help to teachers in classes where several different language backgrounds are represented.

I PRESENTED a paper in 1966 with Margaret Amy Sharp entitled "Problems of Navajo Speakers in Learning English." This paper was intended as a guide to teachers of Navajo children in planning work in English. In the course of further research, I found that the problems in English of all Southwestern American Indian speakers whose English I had an opportunity to observe were similar. I formed this conclusion on the basis of some 1,500 themes written by children from the fourth through the twelfth grades representing speakers of Apache, Havasupai, Hopi, Hualapai, Maricopa, Mohave, Navajo, Paiute, Papago, Pima, Shoshone, Tewa, and Tewa-Laguna, principally during the school years 1967–1970 in both public and Bureau of Indian Affairs schools. There were no errors unique to speakers of any one language background nor any not found in the writings of speakers of all of these language backgrounds. Because of a lack of expert knowledge of the languages involved, I have not attempted explanations of the various features listed except in a very general way.[1] I present this list of predictable problems as a guide to teachers of speakers of Southwestern American Indian languages in planning work in English. I feel that it should be particularly useful in classes containing children of several language backgrounds.

I wish to thank the many teachers and students whose cooperation in submitting materials made my research possible. I also feel it fitting to express my gratitude to the late Edward P. Dozier for the many insights he provided me with in the course of my experience in working with speakers of Southwestern American Indian languages.

PHONOLOGICAL FEATURES

It is a common feature of second-language learning that the learner carries over features of his first language to the second, particularly when the second language contains sounds which do not exist in his first language. In this case, the tendency is for the speaker to substitute the nearest sound in the first language for the new sound in the second. This is readily understandable in spoken language. What frequently happens with speakers who learn a second language purely by ear, however, before they can read or write any language, is that phonological errors later ap-

---

[1] It was pointed out by Dr. Edward P. Dozier in a paper presented at a meeting of the Southwestern American Anthropological Association in Tucson, Arizona, in April, 1971, that Southwestern American Indian languages, although they may fall into perhaps as many as ten different linguistic stocks, or *phyla*, nevertheless share many linguistic features. He outlined the phonological features and a number of morphological and syntactic features which are common to the various languages. Since errors in a second language reflect linguistic features in the first language of a speaker, the findings of my research on the English produced by speakers of the languages I have noted above would certainly reflect the commonality of linguistic features among them as described by Dr. Dozier. See also Dozier (1963:1–3).

pear as spelling errors and as errors in morphology and syntax. Thus the examples below represent errors in written English reflecting the phonological characteristics of the speaker's English. I have used an adaptation of the Trager-Smith phonemic alphabet of American English in the examples.

Phonemes Which Cause Problems

Vowels

i, iy. Some confusion between the simple and complex high front vowel phonemes is apparent in spelling:

> Once there *leave* some people in these houses. (Hopi)
> Don't leave *thes* hole. (Paiute)
> one of *this* games (Papago)
> time for the night watchman to make *he's* rounds (Tewa)
> The bird sees *he's* food. (Navajo)
> *His* got a little girl. (Navajo)

i, e. Some confusion between the high and mid front simple vowel phonemes is apparent in spelling:

> *untell* (for "until") (Maricopa)
> *agin* (for "again") (Shoshone)
> Everybody *well* be pushing to get in line. (Tewa)
> *Will,* I was walking down the street, . . . (Apache)

e, æ. Some confusion between the mid and low front simple vowel phonemes is apparent in spelling:

> I *when* to Phoenix Indian School. (Apache)
> *Want* I was fifteen years old, . . . (Hopi)
> I *attanded* this school. (Navajo)

Consonants

Difficulties with final consonants, particularly those appearing in consonant clusters, would seem to reflect the general scarcity of final consonants and final consonant clusters in the Southwestern American Indian languages. There is also difficulty with phonemic distinctions among the nasals "*m, n, ŋ*", especially in final position, which undoubtedly reflects a lack of correspondence with the occurrence of these nasals in final position in English.

"*p, b, t, d, k, g.*" The stops, especially the voiceless stops "*p, t, k,*" are frequently omitted or confused in final position. Problems with the final "*t, d, əd*" frequently are evidenced in faulty past tense and past participle forms of the verb (see following section on morphological and syntactic features).

They *though* they would play a joke. (Tewa)
For the *pass* years that I have been at this school. . . . (Navajo)
I *though* instead of going to sleep. . . . (Hopi)
I belong to the Papago *tripe*. (Papago)

t, θ, d, ð. "*θ*," the voiceless interdental spirant, and "*ð*," the voiced interdental spirant, do not exist in the Southwestern American Indian languages as phonemes. Thus a common error is the substitution of "*t*" or "*d*" for "*θ*" and "*ð*." This results in occasional spelling errors such as *day* for *they*. The problem is much more common in spoken than in written English, however.

m, n, ŋ in medial position. The most common problem is the intrusion in spelling of an *n* which does not occur in English. This probably reflects the occurrence of nasalized vowels in the first language.

durning the war (Paiute)
I was *seening* the dance (Papago)
On *Many* 4 (Navajo)
It was at *Many* 4 (Papago)

m, n, ŋ in final position. The nasals in final position are frequently confused and occasionally omitted. The syllable *ing* in spelling is frequently omitted, indicating that the syllable is probably not heard and therefore not reproduced in English. (See following section on morphological features.) Related to general difficulty with final consonant clusters is the frequent omission of *not*, or *n't*, in writing:

Maybe *I'n* going, maybe *I'n* not. (Apache)
if *I'n* going or not (Navajo)
We told *hin* to quiet down. (Navajo)
I stay with *then*. (Hopi)
They were later *know* as the Shoshone tribe. (Paiute)
I had *know* the beans were not boiled. (Mohave)
At the *begin* I cried all day. (Havasupai)
I was *play* with my brother. (Navajo)
I *when*, and I found me a job. (Hopi)
I *when* to Phoenix Indian High School. (Apache)
I was so hungry that I did not *mine*. (Tewa)
We *could* (for "could not") walk any further. (Maricopa)
He told me I could try but I *could* do it. (Pima)
I laughed so hard I *could* know what to do. (Apache)

s, z in final position. The voiceless and voiced alveolar fricatives are frequently omitted in final position. Problems with final "*s, z, əz*" frequently are evidenced in faulty noun plural and possessive forms and faulty third person singular present tense verb forms. (See following section on morphological and syntactic features.)

My grandfather *alway* told me. . . . (Navajo)
They *alway* built new things. . . . (Hopi)

Problems with consonant clusters other than those with nasals:

> They *strat* drilling. (Papago)
> My *frist* job. . . . (Paiute)
> He should *pratice* outside. (Tewa)
> He should *pragatists* the summer dance. (Navajo)
> *bast* ball (Pima)
> There is a *lost* games. (For "There are lots of games.") (Papago)
> They got *lot* (for "lost"). (Navajo)

In addition to the above spelling errors, which all reflect some trans-
ference of phonological features, there were also instances of sporadic
spelling errors throughout the materials which did not reflect phonological problems in any systematic way, but there were not nearly so many as
can be related to phonological problems. There were also, of course,
errors of the kind predictable for native-speaking students as well, such
as transpositions not related to phonology (for example, *freind* for *friend*)
and confusion of homonyms (for example, *know, no; too, two, to; for, four*).

MORPHOLOGICAL AND SYNTACTIC FEATURES

As pointed out above, phonological errors in learning a second language often show up as morphological and syntactic errors when the
speaker begins learning the second language before he can read or write
any language. In the case of practically all of the errors below, both a
sophisticated morphological and/or syntactic explanation and a simple
phonological explanation for the errors exist. For example, in the case of
omission of the final -(e)s regular noun plural marker, a common error in
English for Southwestern American Indian speakers, we may say on the
one hand that the error occurs because noun plurality is not marked in a
similar way in the native language of the speaker; on the other hand, we
may say that final consonants might be rare or non-existent in the
speaker's first language and that therefore he perhaps does not hear them
and consequently tends not to produce them in English. However, considering that the characteristic appears in the English of Southwestern
American Indian speakers when the learner, entering school at the pre-
first or first-grade level, is unsophisticated linguistically and probably
not exposed to formal grammatical explanations, and when he cannot yet
read or write any language, it is probable that the errors below are basically related to phonology rather than to a sophisticated carry-over of the
morphological and syntactic features of the first language.

Nouns

Omission of Final -(e)s of the Regular Noun Plural. This undoubtedly
reflects (1) a different way of indicating plurality in the first language;

and (2) a lack of or infrequent occurrence of final consonants and consonant clusters in the first language:

> We all gathered in the auditorium to receive *instruction*. (Apache)
> We did not know which one of the *dormitory* to go to. (Hualapai)
> My grandpa has told me lots of old *storie*. (Navajo)
> I rode horses for two *week*. (Hopi)
> It was hard for me to get along with white *kid*. (Mohave)
> Both of my *grandparent*. . . . (Paiute)
> They only had three *piece* of corn bread. (Papago)
> I wanted to know about other *tribe* of *Indian*. (Pima)

Possessive Forms of Noun: Lack of 's. This undoubtedly reflects (1) a different way of expressing possession in the first language; and (2) a lack of or infrequent occurrence of final consonants and consonant clusters in the first language:

> We got to my *grandfather* house. (Paiute)
> We go to the *teacher* house. (Tewa)
> *Jack* father (Navajo)

Verbs

Lack of Final -(e)d in Past Tense. This undoubtedly reflects (1) that Southwestern American Indian languages have verb systems based on aspect rather than on tense, as in English, so that all tense forms and usages are likely to be difficult for these speakers; (2) that there is a lack of or infrequent occurrence of final consonants and consonant clusters in the first language:

> The next day we all *gather* in the auditorium. (Apache)
> He dumped a bucket of water on me, so each of the girls *surround* him, and we nearly drowned him. (Pima)
> As we got near to Blythe, we *stop* to rest for a while. (Hopi)
> Finally the long evening came and I *help* my mother around the house. (Navajo)
> The next day he went out. On his way he *meet* a man. He *decide* to stay with him. (Mohave)
> Grandmother and him *escape* from the group and lived in a hole near a rock. (Paiute)
> I got up out of bed, *wash* my face. . . . (Papago)
> I told them what *happen*. (Shoshone)
> Then we *stop* to rest for a while it was kind of windy. (Hualapai)

We may note here and elsewhere that a basic problem is the lack of the final past tense marker; this, however, is closely related to the use of the simple verb form of the irregular verb as well in describing past. This results in much apparent shifting between present and past forms in describing past time, and, of course, the errors are not entirely consistent.

Lack of Final -(e)d in the Regular Past Participle. Again, this is undoubtedly due to both a morphological and a phonological feature:

> I did not go home like I was *suppose* to. (Hopi)
> They were afraid that they might be *capture* again. (Paiute)
> I was *puzzle*. (Navajo)

Final Nasal Difficulty Resulting in Faulty Verb Forms: Omission of -ing in Spelling. A characteristic tense formation among these speakers is the use of *was* plus the simple form of the verb, as in "was go" for "was going." More frequently than not, however, the form "was going" is not the correct tense but should have been the simple past form "went." It is possible that *was*, for some linguistic reason, is being used as a past marker. The important point is that the usage is common.

> He *was go* to the trading post. (Apache)
> I *was play* with my brother. (Navajo)
> He *was enjoy* the movie. (Tewa)

Subject-Verb Agreement Errors (Occurring in Third Person Singular Present Tense and Other Forms Showing Agreement: am, is, are; was, were; have, has; do, does; go, goes). Such errors are predictable for all learners of inflected languages:

> The ways of the white man *has* entered the Indian's life. (Hualapai)
> Sand and dirt *was* all around us. (Hopi)
> Others who *has* girlfriends or boyfriends. . . . (Pima)
> They *tells* us stories. (Hopi)
> Our legs *was* aching. (Maricopa)
> He *meet* lots of friends. (Mohave)
> It *take* place at Fort Defiance. (Paiute)
> We *was* going to the trading post. (Apache)
> The beans *was* not boiled. (Tewa-Laguna)
> There *was* steps going down. (Shoshone)

Adjectives

Adjectives present problems only in the forms and comparison patterns of the degrees, as for many young native speakers and generally English-as-a-second-language learners of all language backgrounds. Double comparatives (*more nicer*) and superlatives (*most nicest*) are common, as well as such patterns as "He sings better as I do," and so on.

Adverbs

Occasionally the adjective form instead of the adverb form is used, as is the case with some native speakers, as in "They treated me real nice." As in the case of adjectives, occasionally forms and comparison patterns are incorrect. The most common problem is the use of the incorrect word in "two-word verb" forms such as *get at, get up, get to, get around*, and so on.

Pronouns

There was some confusion in gender distinction between the third person singular masculine and feminine pronoun forms, with a tendency to interchange *he* and *she*, and *his* and *her*. This would reflect a lack of third person singular gender distinction in the first language. This usage was much more common among the younger children than the older ones, and practically nonexistent in the writings of the older students (Grades 7 through 12) which I examined.

Determiners

The articles (*a, an,* and *the*) are frequently omitted by Southwestern American Indian speakers. The omission undoubtedly is due (1) to a lack of such linguistic items in the first language and (2) to the fact that in English the articles are normally unstressed and therefore not accurately heard by the learner. Such usages as below are common:

> White man came and built house. (Papago)
> I stayed there in little town. (Pima)
> Jack has white lamb. (Navajo)
> We went to storekeeper. (Apache)
> In last part of May. . . . (Hopi)
> In afternoon (Maricopa)
> He met lots of friends. (Paiute)
> But *and* Indian. . . . (Hualapai)
> I ate *and* orange. . . . (Navajo)

A confusion between *this* and *these* is undoubtedly in part phonological (the confusion between "i" and "iy" mentioned above). There is also evident some confusion between *this/these* and *that/those* for "close" and "far," as well as between the distinctions for singular and plural, as below:

> *This* old peoples. . . . (Hopi)
> Don't leave *thes* hole. (Paiute)
> I have seen one of *this* games (Papago)
> I have done *this* things many times. (Navajo)
> We had horse-racing and other of *those* stuff. (Havasupai)

Prepositions

Prepositions are difficult for speakers of all language backgrounds in learning English. They are difficult for two reasons: (1) when both the first and the second language contain prepositions, there is rarely a reliable one-to-one dictionary correspondence between them; (2) in English, prepositions are normally unstressed so that in spoken English, they may not be accurately heard. For speakers of first languages which do not contain prepositions, the result in English may be either an incorrect preposition or the omission of prepositions. For speakers of Southwestern American Indian languages, the more common error appears to be the use of an incorrect preposition rather than the omission of a preposition. Typical usages are these:

> *in* about two weeks later (Hopi)
> *on* May (Navajo)
> *on* May (Hopi)
> I went to the place to practice *to* the summer dance. (Navajo)
> After lunch we walked *on* the garden. (Papago)
> *in* somewhere in the town. (Tewa)
> There wasn't another bus leaving *to* Shiprock. (Navajo)
> *To* Texas we visit my aunt's sister. (Apache)
> Next we go *at* store. (Mohave)
> *On* afternoon me and my brother were going to the river. (Hualapai)
> We asked *to* the storekeeper. (Navajo)

Conjunctions

Second language learners of English have difficulty principally with mastering the meanings of conjunctions; younger learners tend to overuse *and* as an introductory word in sentences, as do young native speakers of English. There seemed to be no specific characteristics in the usage of Southwestern American Indian speakers.

Word Order (Arrangement)

There were no typical arrangement problems except for occasional misplacement of the adverbs of indefinite time (*always, never, usually, sometimes,* and so on).

NONSTRUCTURALLY RELATED FEATURES

In the materials examined, there were many instances of fragmentary sentences, run-together sentences, comma splices, excessive coordination, various kinds of punctuation errors, and errors in capitalization and other mechanics. Such errors were much more common among the younger children as compared to the writings of those in the upper grades, as is the case with native-speaking English students in our schools. These mistakes were not systematic or consistently related to structure.

REFERENCES

COOK, MARY JANE AND MARGARET AMY SHARP
    1966   Problems of Navajo Speakers in Learning English. *Language Learning* XVI, 1 and 2: 21–29.
DOZIER, EDWARD P.
    1963   Phonological Characteristics of Southwestern Indian Languages. *The Newsletter*. Division of Indian Education, New Mexico State Department of Education. February: 1–3.

15. *English and Papago Compared*

MADELEINE MATHIOT

Mathiot presents a sketch of the respective phonological systems of English and Papago and then concentrates on a comparison of the most salient grammatical categories of the two languages. Her comparative work on English and Papago needs to be done for other Southwestern Indian languages and it is hoped that this article will serve as a model for other such comparative papers.

This paper is partly based on the research done under contract No. OE-2-14-007 with the Office of Education. It was commissioned by the English for Speakers of Other Languages Program of the Center for Applied Linguistics, in Washington, D.C.

PAPAGO is a Uto-Aztecan language spoken by roughly 14,000 people in Southern Arizona and adjacent portions of the State of Sonora in Mexico. It is related to Pima to the point of being mutually intelligible. Among the better-known other Uto-Aztecan languages are Hopi and Aztec.

The exact number of Papago dialects remains to be ascertained. Joseph, Spicer and Chesky (1949) mention six dialect groups: (1) *Totoguañ* (2) *Kolóodi* (3) *Gigimai* (4) *Kohadk* or *Kuhadk* (5) *Huhuʔula* or *Hohoʔola* and (6) *Huhuʔuwax* or *Hohoʔovax* (see their discussion pp. 66–71 and especially their map p. 67 showing the approximate distribution of the dialect groups on the Papago Reservation). I am acquainted personally with three dialects, primarily with the Totoguañ dialect spoken in the Santa Rosa-Covered Wells area as well as in the San Xavier Reservation near Tucson, and superficially with both the Kolóodi dialect spoken south of Sells all the way to San Miguel and the Huhuʔula dialect spoken in the Pisin Moʔo and Menager's Dam areas.[1] The data in the following discussion are taken exclusively from the Totoguañ dialect of the Santa Rosa-Covered Wells area.[2]

The comparison of English and Papago presented here concerns primarily the basic phonological features of the two languages and their grammatical categories (e.g. number, tense, etc.) whether the latter are expressed synthetically or analytically. In addition, some syntactic patterns that are strikingly different in the two languages are compared. Differences in the lexical structure of the two languages have not been considered.

PHONOLOGY[3]

From a phonological standpoint Papago differs from English by having (a) predominantly monophthongal vowels (b) a contrast between voiced and voiceless vowels (c) lenition rather than voicing in stops (d) preaspiration rather than postaspiration in fortis consonants (e) retroflexion of consonants in the alveolar range (f) a single liquid and (g) automatic breaking up of consonant clusters by insert vowels.

---

[1] I was told by Papagos that Huhuʔuvax is another name for the Huhuʔula dialect group. This remains to be ascertained.

[2] Among other linguists, to my knowledge Kenneth L. Hale has done the most work on Papago. He has been working on the Totoguañ dialect spoken in the Tucson area. The latter has some significant phonological differences from the Totoguañ dialect of the Covered Wells area (see Hale 1965). Dean Saxton has given a phonological description of the Kolóodi dialect (see Saxton, 1963). Other works done on Papago are listed in the bibliography.

[3] The symbols used in the spelling system that I proposed for Papago differ from the symbols presented in the phonological charts as follows: Vowel length is indicated by two identical vowel symbols. Example: *kii* 'house'. The high back unrounded "ü" is spelled "e;" the bilabial fricative "ϕ" is spelled "v;" the apico-domal fricative "š" is spelled "x;" the apico-alveolar lateral flap "ḷ" is spelled "l." Finally, stress is indicated only if it does not fall on the first syllable of the theme.

The above mentioned differences will be elaborated on further below. Unfortunately not enough is known at this stage about intonational and paralinguistic phenomena to include them in the present discussion, although their importance for native-like command of a language may be even greater than that of segmental elements. In the phonological discussion, my own analysis will be used for Papago (see Mathiot, to appear) and the Trager-Smith's analysis as modified by Sledd will be used for English (see Sledd 1959).

Stress

It is commonly accepted that English has three degrees of stress: primary stress, secondary stress and weak stress.

Papago has only two degrees of stress: primary stress and weak stress. In most cases, primary stress falls on the first syllable of the theme.

Vowels

The American English vowel pattern according to Sledd includes the following simple vowels (1959:49):

	Front		Central		Back
High	I		ɨ		U
Mid	ɛ		ə		O
Low	æ	a	ɑ		ɔ
	Unround				Round

and the following diphthongs (p. 54):

Diphthongs ending in I

			UI
			OI
aI	ɑl	ɔI	

Diphthongs ending in U

IU		ɨU
	aU	ɑU

Diphthongs ending in ə

Iə		Uə
ɛə		Oə
æə	ɑə	ɔə

In addition, a feature of length can be associated with both simple vowels and diphthongs (p. 54).

Long vowels	i:	u:	Long diphthongs	i:ə
	e:	o:		e:ə
	ɔ:			

The Papago vowel pattern, (only simple vowels and no phonemic diphthongs)[4] is as follows:

	Voiced				Voiceless
	Front	Mid	Back		Front
			Unrounded	Rounded	
High	i		ü	u	ï
Mid				o	
Low		a			

In addition, a feature of length can be associated with any of the voiced vowels.

As can be seen when comparing the vowel charts of the two languages, on the one hand, in addition to all the diphthongs, Papago lacks completely the following American English vowels: ɛ, æ, ɑ, ɔ, ə and ɨ (see Sledd 1959:49). On the other hand, Papago has two vowels which are absent in English: "ü" and "ï".

Finally, the American English vowels that have Papago counterparts in the same general phonetic range include the following pairs:

English	I	and Papago	i
	U		u
	O		o
	a		a

In each of these pairs the English vowel differs from its Papago counterpart by being laxer. This difference applies equally to both the short and the long vowels.

Consonants

The American English consonant pattern according to Sledd includes the following simple consonants (1959:42–44):

---

[4] Papago has phonetic diphthongs, both rising and falling. The vowels "i" and "u" can function as either onglides or offglides in rising and falling diphthongs respectively. An example of a rising offglide is [gígimai] gigimai name of a dialect group; an example of a rising onglide is: [gegokivio] gegokivio '(you pl.) stand up!'; an example of a falling offglide is: [ʔáuppa]ʔauppa 'cotton wood tree'; an example of a falling onglide is: [łótoguañ] totoguañ name of a dialect group. Some Spanish loan words follow the Papago pattern. An example is Kaviu (Spanish caballo) 'horse'. In other Spanish loan words, one semiconsonant, namely, "y" has to be postulated. Examples are: yaavi (sg.), yayavi (pl.), (Spanish llave) 'key'; payáaso (sg.), papyáyaso (pl.), (Spanish pallaso) 'clown'.

		Bilabial	Labio-dental	Dental or Alveolar	Palato-alveolar	Palatal or Velar	Glottal
Stops	Voiceless	p		t		k	
	Voiced	b		d		g	
Affricates	Voiceless				č		
	Voiced				ǰ		
Fricatives	Voiceless		f	θ s	š		h
	Voiced		v	ð z	ž		
Nasals		m		n		ŋ	
Liquids				r	l		

and the semi consonants "w" and "y."

The Papago consonant pattern includes the following simple consonants:

		Bilabial	Apico Dental	Apico Alveolar	Apico-domal	Lamino-alveolar	Dorso-velar	Laryn-geal
Stops	Tense	p	t			c	k	
				ḍ				ʔ
	Lax	b	d			j	g	
Fricatives		φ		s	ṣ̌			h
Nasals		m	n			ñ		
Lateral flap				ḷ				

and the semi consonant "y" in loans from Spanish (see note 5).

As can be seen when comparing the consonantal charts of the two languages, on the one hand, Papago lacks completely the following American English consonants: v, θ and ð, z and ž, ŋ and w. On the other hand, the following Papago consonants are absent in American English: ḍ, ʔ and ñ. Finally, the Papago consonants that have American English counterparts in the same general phonetic range include the following: (1) among the stops, p, t, k and b, d, g and the two affricates c and j; (2) the fricatives φ, s, ṣ and h; (3) the nasals m and n; (4) the lateral flap ḷ, and, (5) the semi consonant y. The American English consonants differ from their Papago counterparts as follows: (1) In American English the two series of stops and affricates are opposed in terms of voicing and post-aspiration. The same two series in Papago are opposed in terms of lenition pre-aspiration for the fortis consonants, pre-glottalization and varying degrees of voicing for the lenis consonants. (2) Among the fricatives, American English "f" is consistently labiodental and voiceless while its Papago counterpart "φ" is bilabial and may be voiced; American English "s" is palato-alveolar and has no retroflexion while its Papago counterpart is apico-domal and retroflexed; finally, American English "s" and "h" are roughly the same as their Papago counterparts. (3) The same applies to the nasals "m" and "n." (4) In American English there are two clearly distinct phonemes "l" and "r" whereas Papago has a single phoneme "ḷ" the pronunciation of which ranges from something close to American English "l" and something close to American English "r". (5) Finally, the American English semi-consonant "y" has a counterpart in some Papago loans but not in any native words (see note 5).

When it comes to consonant clusters there are two essential differences between the two languages: (1) Papago consonant clusters are usually limited to a maximum of three (see Saxton 1963:31–32) whereas American English has no such limitation. (2) Papago consonant clusters are characterized by an insert vowel which is voiced before a lenis or a voiced consonant and voiceless otherwise, a phenomenon which does not occur in American English.

GRAMMAR

From a grammatical standpoint Papago differs from English by having a much more highly developed inflectional pattern. Many things that in Papago are expressed by inflectional affixes are expressed in English either by separate words (e.g. auxiliaries, particles, etc.) or by lexical means. In addition, Papago has a number of grammatical categories that are absent in English (e.g. aspectual ranking, aspectual number, etc.) and conversely (e.g. tense, gender, etc.).

In comparing the grammatical categories of the two languages, particular emphasis will be put on their respective semantic content since this information is considered essential for the correct use of morphological and syntactic patterns. Here again my own analysis will be used for the Papago data (see Mathiot, to appear). For English I have found Ilyish's description the closest to my requirements (see Ilyish 1965).[5]

Word Classes

According to Ilyish, English has the following word classes (i.e. the so-called major "parts of speech"): (1) verbs (2) nouns (3) adjectives (4) adverbs (5) prepositions (6) pronouns (7) numerals (8) conjunctions (9) particles and (10) interjections (see Ilyish 1965:31–36).[6]

Papago has the following word classes: (1) verbs (2) nouns (3) modifiers (4) postpositions (5) pronouns (6) numerals (7) subject complex words and (8) particles.

As can be seen when comparing the list of word classes in the two languages, on the one hand, certain distinctions present in English are absent in Papago. Thus adjectives and adverbs are subsumed under a single word class, that of modifiers. Conjunctions and interjections are not differentiated from particles which include all noninflected words other than the substitutes (i.e. words which syntactically parallel inflected words). On the other hand, one Papago word class is absent in English: namely, the subject complex words, i.e., words the pseudo-stems of which are constituted by the subject personals which translate into English as 'I', 'he'. Subject complex words combine with verb forms and with particles to constitute verbal phrases analogous to the compound verb forms of English (e.g. *ntp o ñei* 'I might see him'; *nt o ñei* 'I want to see him'; *na*ʔ*ans o ñei* 'I doubt whether I'll see him'). Finally, English word classes that have Papago counterparts are: verbs, nouns, prepositions, pronouns and numerals.

As suggested by the terminology, English prepositions differ from Papago postpositions—among other things—in terms of their position with respect to the noun phrase which they introduce. Thus while English prepositions must occur before the noun phrase which they introduce, Papago postpositions can occur either before or after—the preferred pattern of occurrence being after—that noun phrase.

English pronouns differ from Papago pronouns by being much more

---

[5] Note that Ilyish's description is based on data collected from the literature and that it may be more representative of British English than of American English.

[6] Note that two word classes mentioned by Ilyish have been left out as too controversial: (1) the statives (e.g. 'astir', 'afloat') and (2) the modal words (e.g. 'certainly,' 'probably'). The first, I regard as a type of predicative adjectives, the second, as a type of adverbs.

varied. Thus, some English pronouns correspond to Papago pseudo-stems (e.g. 'I' corresponds to a pseudo-stem in the subject complex words) or to Papago affixes (e.g. 'my' and 'me' correspond to an object personal affixed to either a noun, a verb or a postposition). On the other hand, one type of Papago pronouns, the locationals, correspond to English adverbs of place.

The most striking difference is between English verbs and nouns, and Papago verbs and nouns. It is to be noted that in Papago the verb, and to a certain extent also the noun, cover a wider range of possibilities than in English. Thus, on the one hand, many meanings which in English are expressed by a predicative adjective or a predicative noun are expressed in Papago by a verb form (see below). Examples are: *sgiigi ?o* 'he is fat'; *svegi ?o* 'it is red'; *heg?o vud ñsiis* 'he is my younger brother'; *D (<vud) ?o ?ekeickvadam* 'it is a bicycle'.

On the other hand, a few meanings which in English are expressed by a verb form are expressed in Papago by a noun. Examples are: 'a deer wounded by you' (Papago: *huavi m-mummuda,* lit. 'a deer your act of wounding'); 'he knows how to drive' (Papago: *maac g meli,* lit. 'he knows the act-of-driving').

In the following sections there will be a discussion of the following major word classes of English: verbs, nouns, adjectives and adverbs, and two word subclasses, namely, the personal pronouns and the possessive pronouns. The major word classes of Papago that correspond to them as well as the grammatically relevant minor word classes that are closely associated with each will be included in the discussion.

The Verb

The verb in English is closely associated with (1) personal pronouns, subjects and objects, (2) auxiliary verbs (namely 'have, be, do, shall and will', see Ilyish, p. 28), (3) modal verbs (i.e., 'can, may, must') and (4) the negative particle 'not' (see Ilyish 1965:131–2).

In Papago, the verb is closely associated with (1) the subject complex words which include the subject personals as pseudo-stems as well as pseudo affixes manifesting various aspectual and modal categories, and (2) a few modal and aspectual particles, among which is the negative particle. (It should be noted that the object personals which translate in English as personal pronoun objects are affixed to the verb theme, thus being a part of the inflectional inventory of the verb.)

Ilyish lists the following inflectional categories for the English verb: (1) tense, (2) aspect, (3) correlation, (4) mood, (5) voice, (6) quality (which includes two members, the affirmative and the negative), (7) interrogation, (8) emphasis, and, (9) person together with associated categories.

In my analysis of Papago, the following categories are viewed as being manifested in the verb itself: (1) several verbal number categories; (2) several aspect categories; (3) conjunctivity (which includes two members, the concursive and the correlative); (4) mood; (5) voice and; (6) person together with associated categories. The following categories are viewed as being manifested in the pseudo affixes of the subject complex words: (1) two statement type categories, namely connectivity and statement mode (which includes three members, the assertive, the promptive and the interrogative; (2) three statement qualification categories, namely, attestation, incognizance, and aspectual distance. The following categories are viewed as being manifested in particles associated with the Papago verb: (1) assertion, which includes two members, the affirmative and the negative, and (2) extension.[7]

As can be seen when comparing the list of grammatical categories associated with the verb in the two languages, on the one hand, a single category present in English is absent in Papago. This is tense. On the other hand, several categories present in Papago are absent in English. These are: all the verbal number categories, the three statement qualification categories, one statement type category, namely connectivity and finally extension. English categories that seem to have at least partial counterparts in Papago are: English correlation and Papago conjunctivity; English mood and Papago mood; English voice and Papago voice; English categories of interrogation and emphasis and Papago statement mode; English category of quality and Papago category of assertion; finally, English and Papago person together with associated categories.

In the following discussion only the categories that are present in English or have counterparts in the two languages will be included. The Papago categories which have no counterparts in English will not be discussed.

English Tense

As described by Ilyish, tense "reflects the objective category of time and expresses on this background the relations between time of the action and the time of the utterance" (1965:42). There are three tenses in English: the past, the present, and the future. The present is unmarked. The past is expressed by the forms -ed, -d attached to the verb theme, or, in a so-called irregular way, as in 'wrote'. The future is expressed by the form "will" followed by the verb, as in 'will write'. Instances of the three tenses are shown below.

---

[7] Note that my analysis of Papago particles is incomplete. For a semantic analysis of a Papago particle, see Hale, 1969.

English tenses are rendered in Papago by adverbs of time such as 'yesterday', 'today', and 'tomorrow'.

English Category of Aspect and Papago Aspect Categories

Aspect is usually taken to indicate the way in which the action is shown to proceed. There are two aspects in English: the common aspect and the continuous (also called progressive) aspect. The continuous aspect indicates an action going on continuously during a given period of time; the common aspect indicates an action not thus limited, i.e., neutral as to continuity (Ilyish 1965:83–4). The common aspect is unmarked. The continuous aspect is expressed by the auxiliary verb "to be" and the suffix -ing attached to the verb theme, as in 'am eating', 'is eating', and 'are eating'. Instances of the two aspects in the three tenses are:

	Common Aspect	*Continuous Aspect*
Present	writes	is writing
Past	wrote	was writing
Future	will write	will be writing

Papago has three aspect categories: (1) resumptivity, (2) extensionality, and (3) aspectual ranking. Only extensionality seems to have a partial counterpart in English. This category indicates the duration of the action, or condition, referred to by the verb. There are two members: the durative and the immediative. The durative indicates an extended action or condition. The immediative indicates an immediately following action. The durative is expressed by the suffix -d attached to the verb theme. The immediative is expressed by the suffix -ka²i attached to the verb theme. An instance of the durative is: himad 'being walking'. An instance of the immediative is: himka²i 'Go on, don't stop walking!'.

As can be seen from a comparison of the meanings of English aspect and Papago extensionality, English continuous aspect appears to have a fairly good counterpart in Papago durative aspect. There is no similarity, however, between English common aspect which is neutral as to continuity and Papago immediative aspect which is negatively marked as to duration.

English Category of Correlation and Papago Category of Conjunctivity

According to Ilyish, English category of correlation has to do with the precedence of an action over some moment in time (1965:99). It has two members: the perfect and the non-perfect. The perfect indicates that the action precedes some moment in time; the non-perfect is neutral as to precedence (p. 99). The non-perfect is unmarked. The perfect is expressed by the auxiliary 'to have' and the suffix *-en* attached either to the verb theme or to the stem of the auxiliary. Instances of the two members of the category of correlation in the three tenses and the two aspects are:

TENSE	ASPECT		ASPECT	
	Common	*Continuous*	*Common*	*Continuous*
Present	writes	is writing	has written	has been writing
Past	wrote	was writing	had written	had been writing
Future	will write	will be writing	will have written	will have been writing
	Nonperfect		Perfect	

CORRELATION

Papago category of conjunctivity indicates the way in which the action—or condition—expressed by the verb is conjoined to another. There are two conjunctives: the concursive and the correlative. The concursive indicates the simultaneity of two actions or conditions. The correlative indicates the logical priority of one action or condition over another. The concursive is expressed by the suffix *-c* attached to the verb theme. The correlative is expressed by the suffix *-k* attached to the verb theme. An example of the concursive is: *bei g ʔali pi ha kunc* 'she had a child without being married'. An example of the correlative is: *ʔid ʔo mumku cum si ʔegegusidk* 'he is sick from having overeaten'.

As can be seen from a comparison of the meanings of English correlation and Papago conjunctivity, English perfect seems to have a rough counterpart in Papago correlative with one important difference: in Papago one is dealing with the logical precedence of an action over another action whereas in English (according to Ilyish 1965:99) only precedence in time is implied.

English Category of Mood and Papago Category of Mood

Mood usually is taken to indicate different degrees of reality of an action. The category of mood in English has three members:[8] the indicative, the subjunctive, and the imperative. The indicative mood indicates that the speaker represents the action as real (Ilyish 1965:106). The subjunctive mood indicates that the speaker represents the action as unreal (p. 112). The imperative mood indicates that the speaker represents the action as either an order, a request, or a prayer (p. 111). An instance of the indicative mood is: 'Soames Forsyte *divorced* his first wife, Irene' (p. 106). Instances of the subjunctive mood are: 'I suggest that he *go*';

---

[8] The number of moods outside the indicative and the imperative, in English is a highly controversial problem area. Ilyish only presents the different points of view (see Ilyish pp. 108–115). The position chosen here is that held by most grammarians.

'If he lived here he *would come* at once'. An instance of the imperative mood is: *'Come* here please!'.

Papago category of mood indicates the statement type characterizing the clause of which the verb in question is the predicate. There are three moods: on the one hand, the imperative and the hortative, on the other hand, the indicative. The imperative and the hortative moods indicate two types of command. The indicative mood is neutral as to command. The imperative mood is expressed by the suffix -*ñ*, -*ϕ* attached to the verb theme. The hortative mood is expressed by the suffix -*ʔi*, -*ʔa*, -*ϕ* attached to the verb theme. (Note that when the verb is in the hortative mood, the hortative particle *g* precedes the verb.) The indicative mood is unmarked. An example of the imperative mood is: *himiñ!* '(you sg.) go!'. An example of the hortative mood is: *pi g him!* '(you sg.) don't go!'. An example of the indicative mood is: *hii ʔat* 'he left'.

As can be seen from a comparison of the meanings of the category of mood in the two languages, English imperative mood has a good counterpart in Papago imperative and hortative moods. There is no similarity, however, between English indicative mood which indicates that the speaker represents the action as real and Papago indicative mood which is neutral as to command. Papago inflectional categories do not stress the reality as opposed to the unreality of the action but rather the manner in which the information conveyed by a given statement is attested (cf. the three members of the category of attestation, the evidential, the quotative and the potential) as well as whether or not the speaker is ignorant with respect to the action or condition referred to in a given statement (of the category of incognizance).

English subjunctive mood is rendered in Papago by various particles.

English Category of Voice and Papago Category of Voice

As stressed by Ilyish, there are two main views regarding the category of voice: One is that voice "expresses the relation between the subject and the action". The other is that voice "expresses the relations between the subject and the object of the action" (1965:120). The second view is chosen here.

The category of voice in English has two members: the active voice and the passive voice. The active voice indicates that the subject of the verb performs the action, is the doer. The passive voice indicates that the subject of the verb is not the doer but the goal of the action (p. 121). Examples of the category of voice manifested together with other verbal categories are:

		Active Voice	*Passive Voice*	
present tense	*common aspect*	invites	is invited	
	continuous aspect	is inviting	is being invited	*indicative mood*
past tense	*nonperfect correlation*	invited	was invited	
	perfect correlation	has invited should invite	has been invited should be invited	*subjunctive mood*

In Papago the category of voice indicates whether or not the reference is to a state, or condition. There are two voices: the stative voice and the active voice. The stative voice indicates that the reference is to a state, or condition. The active voice indicates that the reference is to an action, or occurrence. The stative voice is expressed by the suffix *-k, -ka, -ɸ* (i.e. zero) attached to the verb theme. The active voice is unmarked. An instance of a verb in the two voices is *skegaj* 'to be beautiful' for the stative voice and *kega* 'to become beautiful' for the active voice.

As can be seen from a comparison of the meanings of the category of voice in the two languages, English voice has no real counterpart in Papago. English passive voice is sometimes rendered in Papago by the active voice (e.g. *ʔe-ʔo ohon* 'to get (to be) written') or by the stative voice (e.g. *ʔoʔohonas* 'to be written').

English Categories of Interrogation and Emphasis and Papago Category of Statement Mode

According to Ilyish (1965:133–4), English has a category of interrogation and a category of emphasis which include two members each: the noninterrogative and the interrogative for the former, the unemphatic and the emphatic for the latter. Both the uninterrogative and the unemphatic are unmarked. Both the interrogative and the emphatic are expressed by the auxiliary verb "do". An instance of the interrogative is: '*Does* he take . . . ?' An instance of the emphatic is: 'He *does* know.'

Papago category of statement mode is expressed by pseudo prefixes in the subject complex words. It indicates the mode of the statement of which the compound verb containing the subject complex word is the predicate. There are three modes: the interrogative, the assertive, and the promptive. The interrogative indicates that the statement constitutes a question. The assertive indicates that the statement constitutes an emphatic assertion. The promptive indicates that the statement constitutes a way of prompting. The interrogative is expressed by the prefix *n*-, *naʔa*-. The assertive is expressed by the prefix *v*-. The promptive is expressed by the prefix *ñee*-. An example of the interrogative is: *napt o hii?* 'Will you (do you want to) go?' An example of the assertive is: *vant o hii* 'I will (definitely) go.' An example of the promptive is: *ñeept o ñei g maakai*! 'Why don't you see a doctor (i.e. you should see a doctor)!'

As can be seen from the comparison of the meanings of English categories of interrogation and emphasis and Papago category of statement mode, it seems that the two English categories have a good counterpart in two members of the Papago category, namely the interrogative and the assertive.

English Category of Quality and Papago Category of Assertion

According to Ilyish (1965:132), English has a category of quality which includes two members: the affirmative and the negative. The affirmative is unmarked; the negative is expressed by the particles 'do not' or only 'not'. Instances are:

Affirmative	*Negative*
takes	does not take
take!	do not take!
took	did not take
has taken	has not taken
must take	must not take

Papago category of assertion has two members: the affirmative and the negative. The affirmative is marked. The negative is manifested by the particle *pi*. Instances are:

Affirmative	*Negative*
skegaj 'is beautiful'	pi kegaj 'is not beautiful'
him 'is walking'	pi him 'is not walking'

A comparison of the meanings of the two categories shows that English quality has a very close counterpart in Papago assertion.

Person and Associated Categories in English and in Papago

According to Ilyish (1965:130), the -*s* inflection in verbs (e.g. 'live-*s*') conveys four meanings: (1) *third person* (2) *singular number* (3) *present tense* and (4) *indicative mood*.

In Papago the categories manifested in the object personals affixed to the verb theme are the following: (1) person, (2) personal number, (3) reflexivity, (4) definiteness, and (5) humanness.

A comparison of the various categories listed above shows that only two English categories seem to have counterparts in Papago: person and personal number.

According to Ilyish, (a) the category of person manifested in the English verb has two members: third person and non-third person, and (b) the category of personal number has two members: singular and plural.

Papago category of person manifested in the object personals has three members: first person, second person and third person. The first person refers to the speaker or the group with which the speaker associates himself (e.g. 'me' or 'us'). The second person refers to the entity or entities spoken to (e.g. 'you' or 'you-all'). The third person refers to the entity or entities spoken about (e.g. 'him' or 'them').

The category of personal number manifested in the object personals has two members: the personal singular and the personal plural. The personal singular indicates a single referent; the personal plural indicates several referents (e.g. 'him' vs. 'them').

A comparison of the meanings of the categories of person and personal number in the two languages shows that (1) English person has only a partial counterpart in Papago person and (2) English personal number has an exact counterpart in Papago personal number.

Nouns

The noun in English is closely associated with (1) three articles (definite, indefinite and zero) and (2) the possessive pronouns (e.g. 'my').

In Papago, the noun is closely associated with the particle *g* called the noun marker. (It should be noted that the object personals which translate in English as possessive pronouns are affixed to the noun theme, thus being a part of the inflectional inventory of the noun).

Two inflectional categories are commonly accepted for the English noun: (1) nominal number and (2) case (which includes the common case and the genitive case).

Papago has the following inflectional categories: (1) nominal number; (2) alienability, and (3) person and associated categories. In addition it has one incorporated instrumental and five incorporated locationals.

A comparison of the categories listed above shows that, on the one hand, Papago has several categories and inflectional affixes that are absent in English. These are: (1) person and associated categories (manifested in the object personals affixed to the noun theme); (2) the incorporated instrumental; and (3) the incorporated locationals. On the other hand, (1) English category of nominal number seems to have a counterpart in Papago category of nominal number and, (2) English category of case as manifested in the noun seems to have at least a partial counterpart in Papago category of alienability.

It should be noted that in the case of nouns, both in English and in Papago, grammatical categories are not the only significant consideration. There is also the crucial problem of their subclassification. The latter is closely related to the category of number in both languages.

In the following discussion only the distinctions that are present either in English alone or both in English and in Papago will be included. The distinctions that are present only in Papago will be disregarded.

English Articles

Ilyish (1965:53–4) seems to favor the view that there are three articles in English: the definite article "the", the indefinite article "a", and the zero article, i.e. the "meaningful absence of article". The definite article indicates either an "individual object with its own characteristics" (p. 57) or, "what is known already, or at least what is not presented as new" (p. 58). The indefinite article indicates either "some object belonging to that particular class of objects" (p. 57) or, "what is new" (p. 58). The zero article "with a noun in the plural corresponds to the indefinite article with that noun in the singular" whereas the zero article "with a noun in the singular stands apart and does not correspond to anything in the plural" (p. 59).

There is no distinction in Papago which corresponds to the distinction between the definite article, the indefinite article and the zero article in English. The noun marker which is associated with the Papago noun is not in any way correlated with the use of the English articles. It translates in English sometimes by the definite article, sometimes by the indefinite article, and sometimes by the zero article.

English Category of Nominal Number and Papago Category of Nominal Number

It is commonly accepted that English has two nominal numbers: (1) the singular and (2) the plural. The singular indicates that "one object is meant"; the plural indicates that "more than one object is meant" (Ilyish 1965:39). The singular is unmarked. The plural is usually expressed by the suffix "-s" attached to the noun theme. An example of the singular is: 'boy'. An example of the plural is: 'boys'.

Papago category of nominal number indicates both the number of entities and the number of loci (i.e. culturally defined whereabouts) in which these entities are located. There are three nominal numbers: the nominal singular, the nominal plural and the nominal distributive. The nominal singular indicates a single entity and a single locus; the nominal plural indicates several entities and a single locus; the nominal distributive indicates several entities and several loci with indiscriminately either a single entity or several entities per locus. The category of nominal number is manifested by the reduplication of the first syllable of the stem. Plurality is manifested by simple reduplication. Distributiveness is manifested by double reduplication. An example is, for the singular: *daikuḍ*, 'a single chair from a single locus' (such as a household); for the plural: *dadaikuḍ*, 'several chairs from a single locus' (such as a household); for the distributive: *daddaikuḍ*, 'several chairs from several loci' (such as several households).

As can be seen from a comparison of the meanings of the category of nominal number in the two languages, the opposition involving locus present in the Papago category is irrelevant in English. This meaning is conveyed in English, not by the category of nominal number itself, but by adverbial phrases (such as 'from a single household' or 'from several households').

English Noun Subclasses and Papago Noun Subclasses

According to Ilyish (1965:39–44), there are four subclasses of English nouns: (1) count nouns, (2) pluralia tantum, (3) singularia tantum (usually called mass nouns), and (4) mixed nouns. Count nouns occur both in the singular and in the plural. An example is: 'dog' for the singular and 'dogs' for the plural. Pluralia tantum occur only in the plural. Examples are: 'trousers, outskirts, measles'. Mass nouns occur only in the singular. Examples are: 'milk, iron, peace'. Mixed nouns (called by Ilyish collective nouns and nouns of multitude) occur either in the singular or in the plural with the following meaning changes: In the singular they "denote the whole group"; in the plural they "denote the group as consisting of a certain number of individuals" (p. 43).

In Papago there are five subclasses of nouns: (1) mass nouns, (2) aggregate nouns, (3) individual type 1 nouns, (4) individual type 2 nouns, and (5) mixed nouns. Nouns with mass status refer to undifferentiated masses. They occur in the singular and in the nonsingular. This means that in these nouns the opposition of plural versus distributive is neutralized (see also individual type 2 nouns below). An example is: *xuudagĭ* 'water, one body of water' for the singular and *xuxudagĭ* 'several bodies of water' for the nonsingular. Nouns with aggregate status refer to entities that are found in aggregation such as herds or groups. These nouns occur in the nondistributive and in the distributive. This means that in these nouns the opposition of plural versus distributive is neutralized. An example is: *haivañ* 'one cow, several cows from a single herd' for the nondistributive and *hahaivañ* 'several cows from several herds' for the distributive. Nouns with individual status refer to entities that are neither realized as masses nor are part of an aggregation. There are two types of individual nouns: nouns with individual type 1 status and nouns with individual type 2 status. Nouns with individual type 1 status occur in the singular, in the plural and in the distributive. In these nouns all three oppositions are manifested. An example is: *kaviu* 'a single horse' for the singular, *kakaviu* 'several horses with a single owner' for the plural, *kakkaviu* 'several horses with several owners' for the distributive. Nouns with individual type 2 status occur in the singular and in the nonsingular. In these nouns the opposition of plural versus distributive is neutralized (as with mass nouns above). An example is: *ban* 'a single coyote' for the singular, and *baaban* 'several coyotes' for the nonsingular. Nouns with mixed status are those which alternate between individual type 2 status and aggregate status. An example is: *xeeᵖe* 'a single wolf, several wolves in a single pack', *xexeᵖe* 'several wolves'.

A comparison of the meanings of the various noun subclasses in the two languages shows that English count nouns and mass nouns have partial counterparts in Papago individual nouns and mass nouns respectively. However, it should be noticed that, although there is some general correspondence as far as the categories are concerned, this is not necessarily the case with particular instances. Thus in some cases English count nouns correspond to Papago mass nouns. An example is, the English count noun 'cloud' which corresponds to Papago mass noun *ceevagï* (lit. 'cloudiness'). The other English noun subclasses, namely, pluralia tantum and mixed nouns, have no counterparts in Papago.

English Category of Case and Papago Category of Alienability

According to Ilyish (1965:45), English has two cases: a common case and a genitive case. The common case is neutral as to possession. The genitive case indicates possession (p. 48). The common case is unmarked. The genitive case is expressed by the suffix " 's" attached to the noun theme as in 'father's.'

Papago category of alienability indicates whether an association between entities is one of genuine ownership or not. The category of alienability has two members: alienable status and inalienable status. Alienable status indicates that an association between entities is one of genuine ownership; inalienable status indicates that it is not. Inalienable status is unmarked. Alienable status is expressed by the suffix *-ga*. Examples are: *hiañ kii* 'tarentula's burrow (lit. house)' for the inalienable status; *Kelibaḍ Voʔoga* 'Dead-Old-Man's Pond (a place name)', for alienable status.

The above examples show that the English genitive case corresponds to Papago alienable status only to the extent to which the conception of possession coincides in the two languages.

Adjectives and Adverbs

In English as well as in Papago adjectives and adverbs are closely associated with particles indicating different degrees of grading, such as 'more... than' (Papago *baʔij ʔi ...*), 'the most ...' (Papago *xa ʔi si ...*).

It is commonly accepted that some English adjectives and adverbs are inflected for a single category, namely, comparison. This category is here considered part of the broader phenomenon of grading. English category of comparison has two members: the comparative (suffix "er") and the superlative (suffix "est"). In other English adjectives and adverbs the category of comparison is expressed by the use of particles, "more ... than" for the comparative, and "the most" for the superlative. Grading, other than the category of comparison is always expressed by the use of different particles such as "less ... than", "as ... as".

In Papago, all forms of grading of adjectives and adverbs are expressed by the use of particles. In addition, Papago adjectives and adverbs are inflected for a single category, referential number. The latter category has no counterpart in English.

Personal Pronouns and Possessive Pronouns

Three types of English personal pronouns are distinguished here: (1) simple personal pronouns, (2) reflexive personal pronouns, and (3) emphatic personal pronouns.

Simple personal pronouns occur either as subjects of a verb (e.g. 'I want to go'), or as objects of a verb or of a preposition (e.g. 'He saw me'; 'He wants to go with me').

Reflexive personal pronouns occur as objects of verbs or of prepositions (e.g. 'I am washing myself'; 'I am knitting for myself'). Emphatic personal pronouns occur only in apposition to nouns ('I met John himself'; 'John himself came').

English possessive pronouns occur either as objects of a verb (e.g. 'I took mine') or as modifiers of a noun (e.g. 'my house').

Papago forms that translate into English as personal pronouns and possessive pronouns are: (1) personal pronouns, (2) subject personals, and (3) object personals.

Papago personal pronouns denote emphasis. They occur either in apposition to nouns or in apposition to the subject personals or the object personals. Examples are: *ʔaacim ʔOʔodham* 'We Papagos'; *ʔaapiʔi m-ñei* 'saw you in person'; *ʔaapiʔi m-vui* 'with you in person'; *ʔaapiʔi m-kii* 'your own house'.

The subject personals are the pseudo-stems of the subject complex words. Examples are: *ʔañ* 'I . . .'; *ʔapt* 'You (sg.) . . .'.

The object personals are affixed to verbs, nouns and postpositions. Examples are: *ñ-ñei* 'saw me'; *ñkii* 'my house' and *ñvui* 'with me'.

It is commonly accepted that English simple personal pronouns are inflected for four categories: (1) person, (2) case, (3) referential gender, and (4) personal number, and that English reflexive, emphatic and possessive pronouns are inflected only for three categories: (1) person, (2) referential gender, and (3) personal number.

In the pseudo-stems of the Papago personal pronouns, the category of person is manifested together with the following categories: (1) definiteness, (2) humanness, and (3) distantiality. Their pseudo-inflection include: (1) pronominal number and (2) specificity. In addition, they have one incorporated instrumental and several incorporated locationals. In the subject personals, the category of person is manifested together with: (1) personal number and (2) definiteness. In the object personals, the category of person is manifested together with: (1) personal number, (2) reflexivity, (3) definiteness, and (4) humanness.

A comparison of the categories listed above shows that, on the one hand, English has two categories that are absent in Papago, namely case and gender. On the other hand, Papago has several categories and inflectional suffixes that are absent in English. These are: (1) reflexivity, (2) definiteness, (3) specificity, (4) distantiality, (5) the incorporated instrumental, and (6) the incorporated locationals. Finally, two English categories seem to have counterparts in Papago. These are: (1) English person and Papago person and (2) English personal number and Papago personal number.[9]

In the following discussion only the categories that are present in English alone or that seem to have counterparts in the two languages will be included.

English Case

It is commonly accepted that the category of case as it applies to the personal pronouns has two members: nominative case and objective

---

[9] Papago category of pronominal number which emphasizes the number of loci (i.e. culturally defined whereabouts of a given entity) is unique to Papago.

case. Instances are: for the nominative case 'I', 'he', and 'she'; for the objective case 'me', 'him' and 'her'. According to Ilyish (1965:73), the nominative forms are "being gradually restricted to the function of subject, whereas the objective case forms . . . are taking over all other functions."

The category of case has no counterpart in Papago. English nominative case is rendered in Papago by the use of subject personals, the objective case by the use of the object personals.

English Referential Gender

The category of referential gender applies only to the third person pronouns, both personal and possessive. It has three members: (1) the masculine, (2) the feminine, and (3) the neuter. Examples of the masculine gender are: 'he, him, himself' and 'his'. Examples of the feminine gender are: 'she, her, herself' and 'hers'. Examples of the neuter gender are: 'it, itself' and 'its.' The three members of the category of referential gender enter into two contrastive patterns of usage:[10] (1) neuter versus non-neuter and (2) feminine versus masculine. To the opposition neuter versus non-neuter correspond, on the one hand, the semantic opposition non-human versus human, on the other hand, the semantic opposition downgrading versus upgrading. In these semantic oppositions, non-human and downgrading correspond to neuter; human and upgrading correspond to non-neuter. The obvious opposition of non-human versus human corresponding to neuter versus non-neuter is exemplified by the instances in which an animal or an inanimate object is referred to by 'it' whereas a human being is referred to by either 'he' or 'she'. The less obvious opposition of downgrading versus upgrading corresponding to neuter versus non-neuter is exemplified by the instance in which a human being (such as a baby, a homosexual or a corpse) is referred to by 'it' whereas a pet is referred to by either 'he' or 'she'. To the opposition feminine versus masculine correspond, on the one hand, the semantic opposition female versus non-female, on the other hand, the semantic opposition awesomeness versus lack of awesomeness. In these semantic oppositions, female and awesomeness correspond to feminine; non-female and lack of awesomeness correspond to masculine. The opposition of female versus non-female corresponding to feminine versus masculine is exemplified by the instances in which a female being (either human or animal) is referred to by 'she' whereas a male being (either human or animal), or else a being whose sex is unknown, are referred to by 'he'.

[10] The following semantic analysis of American English category of referential gender is my own (see Madeleine Mathiot, *The Semantic and Cognitive Domains of Language*).

The opposition of awesomeness versus lack of awesomeness corresponding to feminine versus masculine is exemplified by the instances in which the sea, a hurricane, a souped-up car, or for that matter the average American car, are referred to by 'she' whereas a friendly old bicycle or a small European car are referred to by 'he'.

Papago has no real counterpart in the English category of referential gender. The Papago category of humanness which stresses the distinction between human and non-human corresponds only to one of the four semantic oppositions involved in the English category of referential gender.

English Category of Person and Papago Category of Person

It is commonly accepted that the category of person manifested in the English personal and possessive pronouns has three members: the first person, the second person, and the third person. The first person refers to the speaker or the group with which the speaker associates himself (e.g. 'I' and 'we'). The second person refers to the entity or entities spoken of (e.g. 'you' or 'you-all'). The third person refers to the entity or entities spoken about (e.g. 'he' or 'they').

The category of person in Papago (see above) is the exact counterpart of the category of person in English.

English Category of Personal Number and Papago Category of Personal Number

As already stated (see above) English category of personal number has an exact counterpart in Papago category of personal number.

Some Syntactic Patterns

Only three syntactic patterns will be compared in the two languages. They are: (1) order, (2) embedding, and (3) the formation of analytic versus synthetic constructions.

Order

In English the major syntactic relations are most commonly expressed by position in the sentence. This results in the relatively fixed order within the sentence of the elements that manifest syntactic relations, namely, the subject (S), the predicate (P) and the object(s) (O). The most common order of these elements is S P O.

In Papago, syntactic relations are often expressed by various patterns of agreement. Thus, verbs inflected for the category of subject number agree in number with the nominal subject. Verbs inflected for the category of object number agree in number with the nominal object.

As a result, the order within the sentence of the elements that manifest syntactic relations is freer than in English. Constructions such as O P S and P O S are common.

It should be noted that when the subject is a subject complex word (SCW), the preferred construction in short utterances is the following: P SCW [O]. Instances are: *hii ?at* 'he left'; *?ii ?at g xuudagi* 'he drank (the) water'.

In addition, and as was already mentioned above, Papago postpositions can occur either before or after the noun phrase which they introduce, the latter construction being the preferred one. Thus, although the construction *daam g do?ag* 'above the mountain' is possible, the preferred construction is *do?ag daam*. By contrast the corresponding English prepositions, as is well known, always precede the noun phrase which they introduce.

Embedding

It is the inclusion of a sentence-like fragment within a sentence or a phrase. An instance is: 'The man *who just came in* is my lawyer.'

Embedding occurs both in English and in Papago with the following difference: whereas the common pattern in English is right embedding, it is left embedding that appears to be the norm in Papago. An instance is: *?id ?atki ?ab si kuava maagina ?ab kuit?ab* 'this car bumped hard against a tree' (lit. 'this bumped hard car tree against').

Analytic Versus Synthetic Constructing

Analytic constructions are those in which certain relations are carried by independent words. Synthetic constructions are those in which the same relations are carried by bound morphemes, i.e., morphemes included in words. As already mentioned above, English has a much less highly developed inflectional pattern than Papago. Another way of stating this fact is to say that English is predominantly analytic whereas Papago is predominantly synthetic.

This difference between the two languages can be illustrated with many types of constructions. Thus to the analytic construction, 'to be beautiful', correspond two types of synthetic Papago constructions, *skegaj* 'to be beautiful' and *kega* 'to get to be beautiful'. To the analytic construction 'to be written' correspond two types of synthetic Papago constructions, *?o?ohonas* 'to be written' and *?e-?o?ohon* 'to get to be written'. To the analytic constructions 'to have a husband' and 'to have a dog' correspond the synthetic Papago constructions *kun* (compare to noun *kun* 'husband') and *gogsga* (compare to noun *gogs* 'dog') respectively. To the analytic constructions 'sees you' and 'with you' correspond the Papago synthetic constructions *m-ñei* and *m-vui* respectively. To the analytic construction 'my house' corresponds the Papago synthetic construction *ñ-kii*.

REFERENCES

DOLORES, JUAN
    1913   Papago Verb Stems. *University of California Publications in American Archeology and Ethnology* 10: 241–263.
    1923   Papago Nominal Stems. *University of California Publications in American Archeology and Ethnology* 20: 19–31.

HALE, KENNETH L.
    1959   A Papago Grammar. Unpublished Ph.D. dissertation. Indiana University, Bloomington.
    1965   Some Preliminary Observations on Papago Morphophonemics. *International Journal of American Linguistics* 31, No. 4: 295–305.
    1969   Papago /čim/. *International Journal of American Linguistics* 35, No. 2.

ILYISH, B. A.
    1965   *The Structure of Modern English*. Moscow-Leningrad.

JOSEPH, ALICE, ROSAMOND B. SPICER AND JANE CHESKY
    1949   *The Desert People, A Study of the Papago Indians of Southern Arizona*. The University of Chicago Press, Chicago.

KURATH, WILLIAM
    1945   A Brief Introduction to Papago, A Native Language of Arizona. *University of Arizona Social Science Bulletin*, No. 13, Tucson.

MASON, J. ALDEN
    1950   The Language of the Papago of Arizona. *University of Pennsylvania Museum Monographs*, Philadelphia.

MATHIOT, MADELEINE
    in   Grammatical Outline in the Introduction to *A Dictionary of Papago Usage*.
    press Publications of the Research Center for the Language Sciences, Indiana University, Bloomington.
    in   The Semantic and the Cognitive Domains of Language. In *Cognition—*
    press *A Multiple View*, Paul L. Garvin, ed.

O'NEALE, LILA M. AND JUAN DOLORES
    1943   Notes on Papago Color Designations. *American Anthropologist* 45: 387–397.

SAXTON, DEAN
    1963   Papago Phonemes. *International Journal of American Linguistics* 29, No. 1: 29–35.

SAXTON, DEAN AND LUCILLE
    1969   *Dictionary. Papago and Pima to English, English to Papago and Pima*. The University of Arizona Press, Tucson.

SLEDD, JAMES
    1959   *A Short Introduction to English Grammar*. Scott, Foresman & Co., Chicago.

WILLENBRINK, ANTONINE, O.F.M.
    1935   *Notes on the Pima Indian Language*. The Franciscan Fathers of California.

16. *Language Pluralism in a Southwestern Pueblo: Some Comments on Isletan English*

WILLIAM L. LEAP

The author's main interests are focused on how a bilingual speaker is able to maintain fluency in more than one language structure. His paper deals with language pluralism at Isleta and suggests that Isletan English utilizes the phonological and grammatical constraints of Tiwa and not of English. Learning English at Isleta, then, seems to be a matter only of learning vocabulary items and indicates that even though languages used in linguistically plural communities may be situationally autonomous, their structures may be shared.

This is an expanded version of a paper originally presented at the annual meetings of the Southwestern Anthropological Association in 1971. The research was funded by a National Science Foundation Dissertation improvement grant (NSF GS-2498) and through personal sources. The author has benefited, from conversations with George L. and Felicia H. Trager, M. Estellie Smith, Elizabeth A. Brandt, Ruth H. K. Landman, and Harvel Sebastian. Many thanks also to the several students and friends at the American University, who assisted on this project. Of course, none of this would have been possible without the unselfish cooperation of my friends at Isleta, who have been so patient during all of the Isleta research.

Isleta, New Mexico, is a Southern Tiwa-speaking pueblo community located some fifteen miles south of the center of downtown Albuquerque. Isleta may be called a community, in that the Isletans vote for, and agree to abide by, the decisions of one common set of governing officials. The pueblo itself, however, is actually an aggregate of five terminologically distinct living areas, two of which merit special mention here. The village (Isl. *natśa'i*), the largest settlement area on the reservation, includes individual house units, the plaza, the community "round house," the two dance kivas, other Indian ceremonial structures, the post office, the CAP (Community Action Program) headquarters, and the Roman Catholic church. South and west of the village lies *Oriabi*, the area originally settled by the Keresan speakers who moved to Isleta from Laguna pueblo in 1882; hence the other name for this area, the Laguna village (Isl. *biernin+təà'i*). Today, however, persons of Keresan and Isletan background have homes within this area.

Surrounding these various settlement areas lie the pasture lands and cultivated fields considered typical for a Southwestern Indian pueblo. Given the state of the market economy, the potential income from small-scale cattle raising and agriculture is no longer sufficient to maintain a family of any size. Other sources of income on the reservation, despite the efforts of the CAP, remain quite meager. The pickle plant has been the only possibility of large-scale employment, but that facility continuously has been opened, maintained, then closed, only to be reopened once again, as persons from outside the community experiment with the factory lease. Isleta has never been a tourist's pueblo; even today only two or three families manufacture pottery or other goods for the sightseer's consumption. All told, there are only four instances of Isletan-owned "private enterprise" on the reservation: two food-vending facilities; the Isleta bakery, supplying most of the Indian bread and pastries consumed at the pueblo; and the art gallery, used by Eddie Shirpoyo as an outlet for the increasingly popular landscapes he produces. The recent opening of the Isleta recreation area on reservation land north of the village has the potential to attract outsiders, thanks to the boating, fishing and picnicking opportunities it offers; since the facility belongs to the people of Isleta, a sense of community responsibility supplies the needed manpower, and only one or two Isleta men have to be "employed" full time.

ISLETANS WORK ELSEWHERE

It is not surprising, then, to find that most of the people of Isleta have turned to nearby Spanish communities or commute as far as Albuquerque or Belen, in order to find employment. Relations between

Isleta and these neighboring communities are more than strictly economic ones. The Roman Catholic church, located on the north side of the plaza within the village, serves a parish that includes persons from Peralta and Pajarito, as well as members of the pueblo community. After completing the elementary program offered by the B.I.A. (Bureau of Indian Affairs) day school on the reservation, Isletan children complete their education in the county high schools of Las Lunas or Peralta. Since the closing of the general store in the village, Las Lunas and Peralta also have begun to serve as shopping centers for the people of Isleta, and several stores specifically have started to cater to the needs of the pueblo housewife.

Thus, while it is certainly correct to say that Isleta is a pueblo Indian community, such a statement does not imply that the people of Isleta live within a cultural vacuum. Formalized and frequent contact with the Anglo-Spanish world has removed virtually all traces of the "reservation Indian" from the Isletan life-style. The observation, then, that "the inhabitants of Isleta are multilingual," comes as no surprise. While the exact situation will vary along generational and familial lines, it is safe to say that most Isletans over the age of twenty-one, and many under that age, have speaking fluency of both Isletan Tiwa and English, and also may have control over the variety of Southwestern Spanish spoken in the Albuquerque area. Families with Laguna background, or close Keresan ties also may speak Laguna Keresan in their homes. All members of the so-called "Laguna Kachina society" at Isleta have some familiarity with Keresan, since their various ceremonials are given in that language. Instances of inter-marriage, as well as long-standing trade relations or friendships serve to link many Isletan families to individuals from other Indian communities; as a result, it is not unusual to find an Isletan who demonstrates knowledge of "some" Navajo, "some" Zuni, or "some" Hopi.

Such an instance of language pluralism is not in any way uncommon to pueblo communities as a whole. Spenser, for example, in his discussion of Keresan phonology, has noted:

> Most Keres today are bilingual. The majority of the older generation speak New Mexico Spanish, while younger people, as a result of compulsory education, are at home in English. A fairly large number of Keres who trade throughout the northern areas of New Mexico at frequent intervals can converse quite adequately in Navaho, Zuni, or one or more of the Tanoan languages. (1946:230).

Hoijer and Dozier, in fact, preceded their discussion of the phonemes of Santa Clara Tewa with this caveat:

> Since our report rests upon data from a single bilingual speaker, our con-

clusions must, of course, be regarded as preliminary. We hope to check them later against materials collected from monolinguals at Santa Clara. (1949:139).

Indeed, as the tone of the present volume would suggest, language pluralism is not in any way uncommon to the modern-day Southwest as a whole.

The fact that this situation is familiar does not make it any less intriguing—the anthropologically oriented linguist always needs to consider the cultural implications of the obvious. In that regard, three lines of investigation would be open: (1) noting that (at least) two historically distinct languages are being spoken, to determine the kinds of reciprocal effects or "interferences" that result from a situation of simultaneous language use; (2) stressing function rather than form, to determine when, and for what purposes, these various codes are employed; (3) and by far the most demanding question, to determine how it is possible for one speaker to control knowledge of more than one language.

FOCUS ON SIMULTANEOUS LANGUAGE USE

The focus initially will be on the first of these approaches, and for only two of the languages in use within the Isletan speech community—Isletan Tiwa and Isletan English. The present discussion is an outgrowth of four years of investigation into the structure of the Isletan "Indian language." Conversations with Isletan informants during these years of grammatical analysis continually pointed to the fact that an Isletan speaks English with some sort of "accent." In January, 1971, having completed a systematic statement of the structure of Isletan Tiwa phonology, it was decided to consider the linguistic nature of this "accent," specifically to see how an Isletan speaker's Tiwa phonological pattern might be interfering with his pronunciation of English utterance materials. The data to be considered, a corpus of some 500 words and sentences, were obtained from a replay of taped interviews with three persons fluent in Isletan and English. Most of the discussions on the tapes had to be carried out in English, since the investigator was not fluent in the Indian language. As a result, the tapes offered a rich variety of English vocabulary items, grammatical constructions, and usage patterns. Tentative conclusions drawn from the analysis of the taped information were systematically rechecked and expanded during the summer 1971 field season, through observations at the Isleta Day School, and additional interviews with four other "bilingual" Isletans. What follows, then, is a preliminary report on this investigation.[1]

[1] The description and analysis of American English phonology as given in Trager and Smith (1951) was used as the "baseline" for the English portion of the

As noted above, the original focus of the investigation was quite limited: to determine the ways in which Isletan Tiwa phonology might interfere with an Isletan's pronunciation of English. It soon became apparent that there was more involved than interference, and that the situation extended beyond the phonological level. The present discussion can make this point most effectively if the course of the original investigation is retraced. Thus, we begin with a consideration of the vowel elements of Isletan Tiwa and Isletan English.

The vowel phonemes of Isletan Tiwa, with their positional variants, are listed below:

i: high, front, tense, unrounded, oral

į: high, front, tense, unrounded, nasal

e: generally, lower mid, front, tense, unrounded, oral; before "m" and "n", with lowered lower high allophone; in some environments, "e" shows a (noncontrastive) phonetic prolongation, whose significance is seen in the following paragraphs.

ę: higher low, front, tense, unrounded, with varying intensity of nasal quality.

ɔ: generally, high central, tense, unrounded, oral, though tongue height and rounding quality may vary in some environments.

ǫ: mid, central, tense, unrounded, nasal in all instances

a: generally, low, central to back, tense, unrounded, nonnasal; with lower mid, central allophone in clusters after "i" and "u."

ą: generally, low, central, tense, unrounded, nasal; with lower mid allophone after "į" and "ų."

u: generally, lower high to higher mid, back, tense, rounded, oral; always higher mid when accompanied by low tone.

ų: generally, lower high to higher mid, back, tense, rounded, nasal; always higher mid when accompanied by low tone.

Note that Isletan Tiwa maintains the usual Tanoan typological distinction between oral and nasal vowel quality, with each series containing elements within five general articulatory positions: high, front; mid to low, front; high to mid, central; high to mid, back; and low, mid to back. Uniquely back segments are redundantly rounded.

Two semivowel qualities also occur in Isletan Tiwa: "y"—front, nonrounded; and "w"—back, rounded; the phonetic height of the semivowel varies with the tongue height of the adjacent vocalic segment. The Isletan Tiwa vowel-semivowel (VS) clusters are: ey, ęy, ɔy, ǫy, uy, ųy, ay, ąy; iw, įw, ew, ęw, ɔw, ǫw, aw, ąw. All of the possible clusters, except for "iy" and "uw", and their nasalized equivalents, actually have occurrence. Several bivocalic (VV) clusters—ie, įę, ia, ɔa, ǫą, ua, ųą—are found also. These varieties of VS and VV clusters represent the only occurrences

discussion, since the only other comprehensive description of the sound pattern of English, while certainly interesting, does not contribute insight into the solution of descriptive problems.

of phonemic (i.e. contrast-making) "lengthened" vocalic sequences in this language.

The vowels of Isletan English may now be considered in the light of this information. As noted, it was originally expected that the Isletan English vowels would show phonetic and distributional resemblance to the elements of the nine-vowel system of Albuquerquian English; where they did not show this resemblance, specific instances of Tiwa-based interference would be seen to condition the exception. There was more to the Isletan English vocalics than originally supposed.

A six-way contrast is maintained by these elements in the following articulatory positions: high, front—"i"; mid, front—"e"; low, front— "æ" high to mid, central—"ə"; high to mid back— "u"; and low, central to back—"a." Three vowel-semivowel clusters—"iw, aw," and "uw"— and two instances of a phonemically distinct "prolonged" vocalic—"e·" and "a·"—complete the vocalic inventory.

The Isletan English materials and their English environmental equivalents are as follows (the order of presentation is Isletan English: Albuquerquian English): iːi; eːi,e; æːæ; əːɨ,ə; aːa,ə; uːu,o; iwːiw;— ːew; awːæw;—əw; awːaw; uːuw; iːih; e·ːeh;—ːæh;əːəh;a·ːah;uːuh; iːiy; e·ːey;—ːæy;—ːəy; a·ːay;—ːuy. Notice that the equivalence is in no way one-to-one, from either a phonetic, phonemic, or allophonic point of view. Several of the English distinctions are subsumed under a single element in the Isletan English system: "u" and "o" correspond to Isletan English "u"; "i" and "ə" to Isletan English "ə"; and so on. Similarly, several of the English vowel clusters correspond to elements with single vocalic status in the Isletan English system.

Likewise, the Isletan English vowels differ from their English counterparts in sheer number (six in Isletan English vs. nine in English), in specifics of muscular tension, range of intra-phonetic tongue height and positioning, and in their allophonic patterning. This lack of correspondence suggests that the vowel system of Isletan English is something quite dissimilar to the system that might be expected for a dialect of English.

The reason for this "deviance" becomes apparent when the Isletan English materials are compared to the vowel system of Isletan Tiwa, as follows (the order of presentation is Isletan English: Isletan Tiwa): iːi; eːe; æːę; əːə; aːa; uːu; iwːiw; awːaw; uwːu (no "uw" in Tiwa); e·ːe (as [ɛ·]); a·ːa. Note that the five oral vowels of Isletan Tiwa are identical in muscular tension, tongue height, tongue position, and (with two exceptions) allophonic patterning, to five of the six vowels of Isletan English. The remaining vowel—"æ," has no correspondence within the Isletan Tiwa oral vowels but does appear to be phonetically identical to the front, low, tense nasalized vocalic, Isletan Tiwa "e." This suggests an interesting sort of "working hypothesis": might the vocalic system of Isletan English be, in actual fact, the result of an "adaptation" of the Isletan Tiwa vocalic system, to the structural (but not necessarily the articulatory) requirements of English utterance phonology? To put it simply, could Isletan English really be English material, pronounced as if it were Tiwa?

Taken in this sense, the two exceptions to the correspondence mentioned above become readily explainable. Isletan English "e" before following "s" and "r" has a tongue position higher than that of the principle allophone of its class, yet not as high a position as is found before following nasal. Isletan Tiwa has the nasal conditioning, but lacks a specific variant in "s" and "r" environments; this would mean, in turn, that such environments *could exhibit* allophonic conditioning without distorting the patterning of Tiwa phonological structure; such a position restriction merely would have to be "accreted" to the existing set of Isletan phonetic distributions.

In addition, Isletan English contains two instances of contrastively lengthened vocalic—"e·" and "a·". Isletan Tiwa has no equivalent of the "a·", and shows only an apparently subphonemic variety of the "e·"— [ε·], as a reflex of vowel-semivowel clusters reconstructable for earlier stages of Isletan Tiwa and still operating in the variety of Southern Tiwa spoken at nearby Sandia pueblo. In all instances, the Isletan English vocalics correspond to clusters of English vowel and post-vocalic "h." Isletan Tiwa "h," however, could not be used to approximate the English lengthener since the Tiwa "h" is consonantal and not semivocalic, and thus the subphonemic lengthener, present in the phonetic inventory, is called into play.

This raises another question: why do only three other vowel-semivowel clusters occur within the Isletan English corpus, given the much larger inventory of such elements in both Tiwa and English? The Isletan English: Albuquerquian English correspondences given above also shed some light on this question.

It must first be recalled that the semivowels of Isletan Tiwa are much more highly syllabic than are their English counterparts—so much so, that in many instances the investigator might be tempted to write both syllabic and non-syllabic offglides as the realization of the post-vocalic semivowel. Thus it is not surprising to find several of the English vowel-semivowel clusters subsumed under a single Isletan English vocalic; an Isletan speaker simply does not hear a sufficient amount of phonetic "stuff" in post-vocalic position to necessitate his use of a separate structural element in these instances.

The remaining gaps in the Isletan English vowel-semivowel inventory occur in those instances where the corresponding English clusters are themselves quite dialectically restricted: æw, uy, əy and æy. While these sequences do occur in Isletan Tiwa, they are not required for phonological contrast in the Isletan variety of English (or in Albuquerquian English, for that matter).

At this point, there is some reason to continue a tentative acceptance of the working hypothesis given above—that the vocalic system of Isletan English might more accurately be seen as a form of the Isletan Tiwa vocalic system, adapted to the structural requirements of English utterance materials. Turning attention to the consonant inventory of Isletan English, this hypothesis can be both strengthened and expanded.

As before, we begin with the Isletan Tiwa details. Isletan Tiwa contains the following consonantal elements in initial and medial positions: p t k—voiceless, fortis stops; č—voiceless, fortis affricate; b d g—voiced, lenis stops; f θ s š x h—voiceless, fortis spirants. In final utterance position, only b d g occur, and do so as voiceless, rather than as voiced, lenis stops. The resonants—m n r l—likewise voiced and lenis in initial and medial positions, occur with voiceless variants in final position. In English, of course, the possibilities for contrast in all three word positions are much more varied, and in final position both voiced and voiceless sounds, as well as stop and spirant sounds, frequently occur.

In Isletan English, however, the Tiwa distributional pattern, rather than the English one, appears to be the rule. The distinction between voiced and voiceless stops, found in initial and medial position, is neutralized, and only voiceless, lenis stops occur in final position. As a result, only contextual information can distinguish between such "minimal pairs" as got and God, pot and pod, cup and cub, and the like when given in Isletan English.

In similar fashion, the final distinction between much and judge is lost, with both words having a voiceless, lenis affricate in word final position. Likewise, the final sounds of boys and horses, give and rough, and smooth and bath are given as voiceless lenis spirants by the Isletan English speaker. Of course, neither voiceless lenis affricates nor spirants occur within the Isletan Tiwa phonological inventory; but their presence in Isletan English (as required by the examples here listed, for instance) does appear to follow Isletan Tiwan phonological rule governing final position consonant phonetics in Isletan Tiwa.

There is more to the argument than this observation, however. If Isletan English has final position voiceless, lenis affricate and apirants, then these (in a distributional sense) must be taken as final position variants of "something." Following the Isletan Tiwa rule, where final voiceless lenis stops are allophones of voiced, lenis stops, the Isletan English final voiceless lenis affricate, and voiceless lenis spirants, become allophones of voiced, lenis sounds. Hence, by extension of an Isletan Tiwa phonological rule, a voiced lenis affricate, "ǰ," and a series of voiced lenis spirants are introduced into the Isletan English phonological structure.

The same argument may be used to account for the presence of the various final position consonant clusters in Isletan English, even though Isletan Tiwa phonology allows only four clusters in that position—-nm, -ng, -rm, -lm. Here, as above, only voiceless lenis sounds, as allophones of voiced, lenis classes, may occur in final position. For a word like English lo*cked*, where neither member of the cluster may occur (phonemically) in that position in Tiwa, the second member of the cluster is deleted, and the first member is "normalized" to its lenis equivalent in the Isletan English inventory. In similar fashion, the final "-st" of English priest will be given as "-z" in Isletan English. Since both members of the "-nz" cluster in English mea*ns* have final position values in Isletan English (through the argument above), "-nz" as a voiceless lenis cluster will appear in the Isletan English equivalent of this word. The same sequence also will occur in the Isletan English pronunciation of hu*nts*, once the noncorresponding "-t-" is deleted, for the same reason as above.

Thus, while the consonants of Isletan English are in many ways similar to those within an English inventory, their distributional patterning is almost identical to that governing consonants of Isletan Tiwa. This observation, when added to the analysis of vowel materials given above, allows us to wonder whether it is appropriate to consider Isletan English phonology as an English phonology at all.

Might the same sort of "conclusion" apply to the grammatical aspects of Isletan English structure? That is, does the composition of Isletan English utterance materials seem to be governed by Isletan Tiwa, rather than English grammatical rule?

At first glance, this might appear to be a pointless question. Certainly, an Isletan English utterance contains recognizable English morphemic materials, and the details of their combination into utterance wholes likewise follows expectable English patterns—except where they do not. In the context of the present article, such exceptions are of particular interest; for each instance of deviation from a more general English usage (what Miss Fidditch [Joos 1962] would call a "mistake") can be accounted for in terms of an Isletan Tiwa grammatical rule.

Thus, for example: "Two women was out there fighting" would

appear to contain an error in number agreement between the (plural) noun and the (singular) verb. Notice, of course, that this sentence designates a situation in which two elements occur together as part of one, interrelated unit. Even though two women are fighting, only one fight (one activity) is going on. Hence the verb, denoting the fighting, is singular, while the noun, denoting the participants, is plural—exactly as occurs in the Isletan Tiwa equivalent of this Isletan English sentence: *wìsiɫiwran ʔìbehúban.* which may be analyzed in the following components:

wìsi-ɫíwran	ʔi-	-be-	-hú-	-ban
two-women	3d per.	—reflexive	—fighting	—past
	dual	each other		tense

The Tiwa sentence clearly denotes that the two women were acting as an interrelated unit, and not as separate entities.

In similar fashion, the "mis-agreement" of an Isletan English sentence like: "Either phrases can be used" can be accounted for, through the use of a Tiwa, instead of English, grammatical perspective. The reference in this sentence is being made to *one* member of a two-member structured set; *phrases* is given as a plural, but the verb and the accompanying modifier are singular, since the individual members of the set and not the set as a whole, are being discussed. Likewise, for Isletan English: "You would not be holding any positions," reference is being made to any one of several members of a common class; the multipleness of the class is marked by the use of the English "-Z_1 plural" morpheme, and the preceding singular modifier focuses the discussion on various members of the multiple, not on the multiple as a whole. The answer to the question, "What corn group does he belong to?"—"He is a blue corn people," would yield to a similar analysis.

The same approach can be used to account for Isletan English constructions like: "The Isleta woman should stick together." The Isletan Tiwa word for woman, ɫìwráde, contains the -Vde "category" suffix, indicating that the reference in question here is to a position or status within the socioculture that any number of eligible individuals may share at a given time. Thus, to speak of the women of Isleta sticking together and acting as a group, would involve reference to the category whole, not to a grouping of individuals. The corresponding sentence in Isletan English, then, contains the seemingly appropriate singular subject form.

Isletan verbs make no distinction between "gender" in the third (or any) person, thus instances of Isletan English "The government will step in and he will help you." Or, "My welfare checks, he is not here yet." are not surprising. Perhaps the absence of the appropriate third person allomorph of the verb to be, as in "That be the governor," or "They be the only ones left," may likewise be explained, since in Isletan Tiwa the prefix on the verb and not the verb suffix indicates person and number—as the detail on the Tiwa example above will indicate.

Numerous sentences in Isletan English contain *-tion* forms in usages that, while not "incorrect" by an English speaker's standards, will strike a non-Isletan as somewhat unusual. "He acts as a protection, not as a law." "Then I had a confusion." "He asked me for the reflection of it." Such derivational constructions in Isletan English are quite similar to the partitive references made, in Isletan Tiwa, by the *na-* prefixed "collectivity" words.

Any kind of foodstuff, be it chili, bread pudding, or cold pizza, may be called *nakár*—food, since food is a sort of collective category not restricted in its membership by contexts of time or space, nor by detail of nutritional composition. In similar fashion, any person can be confused since a state of confusion need not be restricted to specific causes nor to specific sets of circumstances. Thus, to say "I am confused" in Isletan English would not make good Tiwa sense for this would imply that the speaker had a unique possession over this emotional state. A more collective (or "partitive"-like) reference can be made, however, by saying: "I had a confusion," thereby using English grammatical material to signal an Isletan grammatical meaning.

One other Isletan English example may be briefly considered— "idiomatic" expressions like, "His hair was hairy" used to mean that the individual in question has an abundance of hair on his head. Such a construction is not a grammatical mistake, but is nevertheless somewhat peculiar; even so, the usage becomes understandable if considered in Tiwan terms. The Isletan term, *xɔ'i* 'peeling' when used in an anatomical sense, denotes a person's scalp or his skull—i.e. the material that forms the top of his head; hair on one's head may likewise be referred to by this term. This same sort of equation of "scalp," "skull" and "hair," appears to be implied by the wording of the English sentence in question here.

Such scattered examples, of course, cannot serve as the basis for substantive conclusions about the nature of Isletan English grammar, but they can be taken in their suggestive sense, and what they suggest is this: while Isletan English sentences do contain recognizable English morphemes and word constructions, the varieties of constructions into which these elements may enter frequently seem less familiar—each such instance of nonfamiliarity can be accounted for when considered in terms of the details of Isletan grammar. That is, an Isletan English speaker instead of talking "bad" English, may well be talking "good" Indian—using Tiwa grammatical rules and Tiwa phonological potential to generate his conversational material.

Nature of Isletan English

The preceding examples, as well as the other materials in the larger corpus from which they were drawn, lead one to wonder, then, whether Isletan English is really English at all, or whether it might not be more accurately described as an additional variety of Isletan Tiwa—more specifically, the variety of Indian used by an Isletan to communicate, *as an Indian*, with the non-Indian Anglo world. This is not to say, of course, that an Isletan cannot recognize a difference between Tiwa words and English ones, nor should this imply that he cannot distinguish between talking in Indian and talking in English; there certainly are numerous situations (kiva rituals being one) where the exclusive use of one variety, instead of the other, is culturally required. Yet just because the use of the varieties may be in complementary distribution does not necessarily imply that the structural makeup of these codes must likewise be completely distinct.

And, of course, even the usage situations are not always so dichotomous. Isletan English conversations frequently contain whole stretches of Isletan Tiwa utterance materials within the "English" sentences— the phenomenon the literature labels as "code-switching." In the context of the present article, the presence of such "intrusive" materials is hardly surprising: since the phonological detail, and perhaps much of the grammatical structure, of the Isletan phrase and the English environment may be virtually identical, code-switching would merely involve the change in lexical material. (The motivations for such changes, of course, remain to be determined.) In similar fashion, the presence of (Isletan) English words within Isletan Tiwa utterance materials becomes understandable. Given the phonological and grammatical similarities, all that would be remaining would be the addition, to the English lexical items, of the Tiwa morphemic marker appropriate to the given utterance environment—and hence we have the so-called "English loan words" introduced into conversational Isletan.

Of course a number of points remain to be dealt with, and it may be, given the present stage of the analysis, that these points can be raised only as questions for future research. Most important here is the fact that many people at Isleta (especially persons in the 20–40 age bracket) *are* able to speak a variety of English that even Miss Fidditch would approve of, one that contains few (if any) indications of Tiwa influence.

It is important to note, however, that such uses of WASP (White Anglo-Saxon Protestant) English are restricted, in the main, to those situations (primarily professional) where the Isletan wishes to emphasize his role as a fully functioning individual within Anglo society. At home, among Indian friends at work, the WASP style is dropped; conversations with Anglo acquaintances may begin in WASP style, but as the security of friendship is reaffirmed, the Anglo conventions become replaced with Tiwa ones.

Given the argument in the present article, it is worth wondering how an Isletan speaker is able to learn such an "acceptable" English, for to do so, he must overcome the constraints of Isletan Tiwa as well as of its variety of English. This means that in a very real sense, a young Isletan may have to learn two quite structurally distinct usage patterns for the same English lexical inventory. This is not an unfamiliar state of affairs (the parallel to the black English situation is most obvious), but again, its familiarity is not grounds for dismissing the situation out of hand. It is not sufficient merely to recognize that the Isletan may have fluency in two different varieties of conversational English. What we need to know is how this fluency can occur—through what processes, linguistic or otherwise, is such language pluralism possible.

At present, the processional nature of this most extreme example of language pluralism—"pure" English vs. "pure" Isletan—remains an open-ended question, yet not an unanswerable one. We do have a basis from which to start the investigation: for an Isletan, speaking WASP English is not the same thing as speaking Isletan English. Through our understanding of the latter, we know, at least, what is *not* happening in the former situation.

A second question arises here. The argument that Isletan English may have the same linguistic structure as is found for Isletan Tiwa would seem to imply that Tiwa structure has come out of this "accommodation" completely unaffected by English influence. In the long run, this may prove to be a misleading conclusion, since some feedback is expectable. Thus it may not be surprising to find that some of the phonological questions in Isletan Tiwa may be more effectively understood within an English context, rather than strictly a Tiwan one. The subphonemically lengthened variety of Isletan "e" has been treated (as above) as a reflex of an older vowel-semivowel situation, as the comparative data from Sandia would attest. Recalling that the "lengthener" here is called into play in Isletan English as the equivalent of English post-vocalic "h," it could be argued that the lengthened "e" of modern day Isletan Tiwa constitutes the beginnings of a post-vocalic length phenomenon in that language, a third kind of vowel-semivowel cluster. This would reverse the direction of the discussion of Isletan

English "e·" and "a·", of course, but might also suggest, in the process, a way of testing the historical reality of this instance of English-derived influence on Tiwa phonological structure. Should such influence truly be in operation, we should expect that Tiwa "a·" will be the next vocalic to show evidence of a lengthened allophone.

The presence of English influences on Tiwa grammatical structure may be a bit more obvious. Younger speakers of Isletan and English, for example, are frequently found to make the Tiwa singular-plural animate distinction (given as -Vde, -Vn by older speakers—*kabéde*, *kában* 'corn group leader') as *kábe*, *kában*, using the unmarked singular, marked plural convention of English structure; some speakers also use forms like *kábe*, *kábes*, actually introducing the English -Z_1 plural marker into their Tiwa inventory. As a result, the singular forms lose their formal marker of their membership in the "category" noun class, as discussed above; some rearrangement in Isletan noun class semology should be expected to result, a point that will be given close observation in future field seasons.

Whether these instances of "possible" English influence on Tiwa structure require, or will require, a rewording of the tentative conclusions about Isletan English structure remains unanswerable. It is, in any case, safe to say that, at present, the Tiwa-ness of Isletan English is much more blatantly obvious than are any reciprocal effects English may be introducing. The reason this is true at the time of this writing is, of course, a historical one. In a very real sense, it has only been with the speakers of the "parents'" generation at Isleta (persons forty to sixty years of age), that English became the "second" language of the Isletan community; for older generations, Spanish served as the primary non-Indian communication medium, and even today many of the oldest persons at Isleta still retain this Isletan-Spanish fluency.[2] The present under-twenty generation, then, is the third generation to use English as their "second" language. Unlike those who in previous years learned their English in B.I.A. schools and elsewhere, *after* they learned their Indian, this under-20 age group may be the first generation to grow up with speaking control of both Isletan Tiwa and Isletan English, and thereby offer the first situation where complete feedback between Isletan and English structures might be possible.

Learning both English and Isletan does not necessarily imply complete fluency in each of these languages; in not a few instances, a person under 20 grew up speaking English and knowing only enough Indian (as one informant put it) "to get by"—to be able to follow a conversa-

---

[2] Bodine (1968:25) has reported the same situation for Taos, and Brandt (1970:47) describes similar conditions at Sandia.

tion in Indian (even though he may enter into it by speaking English). Even so, if circumstances deem it necessary (or appropriate—as in peer-group situations), he can speak Tiwa though he will admit to feeling selfconscious about it. Attention needs to be paid to this ability differential, but such information should only enhance, and not contradict, the observation of the preceding paragraph.

This growing occurrence of English usage has had an additional manifestation: persons over age 20 (teachers and lay adults alike) readily admit that the children they know speak English without any noticeable difficulty; if anything, they say, the young people's knowledge of Indian needs improving. Given the examples discussed in the present paper, such comments would seem to imply that standards of correctness for Isletan English have been developed within the speech community, standards that are based, however, on Isletan-English, and not Miss Fidditch's, criteria. A historical tradition of Isletan English usage may also be present, which would explain why the young person described above, who speaks fluent English and "little" Tiwa, nevertheless will speak his English with an Indian accent; the English he learns at the pueblo is the Isletan-derived variety. This also may explain why such a young person is able to learn (or re-learn) fluent Tiwa so rapidly when he takes on adult responsibilities within the community. What he needs to learn (and what he will admit to being the least secure about) is lexical data; he already has control over an acceptable Indian phonology and knows many of the Indian grammatical constructions—he learned them both when he learned his Isletan English.

Other Questions Arise

Such consideration of the chronological aspects of language pluralism at Isleta brings up another direction for questioning. If members of the older generation spoke Tiwa and Spanish, might this use of Spanish have had some effect on Tiwa structure in the past, and might such effects enter into the detail of the Isletan English materials dealt with here? On the grammatical level, this remains a point for future research, although it might be noted that the tense distinctions of the Southern Tiwa verb system strongly resemble the distinctions found in New Mexico Spanish. This happens in spite of the fact that several of the morphemic markers for these distinctions have direct phonological correspondence to the tense markers in the other Tanoan languages; the analogy to the Isleta lengthened "e" situation, in its historical and functional senses, should not be disregarded.

On the phonological level, the situation likewise remains to be considered in detail, yet several factors suggest that Spanish phonology has not altered the historical components of Tiwa phonology at all. The vowel qualities of Southwestern Spanish (Trager and Valdez 1935: 34) are most unlike the vocalics of Isletan Tiwa and Isletan English, both in terms of their environmentally conditioned phonetic quality and their relative distributions within utterance materials. While there is somewhat more similarity between Spanish and Isletan English consonant elements, the similarity lies primarily in those phonemes that were introduced into Isletan Tiwa (and the rest of Tanoan) at some time shortly after the contact period; they probably did so, in fact, through mechanisms similar to those given in the discussion of Isletan English final "j," "z," and the like, above. It would appear that, at least on the segmental level, Spanish has contributed to Isletan English phonology only in the ways that it has contributed to that of Isletan Tiwa, and that the effects in the latter instance are quite limited indeed. This would suggest the possibility that an analysis of the phonology of the Spanish of Isleta, New Mexico, might well point to the same sort of conclusions as were reached for Isletan English: Isletan Spanish contains Spanish lexical items, operated upon by Tiwa grammatical and phonological convention. This would imply, in turn, that modern day Isletan Spanish could not be taken solely as a direct descendent of the language of the conquistadores, nor would it necessarily be similar to the Spanish spoken in the communities adjacent to Isleta today.

Results of Analysis

We are now in a position to consider some more general implications that this discussion may have, for the understanding of language pluralism as a general (or potentially universal) language phenomenon. As noted above, to say that an Isletan speaks Indian and English gives only a half-accurate picture. The analysis here suggests, in fact, that our bilingual Isletan is not bilingual in the sense of much of the literature—he does not have control over two separate language structures, but (at best) over two different lexical systems, and he brings to their conversational realization what appears to be a single phonological system and (most probably) one set of grammatical rules. Thus while Fishman may be right in his insistence that bilingualism is really the result of an addition of another situationally-based code to the wealth of intra-linguistic codes already possessed by the speaker (1968:passim), this argument must not lead us to the premature conclusion that these various codes need be as structurally autonomous as they are situationally so. The use of terms like "bilingualism" or "language pluralism" to categorize situations where a speaker uses more than one historically distinct code may, in this sense, be too general and all-inclusive for purposes of descriptive analysis. The data considered here would suggest that degrees of bilingual behavior may be definable on structural criteria, just as is possible in functional perspective (Ferguson 1959) and in terms of fluency criteria (Mackey 1965). The structural aspects of such behavior cannot be underrated; only through attention to such information can we ever hope to understand what happens when languages come into contact—or, to put that more accurately, how speakers respond, as speakers, to the opportunity to talk with persons from outside the speech community, literally on their own terms.

We can also question the advisability of using the terms "first" and "second" languages for anything other than chronological perspective; from the structural point of view, the direction of the subordination may not be consistent from one situation to the next. For Isleta, it does appear that the so-called second language has adapted to the structure of the first, but a different state of affairs is found when the English of the Kalmyk Mongols of Freewood Acres, New Jersey is considered. Kalmyk English contains the segmental phonology appropriate to its regional dialect, but uses the suprasegmental structure more typical of Mongol than of English—one phonemic stress, three levels of pitch quality; phrase and clause constructions formed under pitch-reducing operators, instead of the stress-reducing ones described in Trager and Smith. In similar fashion, their variety of Kalmyk employs English segmentals and Kalmyk suprasegmentals. (Leap, n.d.)

This would suggest that the variety of bilingualism in operation in New Jersey is different from that occurring at Isleta, even though the results—native-English language pluralism—are ostensibly the same in both instances. The reason for such differences may well lie within the whole detail of the acculturational matrix of each area. It would be interesting to see, in that regard, whether the direction of the acculturation reflected within the linguistic sphere would correlate with (and thus predict) the overall tone of that matrix.[3]

THE PROCESS OF BILINGUALISM

For indeed, what has been discussed in this paper was really a problem in linguistic acculturation. Yet, most articles that purport to deal with language and acculturation questions have done so only from a diffusionist's point of view—recognizing that new words have been introduced into a pueblo Indian vocabulary, the authors are content to list and discuss the more picturesque examples. Rarely, however—and

[3] Thus, the details of the English of the Isletan community do appear to resemble the kind of "compartmentalization" that Spicer (1954) and Dozier (1956) find as characteristic of puebloan acculturation as a whole.

Kashru (1965), Kelkhar (1957) and Mireau (1962) stand as three such exceptions—is any attention given to the processes that allow such an ingathering to take place. Thus we know that languages, like the other systems of culture, are able to acculturate; we have yet to understand, in any but the most trivial of senses, *how* this acculturation occurs. To say, in this context, that "words are borrowed" is really to say nothing at all.

As the argument here has suggested, we might well begin with the realization that bilingualism is a process, and not a state. To draw (and rather poorly) an analogy from the rest of anthropology, bilingualism is one means through which a speaker is able to exploit new language environments. Language pluralism (an observational fact) becomes, then, a result—but not the only possible result—of such a process. Working from this point of view, the present paper has attempted to understand the "hows" involved in one instance of language pluralism—the English of Isleta, New Mexico.

REFERENCES

BODINE, JOHN JAMES
  1968 Taos Names: A Clue to Linguistic Acculturation. *Anthropological Linguistics* 10: 23–27.
BRANDT, ELIZABETH A.
  1970 On the Origins of Linguistic Stratification: The Sandia Case. *Anthropological Linguistics* 12: 46–50.
DOZIER, EDWARD P.
  1956 Two Examples of Linguistic Acculturation. *Language* 32: 146–157.
FERGUSON, CHARLES A.
  1959 Diglossia. *Word* 15: 325–340.
FISHMAN, JOSHUA A.
  1968 Sociolinguistic Perspective on the Study of Bilingualism. *Linguistics* 39: 21–49.
HOIJER, HARRY AND EDWARD P. DOZIER
  1949 The Phonemes of Tewa, Santa Clara Dialect. *International Journal of American Linguistics* 15: 139–146.
JOOS, MARTIN
  1962 *The Five Clocks*. Harcourt, Brace and World, Inc., New York.
KASHRU, BRAJ B.
  1965 The Indian-ness in Indian English. *Word* 21: 391–410.
KELKHAR, ASHOK R.
  1957 Marathi English: A Study in Foreign Accent. *Word* 13: 268–282.
LEAP, WILLIAM L.
  1970 The Language of Isleta, New Mexico. Unpublished Ph.D. dissertation, Department of Anthropology, Southern Methodist University, Dallas.
  n.d. Unpublished Kalmyk Mongol field materials.
MACKEY, W. F.
  1965 Bilingual Interference: Its Analysis and Measurement. *Journal of Communication* 15: 239–249.
MIREAU, ERIC
  1963 Concerning Yavapai-Apache Bilingualism. *International Journal of American Linguistics* 29: 1–3.

SPENSER, ROBERT F.
   1946   The Phonology of Keresan. *International Journal of American Linguistics*
          12: 230–236.
SPICER, EDWARD H.
   1954   Spanish Indian Acculturation in the Southwest. *American Anthropologist*
          56: 663–678.
TRAGER, GEORGE L. AND HENRY LEE SMITH, JR.
   1951   An Outline of English Structure. *Studies in Linguistics*, Occasional paper
          no. 3 (Seventh reprinting). American Council of Learned Societies, Wash-
          ington, D.C.
TRAGER, GEORGE L. AND G. VALDEZ
   1935   English Loans in Colorado Spanish. *American Speech* 12: 34–44.

17. *Trilingualism in an Arizona Yaqui Village*

CARROLL G. BARBER

Barber's article deals with the Yaqui Indian community of Pascua in Tucson, Arizona, which was bilingual in Yaqui and Spanish in 1950, while children and most young adults also spoke English. In a study of the meanings attached to the three languages by men of ages eighteen to thirty, he found that each language was associated with definite social relationships and cultural patterns; Yaqui: familial, informal, formal-ceremonial; Spanish: familial, informal, formal-Catholic, recreational; English: mostly formal, educational, economic, legal. An earlier prediction that Pascua was in transition from being bilingual Yaqui-Spanish to bilingual Spanish-English is briefly re-assessed; the transitional period is now seen as having greater length and stability.

This is an abbreviated version of a Master of Arts thesis in Anthropology, University of Arizona (Barber 1952). Both in formulating the problem and in carrying out the field research I was guided and encouraged by Edward H. Spicer, whose deep knowledge of Pascua and Yaqui culture were literally invaluable. I also remain indebted to George C. Barker, whose studies of linguistic behavior in the Mexican-American community of Tucson were of great assistance.

[295]

RESEARCH on multilingualism has increased in both quantity and sophistication in the twenty years since this study was completed. Nevertheless, as a descriptive account of a highly complex and intriguing linguistic situation it may still interest investigators of multilingual societies—particularly persons working in the Southwest.

The data were gathered in 1950–51 in the Yaqui Indian community of Pascua in northwest Tucson, Arizona. At that time, almost all Pascuans spoke Yaqui and Spanish, while the younger ones spoke English as well. I observed the linguistic behavior of the people under a great many circumstances during a nine-month residence in the village and became particularly interested in the way the men from about eighteen to thirty handled their three languages. As far as adults were concerned, it was this group which could most truly be considered trilingual, individual differences notwithstanding. To give historic depth to the study and to supplement my observations, I carried on extensive interviews with twelve men, ranging in age from 19 to 31. They represented perhaps one-sixth of the total of the men of this age group residing in the community, according to a partial census which had just been concluded.

In the brief description below of Pascua as it was in 1950 and in the presentation of the results of the study, the tradition of the ethnographic present has been followed.

PASCUA AND ITS CULTURE

Like other Yaquis in Arizona, those who moved into Pascua in 1922 had come from Mexico during the time when most Yaquis had been driven from their villages in southern Sonora by the Mexican government. Even before the founding of Pascua, Yaquis already had formed small settlements on the outskirts of several Arizona towns, where they attempted to recreate the kind of society they had known before (Spicer 1947). The degree to which the Yaquis of Pascua succeeded in this attempt can be seen in the study by Spicer (1940).

In appearance and in fact Pascua is a poor community. The houses are mostly adobe, the streets are unpaved, there is no electricity or runing water (though pipes were being laid in the 1970s). But its residents are not a random grouping of families with nothing in common but their poverty. Rather, the people are closely linked by kinship ties and most of them are members of household units of more than one elementary family which occupy fenced-in parcels of land. In addition to their kin relationships, all of the people have relations with non-kin through the *compadre* system. As a child grows up he acquires godparents on numerous occasions: baptism, confirmation, marriage, entrance into a ceremonial society, and others. When as an adult, he himself becomes a godparent, he then becomes *compadres* with the parents of the child or other person that he has sponsored.

While in these particulars the society of Pascua does not differ markedly from that of a Yaqui village in Sonora, this is not the case with the ceremonial system. All of the positions and organizations have been retained, but of necessity their former governmental functions have been lost. The ceremonial leaders in Pascua, to be sure, are "community leaders," but they have no formal authority.

Male ceremonial personnel consist of lay priests, or *maestros*, and their assistants: the *matachinis*, a dance society dedicated to the Virgin Mary; and the *fariseos* and *caballeros*, whose patron is Jesus and who are only active during Lent. Men join the three societies through "promise" or vow; when a child is sick and other means of curing seem to have failed, a vow of lifetime service to Jesus or the Virgin in one of the societies may be made by his parents, or an older person may make this for himself. The clowning *pascolas* and the deer dancer, who also appear at ceremonies, have no vows to participate.

Ceremonies take place according to the Roman Catholic calendar, with the greatest emphasis placed on the Lenten season. The so-called Easter ceremony, which includes a series of observances from Ash Wednesday to Easter Sunday, brings back Yaquis from many parts of Arizona and also is well attended by outsiders (Painter 1971 gives an excellent account of these events). The religious beliefs expressed in Yaqui ritual can perhaps best be described as a reworking of Catholic belief in the light of earlier Yaqui religious concepts.

The economic basis of Pascua society is controlled entirely by outsiders. The majority of men work at unskilled or semiskilled jobs, principally on cotton farms or on the railroad. The cotton-picking season from August to January results in a considerable drop in village population as families move to cotton camps north of Tucson. Some have found more permanent agricultural work and live away from the village for most of the year. They still consider Pascua their home, but, like the railroad workers, they only return for family or village ceremonies. Some men have found jobs with local construction companies or the gas and water companies, but only a few have become skilled laborers.

A serious conflict has arisen in Pascua society between ceremonial and economic activity—more accurately stated, between ceremonial leadership and holding a steady job. It is possible simply to participate in ceremonies as a society member and still maintain more-or-less steady employment, and this is the course which most men have taken. But if a man desires leadership, or if it is pressed upon him, he finds that he must either neglect work for at least part of the year or neglect his ceremonial obligations, not only to Yaquis living and dead but to Jesus and Mary as well. The most drastic resolution of the conflict is to deny altogether one or the other set of duties, but either type of denial means sacrifice of one kind or another. This conflict is of course vital to the future of Pascua as a Yaqui community (Spicer 1940:291).

CHILDHOOD TO MANHOOD

Beginning life in the closely knit society of the village, the young men of today began their first extensive contact with the larger society when they entered school. Judged by the expectations of the American educational system, however, the results of their schooling generally have not been happy ones. Few of them finished grammar school; most of them went to school for only part of each school year and did not advance far no matter how many years they attended. Among the men I interviewed, the best record was eight grades completed in eight years of attendance, which is highly unusual; the worst record was four grades completed in twelve years of attendance. The men today regret their spotty education, but neither they nor their parents nor their teachers were prepared to cope with all the problems encountered. Nevertheless, while most of them left school poorly trained in basic skills, the experience was important for other reasons. In their school years, they became acquainted not only with their Anglo teachers, but also with Mexican, and sometimes Anglo, classmates.[1] Many of them learned as much or more on the playground as they did in the classroom.

Not long after they began school they also began to function in the economic world of their parents. Indeed, work and school were often in conflict, and economic necessity was the most common reason for their poor record of school attendance. Most of them worked first with their families in the fields, and at odd jobs, and continued to do so into adolescence. Others, when they were old enough, followed their fathers into construction or railroad work. A far more intensive encounter with the Anglo way of life came with World War II. Less than half of the young men of military age went into the armed services, but their influence on village life as veterans has not been in proportion to their numbers.

The men live today in the kinds of households in which they were brought up as children, although now they are often husbands, fathers, and even household heads, themselves. As adolescents and now as adults

---

[1] Throughout the paper I have used the terms "Anglo" and "Mexican" rather than the cumbersome "Anglo-American" and "Mexican-American." The reference in any case is to cultural heritage rather than citizenship. It might be noted that the term "Anglo" is little used in Pascua; "American" is far more common.

they have come to have an ever increasing number of *compadres* as well. The only outward sign of any weakening of kinship ties are the complaints of older people that young people no longer have any respect. While much of this is easy to discount, it is true that young men show more independence of their families than before.

Even as boys most of the young men had begun to participate in the ceremonial system, and now many of them are active adult members of the three societies. There are some signs that the leadership conflict, indeed, has pushed some of them into responsibility at a younger age than would formerly have been the case, because their family responsibilities are not always as pressing as those of older men. However, for the most part, those young men who participate do so without assuming important leadership roles. Of my sample of twelve, seven were participants, one as a leader.

In belief there seems to be considerable ambivalence. The same man may sound quite proud of Yaqui ritual at one time and slightly apologetic at another. But while participation may have declined in Pascua, this does not mean a trend towards increased Catholic observance. Church-going is generally limited to baptism, confirmation, marriage, and funerals, though a few men go to mass occasionally. The men feel, nevertheless, that they are Catholics.

On the surface the economic picture appears little changed from the prewar years, even for the veterans. As one man says bitterly, "I didn't learn a God damn thing in the army. I had to go back to field work." Still, unlike their parents, they do not accept the situation with resignation, and they avoid field work if at all possible. At the risk of an actual loss of income they may stay in town in case something better comes along, or they may catch the daily truck to the fields one day and pick up a day's labor in town the next. Some of the men in construction work have joined the laborers' union and have achieved more job security and better pay than the other men.

One of the obvious changes since the war is in recreation patterns, and the veterans seem to have been instrumental in this change. Much spare time is still spent in the village, attending household fiestas, playing baseball, shooting dice or playing cards, or just sitting around together to talk, sing, and drink. But the young men also go farther afield, to the movies or to Mexican bars and dance halls. The Saturday night downtown seems definitely a postwar innovation, and several of the veterans claim to have started it. The increased number of cars and the occasional extra few dollars to spend which make this possible may indicate a somewhat improved economic situation in the village, despite what has just been said, or it may indicate a new allocation of resources on the part of an individual. This activity has, of course, increased contacts with outsiders: Mexicans, Anglos, and Papagos.

Being in the lower class economically, and belonging to a minority ethnic group, the young men have sometimes suffered from discrimination. Much of this, to be sure, is because for many Anglos there is little or no difference between Yaquis and lower-class Mexicans. In any case, the men are seldom articulate about this, at least before outsiders, except in specific cases of job discrimination or police mistreatment.

What has been said should help make clear some of the contradictions in the lives of a group of men with the difficult task of adjusting to three cultures. Since this adjustment involves the use of three languages, the following analysis of their linguistic behavior can contribute to a deeper understanding of their situation.

LANGUAGES IN ACTION

Yaqui, Spanish, and English mean much more to a young man in Pascua than three equally good ways to get something said.[2] He has learned them under different circumstances, uses them in different situations, and thinks about them with different attitudes. Following anthropological convention, it can be said that the total of all the associations that one of these languages had with various parts of his life is the *meaning* which that language has for him. What it means to him may not be quite what it means to a brother or a friend, but it should be possible to arrive at a general meaning for each of the languages which is shared by all the young men in the village. The common names of the three languages provide some clues to the more obvious associations which they have—for example, when speaking Spanish, Yaquis refer to their own language simply as *la lengua* (the language), and occasionally when speaking English simply "language." But the names, of course, the men share with the entire community. Therefore, it is necessary to investigate how this particular group of men learned their three languages, how they use them today, and what they say about them for an adequate analysis of the meanings which the languages have for them.

---

[2] To speak merely of Yaqui, Spanish, and English without amplification is of course imprecise, but few descriptive studies of the local varieties of these languages have been made. "Arizona Yaqui" is the best described, having been treated by Kurath and Spicer (1947) and Crumrine (1961). "Southern Arizona Spanish" was first studied by Post (1934); a tentative classification of its varieties has been made by Barker (1947, 1950). "Arizona English" is impossible to define; Tucson, for example, probably has speakers of most of the class, regional, and ethnic varieties of English found in the United States. The speech varieties found in Pascua were more fully discussed in my thesis than is possible here, but the description was based mainly on impression and speculation (Barber 1952).

Learning Three Languages

Yaqui was the first language of all of the men, almost without exception. It is natural that they cannot remember in what language their first words were spoken, but even those who began to speak Spanish when very young say they must have learned Yaqui first, because, for example, "my mother talked Yaqui; my father spoke both Spanish and Yaqui." One man says that he did learn Spanish first, and he still does not speak Yaqui, although he understands it quite well. Why this is so he is not sure and his only explanation is that "maybe they talk to us in that language but we don't get it so they started talking Spanish." Apparently, though his parents knew Yaqui, they spoke Spanish to the children, perhaps on purpose as some parents are doing today. But Yaqui is definitely the native language for the other men, the one they heard at home from their parents and other relatives, including older brothers and sisters.

While they mastered Yaqui structure when they were still quite young, they have of course continually added to their vocabulary. This is not only confined to words newly adopted into Yaqui from Spanish, a process in which the men themselves play an active part, but also native Yaqui words which they have not had the opportunity to hear very often. These are words connected with the former life of the Yaquis which their parents remember and sometimes use, and which they may occasionally hear spoken by Yaquis from Sonora. Unlike their other languages, however, the men have almost no opportunity to learn new words or expressions from reading, since most of them have no familiarity with written Yaqui as used in Sonora and by the *maestros* in Pascua for their handwritten books of hymns and prayers. One or two men have read a few letters written in Yaqui, but that is all.

While Spanish is in almost all cases the second language of the young men they learned it at different ages. Some men say they do not remember whether they first spoke Yaqui or Spanish, but most recall having their first intensive contact with it slightly before or at about the same time that they began to learn English in school, around the ages of five to seven. Progress in Spanish was generally much more rapid than in English, however, since they had more occasion to use it. A few men say that in point of time Spanish is their third language, but this seems questionable.

Some of them first heard Spanish and used it in their families, while others picked it up from Mexicans. In cases where the men learned Spanish quite early it was generally the parents, particularly the father, and other Yaquis, both old and young, who taught them. Those who remember beginning to learn it about five or so often had outsiders for teachers.

The question "when did you first learn Spanish?" is often answered by a remark like, "when I went to school, because there are a lot of Mexican boys around." There are probably no men who did not hear Spanish in their families, but in a great many cases contact with Mexican children in and out of school played a much greater role in their acquisition of the language.

There were considerable differences in the amount of Spanish spoken by the men when they were still children. Some of them associated with Mexicans throughout their childhood in places away from Pascua, and one of these remarked that:

> Well, you see I never lived in the village before I was sixteen. All that time we lived around neighborhoods where we spoke Spanish and that's where we picked it up. Some guys didn't learn it till sixteen or seventeen. That's where we had a little advantage over our own people.

For men this age sixteen or seventeen seems extreme if it was a question of speaking it for the first time, though they may not have mastered it thoroughly until then. One man who had lived in the Yaqui village of Bacatete near Eloy, cut off from contact with Mexican children, said he did not begin to talk Spanish until he came to Pascua when he was nine or ten. When I asked if he did not speak it at all before, he insisted that:

> I began to talk Spanish when I came to Pascua. I used to play with guys but didn't talk it good, like the X's now. You know even Mexicans make mistakes.

Judging from these two cases and others like them, it is hard to generalize concerning the effects of living in Pascua or away on the speed with which they mastered Spanish. It seems safe to say that the more time spent in school the more quickly fluency in Spanish was achieved, since they usually went to school with Mexican children. In a few cases, however, they went to predominantly Anglo schools and did not have this contact.

Regardless of how long it may have taken to learn it, there are few young men who do not speak Spanish easily, and even more than with Yaqui, they are constantly learning new words. The sources for this are quite varied; beyond learning from each other and Mexicans there are also movies and the radio. Tucson has one theater which regularly shows Mexican films, and its five radio stations devote an average of about eleven hours a day among them to Spanish programs. *Reading* is probably not important, since not all of them know how to read Spanish, and not all of those who do, read it very much. What they do read consists of an occasional copy of Tucson or Los Angeles Spanish newspapers, songbooks, and Mexican magazines, especially *policías*. Some use is made of bilingual Spanish and English dictionaries which a few of them own; it is likely that the Spanish-English section is used more often, since it serves the function for them of an ordinary Spanish dictionary.

Learning English usually stretched over a longer period than learning Spanish. Although in some cases the men heard their first English words from members of their families, this was generally not important since it only amounted to something like "I just heard it from them; they told me it was English." School was where the men really began to learn English; they, of course, learned more quickly when they used the language with Anglo kids on the playground as well as hearing it in class. Some of them were able to speak it quite readily when they left school, but others did not know it very well. As one man says, he learned English "just to talk to the teacher." In any case, most of the men look on school as being the principal source of their English.

They are not in agreement, however, whether their knowledge was increased very much after they started to work. This is undoubtedly a reflection of the kind of jobs they took and the kind of relations they had with their employers. While one man says that when he left school, "I was speaking it pretty well because I talked with my boss and learned more from him," another, talking about the Anglos he worked with, says, "I didn't learn much from them. From bosses all that was needed was to understand, no back talk."

For one man contact with employers and other Anglos was no more effective for him than school, for he says about his English:

> I learned it in school but didn't talk it till I went in the army. I was ashamed to talk it. When I went in the army I had to talk it.

Certainly those who went into the armed forces found themselves speaking more English than ever before, and as a rule the veterans today speak it with greater ease than others. The exceptions to this are those who went to school steadily throughout the year for a fairly long period, while in at least one case having been in prison has had much the same effect.

The effects of military life on the veterans' linguistic systems were not confined to increasing their use and command of English. In the first place, they were usually cut off from any contact with Yaquis, and many of them say that when they came home on furlough and when they were discharged it took a little time to get used to Yaqui again. One man tells of meeting two other Yaquis in his outfit, but the encounter did not lead to conversation:

> There were two guys who were Yaquis but they didn't know I was. They used to sit near me when we were playing dice. Sometimes I'd smile when

they said funny words. They always talked Spanish to me. I just wanted to listen. They were always wondering about what their wives were doing.

As this story indicates, military life led to the increased use of Spanish by Yaquis whenever they met Mexican soldiers from various parts of the Southwest. The Mexicans generally thought that the Yaquis were Mexicans too (which would appear to indicate that there was nothing peculiar about the way they spoke). One man says he once told some of them he was Mexican, and "they believed me because I was talking Spanish." Sometimes other men in the barracks would object to the use of Spanish and tell them to shut up or talk English, but some of the veterans report that the other soldiers generally did not seem to mind. A few short-sighted officers discouraged the use of Spanish by trying to get Mexicans and Yaquis not to use it. Besides the Mexicans in their units, some Yaquis met people in Europe or the Pacific with whom they could speak Spanish.

Since the war years, some of the men have been able to escape from the cotton fields and have gotten jobs where they have contacts with English-speakers as fellow-workers as well as supervisors. Despite what some of them say, getting into jobs other than field work has had the effect of increasing their command of English. One man in construction work says, "the words I speak I got on the job—in school a little. On the job I know what they want and what's what." Other contacts with English-speakers also have become wider, though often merely in impersonal relationships like buying things in stores which do not employ Spanish-speaking clerks. At least one man has discovered the value of listening in on conversations for language learning, "I try to get the words what they say when I'm around Americans."

Going to the movies, listening to the radio, and reading also have increased their control of English, but the men themselves are unable to say how important the effect of these activities has been. Almost everyone likes the movies and many men say that they prefer English ones to those that come to the Spanish theater, but as one of them says, "I just go for entertainment. Sometimes you pick up a few words you don't know." Radio is probably less important, because the men listen mostly to Spanish programs because they like the music better. However, some of them also listen to comedians, quiz shows, newscasts, and other English programs. Everyone is able to read English to some extent, but not all of them read much for recreation. Besides daily papers, which some of them buy frequently, comic books, magazines, and paperbacked novels account for most of the reading matter. Comic books are by all odds their favorite reading and large stacks of them are seen quite commonly. Many men say that reading does help their English, and one of them uses comic books to see how to spell words when he writes letters.

A note might be added here that the men are firm believers in the "doctrine of correctness" in regard to all their languages. Much of this must have come from their school teachers in connection with English, but the remarks of older Yaquis about their deficiencies in their own language, or from Mexicans about their Spanish, have undoubtedly played a part too. The result is that many of them feel that they speak all the languages poorly, instead of feeling proud of their accomplishment.

Making Linguistic Choices

The men often find questions about their use of their languages rather ridiculous; naturally they speak Yaqui to Yaquis, Spanish to Mexicans, and English to Anglos. As one of them said, "I could talk to you in Yaqui—you wouldn't understand me." The problem does not seem so simple, however, when it is realized that in many of their social relationships they are dealing with people who speak at least two of their languages. Why then do they choose to speak one language at one time and another at some other time? Equally important, why do they choose to hear one language at one time and another at some other time? These questions can only be answered by seeing in detail just how the languages are used.

Within their families and households, where almost all of the people are Yaquis, except for a very few Mexicans or other Indian relatives by marriage, the young men speak both Yaqui and Spanish. They tend to speak Yaqui most of the time with older people, Spanish most of the time with children, and about the same amount of each with people around their own age. As a result of these tendencies the two languages appear to be used almost equally, though Yaqui is probably spoken with somewhat greater frequency.

A few examples of usage within households will show the kind of facts upon which this generalization is based. One young man in his early twenties, living with his parents and six younger brothers and sisters, speaks both Yaqui and Spanish with his father and oldest sister, but with his mother and the other children he speaks Yaqui almost exclusively. Another man almost always speaks Yaqui with his wife and parents, and mostly Yaqui to his two young children. Four younger brothers also belong to the household; to the two oldest he speaks mostly Yaqui and both Yaqui and Spanish to the youngest ones. A third man, just over thirty, living with his wife's parents, speaks both languages with his wife and father-in-law and mother-in-law, but uses a good deal more Yaqui than Spanish. To his very young children he also speaks both, but here he appears to use far more Spanish than Yaqui. A young widower, living at his parents' home with his two children, a son and daughter, speaks Yaqui "always or almost always" with his sister and mother and mostly Yaqui to his father, but when asked about his children he says, "I got them used to speaking Spanish."

The children of Pascua do not appear to be learning as much Yaqui as some of the above cases would indicate; often they are not really learning to speak it, though they are usually able to understand it. It may be that while parents often use Yaqui when speaking to their children, contacts with other children their own age where Spanish is more and more used, are more decisive and that the parents eventually fall into line. This pattern within the household also prevails in family relationships outside, and presumably for godparents and compadres as well. Thus one man, whose household consists only of himself, his wife and two children, a boy and a girl who are not talking yet themselves, speaks Spanish almost always around his own home but still uses Yaqui at an older relative's house across the street.

In all of these cases, as nearly as can be determined, the usage is reciprocal, that is, all parties to a conversation generally speak the same language. But there are several men who speak Spanish most or all of the time in their families. These men are not merely the few who did not learn to speak Yaqui as children, but men who are quite able to speak it but do not choose to. One man with a wife and two small children living with his mother uses Yaqui very rarely, though his mother and wife often speak it to him. Conversations can be heard in which the man speaks Spanish and his wife Yaqui with neither changing to the language used by the other. This can be illustrated by a brief dialogue at the supper table, which he started by asking a question about the tortillas:

Man in Spanish: Tienen leche, no? (They have milk in them, don't they?)
Wife in Yaqui: Hewi (yes)
Wife in Yaqui: Munim waata? (You want some beans?)
Man in Spanish: Sí (Yes)

Another man, living in a household of ten people, which includes members of four generations, is almost notorious for not speaking Yaqui at home or anywhere else, although before he went into the army he is said to have rarely spoken Spanish. While he says his mother and his wife sometimes complain that he does not answer them in Yaqui when they speak to him, his younger brother excuses himself when he forgets and speaks Yaqui because "he's ashamed to talk in Yaqui to me because he thinks I don't understand it." This is a clear example of accommodation to someone else's linguistic patterns; it is highly unlikely that his brother actually thinks he does not understand Yaqui.

The presence of outsiders may temporarily upset the patterns present in a household when out of politeness Spanish may be used if Mexicans are present, or even English, if the people in the conversation understand it, when Anglos happen to be there. Beyond this, English is almost never used in the home, except occasionally for effect, or for referring to something for which the Yaqui or Spanish word is not known, or for naming dogs. During the war, when men were away from home, English did play a more important role, since men wrote home in that language if they did not know how to write Spanish.

Three languages are used in ceremonies: Latin, Yaqui, and Spanish. Latin is used only by the *maestros* for certain parts of the services, but only they have any real understanding of it. Some songs and prayers are in Spanish, as are a few of the speeches made during the Easter ceremony. But Yaqui is the principal ceremonial language, and it would be difficult or impossible to take part without at least understanding it. Sermons, ritual speeches, and most commands in the societies are given in Yaqui. One person in a position of leadership, however, does use Spanish in place of Yaqui to one or two men who either cannot speak Yaqui or customarily do not. The men, however, do understand it, so this is not absolutely necessary.

Those men who do not participate are under no compulsion to listen to the sermons, some of which are quite long, and if they have the alternative they are more likely to be at the front of the ramada where the *pascolas* and deer dancer are dancing. When the *pascolas* are not actually dancing, they carry on a bantering conversation with each other, at times somewhat indecent, and there is a good deal of joking between them and the crowd. While they sometimes make the concession of talking in Spanish if Mexicans are around, they do not do the same for Anglos. It is for the Yaquis that they say "funny things, so people can laugh." Rarely a little English can be heard, apparently for its humorous effect, as when a *pascola* told his flutist-drummer accompanist, "Come on, boy, let's go!"

At the *pascola* ramada, too, the men also have the chance to hear what must be the oldest Yaqui literature remaining, the songs sung by the deer dance musicians. But if a man is asked if he understands them his reply is likely to be like this: "I think the old men do, I don't think the young guys know, they don't pay no attention." However, the songs are sung to the accompaniment of a water drum, raspers, and the rattles of the dancer himself, so that it may be that there is just too much noise.

Meetings of the ceremonial societies are conducted in Yaqui and

the general procedure is carried over into other meetings, just as ceremonial leaders are still considered to some extent the village leaders.
At such formal meetings, the younger men, who are quite self-assertive
at other times, seem strangely subdued and let the older people do the
talking. They may say no more than the customary greeting, "Dios
emchania," when they enter the group, to which those already present
reply, "Dios emchihiokwe." One notable exception is the *caballero*
captain, who is sometimes in charge of the meetings and interprets when
Anglos are present in some sort of official capacity.

This brings up a final point concerning language and ceremony.
Though it plays no part in ceremonies, English is still necessary for at
least one or two of the leaders since some arrangements have to be made
with outsiders concerning the Easter ceremony. Also, though the Yaquis
sometimes put up with a good deal from the crowds of Anglos who come
to watch, somebody has to be prepared to cope with them if they become too careless.

On the job there may be occasion to speak all three languages,
though the sort of work being done has much to do with it. The composition of the agricultural labor force in southern Arizona, and the linguistic
complications, can be seen in what one man said about the people he met
working in the fields:

> Mexicans, Yaquis, people from Oklahoma—white guys. They all talk
> their languages. White guys always talk to Mexicans and Yaquis in Eng-
> lish. Mexican guys talk to Yaquis in Spanish. Papagos just speak their
> language and English.

Generally Yaquis work together with other Yaquis, often in family
groups during the cotton picking season, or with Mexicans. This means
that the language spoken at work can be either Yaqui or Spanish depending on the people a man is working with. In a group of both Mexicans and Yaquis the choice often depends on whether the Mexicans are
to be included in or out of the conversation. The Yaquis recognize the
value of having a language of their own which gives them a chance to
say things privately no matter how many non-Yaquis are around.
Employers and their agents generally speak English to the men, so they
are forced to use it in return, or at least understand it if the situation
does not call for "back talk." From what the men say, very few of the
Anglos who hire them know Spanish. Probably more Spanish is used in a
normal day's field work than Yaqui and more Yaqui than English, but
since the personnel of the group can vary considerably this is rather
uncertain.

Railroad work in the Southwest traditionally has been done by
immigrants from south of the border and the composition of section and

extra gangs in southern Arizona is still largely Mexican and Yaqui. The amount of Yaqui a man speaks on the gang again depends on the make-up of the group. In one which seems fairly representative there are Mexicans, Anglos, Papagos, Negroes, as well as a majority of Yaquis. In this gang one of the Yaquis says he speaks "English, Mexican, and Yaqui; English to the colored guys, Yaqui to I don't know how many." The fact that Yaqui can serve as well as the other languages for railroad work was mentioned earlier. The foreman of this gang is an Anglo, but "he speaks Spanish a little bit, sometimes we talk Spanish together and sometimes we speak English together." Generally field and railroad work involve a similar division between the amount of Spanish and Yaqui used with fellow-workers, while English is used most of the time with employers, foremen, and the like so that it has become the chief means for communication in employer-employee relationships.

Jobs in town make for a different linguistic pattern, involving the use of hardly any Yaqui, so that unless English is spoken exclusively, the language spoken is "all mixed—Spanish and English." Some Yaqui may be used if two Yaquis happen to be working together, but generally the men find themselves working with Mexicans and English-speakers, either Anglo or Negro. When a man was asked to whom he spoke English he replied, "my employers, a lot of people I work with, colored and white, Indians—other kinds of Indians." A man may work alone with a small-time subcontractor, or in a large crew of workers on a job like a new highway or factory, or in the work gangs of the gas and water companies. The larger the group, and the more unskilled the labor, the greater is the likelihood that it will have many Spanish-speakers, according to the pattern which has long prevailed in Tucson and which is only now beginning to break down. Generally, however, town work of any kind involves speaking a great deal of English, even if much of the talk on the job with other workers is in Spanish. The only outside organization to which any of the men belong is one connected with their jobs, the Tucson local of the AFL Laborers' Union, and the meetings are held in English.

While all of the languages may be used in one way or another while the men are making money, only Spanish and English are used when they spend it. Many of the clothing, food, and other kinds of stores which Yaquis patronize have Spanish-speaking clerks; this is one of the reasons that Yaquis go to them, although most young men are not bashful about going to a store where only English is spoken. The places where men spend their money to have a good time: bars, theaters, dance halls, restaurants, and so forth, are predominantly Spanish-speaking; even theaters showing only English movies sometimes hire Mexican girls as ticket sellers. In these impersonal relationships between buyer and seller there is a considerable amount of mutual identification which takes place almost instantaneously and automatically. A bartender in a Mexican bar will say to his customers "qué quieres?" or "what'll you have?" without conscious thought, and similarly a Yaqui at the ticket window of a theater will say either "quiero un boleto" or "I'd like a ticket." In such cases the person judges the linguistic background of the person he is talking to and accommodates his own usage to this.

In connection with their economic life it is significant that most men say they do their arithmetic in English: "like me, if I had to figure something out, I'd do it in English, that's the way I learned it in school." They often remark that they only know how to count up to ten or twelve in Yaqui, but they are able to do simple arithmetic in Spanish. That many of them do not is symbolic of the fact that most of their economic relationships are controlled ultimately by Anglos, though the reason is undoubtedly that the techniques come easier in the language in which they learned them.

While both work and ceremony bring the young men in contact with older Yaquis, and their life at home with people of all ages, spare time away from home is usually spent with men and women around their own age. On the average, Spanish and Yaqui seem to be used about equally with people their own age within their families, but away from home there is a somewhat greater use of Spanish, perhaps a 60–40 division instead of a 50–50 one, though the figures are only meant to be suggestive. English too seems to play a somewhat larger part here than in situations which involve older Pascuans. The use of the three languages on an informal basis within the village is illustrated by three ways of greeting people and their customary answers, which have the same literal meanings:

Yaqui:	"Haisiwa?"	"Ka hiwa."
Spanish:	"Qué dices?"	"Nada."
English:	"Whaddya say?"	"Nothin'."

Though the English expression is rarely used, except to Anglos, it is probably involved somehow in the process of loan translation which seems evident, though the direction is not certain. The Yaqui form, however, is fairly recent, and older people have been known to object to it.

When the men are asked what language they use most among themselves the answers vary considerably. Almost any of their replies reinforce impressions which an outsider might get at different times, while taken together they point to a somewhat greater use of Spanish than Yaqui, with a minor use of English. A sample of their replies to the question illustrates this:

"Spanish."

"Spanish and Yaqui."

"Some use Spanish, some use language, some use Spanish and the language."

"About half and half."

"Mexican—they use both Mexican and their own language. English—every once in a while they use something."

"When the young guys get together they start talking Yaqui and then Spanish, but I don't know which they use most."

"Now they mostly use Spanish—Spanish all mixed."

It is definite that some use more Yaqui than Spanish, while there are also the men mentioned earlier who speak Yaqui hardly at all. Since others often accommodate themselves to the patterns of these men—"A lot of Yaquis are accustomed to speaking Spanish, I never speak to them in Yaqui"—this brings the Spanish total up.

Beyond the village when they are out for a good time, the men spend most of their time in a Spanish-speaking world. In associating with Mexicans in recreational activities in the places mentioned earlier, as well as at work, the men have increased their use of Spanish. English is seldom spoken prominently in conversations with Mexicans, but Mexicans do show considerable curiosity about Yaqui. This is limited usually to learning a few words and wanting to know what has been said, but it makes for an interesting contrast, which one man has commented on, "I've heard guys say they dislike Yaqui and Mexicans say they wish they could speak it."

English is sometimes spoken on an informal basis with Anglos in the spare time activities of the young men, though the close friendships with Mexicans which many Yaquis have formed are not often duplicated with Anglos. When Yaquis are together with Anglo friends from work or the university, English is almost always spoken if only a couple of people are around. But if the *gringo* knows some Spanish and he is along with a group of several Yaquis, talk lapses back into Spanish with only an occasional remark or explanation in English. In my own experience, I found that if a man wanted to get something across to me that he felt about very deeply he tended to say it in Spanish. There were also times when someone became impatient with me for not speaking more Spanish. They did not expect much as far as Yaqui was concerned, but one man assured me I could learn it in a week.

So far linguistic usage between men and women has not been considered. Apparently the same pattern holds in the main, though one man says that when he is out with girls, even if they are Yaqui, he speaks "every time Spanish." It may be indicative that hardly any of the young men claim to be familiar with romantic songs in Yaqui, although older men know some, while there are very few who do not know a great many in Spanish. But even if Spanish is more important than Yaqui for romantic purposes, it still has to compete with English. Undoubtedly the most intimate relationships formed with English-speakers by most young Yaqui men are with Papago girls; when one man was asked about occasions when he spoke English, part of his answer was "with that heavy-set girl English—I don't understand her language." Even when nothing serious is involved the men still see Papago girls fairly frequently at dances and sometimes they crash Papago parties in South Tucson (where they are not always welcome). Intimate encounters with Anglo women also require English, but they are quite infrequent in Tucson today. Some of the veterans, however, do boast about the past.

Turning to a less pleasant aspect of having a good time, or too good a time, there is the question of what languages are used in their relationships with the law. The Pima County sheriff's department has a few Mexican deputies, and most of the deputized dance hall guards are also Mexican. These men speak Spanish to the Yaquis, occasionally in a mock friendly, and at the same time, somewhat insulting fashion which the men may repay in kind. Anglo deputies and police may know and use a little Spanish, but generally they conduct their business with Yaquis and Mexicans in English. But while a man may be arrested in either Spanish or English, legal procedures beyond this are conducted in English. Spanish interpreters are available during trials, but one man who had been tried for a fairly serious offense, though he spoke Yaqui and Spanish to friends who were there, did not want to testify in Spanish. He sounded rather proud when he told me he had not had an interpreter, though they asked him if he wanted one.

* * *

Before closing this discussion, perhaps one clarification should be made. It has been said that in many situations both Spanish and Yaqui, or more rarely Spanish and English, are used, and the men themselves have been quoted to the effect that their usage is "mixed." When one of the men was asked what he used most around the home, his brother replied, "todo revuelto, *mixed*, qué no?" ("all mixed up ... isn't it?"). This does not mean, however, that every sentence is a mixture of languages and that it is impossible to say what language is being spoken. Being mixed really means that they switch back and forth between Spanish and Yaqui, and it is often difficult to determine why this is done. Some switching is of course explained on the basis of letting outsiders into the conversation or of keeping them out, but this cannot explain switching when outsiders are not around. One man will say that he switches because it is easier to talk about something in Spanish than in Yaqui, for example, while another will say that all of the languages serve equally well for all occasions.

The Meanings of the Three Languages

It is interesting to compare the associations described above with what the men themselves say and do in regard to language. There appear to be no major contradictions—although there are some minor ones which need explanation—so that increasing confidence can be placed in the analysis.

The story is clearest for Yaqui. It is intimately associated with those things which are particularly Yaqui, particularly the social organization and ceremonial system of Pascua. The social associations are no less apparent. Relationships with all adult Pascuans, especially those older than the young men, are more frequently conducted in Yaqui than in Spanish, and in general all relationships with Pascuans are characterized by the use of Yaqui, even though it is not used exclusively. These are informal relationships with their families and friends, the ones in which the men feel most natural and comfortable. Even formal relationships, concerned mainly with aspects of ceremony, are still to a large degree personal and differ from outside relationships which may be both formal and impersonal. Finally, Yaqui is the "official language" of Pascua, the language used in circumstances when the village acts as one, as in the Easter ceremony.

Thus it has come about that to the people of Pascua, failure to speak Yaqui can be enough to remove one from the society. They actually put this in so many words; of one family, which uses a minimum of Yaqui, but by no means none at all, I have heard it said, "son mexicanos, no hablan la lengua" (they're Mexicans, they don't speak Yaqui). The explanations others give for this failure reveal the same attitude. Of those men who do not or only seldom speak Yaqui, one of the men says that it is because "they want to be Mexicans, they're ashamed to be Yaquis and try to deny they're Yaquis—that's the way I get it." At certain times these people indicate by their behavior that this is true. One man is supposed to have had a violent fight with his mother because she asked him, in front of some Mexican girls, to take some fiesta groceries home. It was not what she asked that made him mad—it was that she said it in Yaqui and exposed him.

However, this need not prove a complete denial of his Yaqui heritage. Some people have done this, but the means they used are the only effective ones: moving out of Yaqui society altogether. Some men, however, do prefer that their Mexican friends, male or female, not know that they are Yaquis, and they will sometimes deny outright that they are. This is criticized not only by older people but by many younger men as well. The man so vigorous in his denunciation of those who refuse to speak Yaqui does his best to puncture any such pretensions:

> If I'm with Mexicans and a Yaqui comes up and talks to me in Spanish, I always answer in Yaqui. They say it's a good thing to do if you're Yaqui to speak it. Like the Chinese—they don't hide their language.

There does not seem to be any reason to refuse to speak Yaqui at home only to fool Mexicans, but one man who does this did give some indication of his reason when he said that if he spoke Yaqui at home, "I'm afraid I'll start talking to Mexicans in Yaqui." When asked if that would be bad he said "no, it ain't bad, but—" and never finished. He admitted speaking Yaqui when drunk, however, and it was also said of another man that, "when he's sober he speaks Spanish, but when he's high he starts speaking Yaqui." The latter man, though he speaks Yaqui at home, is one who might be classified merely as one not accustomed to speaking much Yaqui, since he grew up away from the village. But there is the suggestion of some amount of conscious or unconscious control over the use of Yaqui when he is with outsiders.

Another statement by the pro-Yaqui man quoted earlier implies a connection between the language and religious participation. Speaking of one family, he said, "they can speak it too, but they just don't want to, they got in another religion and don't use it." How far a denial of Yaqui religion is correlated with a refusal to speak Yaqui is hard to say. First, there is at least one man who cannot speak Yaqui but still participates in the ceremonies; however, inability to speak Yaqui rather than refusal is involved here. In all other cases known to me, men who speak a noticeably small amount of Yaqui are also men who do not participate in the ceremonies, but the reverse does not hold true since many non-participants speak Yaqui regularly, both at home and in town.

There is a further complication in that not all the men who will not speak Yaqui receive the same amount of criticism. It seems likely that a public denial of being Yaqui at some time or other which the men know about is necessary to call forth the real scorn of other Yaquis; if men merely wish to give the impression that they are not Yaqui, but will admit it if pressed, people seem somewhat tolerant. As has been seen, other Yaquis may even speak Spanish to them because they seem to prefer it.

Perhaps too little emphasis has been placed on the positive use of Yaqui to identify oneself as a Yaqui, instead of avoiding the language to forestall such identification in the eyes of Mexicans. This can be a matter of practicality as well as pride. One man tells how he once spoke Yaqui to a policeman to prove to him that he was a Yaqui and not a north Tucson Mexican, and that it was therefore quite proper for him to be with some south Tucson Yaquis regardless of what the policeman thought.

The cultural associations which the men have with Spanish are naturally with those aspects of Mexican-American culture with which they are most familiar. Outstanding are the recreation patterns and the Roman Catholic church of which they feel themselves a part. Young Yaquis drink in Mexican bars, dance in Mexican dance halls, sing Mexican songs, and go to Mexican churches, meaning those with Spanish names, on the occasions when they do go. Social relationships associated with Spanish, like Yaqui, are chiefly informal ones. It has been seen how Spanish competes with Yaqui in most informal relationships within Pascua and it is associated with friendly relationships with Mexicans outside, both at work and in town. The tendency, wherever possible, to use Spanish with Anglos when friendship is involved emphasizes the connection between Spanish and easy-going, face-to-face relationships. Most important, however, as much or more than Yaqui, Spanish is associated with their relationships with other young men and women in the village, the group they naturally identify with most readily.

The men generally show a great attachment for Spanish, and all of them definitely prefer it to English. Their defense of their right to speak Spanish in the army, and earlier at school, despite considerable pressure, is indication enough of this. It is not strange that they find it much more expressive than English, because they know it better. However, it might be ventured that many of them also feel it to be more expressive than Yaqui for certain purposes. It would be unwise to do more than suggest this as a possibility, but a few men say they find it easier than Yaqui, which does not seem to be a mere reflection of their relative ability in the use of the two languages.

One man asked me once whether I thought English or Spanish had the most expression and when I said English for me, he replied that he thought Spanish did: "I think you get more out of a song in Spanish than in English—more meanings, expressions, rememberings of places." When I asked what about Yaqui, he replied, "I don't know any Yaqui songs—maybe if I lived in Sonora or if only Yaquis lived together." As for a different kind of expression, the men certainly find it easier to swear, cuss, and insult somebody in Spanish than in Yaqui, since the latter seems to have few words of this sort. But in this regard the men's English vocabulary is as wide as their Spanish one.

There is also the question of the use of the slang vocabulary associated with Pachuco, the "language" of Mexican street gangs, which has been described by Barker (1950). One of the men, when asked what language the young men preferred, answered that "Pachuco is most popular, even with the girls." This is certainly going too far, since many men deny having anything to do with it. And even this man recognizes that it is out of place when speaking to certain people. He once shouted "orale pues" (hey, there), a Pachuco greeting, at a passing car. Then he looked rather sheepish and said that he thought it was a friend of his, but that actually it was the friend's father.

English, finally, is associated with certain aspects of their lives which are governed to a greater or lesser extent by Anglo culture. The parts of this culture which are and have been important in their lives are few but potent: formal education, the economic structure, law enforcement, and military service. The relationships with Anglos based on these have usually been formal and quite often of a superior-subordinate kind, with the Yaquis occupying the latter position. Teachers, bosses, cops, and army officers are the sorts of people the men have had occasion to speak English to, and to a considerable extent they are the people who taught them English in the first place. At times, some of them have even tried to force the Yaquis to use it. It would not be surprising if this had left a bad taste in the Yaquis' mouths and had even inhibited their mastery of the language. Yaquis, of course, have also had friendly, casual relations with Anglos as fellow-workers and fellow-soldiers through the common medium of English. There is in addition, the use of English under pleasant circumstances for some of the men when they are with English-speaking girls.

In Pascua today there are two attitudes concerning English, which might be called the emotional and the practical, and which sometimes appear to be in conflict. I have heard older people say that just because a man spoke English well it did not mean he was any good, and there seems to be a bit of a sneer in the slang phrase "qué mascas el totacho tú también?" (so you speak English too, huh?). I have been assured, however, that no one is ever made fun of for speaking English well, but only if he thinks he does when he actually does not. It can be suggested, nevertheless, that the anti-English attitude may sometimes adversely affect the standing of a man with a good command of English; on the other hand this may involve nothing more than jealousy.

Among younger men the so-called practical attitude seems to be dominant. One person even says that the language he likes best is English—and he is one who has a fair amount of difficulty with it—"because there are a lot of English people. Anywhere you go you can talk English in this country." And another says, "I don't like Spanish—Spanish you can't use everywhere. English you can use everywhere; that's why I want to learn it more." There is an immediate association here between knowing English and mobility. But it also seems justifiable to see in these answers a more basic association between English and having a good job—and therefore being able to travel.

This interpretation is reinforced by the close connection in Anglo culture between literacy and jobs, and for the young men in Pascua, literacy is predominantly associated with English. Almost all of them are literate in English (ignoring the degree), some are literate in Spanish, but almost none in Yaqui. Even letters home are written in English, when the man cannot write in Spanish. (Ironically, one veteran tells of writing a letter for an Anglo soldier to his family in Oklahoma, because the man could not write it himself.)

* * *

It cannot be claimed that the foregoing analysis of the meanings of the three languages has discovered all of the associations they have for the young men, but it appears generally valid and consistent. Since each of the languages is associated with a vital part of their lives, this discussion can perhaps be summed up in the words of one of the men: "It's no good to talk one language. You have to know two or three."

Trilingualism and the Future of Pascua

The concluding paragraph of my earlier report stated: "Trilingualism is a transitional phase in the linguistic history of Pascua. The village began as a bilingual community and after the trilingual period has passed it will again be bilingual, but the languages this time will be Spanish and English rather than Yaqui and Spanish." Paradoxically, it is implicit in this prediction that for a period Pascua would become more, rather than less, trilingual than it was in 1950.

Ideally, an attempt should have been made to bring the results of my original study up to date to see to what degree this might be true, but several considerations made this impossible. Even had time allowed, a proper restudy would have required an examination of the linguistic behavior of men ranging in age from about eighteen to fifty, in order to include both the young men of 1950 and those of the 1970s. Further, it would have been complicated by the fact that there are now two Pascuas. New Pascua is southwest of town on land deeded by the federal government, while Old Pascua remains at the same location. In my brief contacts with residents of the two communities I have seen nothing to indicate that the trend discerned a generation ago has been altered or reversed. Nevertheless, I did seriously underestimate the tenacity of Yaqui tradition in my earlier thinking.

* * *

Speaking of the two communities as one in order to avoid confusion, it can be assumed even without further investigation that in the last twenty years Pascua has become increasingly trilingual, whatever the degree might be. Older persons have died, children have been going to school, and all of the people have had a growing exposure to Spanish and English in this period. There is no way to estimate the number of those who have left the community for good because the culture has no more hold on them—a process noted long ago by Spicer (1940:308)— but whatever the number their departure could also tend to increase the trend to trilingualism if they were among those who had already dropped the use of Yaqui. Given the apparent vitality of Yaqui culture in Tucson today, Pascua will remain trilingual for considerably longer than was anticipated twenty years ago. Indeed, it must remain trilingual if it is to survive as a distinctly Yaqui community.

REFERENCES

BARBER, CARROLL G.
  1952 Trilingualism in Pascua: The Social Functions of Language in an Arizona Yaqui Village. M.A. Thesis, Department of Anthropology, University of Arizona, Tucson, Arizona.
BARKER, GEORGE C.
  1950 Pachuco: An American-Spanish Argot and Its Social Functions in Tucson, Arizona. *University of Arizona Bulletin*, Vol. 21, No. 1, Tucson, Arizona.
  1972 Social Functions of Language in a Mexican-American Community. Anthropological Papers of the University of Arizona, No. 22, Tucson, Arizona.
CRUMRINE, LYNNE S.
  1961 The Phonology of Arizona Yaqui. *Anthropological Papers of the University of Arizona*, No. 5, Tucson, Arizona.
KURATH, WILLIAM, AND EDWARD H. SPICER
  1947 A Brief Introduction to Yaqui, a Native Language of Sonora. *University of Arizona Bulletin*, Vol. 18, No. 1, Tucson, Arizona.
PAINTER, MURIEL THAYER
  1971 *A Yaqui Easter*. University of Arizona Press, Tucson, Arizona.
POST, ANITA C.
  1934 Southern Arizona Spanish Phonology. *University of Arizona Bulletin*, Vol. 5, No. 1., Tucson, Arizona.
SPICER, EDWARD H.
  1940 *Pascua: A Yaqui Village in Arizona*. University of Chicago Press, Chicago.
  1947 Yaqui Villages Past and Present. *The Kiva*, Vol. 13, No. 1.

PART III

SUGGESTIONS FOR FURTHER RESEARCH

18. Toward an Inventory of Interdisciplinary Tasks in Research on U.S. Southwest Bilingualism / Biculturalism

JACOB ORNSTEIN

Ornstein's article presents an overview of urgent tasks in the investigation of bilingualism and biculturalism that should be worked on through an interdisciplinary approach. It is an inventory of some sixty specific research targets in the related fields of linguistics, bilingualism, psychology, sociology, anthropology, and education. It also stresses the desirability of a consortium of scholars and schools in the Southwest to facilitate the exchange of ideas dealing with bilingualism in this area.

This paper was presented at the joint annual meeting of the American Ethnological Society and the Southwestern Anthropological Association, April 29–May 1, 1971, Tucson, Arizona. Appreciation is expressed for support received through grants from the University of Texas-El Paso Research Institute and the Hogg Foundation for Mental Health. Thanks also go to the following faculty members of this university: Paul W. Goodman, Rex E. Gerald, Edmund B. Coleman, Philip Himelstein, Eldon E. Ekwall, Oscar T. Jarvis, as well as to Bernard Spolsky, University of New Mexico.

[321]

THIS PAPER is distinguished by one feature: more attention is paid to detailing states of ignorance than to the exalted status of our knowledge of Southwest bilingualism. Returning to this area after a twenty-year absence in 1968 and helping initiate our school's modest program of Sociolinguistic Studies on Southwest Bilingualism, I have become increasingly impressed, if not overwhelmed, by the complexity of the interrelationships of bilingualism and its analog, biculturalism.

One positive result of this feeling was, however, my compilation of an inventory of desiderata, or research sub-tasks crying for attention. Intended to be more suggestive and catalytic than comprehensive or definitive, it is offered in this paper as an appendix. Perhaps on the principle of an informal regional "consortium" those who are research-minded can exchange findings and data, as indeed I've already begun to do with colleagues at the University of New Mexico and elsewhere.

The remarks herein can then be brief indeed, mostly intended to flesh out the framework a bit more since the task inventory, with over sixty items in various disciplines, is intended for reading and consideration in the solitude of your studies.

It occurs to the writer that the study of bilingualism/biculturalism has much in common with the field of reading. Although a reading specialist may dwell on eye movements, attention span, and acceleration through tachistoscopes and other devices, neglect of the inextricably intertwined psychological, sociological and ontological factors would reduce such an "expert" to the status of a rather superficial mechanic. So it is with bilingualism/biculturalism whose parameters are so ill-defined, and which perhaps is too important or too complicated to be left only to linguists or psychologists. Although bilingualism was for long a peripheral study undertaken by few research linguists, it was eagerly seized upon in the 1950s and 1960s by the new breed of psycholinguists. Nevertheless, the expected breakthroughs defining the nature of bilingualism through the union of the two sciences simply have not emerged. While psycholinguistics is a valuable sub-discipline, it appears to the writer that it was simply oversold during its heyday and unrealistic expectations tend to lead to a "confidence gap."

As for linguists and language specialists themselves, it is important to keep in mind that as William Mackey, Director of the International Centre for Research on Bilingualism at Laval University, Quebec, has pointed out, it was not until very recent years that linguistic diversity has earned respectability as a specialty for serious scholars, few of whom would have been so foolhardy even twenty years ago to stake their entire reputation on its pursuit. Further, in his French-English booklet, *Bilingualism in the Modern World/Le Bilinguisme dans le Monde Mo-*

derne: Phénomène Mondial, he rightly emphasizes that monolingualism was regarded by linguistic scholars as the normal language condition (1967:12–13). As a result, they had concentrated on analyzing the speech of the idealized "educated native speaker" (usually themselves), rather than acknowledging that multilingualism is perhaps more common than its opposite in the world's regions. We need only to read the newspaper to see, nevertheless, that even in such technologically advanced nations as Canada and Belgium, not to speak of polyglot India, violence and threats of secession recently have become exacerbated. In the wake of serious disorders and killings in Canada, the Royal Commission on Bilingualism and Biculturalism was appointed which by now has issued four impressive reports (1965) on the problem. In Belgium, rioters have more than once disrupted church services, and the entire constitution has been restructured and political districts reapportioned, because of conflict between Flemish-speakers and French-speaking Walloons, not to speak of a smaller minority of Germans, some 30,000 in all.

Returning now to our own Southwest, there are enough tasks here for the study of bilingualism/biculturalism to involve hundreds of individuals for goodness knows how many lifetimes. Whether it is always realized or not, this is geographically and otherwise the nation's largest area of linguistic and cultural diversity. Ordinarily the five states of Colorado, Texas, New Mexico, Arizona, and California are considered to be the Southwest, and a detailed breakdown of ethnolinguistic groups here shows much more than the estimated 6 million Mexican-Americans who deservedly are receiving unprecedented attention both by scholars and political and social activists. There are also several hundred thousand American Indians, and according to Carl Voegelin, as many different Indian languages are spoken as there were two centuries ago (1967:449). Add to this varying numbers of speakers of Basque, Czech, Slovak, Polish, Sorbian (a vestigial Slavic language in Texas), Yiddish, German, Armenian, Syrian-Lebanese, Arabic, Greek, and numerous dialects or lects[1] and sub-dialects of these languages. Finally, consider English, with a distribution of varieties based on Northern and Southern Midland, or a combination of both, and an intensely divergent ethnolinguistic picture emerges.

Aside from descriptions of the linguistic communication networks, or the needed elucidations of the distribution, function, and vitality of the languages of the Southwest, there is, in general, a crying need

---

[1] I am indebted to Charles-James Bailey, now at Georgetown University, for the term *lect* which, according to him, has by now some limited use because of its rejection of some of the objectionable overtones of *dialect*, and which was apparently coined by G. B. Milner and A. A. Afendras. (Cf. Working Papers in Linguistics, University of Hawaii, volume 2, May, 1970.)

for up-to-date descriptions of the language varieties of the area, particularly viewed against a multilingual framework. Yeoman work has been done by Glenn Gilbert, now at Southern Illinois University, and one may mention his *Linguistic Atlas of Texas German*, just published by the University of Texas Press (1971), and his edition of *Texas Studies in Bilingualism*, with 13 essays on Romance, Germanic and Slavic immigrant languages spoken in Texas, Louisiana, and Oklahoma, printed in Berlin the year before (1970). A beginning also has been made in the crucially vital task of recognizing Southwest Spanish varieties as something more than a border "lingo" for derisive and contemptuous treatment. Daniel Cárdenas, of Long Beach State College, California, recently completed a sketch of U.S. Spanish, including the Cuban, Puerto Rican, and Mexican-American varieties, and titled *Dominant Spanish Dialects Spoken in the United States* (1970).

At the 1971 annual meeting of the Southwestern Anthropological Association several speakers addressed themselves to the problem. Upon reading the abstracts distributed before the meeting, I was struck by the fact that almost one hundred percent of the speakers in the symposium on Bilingualism in the Southwest devoted significant portions of their papers to acute contemporary issues involving Spanish and Indian language varieties and their use, in our own region. Among these, Arnulfo Trejo's poignant title, "Chicano Spanish Vies for Recognition," indicates that the time for ostrich-like, rigidly academic treatment of Spanish in the Southwest is coming to an end. Incidentally, Professor Trejo came in for favorable mention in the essay by Jerry Craddock, University of California-Berkeley, titled "Spanish in North America," published in the tenth volume of *Current Trends in Linguistics*, edited by T.A. Sebeok. Craddock singled out Trejo's *Diccionario etimológico de la delincuencia*, published in Mexico City (1951), and also cited his unpublished dissertation, *Vocablos y modismos del español de Arizona* (1951). Unfortunately the results of studies performed according to modern linguistic procedures on Southwest Spanish are extremely difficult of access, consisting mostly of unpublished master's theses and doctoral dissertations, augmented by a sparse number of published articles.

Scholarship as usual is not, however, the order of the day, and civil rights movements and the demands of minorities for greater recognition of their languages and cultures, as well as more representation in the vocational and general mainstream, are being reflected in an unprecedented demand for more information on the so-called "social dialects" spoken by such groups. Unfortunately, programs under the aegis of the Office of Economic Opportunity, Office of Education, and other entities simply do not have available the sort of data base, for such intervention programs as Upward Bound and Bravo, that can come only with serious research. The result of this is that numerous "experts" predicate their guidelines on "top of one's head" expertise, often gained by merely living close to a minority or being a member of it. While such "knowledge" has an important place, scientifically obtained documentation has no substitute.

Thus it is that nonstandard speech varieties of urban and rural blacks and whites, and other groups now have a high priority. Nevertheless, the securing of grant money is another matter, requiring a time-consuming, highly formalized application procedure which understandably rankles scholars who do not conceive their roles as mere fund-raisers. It may be of interest to point out that Georgetown University's School of Languages and Linguistics recently received a grant of more than $400,000 from the National Science Foundation to analyze for educational purposes the speech of nonstandard speakers of English in the Nation's capital. Lest this cause a spate of applications to be sent to government agencies, I must counsel readers that the road to such grants is usually a most arduous one—and I believe that the above award was some three or four years in the making. Let those who can and will, pursue this avenue, while, it appears realistic, most of the tasks of cross-cultural research in the Southwest must be carried out by interested persons with local resources, perhaps cooperating on a sort of regional consortium basis. At the same time, the tiny minority of our colleagues willing to brave the rigors of proposal preparation can indeed bring benefits to their home institutions.

Another problem, aside from the securing of funds, is the difficulty of collaborating with several scholars in other disciplines, which cross-cultural research demands. By nature scholars are hardly gregarious but rather solitary workers, imbued with a missionary sense of the importance of their own subject. Again, here we can suggest only that those who can, should commit themselves to this approach, while the remainder can carry out their missions by themselves, often with modest clerical assistance and graduate student involvement.

It is appropriate now to glance at the inventory itself with only a partial listing of what appears to the writer, with some assistance from colleagues in other disciplines, to be the most urgent desiderata in bilingual/bicultural research in the Southwest. Some 60 targets are outlined in half a dozen disciplines, although this is by no means exhaustive. The entire idea of the inventory is only to provide a working tool for potential investigators, and indeed a list which can be handed to colleagues, graduate students, public school teachers, etc., who might be interested in pursuing some of the problems. Continuing revisions and additions are needed in the manner of MIT economist Max Millikin's system of "successive approximations." Aside from this, the compiling of the list has made the writer more aware of the lacunae in this field than ever before, as well as of some cogent realizations that he would like to share in the space allotted.

First of all, some remarks about languages and linguistics are worth making. Interestingly enough, it was several anthropologist-linguists who borrowed from both disciplines to write the most extensive analysis of the linguistic communication network of any area in the Southwest. This is "The Language Situation in Arizona as Part of the Southwest Culture Area" by Voegelin, Voegelin, and Schutz (1967:403–51), appearing in *Studies in Southwestern Ethnolinguistics*, edited by Hymes and Bittle (1967). Replications of this study badly need to be made for the entire region.

There is little need here to repeat the list of desiderata appearing under "Linguistically Oriented Studies" in the inventory. Yet something ought to be said about what is probably the most neglected area of all. It is the one embracing a wide range of verbal skills not controlled by middle-class speakers and largely unknown to them. In his work *The Study of Non-Standard English*, Labov (1969:37) points out the need to investigate and utilize such vernacular styles, applicable of course to languages other than English:

> In the urban ghettos, we find a number of speech events which demand great ingenuity, originality and practice, such as the system of ritual insults known variously as *sounding*, signifying the dozens, etc.; the display of occult knowledge sometimes known as rifting; the delivery, with subtle changes, of a large repertoire of oral epic poems known as *toasts* or *jokes;* and many other forms of verbal expertise quite unknown to teachers and middle-class society in general.

This of course applies just as aptly to other ethnolinguistic groups in the Southwest. Burling, an anthropologist, in his recent book, *Man's Many Voices* (1970:135–37), urges that more attention be paid to "pig latins" and simple metrical verse, of playful or aesthetic type, for the light it might throw on the phonological and syntactic units of various languages. It goes without saying that a truly scientific up-to-date study of the status and influence of *Pachuco* or *Tirilón*, by whatever name it is called, needs to be made, particularly as regards the diffusion of its lexical elements in informal spoken codes of Southwest Spanish.

The distinguished linguist and dialect scholar, Einar Haugen, (1970:20), who pioneered in the development of bilingual studies when these were very low on the scholarly totem pole, had the following to say in his review of bilingual research in America during the 1950's and

1960's for the tenth volume of *Current Trends in Linguistics:*

> In Amerindian studies the main thrust now, as earlier, was on the description of language structures, with no special consideration of language contacts. Since Casagrande's study [on Comanche], no full-scale attack on the topic was attempted, despite the evidence that Indian languages were being acculturated and displaced. Two studies by Americans on the parallel Mexican phenomena did appear, Diebold's on Huave (1961) and Law's on Nahuatl (1961).

Is it not time for workers in both anthropology and linguistics to concern themselves with a broad spectrum of problems in their own back yard which we grossly term bilingualism/biculturalism and, somewhat less, with purely descriptivist activities in the venerable tradition of Franz Boas?

What do anthropologists themselves opine? Edward P. Dozier (1965:400, fn 7) ventures that:

> Contrastive studies of the responses of groups within the Southwest is an open field; there might result typologies of acculturative style, as expressed in linguistic data.

William Madsen (1964), in *The Mexican-Americans of South Texas*, details the results of the four-year Hidalgo Project on Differential Culture Change and Mental Health with ethnographic field work in four communities of Hidalgo County, Texas, ranging from a rural folk society of Mexican-Americans to a bicultural urban center, indirectly offering a pattern in need of replication for other localities of our region, and in which a number of disciplines are represented, including the collaboration of a folklorist. Stanley Newman has spoken of the possibility of an "areal approach," first suggested by George Trager in 1939 and championed ever since by Carl Voegelin, who proposed that rather than specializing in, let's say Athabascan languages, a student might become an expert merely in Southwest languages. At the same time he saw excellent possibilities in linking the areal perspective with typology, declaring that, "The most efficient area for experimentation with typology is the Greater Southwest, including the Great Basin" (Newman 1967:5).

One of the most challenging appeals to anthropologists is that of Dell Hymes, who in a recent essay titled, "Sociolinguistics and the Ethnography of Speaking," has the following to say:

> Anthropology has here a special opportunity, and one might say, even responsibility. Of the sciences concerned with men, it has the closest and fullest ties with linguistics. In principle, it already recognizes linguistic research as part of its concern, already includes some acquaintance with language and linguistics as part of its training. The required combination of training in linguistics and in social analysis perhaps can be effected

under the aegis of anthropology more readily than any other. (Important here also is the humanistic aspect of anthropology, its ties with attention to texts and verbal art. There being a social need for such training, anthropology would enhance its recognized relevance in sponsoring it (1969).

Emphasis on such humanistic problems would, according to him, establish a new center of unity which would be, " . . . in some respects but a renewal of some of anthropology's oldest concerns at the center of contemporary social and scientific problems" (1970:42). Moreover the University of Pennsylvania anthropologist offers us an expanded horizon through his invitation to look much beyond linguistic structures themselves and the socio-cultural features of a speech community to analyses of the "ethnography of speaking" in which the structure of conversational interaction is examined thoroughly as part of ethnography, and in his own words, " . . . to insist on understanding discourse structures as *situated*, that is, as pertaining to cultural and personal occasions in which part of their meaning and structure lies. There is yet relatively little work that integrates both aspects" (1970:18).

As for sociology, its interest in embracing linguistics has been notoriously slow, despite the fact that they are both generalizing sciences. In America at least it was not until sociologist Joyce Hertzler (1953), wrote his programmatic article, "Toward a Sociology of Language," followed by his book of the same title in 1965, that the long overdue synthesis materialized. Nevertheless as late as five years ago, Allen Grimshaw (1967:191), a colleague of the former, lamented that, "Most sociologists have only the vaguest idea of the activity carried on in the growing academic subdiscipline labelled sociolinguistics." Moreover, he noted that they even confuse it with traditional ethnographic work, transformational grammar, or social psychology, whereas—and here he furnishes an apt definition, "Sociolinguistics attends to these reflections of social structure which are revealed in language particularly in speech usages, and is concerned neither with motivation nor with conscious behavior."

By now, as is becoming well known, at least half a dozen models of sociolinguistic investigation into linguistic diversity exist, although some represent modifications of former patterns. One underlying concept, nevertheless, links them all organically and ideologically. It is the conviction that language is not a unitary corpus derived from an idealized educated speaker but a complex of codes with features correlating with the socioeconomic characteristics of the groups using them. Neat cut-off points, research shows us increasingly, are less typical than a linguistic continuum in which the various codes controlled by the same individual frequently intersect.

At any rate, one may mention the models elaborated in Great Britain by Bernstein (1961) and Lawton (1968), in the United States by Gumperz (1967) and Hymes (1967). Of widespread application is that of Labov (1966), making use of the concept of the linguistic variable, and employed with variations by Shuy, Wolfram and Riley (1968), and Fishman (1968).

Of particular interest to us in the Southwest, because of its concern with Spanish-English speakers (in this instance Puerto Ricans) is Joshua Fishman's broad gauge *Bilingualism in the Barrio* (1968), an interdisciplinary team study of the psychological, sociological, and linguistic features of 431 subjects residing in four adjacent blocks of Jersey City. Lamentably, however, although so desperately in need of similar investigations, very little is in progress in the Southwest, with some notable exceptions, such as Michel's work on five-year-old Mexican-American bilinguals (1969), Galván and Troike's research in black, poor white, and Mexican-American social dialects (1969), all in Texas.

As for the Sociolinguistic Studies on Southwest Bilingualism at the University of Texas-El Paso, this represents but the tiniest thrust in an immense sea—or better, desert—of desiderata. Descriptions of the work are found in several recent publications (Ornstein 1970a, 1970b, 1970c, 1971). Our own project involves individuals from other departments, such as Gary Brooks, an educational administration expert, Bonnie Brooks, an educational psychologist, and Paul W. Goodman, specializing in the sociology of poverty. At the present time, this team of specialists and I are taking a stratified random sample of the student body at our university. We are attempting to measure the linguistic and sociopsychological characteristics of the Mexican-American bilinguals using the so-called Anglos as controls. As we have already suggested, one distinguishing feature of sociolinguistic field work in bilingualism is its attempt to relate a selected group of significant linguistic variables to selected social variables of the socio-economic class of the subject. A comparison of these factors in samples of both Mexican-Americans and Anglos ought to be revealing. Moreover, this team of four has devised and copyrighted the *Sociolinguistic Background Questionnaire: A Measurement Instrument for the Study of Bilingualism* (Brooks, Brooks, Goodman, Ornstein 1970). This contains two parts, of which the first includes some 90 questions on demography, language use, and attitudes and the like, while the second focuses on oral and written elicitation in both Spanish and English (often realized, of course, with abundant codeswitching).

Our inventory is quite rich in topics under a predominantly sociological rubric. Mention also should be made of the expansion of studies of what is coming to be known as "border sociology," particularly apt in an area of multiple contacts such as ours. There are by now a small corps of specialists in this area, such as Ellwyn R. Stoddard, an associate professor at my school, who has described his research in various articles (1969), as well as in a forthcoming book on self-identity problems of Mexican-Americans. Having read goodly portions of these, I can vouch for a truly interdisciplinary approach of Professor Stoddard, in which even language problems, often brushed off in cavalier fashion, come in for serious consideration as an integral and often decisive component of "border cultures." Hopefully the Border State Consortium for Latin America, to which the University of Arizona, the University of New Mexico, San Diego State College, and my own school belong, will succeed in giving a bit more direction and coordination to such studies.

Psychologists during the past two decades have been active in so many areas impinging on language and culture that no adequate discussion is possible here of the research and its merits, particularly in the fields of verbal learning and the description of bilingualism. There is however, still an enormous amount to be done in cross-cultural testing of aptitudes, personality assessment, and the like. Educators have now recognized the dissatisfaction of "minorities" with stereotyped "Dick and Jane" texts and tests which assume middle-class Anglo-American schooling. There also have been formidable attacks upon the long revered intelligence tests and other measuring instruments as being discriminatory, and attempts to encourage "culture-fairness" in this area have flourished. At the University of New Mexico, Garland Bills has devised an entrance examination for Spanish-speakers, which, for example, takes cognizance of the fact that a considerable number of prospective enrollees speak only nonstandard varieties of both Spanish and English. Similar work also has been going on at California State College at Fresno.

The inventory details some of the desiderata in the psychological field; none appears to loom more important at present than those within the "new frontier" of cross-cultural investigation. Some insight into the complexity of such tasks is afforded by Wayne Holtzman, an educational psychologist and developer of the Holtzman Inkblot technique for personality assessment, built on the Rorschach Test. For some years he co-directed with Dr. Rogelio Díaz Guerrero a cross-cultural longitudinal study of 800 youngsters, half of them in Austin, half in Mexico City. Beginning in the first grade and yearly for six years, each participant was subjected to a battery of psychological tests of cognitive, perceptual, and personality type, devised largely in the English-speaking world, but modified for Latin Americans, with supplementary consultation with parents for views of life styles.

At any rate, Holtzman describes the above investigation in two articles titled "Cross-Cultural Research on Personality Development" (1965) and "Cross-Cultural Studies in Psychology" (1968). These essays, moreover, are revealing to us for their insights into the complex nature of such undertakings, naturally reflecting that programs of trans-cultural research are far more difficult of execution than of conception. For one thing, the unconscious cultural bias of the investigators themselves constitutes a built-in obstacle (1968:87). For another, sub-cultural variations within a nation itself are often, if not always, numerous and significant. In urban settings, particularly, these can be more severe than those perceived across countries (1968:85, 1965:72–73). Both linguists and anthropologists have tended to "load" research and findings by seeking out the quaint and the exotic in remote and "primitive" locales such as Samoa, the African bush, the Amazon hinterlands, the Hebrides, etc., in a quest for small tribes or peoples in supposedly Rousseau-esque conditions little touched by the trappings and pressures of technological civilization. As recent research on "language universals" is tending to show, languages of no genetic affiliation can be, and are, similar in striking ways. Likewise Holtzman points out that such studies as the one by R. R. Sears has given convincing evidence that, for example, the three motivational variables of aggression, dependency, and competition, are probably transcultural in nature (1965:69), and it may be assumed that other traits are as well. All in all, Holtzman underlines that the severe obstacles are basically the confounding of cultural variables, the lack of comparability in psychological examiners or research assistants, and the lack of semantic equivalence in instruments and methods for collecting data—in other words, language and dialect barriers of various sorts. Aside from such methodological hurdles, he notes that, "The main difficulty with pan-cultural psychological research is the frustrating lack of dependable data on a large and representative sample of world cultures" (1965:89). And this despite the existence in the United States of an impressive body of information on over a hundred countries in the Human Resources Area Files, housed mostly in New Haven.

Finally, a word about the most demandingly cross-cultural discipline—the rapidly developing "ethnic studies" concept. As is well known, Mexican-American, Chicano, Black, Indian, and just plain "ethnic studies" centers and departments have been springing up almost overnight, but their growth is badly impeded by the lack of the underpinnings of a firm documentary research base as well as technical skills of information handling techniques which mark other more traditional studies which have matured over a longer period of time. Philip D. Ortego, acting executive director of the University of Texas-El Paso

Chicano Affairs Program, has commented, "Our requirements, beyond the purely political and programmatic, are extremely numerous and in many fields. There is need for studies of both diachronic and synchronic nature of the socio-cultural record of Mexican-Americans, as well as for syntheses of writings on the characteristics of this group. Such syntheses, in particular, constitute an urgent priority."[2]

Similar sentiments were voiced by David Sánchez, Chairman of the Department of Ethnic Studies, San Diego State College, not long ago.[3] Likewise, Américo Paredes, Director of the Mexican-American Studies Program and editor of the *Journal of American Folklore* in Austin, has emphasized the need for exploring the poorly known annals of the Mexican-American in the Southwest.[4] For some important events, he has noted, only dry official or police records exist, despite the fact that unwritten ballads or *corridos*, as well as word-of-mouth transmission have by no means left them unobserved.[5] A study by Dr. Paredes titled, *With His Pistol in Hand*, issued by the University of Texas Press in 1958, is one of the few linguistic-literary studies of the folk hero Gregorio Cortez. Much of the important data needing analysis in ethnic studies is only available in disparate sources, including mimeographed newsletters and publications, not to speak of personal interviews in which knowledge of contemporary dialects, such as Southwest Spanish, is essential, lest a real linguistic barrier impede such efforts. In this connection, also, the Modern Language Association, now seeking to represent Mexican-American, Indian, and other cultures more fully, had this to say in a recent *MLA Newsletter* (1970) in an item commenting on the efforts of two Hispanists, Carlos Blanco-Aguinaga and Arturo Madrid, who

> . . . stressed the need to secure travel subventions for the participants to this and other meetings (since most are young and the meetings are not "scholarly" in the traditional sense), and also for Spanish departments to give specific attention to Chicano and related studies.

Incidentally, a rapid search for treatises on popular Mexican-American folk literature yields only a handful of titles such as those by Espinosa (1937), Campa (1934, 1946), Rael (1939, 1942, 1951), Tully and Rael (1950), and Paredes (1958a, 1958b). It is surprising how little attention folk topics, including the visual arts, receive in general in our Southwest.

All in all, it might be well to conclude my discussion here with only the reiterated comment that its entire purpose has been to insist on the

[2] Conversation with Dr. Philip D. Ortego, April 22, 1971.
[3] Conversation with Prof. David Sánchez, December 23, 1970.
[4] Conversation with Dr. Américo Paredes, April 22, 1971.
[5] By way of exception, at the April 20, 1971 meeting of Sigma Delta Pi, Spanish honor society, University of Texas-El Paso, Mrs. Janice Keller presented a program on *"Santos—Folk Art of the Southwest."*

realization that our "data base" on Southwest bilingualism/bicultural-
ism is inexcusably faulty. Moreover, despite the difficulty of an interdisciplinary approach to cross-cultural research, it seems the *modus
operandi* most favorable for filling the lacunae.

APPENDIX

Tentative Inventory of Interdisciplinary Tasks in Cross-
Cutural Research on Southwest Bilingualism/Biculturalism

A. *Linguistically Oriented Studies*

   a. *Descriptions*
   1. The two main dialects, General Southwest Spanish and North New
      Mexico-South Colorado (Phonology, Grammar, Lexicon);
   2. Sub-dialects of Spanish and English, and other language varieties;
   3. Pachuco (Tirilón) and other special varieties such as Trader Navajo;
   4. Inventories of nonstandard, stigmatized features in spoken and written
      English and Spanish of representative socio-economic groups (with varia-
      bles of age, urban vs. rural location, etc.);
   5. Leading dialects and their Southwest variations of other standard lan-
      guages: Arabic, Armenian, Greek, Yiddish, Polish, Czech, Slovak, Hun-
      garian, Wendish (Sorbian), Basque, American Indian;
   6. Spanish and English "bilingual dialects" and their norms;
   7. Replication of pertinent tasks 1-4, wherever feasible, for standard lan-
      guages of (5);
   8. Investigation of "substratum theory" in selected localities;
   9. Status of reduction to writing of Indian languages (on continuing basis);
   10. Status of standardization, codification and other "language engineering"
       efforts as applied to Indian languages;
   11. Descriptions of "language situations" by state and smaller regions, on
       largely sociolinguistic basis;
   12. Contrastive semological (semantic) problems, including those of semantic
       shift as regards the above language varieties;

   b. *Bilingualism*
   13. Rising status of Southwest Spanish and other regional varieties, and the
       influence of *chicano* and similar movements;
   14. Creoles, pidgins, calós, argots and other contact vernaculars;
   15. Pig latins and other playful and aesthetic varieties;
   16. Taxonomies of regional kinesics and other paralinguistic features of
       Southwest language varieties;
   17. Loyalties to ancestral vs. English language for ethnic groups mentioned
       in (a) above;
   18. Formal and informal language maintenance efforts of the various groups;
   19. Distributive roles of ancestral language(s) and English in Southwestern
       communication networks (small groups, etc.);
   20. Patterns of bilingualism (stable, transitory, incipient, evanescent, etc.)
       by various groups (differentiated according to such variables as age, sex,
       occupation, urban vs. rural location);
   21. Patterns of language dominance in individuals, over-all and in terms of the

4 skills: speaking, understanding, reading, writing of each language in relation to the other(s);

22. Identification of contact situations involving above languages.

B. *Psychological Issues*

23. Reaction-time studies of bilinguals to stimuli in different language-pairs;
24. Semantic differential experiments (of Osgood and other types);
25. Experiments testing Whorf-Sapir hypothesis in different ethnolinguistic groups;
26. Testing of Compound vs. Coordinate and of "balanced bilingualism" theories;
27. Psychological aspects of code-switching and mixing (degrees of awareness of process, intentionality, evaluative judgments, etc.);
28. Attitudes toward standard languages vs. regional varieties;
29. Longitudinal case studies of ontogeny of bilinguals of different regional groups;
30. Special characteristics of trilinguals, quadrilinguals and other polylinguals;
31. Emergent *chicano* attitudes (and parallel ethnic groups) as they relate to ancestral language use;

C. *Sociological Aspects*

32. Assimilation and its relation to ancestral language use;
33. Language learning in school vs. family vs. physical environment;
34. Cultural conflicts stemming from clash of value systems;
35. Contemporary status of N. New Mexico-S. Colorado "Spanish-American" sub-culture (as contrasted to Mexican-American types);
36. Comparisons of work ethos of various ethnolinguistic groups;
37. Effects of social mobility, urbanization, industrialization on loyalty to ancestral languages and cultures (especially on language use);
38. The linguistic/cultural component in poor self-image of minority group individuals;
39. Experience in armed services and its effects (linguistic, etc.);
40. Re-examination of status of concept of *machismo* and its effects on life style (incl. language use);
41. Effects of English mass media on traditional subcultural institutions and customs;
42. Features of the supposed hybrid "border culture" (language, customs, etc.);
43. Studies utilizing existing demographic data for correlations with linguistic behavior;
44. Acculturation patterns and rates among leading ethnic groups;
45. Emergent patterns of social stratification (urban and rural);
46. Sociological aspects of emergent *chicano* culture and its Indian and other counterparts (including life styles, language use, etc.);
47. Sociological content analyses of *chicano* and other "emergent" literatures of Southwest;

D. *Anthropology, Ethnology*

48. Intermarriage patterns and recent effects;
49. Popular religious systems and practices and language use;

50. Popular medicine and witchcraft practices (incl. language formulas and stylistic conventions in rituals);
51. Neglected verbal art forms (with special attention to linguistic styles);
52. Folk poetry and balladry (including Spanish *corridos*) and linguistic analysis;
53. Collation, analysis (with computer use) of folk literature forms, Mexican-American, Indian, others);
54. Publication of results of (53) in various media ranging from paperbacks, illustrated children's books, popular anthologies, to scholarly reports and monographs (and including radio and TV utilization);
55. Visual folk arts and their linguistic reflexes (*santos, retablos, bultos,* etc.);

E. *Educational Problems* (With constant reference to culturo-linguistic features)

56. Comparative studies of minority students in:
    (a) Overall school performance;
    (b) Standardized tests (of "IQ" type in general use);
    (c) Dropout rates
    (d) Certificate and degree completion times;
    (e) College admissions, including graduate schools;
57. "Culture-fairness" in testing;
58. Longitudinal and in-depth studies of adjustment and guidance problems of "representative" bilinguals or minority students;
59. Development of criteria for training minority group guidance personnel;
60. Experimentation and development work on such pedagogic curricular problems as:
    (a) English-as-second-language or native language as point of departure in kindergarten and first grade;
    (b) Total vs. modified bilingual schooling; evaluations by independent judges;
    (c) Strategies for teaching nonstandard dialects of both Spanish and English alongside standard ones;
    (d) Different types of treatment for dealing with deficient English communication skills at various levels (remedial, enrichment, etc.);
    (e) Comparative strategies for strengthening reading skills among bilinguals (role of dominant language or dialect, etc.);
    (f) Practical implications in applied classroom terms of *lectalism* without control of any standard language;
    (g) Use of various types of folk literature (Navajo, Zuni oral tales, etc.) for different components of instruction;
    (h) Development and testing of innovative approaches, including flexible scheduling, individualized learning (including programmed instruction, out-of-school learning and work study, credits by examination, etc.) for special needs of bilinguals and bidialectals;
    (i) Creation of broad range of tests and textual materials specifically intended for minority groups, with constant evaluation of same.
61. Strategies for teaching Spanish to Spanish-speakers and parallel situations with other ethnic groups;
62. Methods of teaching of Chicano cultures and literatures and their counterparts;

F. *Miscellaneous*

63. Creation of special data banks for broad categories detailed above (in cooperation with ERIC system, Languages of the World Files, Indiana Univ., International Center for Research on Bilingualism, Université Laval, Quebec.

REFERENCES

AARONS, ALFRED C., BARBARA Y. GORDON, AND WILLIAM A. STEWART. EDS.
  1969 Linguistic-Cultural Differences and American Education. Special Anthology Issue. *Florida FL Reporter*, Spring/Summer 7.
BERNSTEIN, BASIL
  1961 Social Class and Linguistic Development. In *Education, Economy and Society*. A. H. Halsey, J. Floud, and D. A. Andersen, eds. The Free Press, Glencoe, Illinois.
BROOKS, BONNIE S., GARY D. BROOKS, PAUL W. GOODMAN, AND JACOB ORNSTEIN
  1970 Sociolinguistic Background Questionnaire: A Measurement Instrument for the Study of Bilingualism. University of Texas at El Paso. Mimeographed.
BURLING, ROBBINS
  1970 *Man's Many Voices: Language in Its Cultural Context*. Holt, Rinehart and Winston, New York.
CAMPA, ARTHUR L.
  1934 Spanish Religious Folk Theatre in the Spanish Southwest. *University of New Mexico Bulletin, Language Series* 5: 1-2.
  1946 *Spanish Folk Poetry in New Mexico*. University of New Mexico Press, Albuquerque.
CÁRDENAS, DANIEL N.
  1970 *Dominant Spanish Dialects Spoken in the United States*. ERIC Clearinghouse for Linguistics, Washington, D.C.
CRADDOCK, JERRY
  1970 Spanish in North America. (Prepared for *Current Trends in Linguistics*, vol. 10. Thomas A. Sebeok, ed. Mouton, The Hague.)
DOZIER, EDWARD P.
  1967 Linguistic Acculturation Studies in the Southwest. In *Studies in Southwestern Ethnolinguistics*. Dell Hymes and William E. Bittle, eds. Mouton, The Hague. pp. 389-402.
ESPINOSA, JUAN
  1937 Spanish Folk Tales from New Mexico. *Memoirs of the American Folklore Society*, 30.
FASOLD, RALPH W.
  1970 Two Models of Socially Significant Variation. *Language* 46: 551-563.
FISHMAN, JOSHUA A., ROBERT L. COOPER, AND ROXANA MA, EDS.
  1968 *Bilingualism in the Barrio. The Measurement and Description of Language Dominance in Bilinguals*. Final Report, Contract No. OEC-1-0628-0297. 2 vols. Office of Education, Washington, D.C.
GALVÁN, MARY M. AND RUDOLPH C. TROIKE
  1969 The East Texas Dialect Project: A Pattern for Education. In "Linguistic-Cultural Differences and American Education." Aarons, et al., eds. Special Anthology Issue. *Florida FL Reporter*. Spring/Summer 7: 29-31, 152-153.
GILBERT, GLENN
  1970 *Texas Studies in Bilingualism*. Walter de Gruyter, Berlin.
  1971 *Linguistic Atlas of Texas German*. University of Texas Press, Austin.
GRIMSHAW, ALLEN E.
  1967 Directions for Research in Sociolinguistics: Suggestions of a Nonlinguist

Sociologist. In *Explorations in Sociolinguistics*. Stanley Lieberson, ed. Indiana University Press, Bloomington. pp. 191–204.

GUMPERZ, JOHN J.
1967 On the Linguistic Markers of Bilingualism. In "Problems of Bilingualism." John Macnamara, ed. Special Issue. *Journal of Social Issues*. 23: 48–57.

HAUGEN, EINAR
n.d. Bilingualism, Language Contact and Immigrant Languages in the United States: A Research Report 1956–1970. (Prepared for *Current Trends in Linguistics*, vol. 10. Thomas A. Sebeok, ed. Mouton, The Hague.)

HERTZLER, JOYCE
1953 Toward a Sociology of Language. *Social Forces* 32: 110–119.
1965 *Toward a Sociology of Language*. Random House, New York.

HOLTZMAN, WAYNE H.
1965 Cross-Cultural Research on Personality Development. *Latin American Monograph Series: Institute of Latin American Studies*, Austin, Texas, No. 25. (Reprinted from *Human Development*, Basel, New York, 1965, 8: 65–89.)
1968 Cross-Cultural Studies in Psychology. *Institute of Latin American Studies, Austin, Texas, Offprint Series*, No. 78. (Reprinted from *International Journal of Psychology* 3: 83–91.)

HOLTZMAN, WAYNE H., J. S. THORPE, JON D. SCHWARTZ, AND E. WAYNE HERRON
1965 *Inkblot Perception and Personality*. Hogg Foundation for Mental Health, Austin, Texas.

HYMES, DELL
1967 Models of the Interaction of Language and Social Setting. In *Problems of Bilingualism*. John Macnamara, ed. pp. 8–28.
1969 Sociolinguistics and the Ethnography of Speaking. (A paper presented at the annual conference of the Association of Social Anthropologists, University of Sussex, April. Accepted for publication in *Linguistics and Social Anthropology*. Edwin Tavener, ed. Tavistock Press, London.)

HYMES, DELL AND WILLIAM E. BITTLE, EDS.
1967 *Studies in Southwestern Ethnolinguistics*. Mouton, The Hague.

LABOV, WILLIAM A.
1966 *The Social Stratification of English in New York City*. Center for Applied Linguistics, Washington, D.C.
1969 The Study of Non-Standard English. ERIC Clearinghouse for Linguistics, Center for Applied Linguistics, Washington, D.C.

LABOV, WILLIAM A., PAUL COHEN, CLARENCE ROBINS, AND JOHN LEWIS
1968 A Study of the Non-Standard English of Negro and Puerto Rican Speakers in New York City. Cooperative Research Project No. 3288. Office of Education, U.S. Department of Health, Education and Welfare. 2 vols. Mimeographed. (Available from U.S. Regional Survey, 3812 Walnut St., Philadelphia, Pa., 19104)

LAWTON, DENIS
1968 *Social Class, Language and Education*. Schocken Books, New York.

MA, ROXANA AND ELEANOR HERASIMCHUK
1968 Linguistic Dimensions of a Bilingual Neighborhood. In *Bilingualism in the Barrio*. Fishman, et al., eds. Language Sciences Series, University of Indiana Press, Bloomington. pp. 636–835.

MACKEY, WILLIAM F.
1967 *Bilingualism in the Modern World/Le Bilinguisme dans le Monde Moderne: Phénomène Mondial*. Harvest House, Montreal, Canada.

MADSEN, WILLIAM
1964 *The Mexican-Americans of South Texas*. Holt, Rinehart and Winston, New York.

MICHEL, JOSEPH
  1969 A Pilot Project in Recording the Speech of the Five-Year-Old Texas
        Spanish-English Pre-School Bilingual Child. In "Linguistic-Cultural
        Differences and American Education." A. C. Aarons, et al., eds. Special
        Anthology Issue. *Florida FL Reporter.* pp. 15–17, 20.
MODERN LANGUAGE ASSOCIATION
  1970 MLA Newsletter, November, No. 5.
NEWMAN, STANLEY
  1967 Introduction. In *Studies in Southwestern Ethnolinguistics.* Dell Hymes and
        W. E. Bittle, eds. Mouton, The Hague. pp. 1–12.
ORNSTEIN, JACOB
  1970a Language Varieties Along the U.S.-Mexican Border. ERIC ED, 032
         (February). (Accepted for publication in *Proceedings of the Second In-
         ternational Congress of Applied Linguistics*, September 9–12, 1969. John
         L. M. Trim, ed. Cambridge University Press.)
  1970b Sociolinguistics and New Perspectives in the Study of Southwest Span-
         ish. In *Studies in Language and Linguistics 1969–1970.* R. W. Ewton Jr.
         and Jacob Ornstein, eds. Texas Western Press, El Paso. pp. 127–184.
  1970c Sociolinguistics and the Study of Spanish and English Language Varie-
         ties in the U.S. Southwest: A State of the Art Paper with a Proposed
         Plan of Research. Written for Southwestern Cooperative Educational
         Laboratory, Albuquerque. (To appear in "Social Dialects in the Spanish-
         Speaking World: Three Cases." Jacob Ornstein, ed. *Janua Linguarum,
         series practica.* Mouton, The Hague.)
  1970d Toward a Classification of Southwest Spanish Non-Standard Variants.
         (A paper presented at the summer meeting, July 27–29, of the Linguistic
         Society of America. To appear in *Linguistics*, The Hague.)
  1971   Sociolinguistic Research on Language Diversity in the American South-
         west and Its Educational Implications. *Modern Language Journal* 55:
         223–229.
PAREDES, AMÉRICO
  1958a *El Cowboy Norteamericano en el Folklore y la Literatura.* Institute of
         Latin American Studies, Austin, Texas. Offprint Series, No. 22.
  1958b *With His Pistol in His Hand.* University of Texas Press, Austin.
RAEL, JUAN B.
  1939 Cuentos Españoles de Colorado y de Nuevo Méjico. *Journal of American
        Folklore* 52: 227–323.
  1942 Cuentos Españoles de Colorado y de Nuevo Méjico. *Journal of American
        Folklore* 55: 1–93.
  1951 *The New Mexican Alabado.* Stanford University Press, Stanford, Cali-
        fornia.
ROYAL COMMISSION ON BILINGUALISM AND BICULTURALISM
  1965 *Preliminary Report of the Royal Commission on Bilingualism and Bi-
        culturalism.* Queen's Printer, Ottawa.
SHUY, ROGER W., WALTER A. WOLFRAM AND WILLIAM A. RILEY
  1968 *Field Techniques in an Urban Language Study.* Center for Applied Lin-
        guistics, Washington, D.C.
STODDARD, ELLWYN
  1969 The Contribution of U.S.-Mexican Border Research to the Field of Latin
        American Studies. *Journal of Inter-American Studies* 11: 477–488.
  n.d. *Mexican-Americans.* Random House, New York.
TREJO, ARNULFO D.
  1951 Vocablos y Modismos del Espanol de Arizona. Unpublished PhD disserta-
        tion. Mexico City College, Mexico City.
  1968 *Diccionario Etimologico Latino Americano del Lexico de la Delincuencia.*
        Uteha, Mexico.

TULLY, M. F. AND J. B. RAEL
  1950 *An Annotated Bibliography of Spanish Folklore in New Mexico and South-ern Colorado.* University of New Mexico Press, Albuquerque.
VOEGELIN, CARL F.. F. M. VOEGELIN AND NOEL W. SCHUTZ, JR.
  1967 The Language Situation in Arizona as Part of the Southwest Culture Area. In *Studies in Southwestern Ethnolinguistics.* Dell Hymes and W. E. Bittle, eds. Mouton, The Hague. pp. 403–451.

Index